Happy

Enjoy many scrumptuous

culinary delights –

and do share !

Love Josh & Dan

MANGOES & CURRY LEAVES

ALSO BY JEFFREY ALFORD AND NAOMI DUGUID

HOMEBAKING
The Artful Mix of Flour and Tradition Around the World

HOT SOUR SALTY SWEET
A Culinary Journey Through Southeast Asia

SEDUCTIONS OF RICE

FLATBREADS & FLAVORS
A Baker's Atlas

Photographs copyright © 2005 by Jeffrey Alford and Naomi Duguid/Asia Access,
with the exception of those copyright © 2005 by Richard Jung, as follows:
Pages 4–5; 16; 20; 24–25; 26; 29; 31; 35 *(left)*; 50–51; 52; 62; 65 *(left)*; 74; 78–79; 81; 91 *(left)*; 106–107; 108; 113;
122–123; 132 *(right)*; 138–139; 140; 151; 163; 167; 169; 174–175; 176; 183; 190; 195; 200–201; 202; 206–207; 216; 221 *(left)*;
226–227; 229; 236; 237; 246; 252–253; 254; 270; 277; 282–283; 284; 291; 309; 314–315; 317; 321; 322; 336–337; 339

Studio food styling by Susie Theodorou, assisted by Beth Pilar
Studio prop styling by Gabi Tubbs

Map on page 7 copyright © 2005 by Rodica Prato

Library and Archives Canada Cataloguing in Publication
Alford, Jeffrey
Mangoes and curry leaves : culinary travels through the great subcontinent / Jeffrey Alford and Naomi Duguid.
Includes index.
ISBN 0-679-31280-3
1. Cookery, Indic. 2. South Asia—Description and travel. I. Duguid, Naomi II. Title.
TX724.5.I4A74 2005   641.5954   C2005-903765-2

Printed in Singapore
10 9 8 7 6 5 4 3 2 1

Book design by Level, Calistoga, CA

MANGOES & CURRY LEAVES

CULINARY TRAVELS THROUGH THE GREAT SUBCONTINENT

JEFFREY ALFORD & NAOMI DUGUID

Photographs by Jeffrey Alford & Naomi Duguid

Additional photographs by Richard Jung

RANDOM HOUSE CANADA

CONTENTS

PREFACE

It's a long way from where we live in Toronto to the Subcontinent. If we fly through Europe, it takes us eight hours to get to Frankfurt, then two hours of layover, and then another eight hours to Mumbai (Bombay) or Delhi. Sometimes we fly west, across the Pacific, then through Thailand, and it takes six to eight hours longer. Either way, it's a long trip, and though we get tired on the airplane, there's a part of us that likes its being long, and likes being a little bit uncomfortable. When we're in the airplane trying to find yet another awkward position in which to sleep, we're reminded that, yes, the Subcontinent is a long way from where we live, *it's halfway around the world!*

We've been making trips to the Subcontinent, separately and together, for thirty years. We first started traveling there right after university, as backpackers, having heard and read so many travelers' tales. Our earliest trips were long journeys filled with high highs and sometimes very low lows, times we'll never forget. But as we've gotten older, and especially since we've become parents, our trips have become a little less roller coasterish, and generally shorter, though in some ways almost more intense and filled with more emotion. A trip to the Subcontinent has become a great gift; we come home feeling more alive, more connected.

In the Subcontinent, we're continually amazed at just how good common everyday food is. Whether a simple meal of rice and lentils, or a tender grilled fish served with a hot tandoor bread and a coriander chutney, food doesn't have to be elaborate to be good, or to be special. If there's any one thing we've observed in eating our way around the Subcontinent, it's that there's tremendous creativity and harmony in the way food is prepared on an everyday basis. Like all good food (and good cooking), it's at the same time both simple and complex, faithful to tradition yet ever evolving.

This book is all about the food of the Great Subcontinent as seen through the eyes of two people who aren't from the Subcontinent. It's a book about tasting the food as travelers and as cooks, whether we're poking around the main market in Thiruvananthapuram (Trivandrum) or Kathmandu or we're at home in our kitchen. We can't pretend to know all about this incredible food from the inside out, but we do know it intimately from the outside looking in. From Sri Lanka to Bangladesh, from India to Nepal to Pakistan, this book is but a taste of one of the most extraordinary culinary regions of the world, served with a little slice of life on the side.

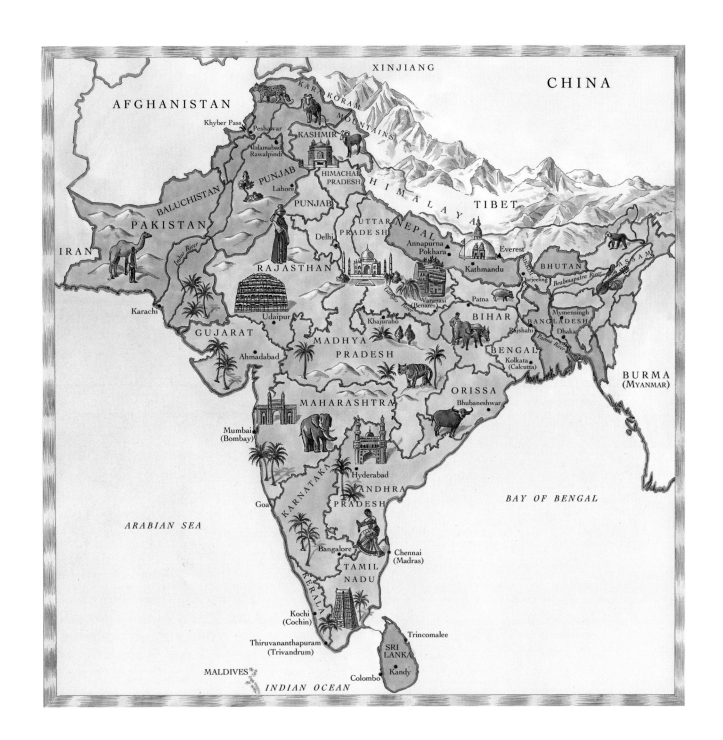

XINJIANG

CHINA

AFGHANISTAN

KARAKORAM
Khyber Pass
Peshawar
MOUNTAINS
KASHMIR

Islamabad
Rawalpindi
HIMACHAL
PRADESH
H I M A L A Y A
TIBET

PUNJAB
Lahore

BALUCHISTAN

PUNJAB
Delhi
UTTAR
PRADESH
NEPAL
Annapurna
Pokhara
Everest
BHUTAN
ASSAM

PAKISTAN

IRAN

Indus River
RAJASTHAN

Kathmandu
Darjeeling
Brahmaputra River

Karachi
Ganges River
Varanasi
(Benares)
Patna
BIHAR
BANGLADESH
Mymensingh

Udaipur

GUJARAT
Khajuraho
Rajshahi
Dhaka

Ahmadabad
MADHYA
PRADESH
Padma River
BENGAL

Kolkata
(Calcutta)

MAHARASHTRA
ORISSA
Bhubaneshwar
BURMA
(MYANMAR)

Mumbai
(Bombay)

Hyderabad
KARNATAKA
ANDHRA
PRADESH
BAY OF BENGAL

ARABIAN SEA

Goa

Bangalore
TAMIL
NADU
Chennai
(Madras)

KERALA

Kochi
(Cochin)

Thiruvananthapuram
(Trivandrum)
Trincomalee

SRI
LANKA

MALDIVES
Colombo
Kandy

INDIAN OCEAN

THE GREAT SUBCONTINENT

In geological terms, the Subcontinent is a story almost too good to be true.
A hundred million years ago, it was attached to the eastern part of Africa,
but then it gradually separated, floating atop a tectonic plate moving slowly
north-northeast across what was then the Sea of Tethys. Around forty
million years ago, this floating subcontinental plate collided with the Asian
plate, and when these two giants met, like two speeding vehicles meeting
head on, they collided with such force that the sea bottom around their
edges rose and buckled. On the Asian side of the collision (present-day
Tibet), the land rose up into a plateau almost three miles high, and on the
Subcontinent side, the land rippled up into ranges of mountains, the highest
mountains in the world, the Himalaya and the Karakoram.

If you hike in the high ranges of the Himalaya, amid all the rock, snow,
and ice, it's still possible to find fossils of seashells, even sometimes a pale
pinkish coral, left from the ancient Sea of Tethys. If you travel in the northern
parts of Pakistan, in the Karakoram range, there are times when you're
surrounded by unbelievably massive mountains of rock, and in places you can
see where "rivers" of rock, like flows of lava, met and crashed into each other.

Geologically speaking, the Himalaya is a young range of mountains, still
growing, but the Subcontinent in people terms is anything but a young place.
When the two continents collided and the mountains were born, rivers began
flowing down toward the sea, making fertile land and eventually giving rise
to great civilizations. The Harappan civilization, which flourished on the
banks of the Indus River (in present-day Pakistan) from 2500 to 1550 B.C.,
was a civilization as developed in every way as those along the Euphrates

and the Nile. Far from the Himalaya, in the tropical climes of the southern parts of the Subcontinent, the highly civilized kingdom of Anuradhapura, on the northern plains of Sri Lanka, existed for nearly fifteen hundred years, beginning in the fourth century B.C.

The present-day Subcontinent is made up of seven countries: Pakistan, India, Nepal, Bhutan, and Bangladesh on the mainland, and the island nations of Sri Lanka and the Maldives (see map, page 7). The northernmost edge of the Subcontinent lies somewhere not far from the latitude of Santa Fe, New Mexico, and its southernmost tip extends south of the latitude of Panama, three degrees north of the equator. The total area of India is approximately one third the size of the continental United States; that of the entire Subcontinent is roughly half the area of the continental United States. The population of the United States is now around 293 million, but the Subcontinent has nearly five times as many inhabitants: about 1.4 billion.

Life in the Subcontinent, especially agricultural life, revolves around weather and the seasons. In most parts of the region, the seasons are marked by wet and dry as much as—or more than—by temperature. Wet and dry are largely determined by the seasonal winds called *monsoons*. Most of the Subcontinent is watered in the June-to-September season of the southwest monsoon, the prevailing wind that flows over the region from the southwest in those months, bringing moisture from the Indian Ocean. In the October-to-January period, the monsoon winds blow from the northeast across the Bay of Bengal, bringing rain to the east coasts of India and Sri Lanka.

In the tropical south of India, and in most of Sri Lanka, temperatures are fairly constant year-round, around 86° to 90°F, so rainfall is the primary way of marking the two main seasons: wet and dry. In the northern plains of India, and in Bangladesh, Bhutan, Nepal, and Pakistan, there are three (or four) seasons: summer (hot season), rainy season (monsoon season), and dry season (fall and winter), and in some areas, a cold season.

The hottest season, summer, is the period before the monsoon rains come. In most places it lasts from early March until sometime in June. It's marked by baked dry earth (except where there is irrigation) and hot winds. Once the monsoon comes and brings rain, the land turns green. As the rains taper off in September, and things dry out, it's harvesttime for the main rice crop and time to plant cooler-season vegetables and winter wheat. The air is clear and the temperatures moderate. In the hills and mountains, there is also a cold season, from December to mid-February, and then things start warming up again.

The most pleasant time to visit is dry season (in most parts of the Subcontinent, that is late September to February, the months after the southwest monsoon ends), for temperatures are generally moderate and skies clear. Nonetheless, the rainy season can be a very dramatic and exciting time. There are usually downpours, then clear periods, then a buildup of clouds and then more rain. The hot summer months of March until June can be grueling because of the heat, but summer has its compensations: It has its own beauty, and it's the season for mangoes and a number of other fruits.

THE PEOPLE

Figuring out who's who in the Subcontinent is not an easy task even for people who live here, let alone for foreigners. After more than five thousand years of human habitation and wave after wave of invaders and wanderers, and with a physical geography (deserts, thick jungles, steep mountains) that in some regions reinforces extreme isolation, it's no wonder that the Subcontinent is one of the most diversely and richly populated places on earth.

One way to begin to appreciate this incredible diversity of ethnicity and culture is through language. India has fourteen major languages and more than a hundred others. Nepal, a country roughly the same size as the state of Iowa, has more than fifty different languages. Over time, each deep Himalayan valley gave rise to a distinct culture, each relatively isolated from the next. The same is true in the mountainous regions of northern Pakistan. Perhaps the greatest cultural diversity anywhere in the Subcontinent is in the extreme northeastern part of India, in the states of Assam, Nagaland, Arunchal Pradesh, and Manipur. Here, as in the nearby Himalayan foothills of southwestern China and the neighboring areas of northern Myanmar, tribal groups make up a majority of the population.

Just as we can group language families in Europe and the Mediterranean (the Romance languages, the Arab languages, the tongues with German roots, the Celtic languages, and so on), so too we can make approximate groupings of languages in the Subcontinent and gain some sense of the cultural map. Some languages, such as Punjabi and Bengali, cross international and state borders, while others are quite local.

Across the northern part of the Subcontinent, the major languages are Indo-European, and many of them have Sanskrit roots, rather as the Romance languages have Latin roots. They're written in a variety of different scripts, and each has a particular literature and a culture associated with it, and millions of native speakers. Some may have some similar vocabulary (as do Spanish and Italian, for example), but they are distinct languages. They include Hindi, one of the two official languages of India (the other is English); Bengali, the language of Bangladesh and of most of the Indian state of Bengal; Gujarati; Oriya, the majority language in the state of Orissa; Marathi, dominant in Mumbai (Bombay) and Maharashtra; Punjabi, spoken in both the Indian and Pakistani parts of the Punjab; Kashmiri; Sindhi, the

Woman and child in a village near Kaziranga National Park in the state of Assam, India. OPPOSITE, LEFT: *Two Tibetan men at the Nepal–Tibet border near Burang, western Tibet. Nepalis and Tibetans come here in the summer to trade salt and wool from Tibet for wheat flour and simple consumer goods from Nepal.* RIGHT: *Village women in the Khajuraho area, Madhya Pradesh state, India.*

dominant language in Pakistan's Sind province; Assamese; and Nepali. The majority language in Sri Lanka, Sinhala, is also Indo-European. Other Indo-European languages, from the Iranic branch of the family, are found mostly in Pakistan: Urdu, the majority language there, with Arab and Persian rather than Sanskrit roots, and written in Arabic script; Baluchi, the dominant language in the province of Baluchistan; Pushtu, spoken on the northwest frontier and into Afghanistan; and Wakhi, spoken in northern Hunza.

In the south, in the Indian states of Tamil Nadu, Kerala, Karnataka, and Andhra Pradesh, the majority languages are Dravidian, a language family outside the Indo-European group. They include Tamil, the majority language in Chennai (Madras) and Tamil Nadu, which is spoken by the large Tamil population of Sri Lanka; Malaylam, the language of Kerala; Telugu, the majority language in Andhra Pradesh; Kannada, the majority language in Karnataka; and Gondi, the language of a large tribal group in the northern Deccan.

In the northern hills and mountains of India and Nepal, a number of languages of the Tibeto-Burmese family are spoken, while in the hills of Orissa and Jharkhand (south of Bihar) as well as up through the northeast

provinces of India and in small pockets in Bangladesh, there are people who speak a variety of languages unrelated to any of the others.

The Subcontinent's rich tapestry of people and culture is evident in almost all aspects of life, including religion. While the majority of people are Hindu (belonging to many different sects and groups), the region as a whole also has the largest number of Muslims in the world (more than three hundred fifty million), some Sunni, some Shia, some Ismaeli (followers of the Aga Khan). The Sinhalese in Sri Lanka follow Theravada Buddhism, and many of the trans-Himalayan peoples in Nepal and India follow Mahayana Buddhism. Sikhism has more than nineteen million followers in the Punjab and all across India. There is an important Zoroastrian (Parsi) population in the Mumbai (Bombay) area, and pockets of Christianity exist in almost all regions, most notably in Kerala, Sri Lanka, and the tribal areas of northeast India.

Nearly 75 percent of people in the Subcontinent still live in rural villages, although the urban population is more than three hundred million. And in all this great mix of people, there are many tribal peoples who live in remote (and not so remote) regions, their lives relatively isolated from the dominant cultures.

A simple lunch made by a settled Ribari woman in a village near the Pakistani border in northwestern Katchh, in the state of Gujarat. On the left are millet skillet breads; lower right is a simple potato curry (see Katchhi Village Potato Curry, page 150) and above it, chopped onions to be eaten as a fresh condiment.

THE FOOD

Generalizations about food in the Subcontinent aren't easy because, for starters, it's a very big place! We feel we could travel a lifetime here and still not be comfortable making such generalizations. And this is not only a result of the Subcontinent's size and scale, but also a product of its history and culture. It's very easy in the Subcontinent for a region (or a group) to subdivide into subregions and then into sub subregions. It's something that perhaps all old civilizations share, a long layering of history and culture over time. But, to do the best we can, here goes.

Pakistan, in the northwest corner of the Subcontinent, has widely varied terrain and climate: high cold mountains and hot dry deserts, fertile plains and deep isolated valleys. What people eat in the southern city of Karachi differs from the food of Lahore, the capital city of the fertile Punjab, and also from the food of the Hunza Valley in the mountainous north, and that of the Baluchi desert on the border with Iran. Pakistan is also in part a country of immigrants, Muslims who moved (bringing their culinary traditions with them) from many parts of India, especially Mumbai (Bombay), Hyderabad, and the eastern Punjab, at the time of Independence in 1947, when British India was partitioned into Pakistan (East and West) and India. Since most of the population of Pakistan is Muslim, very little pork is eaten anywhere, but lamb, goat, and beef, as well as chicken, are eaten by those who can afford it. Pakistan is just across the mountains from Afghanistan, and, like its neighbor, has had wave after wave of invaders passing through, from Alexander the Great to the Moghul conquerors. Central Asian influence is apparent in the widespread use of the large vertical clay ovens known as *tandoors* for baking bread and cooking meat and rice dishes. Flatbread is the staple, either unleavened rotis (skillet flatbreads) or tandoor-baked naan. Rice cooked with meat and aromatics, especially onions, as *pulao* or biryani, using techniques very like those used in Iran and Central Asia, is eaten at some meals and on special occasions. Meat, mostly goat or beef, sometimes chicken, is cut into pieces and marinated, then grilled over a fire or cooked in a tandoor oven, or it is simmered with onions and spices to make a curry. In the Hunza Valley and other isolated mountain regions, dried fruit and wheat are staples.

Unlike Pakistan, which has been a passageway for ideas and invaders, and is on several trading routes between the Subcontinent and Central Asia, the kingdom of **Nepal** has long been fairly isolated from its neighbors. Until fifty years ago, connections in and out of Nepal were by rough tracks, traveled by people and animals on foot. And within the country, as in Pakistan, the rugged terrain means that small pockets of different cultures stay isolated from one another, their only contact through the occasional trade caravan passing through (rather as the different valleys of Switzerland remained very isolated until after the middle of the nineteenth century). In the mountain communities, this isolation, as well as extremes of climate, means that the food choices are limited. The staple foods are rice, millet, lentils, and vegetables, with which Nepali cooks work very inventively. In the main valleys, around Kathmandu and Pokhara, there's a wider range of vegetables, and dairy products are also available. Wheat is grown in some valleys, so chapatis (skillet flatbreads) are a staple. The most common cooking oil is mustard oil, and flavorings include onions, garlic, and several locally available souring agents, as well as dried spices such as cumin and black mustard seed. Beef is not eaten, but water buffalo meat, as well as chicken, pork, and some wild game, is appreciated when available.

The mountain kingdom of **Bhutan** has also long been isolated from the outside world. Bhutan lies on several trading routes between Tibet and India, but even these have been closed since the Chinese took control of Tibet in the 1960s. The population is primarily Tibetan-style Buddhist, but over time a large number of Nepalis have moved to Bhutan for work, bringing their food traditions with them (much of the Nepali population has recently been ejected by the Bhutanese government). Bhutan has steep north-south valleys, some of them with relatively mild climates that favor farming. People also live at higher elevations near the Tibet border, as in Nepal. The staple foods grown in the valleys are rice and buckwheat. Hot red chiles are widely grown and dried for use throughout the year. Meat of all kinds (when available), green vegetables and root vegetables, fresh cheese, and potatoes make up the diet. Ingredients are usually boiled together in a kind of stew, spiced with salt and hot chiles, and eaten with the distinctive red rice of Bhutan.

Whereas Pakistan, Nepal, and Bhutan are mountainous, **Bangladesh** is quite different, absolutely flat. And whereas much of Pakistan is a desert, Bangladesh is well watered by huge rivers and abundant rainfall. The soil in Bangladesh is fertile, because it's alluvial and often renewed by rivers in flood that deposit their silt as they retreat. The staple food is rice, widely grown, along with a wide assortment of greens, fruits, and vegetables that flourish in every season. Freshwater fish are a favorite, prepared in many different ways; some seafood is also eaten. Because the majority population is Muslim, beef, chicken, and goat are eaten, but pork is not. Bangladesh has a distinctive cuisine that resembles that of the Indian state of Bengal, with which it shares a culture and history. Mustard oil is a common cooking oil and flavoring, and the Bengali five-spice mixture known as *panch phoron* is often used to flavor cooking oil before other ingredients are added. In contrast to the Hindu cuisine of Bengal, onions are used in great quantity as both a flavoring and ingredient. Dishes are eaten sequentially at a meal (rather than, as in much of the region, being intermingled), most often accompanied by rice. There's a taste for bitter and also for a touch of sweet in many dishes, as well as a tradition of sweets made with fresh cheese.

Although the island nation of **Sri Lanka** is not large, at the center of the island is a massif that rises to more than seven thousand feet. The area in the mountains thus has a temperate climate where northern European crops such as cabbages and beets grow well, while along the coast, and at lower elevations, there is an amazing variety of tropical and subtropical fruits and vegetables, as well as coconut palms. As a result, cooks work with a wide array of ingredients. The Sinhalese population is mostly Buddhist; Sinhalese cuisine includes meat and fish, but there's also a large repertoire of lightly cooked vegetable dishes known as *mallum* or *mallung*.

Beef is, however, forbidden to the largely Hindu Tamil population of the island. Tamil dishes such as *idli* (a steamed bread) and *dosa* (a crepelike bread), which originated in southern India, are common. The Sri Lankan dish called *hoppers* (a leavened skillet bread) is thought to be a Tamil addition, its name deriving from the Tamil word *appam*. About 11 percent of the island's people are Muslim, to whom pork is forbidden. Rice is the staple food throughout the island, eaten with a variety of curries and the chile-hot salsas called *sambols*. Coconut milk is widely used in sauces, and grated coconut is often part of the flavoring or the thickening of a dish. Another distinctive Sinhalese flavoring is Maldive fish, small chunks of dried tuna with a salty pungent taste, which are crumbled into dishes to give an appealing smoky-salty flavor, much as fish sauce and its relatives are used in the cooking of Southeast Asia.

In southern India, in both **Kerala** and **Tamil Nadu,** the cooking in some ways resembles the cooking of Sri Lanka, with widespread use of coconut milk and grated coconut. Rice is the staple, at the center of the main meal, accompanied by a wide array of curries and sauces, which are blended into it by each diner as he or she eats. The Hindu population of both states is largely vegetarian, with an inventive repertoire of dishes based on rice and other grains, dal, fruits, and vegetables, although many Hindus in Kerala also eat fish. Kerala is also home to a large Syrian Christian community, descendants of early converts to Christianity, who eat meat and fish of all kinds.

The adjacent states, working northward, are **Karnataka** and **Goa** on the west coast, and **Andhra Pradesh** to the east, where, once again, the tropical and subtropical location means that the staple food is rice and that coconut plays an important role. *Dosas* and *idlis* are common snack foods. Many people are vegetarian, though not so much in Goa: Goa was for a long time a Portuguese possession, and the result is a fusion culinary tradition and a large Christian population that eats beef and pork as well as fish and chicken. Hyderabad, capital of Andhra Pradesh, was, like the northern cities of Delhi, Agra, and Lucknow, ruled by descendants of the Moghul conquerors, so the food of the (largely Muslim) elite there is very Moghul-influenced (see Glossary), but with a fascinating infusion of tropical ingredients.

Mumbai (Bombay) and **Maharashtra,** the state that surrounds it, have a subtropical ambiance that reminds us of Los Angeles. Every kind of food from all over India can be found there, but local cooking includes the cuisines of several distinct communities that have been long settled in the region: the Parsis, Zoroastrians who came from Persia (Iran) a millennium ago, and whose food is subtly spiced and nonvegetarian; Gujaratis; and Marathas. North of Maharashtra is **Gujarat,** on India's northwest coast, with strong vegetarian traditions and a distinctive cuisine. Gujarati food is generally mild tasting, and meals come with a subtle balance of sweet, tart, and mildly hot. Legumes (dals) find their way into breads and sweets, as well as snacks and main dishes; the assortment of flatbreads is astonishing.

Northeast of Gujarat is the desert state of **Rajasthan**. The ruling Rajput caste is a Hindu warrior caste, with a meat-eating and hunting tradition. Lower-caste Rajasthanis are likely to be vegetarians, with a more chile-hot palate than that of Gujarat and a dependence on sorghum, millet, and corn, as well as on wheat, for making staple breads. Rajasthan suffers periodic droughts, so agriculture can be precarious; many people here and in the western part of Gujarat are nomadic or seminomadic, their living dependent on herds of goats, sheep, or camels. The food of nomads is of necessity simple, but it can also be delicious and inventive.

In the fertile valleys of mountainous **Kashmir,** in the northwest corner of India, the Muslim majority and Hindu Brahmin minority share overlapping culinary traditions, including rich *pulaos* made with lamb or chicken, delicately spiced kormas and *koftas,* sauces enriched with yogurt, simmered vegetable dishes, and an array of interesting flatbreads. Like those in the Himalayan communities in Nepal, people living at higher elevations, in the mountains of Ladakh and in Baltistan, eat barley rather than wheat or rice and, as Tibetans have done for centuries, depend on dried fruits, dried meat, dried vegetables, tea, and butter during the long cold winter months (see "Rebirth," page 184).

In the **plains of northern India** from the Punjab in the west over to the border of Bengal in the east, wheat generally grows well and so, as in Pakistan, the staple food is flatbreads such as chapati. The breads come hot to the table and then are torn into pieces that are used to scoop up mouthfuls of dal and curry and accompaniments. As in Pakistan, Moghul influences abound (spicing often includes cinnamon and cardamom, and yogurt plays a big role). The Muslims, Sikhs, and nonvegetarian Hindus eat tandoor-cooked kebabs, rich simmered lamb and chicken curries, tandoor-baked naan, and complex flavored rice dishes in the *pulao*-biryani tradition. The cities of Lucknow (capital of the pre-Independence kingdom of Oudh), Delhi, and Agra are particularly famous for their Moghul-style cuisines.

In the Indian **Punjab,** with its fertile agricultural land and long-settled traditions, the menu tends to have more vegetables and meat in it than the Pakistani Punjabi menu. Interestingly, Punjabi cuisine, both the Pakistani and Indian versions of it, was the first subcontinental cuisine to make its mark in North America. It remains the most familiar, with its vegetable dishes such as *muttar paneer* (cheese and pea curry) and *aloo gobi* (potatoes and cauliflower) and its meat dishes such as *saag gosht* (spinach and lamb curry).

East of Delhi is the state of **Uttar Pradesh,** and east of that the state of **Bihar,** places that, together with the state of **Madhya Pradesh,** we think of as the heartland of North Indian cooking. They are located on the Gangetic Plain, the fertile region watered by the Ganges River and its tributaries, and have been continuously inhabited for millennia. The majority population of both states is Hindu and very traditional, so there is a large repertoire of vegetarian dishes. Meals are traditionally served on a *thali* (a metal tray). A stack of fresh chapatis or other flatbread, one or two different dals, several vegetable dishes, one or two pickles or chutneys, a crisp *papad*, and a simple sweet make up the meal.

East and northeast of Bihar lies the Indian state of **Bengal**. In the mountains the food resembles that of Nepal and Bhutan, with small pockets of Bhutanese, Sherpa, Gurka, Lepcha, and other mountain peoples, depending on wheat, potatoes, and hardy vegetables, as well as on dried meat and some rice. The low-lying parts of Bengal are, like Bangladesh, fertile and well watered. The food of Bengal is a close cousin of Bangladeshi food, with rice the staple, a large repertoire of fish dishes and vegetable dishes, and the widespread use of mustard oil as a cooking medium and flavoring, but with much less use of onions, at least by the Hindu majority. **Orissa,** the state to the south of Bengal, has similar food traditions along its coastal plain, but inland in the mountains the population is largely tribal (see "Orissa," page 274), subsisting on local gathered foods and very simple dishes.

Star Fruit Chutney (page 34). OPPOSITE, LEFT: *Banana-Jaggery Fritters (page 330) along with a glass of Tamarind-Mint Tea (page 313); they rest atop our granite mortar from Bengal.* RIGHT: *Prawn White Curry (page 217).*

IN OUR KITCHEN

We both started cooking Indian food when we were in our late teens and early twenties, several years before first traveling to South Asia. Naomi, as a student in London for a year, lived in a hostel in Bayswater, where she had a good introduction to the food of the Subcontinent through meals in small, inexpensive Indian and Pakistani restaurants. It was there that she tasted her first *thali* meal and encountered her first pork vindaloo.

I was living in Laramie, Wyoming, light-years away from even a whiff of ground coriander seeds and fresh curry leaf. But with my friends Mark and Barb, I discovered a restaurant in Boulder, Colorado, a hundred twenty miles away, serving Indian and Sri Lankan home cooking. It was called the Indo-Ceylonese, as I remember, and it was run by a family from Sri Lanka. The owner would bring each dish family-style to the table and announce its name as he put it down. For us, it was incredibly exotic, and an adventure: After eating there, we would replay our meal for weeks on end and look forward to the next.

Spurred on by our restaurant meals, we bought a paperback cookbook called *Indian Cookery,* by Dharamjit Singh, and began cooking our way through it (I still have it, tattered and discolored). Mark and Barb lived in an old Laramie house with a formal dining room, and on weekends we'd gather at their house and each work on a different recipe or two, then eat our Indian feast in the dining room. The whole time, we'd talk about what to cook next time and what we'd try on our next trip to the Indo-Ceylonese.

For both of us, there's always been an element of pilgrimage in the cuisine of the Subcontinent; for Naomi in London and for me in Wyoming, first tasting the food and then needing to go, needing to taste the food firsthand. But the pilgrimage over time has worked both ways: It means traveling to the region to seek out the food and then also bringing it back home. How we eat, how we think about food, and how we cook have all been deeply influenced by eating and traveling in the Subcontinent.

Nowadays at home, unlike earlier days, we seldom cook an "Indian" or a "Sri Lankan" feast, covering the table with a great many dishes. Like most North American families, we run around in different directions all day long and then panic when suddenly it's dinnertime. So we put on rice to cook, and maybe a quick dal (a lentil-based dish) and use a mortar and a pestle to pound a fresh chutney; maybe we'll make a salad or some stir-fried greens. On days we manage to think about dinner in advance, we might make a Sri Lankan curry, such as the okra (ladies' fingers) curry that we especially love, but again, usually we'll serve it simply with rice and a chutney, maybe a little grilled meat.

Our meals are simple in part because our daily lives are busy, but also in large part because we like them that way. When there are three or four big curries on the table, they sometimes compete with one another, and no one shines individually the way it should. Indian "buffet," a common restaurant lunch here in Toronto, is, we think, sometimes a mistake for a restaurant

trying to advertise its food. The food may be good, but the presentation brings it down; tastes get muddy and lose their distinctiveness.

When we're traveling in the Subcontinent, most of our memorable meals, and memorable dishes, are enjoyed in neighborhood restaurants or in village homes, and it is this food we try most to duplicate at home. We remember a cucumber salad made in a mountain village in Sri Lanka, or a plate of seasoned rice flakes served for breakfast in a tea shop in Udaipur. When we serve some of these dishes to friends and then ask them where they think the food is from, often they have no idea. "But it's good," they'll say, as they go for more. The Subcontinent has so long been associated with curry—and there is, of course, an infinite number of delicious and inventive curries— but there's also a world of good food and different dishes that have nothing at all to do with curry.

One thing we've learned from cooking food from the Subcontinent is how to get different tastes to come forward, to pop, to sparkle. We learned when cooking Southeast Asian food to balance the flavors of hot, sour, salty, and sweet in order to make flavors pop. In South Asian cooking, it's much the same, a process of balancing and then highlighting tastes. Now we are never without tamarind pulp to sour a dish, or frozen grated coconut to sweeten and mellow, or a selection of dried and fresh chiles for heat. We also keep onions and garlic, limes, and fresh coriander or mint on hand, as well as fresh curry leaves (stored in the freezer) and whole spices

(coriander, cumin, black mustard, fennel, nigella, and fenugreek seeds and cinnamon or cassia stick, bay leaves, turmeric powder, and asafoetida).

A particularly ingenious South Asian technique for getting flavor to come forward is called *tempering*. After a curry or a dal has been simmered until done, and just before it's served, some garlic and/or onions (or shallots) are sautéed in oil in a separate skillet, one or more dried spices are added to the oil, and then they are cooked briefly, enough to bring out flavor, then the contents of the skillet are mixed into the long-cooked dish. Tempering highlights flavors that have already cooked into the dish, bringing them forward freshly just before serving.

Cooking food from the Subcontinent doesn't, in most cases, require kitchen equipment that doesn't already have a place in a North American kitchen. We use our *cast-iron skillets* a lot, and good *heavy pots (with lids)* for cooking rice and long-simmered dishes, and a *wok*. We use the wok for dishes that in the Subcontinent are traditionally cooked in a *karhai*, a shallow wok-shaped pan that in Britain is widely known as a *Balti pan*. For flatbreads such as chapatis, we use a dependable old *cast-iron griddle,* and we roll them out with a tapered-at-the-end rolling pin, sometimes called a *French pastry pin*. If you have access to a South Asian grocery, it's fun to explore the different cookware that is available, and if the price is right, to take home a *steamer* for making the dumplings called *idlis* or a *hopper pan,* but, all in all, there is not a lot of special equipment needed.

One tool we rely on is a good *mortar* with a *pestle*. Actually, because these can work in such different ways, we've ended up with several different kinds. One time we brought home a flat stone mortar from Kolkata (Calcutta) in our luggage (since then we've seen similar mortars for sale in Indian grocery stores here). We love it. A long rounded bumpy stone is used as the pestle on top of the flat roughened surface of the mortar (see photograph, page 17) and works beautifully for grinding garlic or ginger or herbs to a paste or grinding spices to a powder. For small home-style quantities, it's much faster than even an electric grinder or mini-processor.

Local ethnic grocery stores are a good place to look for mortars and pestles. We have stone mortars and pestles that we've picked up in Mexican grocery stores, and deep ceramic mortars from Thailand that we've bought here at Asian markets. You can also improvise: Once when we were camping, we found two good stones, one flat and one round; we washed them off, and they worked well. *An electric spice grinder* is a wonderful thing to have in the kitchen (we have two, one for coffee beans and one for spices), but a good mortar and pestle are worth their weight in gold (well, not quite), and they're fun.

Here in Toronto where we live, finding ingredients for cooking South Asian food is not a problem because there are pockets of South Asian groceries all around the city. But when we are in Laramie, Wyoming, for example, some ingredients for some recipes are not available, not even a hundred miles away. We've tried to give options and substitutions for these ingredients in the recipes and Glossary, but it always seems most important to give the original version first, then to suggest alternatives. We've also found that what's locally available is changing all the time, and that is especially true of fresh Asian ingredients. If you don't have easy access to ingredients, we highly recommend mail-ordering food from Kalustyan's, a grocery in New York City (www.kalustyans.com). Kalustyan's sends food all around North America, at very reasonable prices. It can also help you locate South Asian kitchen equipment.

Last but not least, like most home cooks, we find that we return regularly to a group of tried-and-true recipes (see "Food for Every Occasion," pages 20–23), getting to know a few recipes by heart that we can cook up without having to think, recipes for which we develop reflexes and intuition. These recipes take a place in our cooking repertoire, and we serve them with other favorite dishes from Italy or Ontario or Thailand. They become partly ours, and they then inspire us to go looking for more.

LEFT: *A Hindu worshipper descends the steps of a temple in Khajuraho, in Madhya Pradesh, India.* RIGHT: *Green cayenne chiles at a market in Udaipur, in southern Rajasthan.*

A NOTE ABOUT CHILES

The food of the Subcontinent has a reputation for chile heat, but on the scale of "hot cuisines," many of the dishes we eat in the Subcontinent aren't particularly hot. It's true that a little fresh green cayenne chile or powdered dried cayenne finds its way into many dishes. Like salt, a little chile gives an edge and can highlight and extend flavor. It's part of the array of seasonings and flavors used by cooks in the region, and it's up to the cook to decide how intense a heat he or she wants.

So although chiles are an important ingredient in many dishes, seldom is the chile heat overpowering, especially compared to the fiery dishes of Thailand, or Mexico, or parts of Indonesia. One exception is Sinhalese cooking, in Sri Lanka, which uses fresh hot chiles and can be intensely hot, especially the condiments called *sambols*.

Chiles play an interesting role in flavor, as do other "heating" spices such as black pepper and ginger. The heat seems to help flavors linger on the tongue, blending and extending them. Eating chiles also gives many people a sense of physical well-being, apart from the pleasures of flavor enhancement.

For the recipes in this book, we calculated the heat for our own taste, then reduced it just a bit. We do like chile heat at almost every meal, and probably at a level similar to many home cooks in the Subcontinent. But giving reliable chile heat in recipes isn't always easy. A package of dried red chiles from Thailand doesn't necessarily have the same heat as a package of dried red chiles from India, nor do two different packages from the same country. We also find cayenne powders can be wildly different. And when we enter the realm of fresh chiles and their various names and corresponding degrees of heat (with and without their seeds), the variation gets even less predictable.

How to find a chile amount that works for you? One way is to make your own cayenne by finely grinding the dried red chiles that you have regular access to, and then whenever you are in doubt, use what you're accustomed to. Try to buy the same kind of fresh green or red cayenne chiles each time, so you're familiar with their degree of hotness. *Most important of all, if you're making a dish for the first time (especially if you're making it with guests coming over for dinner), look at what is written in the recipe and reduce it. You can always add a little chile heat later, when you taste it before serving, simply by adding a pinch of cayenne powder.*

The standard fresh red or green chile we call for is the cayenne chile— shiny, long, slightly curved, and pointed (see photograph above). If you take out the seeds and membranes, there's much less heat (see Glossary under Chiles for detailed instructions). You can substitute the same number of serranos, for the same heat, or use jalapeños, which are milder and have a different taste.

Do remember all those words of caution about washing your hands and not touching your eyes after handling fresh chiles, and be sure to wash your cutting board and your knife after chopping them.

Sri Lankan Beef Curry (page 278)

FOOD FOR EVERY OCCASION

FOR A LAST-MINUTE WEEKNIGHT SUPPER

Pea Tendrils with Coconut (page 71)

Mountain Dal (page 182) with Bhutanese
    Red Rice (page 83) or white rice

Quick Tamarind Pulao with Curry Leaves (page 98)

Bangla Dal with a Hit of Lime (page 178)

Cumin-Coriander Beef Patties (page 268)

Pea Shoots for a Crowd (page 161) or Stir-fried Greens,
    Bangla Style (page 165)

TO DELIGHT CHILDREN

Gita's Luchis (page 115) or Savory Deep-fried
    Street-Side Breads (page 134)

Yogurt-Marinated Chicken Kebabs (page 239)

Cumin-Coriander Beef Patties (without the onion; page 268)

Home-Style Jalebi (page 319)

Mango Ice Cream with Cardamom (page 324)

Banana-Jaggery Fritters (page 330)

FOR A FEAST WITH GUESTS

Cashew-Coconut Meatballs (page 262), followed by Baked Goan Fish with
   Fresh Green Chile Chutney (page 205), Spicy Banana-Yogurt Pachadi
   (page 70), and Fresh Bean Sprout Salad (page 55), all served with
   plain rice and with crispy Papads (page 289) for crumbling over;
   for dessert, Silky Goan Pudding (page 331)

Spicy Chickpea Fritters (Vadas) (page 286) served with Andhra Spiced
   Eggplant (page 49) to start, followed by Duck Vindaloo (page 251),
   New Potatoes with Fresh Greens (page 154), Spiced Grated Carrots,
   Kerala Style (page 143), and Nepali Green Bean–Sesame Salad (page·
   76); for dessert, Mango Ice Cream with Cardamom (page 324)

Pakistani Lamb Pulao (page 104) with Hot Sweet Date-Onion Chutney
   (page 28), Fresh White Radish Slices with Salt (page 54), Zinet's Young
   Ginger Pickle (page 346), and Cucumber Raita (page 67); followed by
   Creamy Pudding with Mace and Cardamom (page 334)

Crisp-Fried Okra Tidbits (page 288) as an appetizer, followed by Lamb
   Slipper Kebabs (page 257) with Home-Style Tandoor Naan (page 116),
   Cachoombar (page 57), Tamarind Potatoes (page 152), and Star Fruit
   Chutney (page 34); with Gulab Jamun (page 318) for dessert

AROUND THE GRILL

Tikka Kebabs (page 256), with Hot Sweet Date-Onion Chutney (page 28)

Nepali Grilled Chicken (page 238)

Yogurt-Marinated Chicken Kebabs (page 239)

Grilled Marinated Beef (page 272), with Star Fruit Chutney (page 34)

Himalayan Grilled Tomato Sauce (page 94)

Bangla-Flavored Grilled Zucchini (page 144)

UNUSUAL TECHNIQUES TO TRY

Slow-Cooked Wheat Berries and Lamb with Fresh Mint (page 266)

Spiced Rice-Potato Dosas (page 114)

Dhokla (page 125)

Tamarind-Mint Tea (page 313)

Home-Style Jalebi (page 319)

VEGETARIAN FEASTS

Nepali Polenta with Himalayan Grilled Tomato Sauce (page 94), served with Pea Shoots for a Crowd (page 161), Mountain Dal (page 182), and Chapatis (page 110); followed by Sweet Yogurt Sundae with Saffron and Pistachios (page 323)

Simmered Kashmiri Paneer (page 171), Cauliflower Dum (page 148), and Katchhi Village Potato Curry (page 150), served with Stir-fried Rice and Dal (page 96), with Tart Mango Salsa (page 48) on the side; followed by Silky Goan Pudding (page 331)

Sweet Sev with Raisins (page 287), followed by Sri Lankan Fenugreek Dal (page 179), Spiced Cabbage Salad (page 77), and Sri Lankan Village Salad (page 66), served with Gita's Luchis (page 115) or Hoppers (page 121), with crispy Papads (page 289) for crumbling over; for dessert, Coconut Custard (page 335)

Bangla-Flavored Fried Zucchini (page 144), Hasna Begum's Mixed Vegetable Curry (page 164), Aromatic Pumpkin and Coconut (page 160), and Bangla Dal with a Hit of Lime (page 178), all served with rice; followed by Sweet and Creamy Rose Water Dumplings (page 328)

FOR A SPECIAL BREAKFAST OR BRUNCH WITH FRIENDS

Eggs with Curry Leaves (page 234), with Chapatis (page 110) or Cumin-Flecked Skillet Breads (page 126); followed by Sweet Yogurt Sundae with Saffron and Pistachios (page 323)

Andhra Scrambled Eggs (page 235) with Chapatis (page 110) or Home-Style Tandoor Naan (page 116); followed by Mini-Crepes in Syrup (page 320) and Banana Lassi (page 308)

Darjeeling Market Tibetan Breads (page 136), with Watercress and Shallot Salad (page 55), served with juice from Hunza Apricot Nectar (page 312); followed by Creamy Pudding with Mace and Cardamom (page 334)

Semolina Uppuma (page 92) with all the trimmings, served with Cardamom Chai (page 305); followed by Mango Ice Cream with Cardamom (page 324)

FAVORITES FOR A POTLUCK

Aromatic Pumpkin and Coconut (page 160)

Mountain Dal (page 182) or Udaipur Urad Dal (page 189)

Ginger-Lamb Coconut Milk Curry (page 261)

Tamarind Potatoes (page 152)

Chicken Biryani, Dum Style (page 102)

Pork Curry in Aromatic Broth (page 279)

Cauliflower Dum (page 148)

CHUTNEYS, SALSAS & SAMBOLS

WE'RE SITTING IN A SMALL BUSY RESTAURANT

at lunchtime in Ahmadabad (in India's Gujarat state) or Kochi (formerly Cochin, in Kerala); or we're listening for the arrival of the meal-service person as we're being rocked along in the train heading south to the city of Chennai (formerly Madras); or we're in a stone house in a Nepalese mountain village at the end of the day with the aromas of supper bubbling from the cookfire. In each

Green papaya

situation, it always includes a chutney or a sauce or a chile paste (or maybe two or three), a small, often colorful dollop of intense flavor. On the street, at a stall selling between-meal snacks, such as pakoras (battered deep-fried vegetables) or *idlis* (freshly steamed rice breads) or *kachoris* (deep-fried filled breads), or *dosas* (savory crepelike breads), or any number of others, it's the same. The food, often freshly fried, hot and steaming, comes with a splash of bright green coriander chutney or a drizzle of tamarind sauce, or a dash of coconut chutney spiked with green chiles.

We all eat because we're hungry. But what we find we hunger for isn't just food to fill our bellies, it's also intensity of flavor and the chance to explore flavor combinations as we eat. And that's where chutneys and sauces come in. They're the smallest servings in the meal, yet they always play a big role because they're such generous providers of pleasure. For us these "sides" of flavor are among the most exciting foods we meet when we're traveling and the most fun to make and to serve once we get back home.

We serve them as condiments or extra flavors with all kinds of foods, not just with meals based on the repertoire of the Subcontinent. They can help heighten the taste of grilled meat or vegetables, for example, or give everyone at the table a chance to add a hit of chile heat or sweet tartness to a mouthful of rice. Some chutneys and *sambols* also make a good dip for bread and for deep-fried snacks. For example, *sambols*, flavorful inventive chile pastes that are freshly ground and based on hot chiles and onions, are a traditional accompaniment for Sri Lankan hoppers (soft-textured savory pancakes), and tamarind sauce is a classic dressing for samosas.

We had to cut back on the recipes in this chapter: It threatened to take over the book, in fact. There's such a variety out there, from Sri Lankan *sambols* to chutneys of all kinds, both freshly assembled mixtures and bottled sauces. In southern India, the chutneys are often made of ground or chopped ingredients "tempered" with hot spiced oil, coconut chutney, for example. In northern India, and in Bangladesh, Pakistan, and Nepal, there are fresh herb-based and fruit-based chutneys, as well as cooked condiments, such as tomato chutney.

Each chutney and sauce in this chapter is a way of adding dash and excitement to a meal, be it a simple supper or a multicourse feast. We've included a large number of these fresh chutneys that you can toss together at the last minute, like small high-intensity salads. And there are several cooked chutneys and sauces that can be made ahead and then brought out when you want the hit of flavor they provide. We've also included a spiced roasted eggplant puree that we serve as a chutney. (In addition, there are yogurt-based sauces in the next chapter, Salads, and a number of other chutneys appear elsewhere in the book as accompaniments; see the Index for a complete list.) Some sauces and chutneys are chile-hot, some are sweet, some are tart, and many are a combination: for instance, sweet-tart, such as our star fruit chutney, or sweet-hot, such as date-onion chutney.

Rural Bengali woman

HOT SWEET DATE-ONION CHUTNEY

· · · · · · · · · · · ·

There's nothing better than having lots of condiments, little tastes of this and that, on hand to dab on during a meal, especially on rice. This unusual onion chutney (*kanda ni chutney* in Parsi) keeps well in the refrigerator, and it gives a delicious hot-and-sweet kick to any mouthful. The dates have a smoky sweetness, and the chiles a fresh heat.

3 dried red chiles, stemmed

2 tablespoons raw sesame oil, or vegetable oil, or ghee

1 large white onion (about ½ pound), coarsely chopped

½ teaspoon salt, or to taste

¼ cup chopped pitted dates

Put the chiles in a small bowl, add 1 cup hot water, and set aside to soak for 10 minutes. Meanwhile, heat the oil in a wok or karhai (see Glossary) or a wide heavy skillet over medium-high heat. Add the onion and salt and cook until the onion is well touched with brown, about 10 minutes. Remove from the heat and set aside.

Drain the chiles, place them in a food processor, add the chopped dates, and process for 30 seconds to finely chop. Add the onion mixture and process for about 15 seconds to chop and blend the ingredients. *Alternatively*, place the drained chiles on a flat stone mortar and grind to a paste with the pestle, add the dates and grind, and finally, add the cooked onion mixture and coarsely grind, leaving some small chunks.

Taste the chutney for salt, and adjust if necessary. Serve in a condiment dish. (Store leftovers in a well-sealed glass jar in the refrigerator for up to several weeks.) MAKES 1 CUP; SERVES 6

Delicious with tart flavors such as Bangla Dal with a Hit of Lime (page 178) or Duck Vindaloo (page 251), and with rice dishes.

Fresh Coriander–Peanut Chutney on seared halibut

FRESH CORIANDER-PEANUT CHUTNEY

· · · · · · · · · · · ·

When we think about the food of the Subcontinent, we often think of dried spices like black mustard seed, cumin, coriander, and turmeric, but fresh herbs also play a big role in flavor, and nowhere more so than in fresh chutneys. This beautiful, quickly assembled, bright green chutney comes from Gujarat state, in the western part of India.

Like most fresh chutneys, it is traditionally made using a stone mortar and a pestle, but a food processor does just as good a job of grinding the ingredients. The peanuts essentially disappear during processing, leaving no trace of graininess, just a hint of flavor and a subtle thickening of the sauce. Flavors are bright and clean, with a hit of fresh-chile heat, and the tartness of lemon juice nicely balanced by a little sugar.

2 cups coarsely chopped coriander leaves and stems (about 1 large bunch)

3 to 5 green cayenne chiles, or substitute serrano chiles, seeded

2 tablespoons boiled skinned peanuts (see Glossary), or substitute unsalted roasted peanuts

1 teaspoon sugar

½ teaspoon ground cumin

About 3 tablespoons fresh lemon juice

About ¼ teaspoon salt

Place the coriander leaves, chiles, and peanuts in a food processor, add the sugar and cumin, and process to a smooth paste. Transfer to a bowl and stir in 3 tablespoons lemon juice and ¼ teaspoon salt. Taste and adjust seasonings and the balance of tart and sweet as you wish. Note that the fresh flavor gets a little dulled after a few hours, so it's best to serve this shortly after you make it. MAKES A SCANT 1 CUP; SERVES 4 AS A DIP AND 6 AS A DRIZZLED-ON FLAVORING

Serve to accompany rice dishes such as Stir-fried Rice and Dal (page 96) or as a dip. Coriander chutney is a traditional accompaniment for deep-fried snacks such as pakoras (see page 298) or samosas (page 296)— drizzle it over or else dip them in the sauce—and for the Gujarati steamed bread called dhokla (page 125). We also like it drizzled on grilled fish.

COCONUT SAMBOL

. . . .

Sambols in the Subcontinent come primarily from Sri Lanka and are not to be confused with the *sambals* in Indonesian/Malaysian cooking, though they are, presumably, related. A Sri Lankan *sambol* resembles a Mexican salsa or a *jaew* from Laos, for it is most often made with uncooked ingredients, such as fresh or dried chiles, shallots, and garlic, that are traditionally ground with a stone mortar and a pestle, then mixed with an acid such as lime juice. The grinding brings out the full flavor of the ingredients and makes for a moist, coarse paste, like a dryish salsa.

In Sri Lanka there are three very common *sambols* that we think of as the Big Three: coconut *sambol* (*pol sambol*), red onion *sambol* (*lunumiris*), and hot-sweet *sambol* (*seeni sambol*). These end up on the table, either separately or together, with snacks and/or meals, and their individual characters depends upon the cook who makes them.

This coconut *sambol* has an intense heat, so servings are small—rather like horseradish or hot mustard. It's traditionally made with grated fresh coconut, which is abundant everywhere on the island. At home we usually use frozen grated coconut, or rehydrated dried coconut, because good-quality fresh coconut can be hard to find. As with all *sambols*, it's fun to grind the ingredients by hand if you have a good stone mortar and a pestle, but a food processor also works well and quickly.

6 tablespoons fresh or frozen grated coconut or
    ¼ cup dried shredded coconut
¼ cup water (if using dried coconut)
½ teaspoon coarse salt
3 or 4 dried red chiles, stemmed
5 or 6 black peppercorns or scant ¼ teaspoon freshly ground
    black pepper
1 garlic clove
½ cup chopped shallots
About 2 tablespoons fresh lime juice

If using dried coconut, place it in a small bowl with the water to soak for a few minutes.

If using a flat stone mortar and a pestle, put the coarse salt on the mortar, then grind the red chiles into the salt. Add the peppercorns or ground pepper and grind in, then grind in the garlic. When you have a thick paste, add the shallots and continue to grind until well mixed. Add the coconut and grind it in, then add the lime juice and mix well.

If using a food processor, grind the black peppercorns, if using, in a spice/coffee grinder, then add all the ingredients to the food processor and process to an almost uniform paste.

Serve in a small condiment dish. This *sambol* will keep for 1 or 2 days if refrigerated.   MAKES A SCANT ½ CUP; SERVES 4

Serve as a spicy-hot condiment with grilled or roasted meat or with Hoppers (page 121).

CLOCKWISE FROM LEFT: *Sri Lankan Seeni Sambol (page 33), Red Onion Sambol (page 32), and Coconut Sambol*

MINT SAMBOL

. . . .

Whenever you have good fresh mint available, make this *sambol* to accompany almost any meal. It has a refreshing taste, and, like most other *sambols*, it's so easy to make.

1 teaspoon coarse salt
5 or 6 black peppercorns or scant ¼ teaspoon freshly ground black pepper
1 large or 2 small garlic cloves
2 to 3 green cayenne chiles, or substitute serrano chiles,
**   coarsely chopped**
½ cup chopped red onion or shallots
1 cup loosely packed fresh mint leaves
About 1 tablespoon fresh lime juice

If using a flat stone mortar and a pestle, put the coarse salt on the mortar and grind the peppercorns (or pepper) into the salt. Add the garlic and chiles and grind into a thick paste. Add the chopped onion or shallots and grind in. Finally, add the mint and lightly pound to mix it in. Transfer to a small bowl, add the lime juice, and mix.

If using a food processor, grind the black peppercorns, if using, in a spice/coffee grinder, then add all the ingredients to the food processor and process to an almost uniform paste.

Serve in a small bowl.   MAKES A SCANT 1 CUP; SERVES 4 TO 5

Serve as a condiment to accompany lamb or fish, or grilled vegetables.

RED ONION SAMBOL

. . . .

The Sinhalese name for this *sambol*, *lunumiris*, is such a great-sounding word. In fact, because *lunu* means "onion," and *miris* is "chile," it means "onion-chile," a perfect name for almost any *sambol*. We use red onions or Asian shallots.

This is probably our favorite of Sri Lanka's Big Three *sambols* (see page 30), so simple and direct, so absolutely addictive and delicious. Like coconut sambol, it's a dense hot paste, spiked with fresh lime juice, and serving sizes are small: teaspoon- to tablespoon-size dollops. *Lunumiris* is traditionally made with Maldive fish, which gives it a salty, smoky back-taste, but we find we prefer it without. If you want to try the traditional version, finely chop 1 teaspoon Maldive fish or bonito flakes and stir it in. PHOTOGRAPH ON PAGE 31

½ cup coarsely chopped red onion or Asian shallots
2 green cayenne chiles, chopped
1 tablespoon fresh lime juice
½ teaspoon salt

Using a food processor or a stone mortar and a pestle, process or grind all the ingredients to a rough paste.

Serve in a small condiment dish.   MAKES A GENEROUS ½ CUP;
SERVES 4 AS A CONDIMENT, 2 AS A DIP

Serve as a chile-hot condiment with savory dishes or as a dip for Hoppers (page 121).

SRI LANKAN SEENI SAMBOL

. . . .

This is perhaps the most famous of the Big Three *sambols* (see page 30) of Sri Lanka. Unlike the other two, which are uncooked, it's slow cooked to a dense mass. Flavors are very hot as well as sweet and aromatic. This recipe makes a relatively large quantity; store it in a glass jar in the refrigerator and bring it out as a condiment with any meal. Put it out in a small bowl with a serving spoon so guests can dollop a little on the side of their plates, as they would hot mustard or horseradish.

PHOTOGRAPH ON PAGE 31

¼ cup coconut oil or vegetable oil

3 cups packed thinly sliced red onions or shallots

¼ cup minced garlic or garlic mashed to a paste

2 tablespoons minced ginger or ginger mashed to a paste

8 fresh or frozen curry leaves

4 to 8 dried red chiles, stemmed and broken into pieces

1 teaspoon Maldive fish, or substitute bonito flakes,
    ground to a powder (optional)

1 teaspoon ground cinnamon

⅛ teaspoon ground cardamom

⅛ teaspoon ground cloves

¾ cup canned or fresh coconut milk

½ to 1 teaspoon sugar

½ teaspoon salt

2 tablespoons fresh lime juice, or to taste

Heat the oil in a large heavy saucepan over medium-high heat. When it is hot, add the onions or shallots, the garlic and ginger, and cook, stirring frequently, until very soft and turning golden brown, 10 to 15 minutes. Lower the heat, add the curry leaves, dried chiles, fish, if using, cinnamon, cardamom, cloves, and coconut milk, and bring just to a simmer. Simmer over low heat for about 30 minutes, stirring occasionally to make sure the *sambol* is not sticking. Remove from the heat, add the sugar, salt, and lime juice, and stir to mix well. Transfer the *sambol* to a food processor and process to a smooth puree.

Transfer the *sambol* to a jar and let cool. Seal lid tightly and store in the refrigerator. It will keep for a month or more if refrigerated.

MAKES ABOUT 1 ½ CUPS

Serve to accompany mild-tasting dishes, such as Cauliflower Dum (page 148) or Aromatic Pumpkin and Coconut (page 160), for a chile-hot contrast, or as a dip for Hoppers (page 121) or Idlis (page 120), or, less traditionally, for tortilla chips or pita bread wedges.

STAR FRUIT CHUTNEY

· · · · · · · · · · · ·

In early rainy season in Bangladesh, the sky is liable to darken suddenly with a huge cloud, then let loose a deluge. People take shelter, or else walk on in the downpour, getting soaked through. Muddy-brown streams of water flow along the edges of the road. Once the rain stops, the sun reappears, and soon a mist starts rising off the wet pavement.

A couple of years ago, I was caught in one such downpour at a local market in the capital, Dhaka. Once it stopped, I began to pick my way along the street between the fresh puddles. I got distracted by a man selling star fruit chutney, aromatic and inviting. I bought some, on a piece of banana leaf, to eat as a snack with my fingers. Each mouthful was tart-sweet and savory, flavored with mustard oil and warm spicing, with a medium heat. This is our version of that rainy-day discovery.

PHOTOGRAPHS OPPOSITE LEFT AND ON PAGE 16

1 medium-large or 2 small green or yellow star fruit ($^1/_2$ to $^3/_4$ pound)

2 tablespoons mustard oil

$^1/_4$ teaspoon black mustard seeds

$^1/_4$ teaspoon nigella seeds

$^1/_4$ teaspoon cumin seeds

Generous $^1/_2$ cup chopped shallots

2 green cayenne chiles, seeds and pith removed, thinly sliced

$^3/_4$ teaspoon salt, or to taste

1 or 2 lime wedges (optional)

Using a paring knife, trim the very finest tough edges off the five "wings" of the star fruit and discard. Trim off a narrow slice at each end of the fruit, then slice the fruit crosswise into thinner-than-$^1/_4$-inch-thick slices. Save 1 or 2 whole stars for garnish, if you wish, and chop the remaining slices into bite-size pieces. Set aside.

In a wok or karhai (see Glossary) or in a heavy skillet, heat the mustard oil over medium-high heat until hot. Toss in the mustard seeds, and when they start to sputter, add the nigella and cumin seeds. Stir briefly, then add the shallots and chiles and stir-fry until the shallots are tender and starting to change color, about 5 minutes.

Add the chopped star fruit and salt and cook, stirring and turning to coat the fruit with the flavorings and to expose it to the heat, for 4 to 5 minutes, until the fruit is softening. Turn the chutney out onto a plate and taste for seasoning and for tartness; if the fruit tastes sweet rather than a little tart, squeeze on some fresh lime juice just before serving.

SERVES 6 TO 8 AS A CHUTNEY, 4 AS A SMALL SALAD

Serve as a condiment for rice dishes or fish or grilled meat, or as an intense palate-freshening salad, a contrast for a meal of mild flavors.

OPPOSITE, RIGHT: *A tabla (drum) maker sits by his shop at the Bangladeshi village of Damrai, about an hour north of the capital city, Dhaka.*

FIRST TRIP

The other night we went to our friends' house for dinner. We were invited because they're planning a trip to India and Sri Lanka, and we, like the ten or twelve other people invited, have often been to the Subcontinent. The idea was that we could all give travel advice and have a good time. And we did have a good time, and give lots of travel advice, but the evening was a little awkward.

People travel to the Subcontinent for so many different reasons. The dinner party crowd was a perfect example. There was a videographer, a temple enthusiast, a human rights worker, a dancer, a photographer, and an Indian crafts-store owner. And because many of these people have been going to the Subcontinent regularly since the early 1970s, there were inevitably strongly held feelings and conflicting views.

"You must travel only by train," someone insisted.

"Don't go to Kerala, go to Karnataka."

"Eat only in Brahmin restaurants."

"Go to Sri Lanka first, not the other way around, because otherwise you'll be comparing it to India."

The discussion could have continued all night, and probably for days on end, because travel to the Subcontinent is one of those subjects that gets people going. But it was a little awkward, and I think we weren't the only ones who found it so. Everyone in the room knew very well that what works for one person may not work for someone else.

When we first began traveling in the Subcontinent in the mid-1970s, the other travelers we most often met divided somewhat equally between hash-smoking hippies and yoga-meditation types, coming predominantly from England, Italy, and France, and, to a lesser extent, Australia. Then, as trekking in the Himalaya became fashionable in the 1980s, more Americans and Canadians started coming, mainly to Nepal. And during this time, if we visited Buddhist sites and Kolkata (Calcutta), we'd always be sharing the hotels with young people from Japan.

But all that started to change in the 1990s, and the scenario keeps changing in leaps and bounds. Places like Rajasthan and Kerala (two Indian states) are now major tourist destinations for visitors from around the world. Charter planes arrive in Goa (the old Portuguese colony on the west coast of India) all winter long from Europe, and even from the United States, heading for the state's many famous beaches.

Tourism has increased at a rapid rate, and for good reason. The infrastructure supporting tourism has improved dramatically and will likely continue to do so. Railway bookings can now be made on the Internet, something that seems almost incomprehensible to anyone who traveled here years ago and vividly remembers waiting for hours in long lines at railway stations only to find the train already fully booked. Also thanks to an Internet-savvy Subcontinent, it's now possible to book hotel rooms (even ten-dollar-a-night rooms) on the Web; it's even possible to arrange for a car and driver. At the expensive end of the travel spectrum, the Subcontinent now has some of the most beautiful, unique, and luxurious hotels in the world.

If you're planning a first trip to the Subcontinent and, like us, you're traveling a lot for food, we have certain advice to offer here, and many more bits that you'll see pop up throughout the book, as well as in "Notes on Photographing the Subcontinent" (page 366). All these suggestions are things that work for us, and they may or may not work for you. Our only real advice is to have fun, because if you do, you'll be ready to go back!

Look for local cookbooks (many of our favorites are listed in the Bibliography). Local and regional publishing is an art form in the Subcontinent, and a gold mine for local cookbooks; many of them are published in English. Scour every bookseller, from streetside kiosks to fancy urban bookstores (and check out locally produced music CDs at the same time). Stop in at local culinary schools and home economics departments, and ask if they put out their own cookbooks. Once you have your hands on a good local cookbook, take it with you everywhere you go, from restaurants to shops to hotel lobbies, and ask any nice person where you might find a specific dish, showing them the recipe. Get on the recipe trail, and it will almost always lead to something fun (and delicious!).

Food that's expensive isn't always the best. Get relaxed (if you aren't by nature) with finding little neighborhood places to eat. It's just like finding a good local diner or café anywhere in the world: Look for places that are busy. If you're staying in a heavy tourist area, or in an expensive hotel, try to get outside the invisible arm's length of the area or hotel before looking for a place to eat. We're not big fans of expensive restaurants in South Asia because we find that the food often is overrich, too cluttered in taste, working too hard to impress.

For health safety reasons, set some rules about what you'll eat and drink. We usually don't eat uncooked salads and vegetables; we avoid ice and ice cream; we eat only fruit we can peel; and we try to eat food hot and freshly cooked. But beyond that, try not to be anxious.

And last but not least, when it comes to food, be sure to search out local breakfasts. Some of the best food in the Subcontinent is served for breakfast, often very early in the morning. Seek out a local restaurant or a busy tea shop, and then show up as soon as you wake up in the morning. Trying something new, and sometimes spicy, for breakfast is one of those "travel things" that many people find difficult to do at first, but in the Subcontinent, when you make the effort, it's often richly rewarded.

Oh, and how long to stay on a first trip? As long as possible. Two weeks, coming all the way from North America, is pushing it on the short side, but if that's all the time you have, we think it's still worth going. Three weeks is more practical, and anything longer just gets better and better.

There's one thing more to consider, and that's how to spread your time. Two weeks in Varanasi or Chennai (what used to be called Madras) can be a good long time, doing little side trips and generally hanging out. But if you travel from New Delhi to Agra to see the Taj Mahal, then to Rajasthan, then perhaps to a little beach in Goa, and then catch the plane and fly back home, all in two weeks, chances are you'll come home a whole lot more tired and stressed out than when you left. Try not to get too ambitious travelwise (chances are the Taj will still be there next time you visit). Leave plenty of room for those local tea shops and gorgeous red dusty sunsets.

Or at least that's what works best for us.

COCONUT CHUTNEY

. . . .

Coconut chutney accompanies many of our favorite meals in the southern part of the Subcontinent, especially *dosas* (see page 112), *idlis* (see page 120), and the deep-fried South Indian snacks called *vadas* (see page 286). It's an easy way to bring flavor and freshness to the table, with a little chile heat and a good balance of tart and sweet. The chutney can be thick with coconut or very liquid; it's up to the cook.

Traditionally coconut chutney, like many other South Indian dishes, is flavored with a little dal that is roasted in a skillet. It gives a pleasant toasted flavor, a mellow nuttiness, and also a little crunch. You can grind it in a spice grinder as we do, or leave it whole and crunchy, or omit it, as you please.

1 teaspoon tamarind pulp

1 tablespoon hot water

1½ cups fresh or frozen grated coconut

1 teaspoon grated ginger or ginger mashed to a paste

2 to 3 green cayenne chiles, or substitute serranos,
roughly chopped

½ teaspoon salt

TEMPERING

1 tablespoon coconut oil or vegetable oil

1 teaspoon black mustard seeds

2 teaspoons toovar dal or urad dal (see headnote),
coarsely ground (optional)

10 fresh or frozen curry leaves

Blend the tamarind pulp into the hot water in a small cup and let it stand for several minutes to soften. Place a small sieve over a bowl and press the tamarind mixture through it. Discard the pulp.

Place the tamarind liquid in a blender, add the grated coconut, ginger, green chiles, and salt, and blend well. Transfer to a small bowl and set aside.

Place a small skillet over medium-high heat and add the oil. When the oil is hot, add the mustard seeds, dal, if using, and curry leaves and stir-fry for 1 to 2 minutes, until the seeds have popped and the dal is toasted. Immediately pour the oil onto the coconut mixture and stir thoroughly. Serve at once. MAKES ABOUT 1½ CUPS; SERVES 6 TO 8

Serve as a dipping sauce or condiment to accompany Spicy Chickpea Fritters (page 286), Home-Style Dosas (page 112), or Idlis (page 120), or simply with a rice dish such as Quick Tamarind Pulao with Curry Leaves (page 98).

Bicycles play many roles in the Subcontinent. Here, in a Muslim neighborhood near one of the city gates of Ahmadabad, capital of the state of Gujarat, a bicycle is being used as a drying rack in the late afternoon sun.

GUJARATI MANGO CHUTNEY

· · · · · · · · · · ·

The manager of the hotel where I stayed in Ahmadabad, a man named Chirag, invited me to his house to learn some home-style Gujarati dishes from his wife, Riku. It was a great afternoon, made even more delightful by Riku's father and mother, who also contributed their ideas about food in Gujarat.

This delicious crowd-pleasing chutney was described to me by Riku's mother, a charming woman. It's the family's favorite chutney, and whenever green mangoes are available, she makes jars of it. She told me to use equal weights of chopped mango and sugar, but the green mangoes she works with are much more tart than those we find here. As a result, we've altered the proportions to suit the mangoes we can find in North America, which tend to be unripe sweet mangoes (rather than unripe tart magoes), with mostly green skins and flesh turning to yellow inside. (If you start with completely green and very tart mangoes, increase the sugar to 3½ cups.)

Since the green mangoes here are partway ripe, they're also juicier than very green mangoes, so the chutney takes a little time to cook down. But it doesn't need close supervision—as long as you have a very heavy pot and set it over medium-low heat, it can simmer and cook down while you do something else.

We like the chutney with a little chile heat, just enough to warm the back of the throat, but without intensity. You may wish for more. Because the cayenne gets added at the end, it's easy to add a little, then taste and decide if you want a hotter chutney.

The chutney can be bottled in sterilized jars like jam and keeps well. We find it makes a great gift, so we never keep them for long.

6 cups chopped peeled unripe mangoes (about 6 medium mangoes)

2¹/₂ cups sugar, or more to taste (see headnote)

2 tablespoons salt

¹/₂ cup peanut oil or vegetable oil

1 tablespoon black mustard seeds

¹/₄ teaspoon asafoetida powder

2 teaspoons cumin seeds, crushed or ground

2 cloves

One 3-inch cinnamon or cassia stick

¹/₂ teaspoon turmeric

¹/₂ to 1 teaspoon cayenne

Place the mangoes in a large bowl, add the sugar and salt, and mix well. Set aside.

In a wide heavy 4-quart pot, heat the oil over medium-high heat. Add the mustard seeds and cook until they pop (place a lid over to prevent splattering). Once the seeds stop popping, lower the heat to medium and sprinkle on the asafoetida powder. Add the cumin, cloves, and cinnamon stick and stir, then add the mango-sugar mixture. It will be quite liquid, because the sugar and salt draw liquid out of the chopped mangoes. Bring to a boil over medium-high heat, stirring, then lower the heat to maintain a strong simmer. Stir in the turmeric and simmer, uncovered, until most of the liquid evaporates and the mixture thickens, about 1¹/₂ hours, or perhaps a little longer. (If your mangoes are very green, they will give off less liquid and the mixture will cook down more quickly, in less than an hour.)

When the chutney has boiled down so that it is a thickened blend of fruit and liquid, add ¹/₂ teaspoon cayenne, stir it in, and then taste for heat. Add a little more cayenne, if you wish, then remove from the heat.

Sterilize four 1-cup jars with lids. Bring the chutney back to a boil, then use a sterilized ladle to spoon the mixture into the jars. Top with sterilized lids. The fourth jar may not be quite full, so it won't seal; use that one first. Refrigerate jars after opening.   MAKES ABOUT 4 CUPS

Serve as a dip for plain breads or as an intensely flavored condiment with any meal.

QUICK RAJASTHANI-STYLE GREEN MANGO CHUTNEY: Here's another version of cooked green mango chutney that takes only 10 minutes or so of cooking. Heat ¹/₄ cup oil in a small wide heavy pot over medium-high heat. Add 1 teaspoon fennel seeds and ¹/₂ teaspoon nigella seeds and fry briefly, then toss in 2 cups chopped peeled green mangoes and cook for several minutes, until starting to soften. Add 1 tablespoon ground coriander, ¹/₂ to 1 teaspoon cayenne, ¹/₂ teaspoon turmeric, ³/₄ cup sugar, and 1 teaspoon salt and cook over medium heat, stirring, until the sugar has completely dissolved and the mixture is bubbling. If your mangoes are very green and tart, you may need to add another ¹/₄ cup sugar and up to ¹/₂ cup water so the sugar will dissolve; if your mangoes are at all yellow, they will give off plenty of liquid. Remove from the heat. Serve warm or cool; store in a tightly sealed jar in the refrigerator.

MAKES ABOUT 1¹/₂ CUPS

Serve as above.

EVERYTHING IS EXCITING ABOUT ARRIVING IN THE SUBCONTINENT, no matter where we are: Delhi, Kolkata (Calcutta), Colombo, Kathmandu, Dhaka. Coming from North America, or from Europe, or from Hong Kong or Bangkok, everything looks different, smells different, even the air feels different. Often we arrive late at night and there's an awkward time of finding our way when a city is asleep, but even so, we're excited.

There are, of course, a few little details to look after. Money, for example. We have to change money, dollars for rupees (or takas in Bangladesh), which isn't usually a problem, but when we change a few hundred dollars at an airport bank, or with a money changer, we end up with large denominations like thousand-rupee notes (right now worth about twenty dollars in India). This is "big money," but what we need most is "small money," one-rupee, five-rupee, ten-rupee notes, money for rickshaws and tea, for beggars, and for fresh pakoras served hot with a little chutney on the street corner. The Subcontinent is always short on small money, always short on change. With only big money in our pockets, we might as well be carrying Monopoly money.

So the first order of business is to get small money, and then more small money, until our pockets bulge with coins and paper money—ones, fives, and tens, crumpled and worn, looking a century old. It's not easy, first trying to break the big bills, always stubbornly insisting that's all we have. We never admit that we have small money, never, until our pockets bulge!

Small Money

Mild green chiles for sale at an afternoon market in Kandy.
OPPOSITE, LEFT: *Market scale in Kandy, Sri Lanka.* RIGHT: *Small money in Sri Lanka.*

TOMATO CHUTNEY

· · · · · · · · · · · ·

On a recent trip to Orissa (see page 274), spent driving almost all day every day for nearly two weeks in the mountains in the southern part of the state, I had consistently good food, but unfortunately I learned very few of the classic Oriyan dishes. Ranjan, my driver and guide, was an incredible companion when it came to tracking down anything related to food and agriculture, even if it meant stopping the car (for the twentieth time in a morning) to walk across a field to identify a type of legume we hadn't seen before, but he was at a complete loss when it came to describing how a particular Oriyan dish might be made. He'd always look at me as if to say, "It's good, just eat it."

The day we had this tomato chutney in the town of Jeypore, I liked it so much that I kept asking and asking until finally Ranjan went into the kitchen and requested that the cook come out. The cook explained and Ranjan translated, and after I at last had good notes and had said thank you to the cook, Ranjan again looked over at me and gave me the look: "It's good, just eat it."

The chutney has a coarsely pureed texture, like a cooked salsa, a great aroma from the curry leaves, a little sweetness from the simmered onions, and a fair amount of heat from the ginger and chiles. PHOTOGRAPH ON PAGE 291

Scant 2 tablespoons raw sesame, coconut, or vegetable oil

About 2 cups thinly sliced onions

4 to 5 green or red cayenne chiles, seeded and coarsely chopped

1 tablespoon minced ginger or ginger mashed to a paste

3 to 3¹/₂ cups finely chopped tomatoes

1 teaspoon salt, or to taste

TEMPERING

1 tablespoon raw sesame, coconut, or vegetable oil

1 teaspoon black mustard seeds

1 teaspoon urad dal, coarsely ground (optional)

8 to 10 fresh or frozen curry leaves

In a large skillet, heat the oil over medium-high heat. When it is hot, add the onions, chiles, and ginger and stir-fry for 4 to 5 minutes, until the onions have softened a little. Add the chopped tomatoes and salt and cook for another 5 to 7 minutes, stirring occasionally, until the tomatoes are well softened.

Transfer the mixture to a blender or food processor and blend to a chunky puree, or transfer it to a large mortar and roughly grind it with the pestle. Turn out into a bowl.

To temper the chutney, heat a small skillet over medium-high heat and add the oil. When the oil is hot, add the black mustard seeds, urad dal, if using, and curry leaves and cook for 1 minute, then stir into the tomato mixture. Serve warm or at room temperature.

MAKES ABOUT 3 CUPS; SERVES 6 TO 8

Serve as you would a tomato salsa: as a dip for crackers or flatbreads, or as a moistening condiment sauce to accompany rice or grilled meat (Cumin-Coriander Beef Patties, page 268, for example).

TAMARIND SAUCE

. . . .

One winter afternoon I spent several hours watching and photographing the cook at Lala restaurant, a little street-side café in the main bazaar in Udaipur. He worked outdoors in the street, deftly and quickly, first shaping and frying *kachoris* (see page 134), then stirring up a large batch of tamarind sauce in a huge restaurant wok.

Though it's generally called tamarind chutney, this is really a sauce, a thickened liquid that's a great all-purpose Gujarati-style condiment. It has some chile heat, and a good, blended balance of tart and sweet, so neither predominates. We've followed the Lala cook's method but adapted both it and the quantities of ingredients to the home kitchen.

2 tablespoons tamarind pulp

1 cup hot water

2 tablespoons chickpea flour (*besan*)

¼ cup cold water

2 tablespoons vegetable oil

1 teaspoon black mustard seeds

1 teaspoon ground fennel

½ teaspoon cayenne

½ teaspoon turmeric

½ teaspoon salt

1 tablespoon sugar

Chop the tamarind pulp. Place it in a bowl with the hot water to soak for a few minutes, then mash with a fork. Place a sieve over a bowl and press the tamarind through the sieve, using the back of a wooden spoon. Discard the pulp and set the tamarind liquid aside.

Place the flour in a small bowl and stir in 2 tablespoons of the cold water to make a smooth paste, then stir in the remaining 2 tablespoons water to make a smooth batter. Set aside.

Heat a wok or karhai (see Glossary) or a heavy skillet over high heat and add the oil. Toss in the mustard seeds and lower the heat to medium-high. As soon as the seeds stop popping, toss in the fennel, cayenne, turmeric, and salt, stir to mix well, and then add the reserved tamarind liquid. Bring to a boil. Add the batter and stir to mix well, then add the sugar and stir. Bring to a vigorous boil and cook hard for 5 minutes, stirring to keep the mixture from sticking. Lower the heat and simmer for another 5 minutes.

Turn the sauce out into a small bowl and serve. Store leftovers in a well-sealed glass jar in the refrigerator. MAKES ABOUT 1 CUP; SERVES 6 TO 8

Serve as a condiment sauce with fried snacks such as Fennel-Flecked Potato Samosas (page 296) or Savory Deep-fried Street-Side Breads (page 134) with Dhokla (page 125), and with rice meals.

I meet Sam most every night at the Pub Royale on the ground floor of the old colonial Queen's Hotel, in Kandy (the former Sinhalese capital, in the hills of Sri Lanka, about three hours' drive inland from the coast). Sam doesn't drink, but he comes to the pub to watch the news and cricket on the television. Every year he comes to Kandy for a month on holiday from Colombo, Sri Lanka's present-day capital city. Sam is a tax accountant, so he flees the city the moment tax season is over. This is his twentieth year at the Queen's.

Sam and I were born in the same year, 1954. When we first discovered it, his already big round eyes grew as big as pumpkins, and he stood straight up from his bar stool. Birth dates are important to Sam because he's a numbers guy. He was born on February 26. Two plus six makes eight, so he's an eight, and eights are leaders, Sam tells me, but they are also bad marriage prospects because they might change careers at any time. Not that Sam has changed careers, but he is a bachelor. A successful, nice, intelligent, almost-fifty bachelor isn't that common in Sri Lanka, I wouldn't think. I quiz him on it often; twice he was in love, but each time she married someone else. I was born on July 9, so I'm a nine. Hitler was a nine, Sam says, and so is the leader of the Tamil Tigers (who fought an often-vicious civil war for an independent Tamil state in northeastern Sri Lanka).

Sam and I first met over hoppers and *sambol*. I was sitting at one end of the bar and he at the other. It was my first night in town, and I ordered fresh, steaming-hot hoppers (savory flour-and-coconut-milk pancakes) that were being made at the entrance to the pub. The hoppers arrived with *seeni sambol* and *lunumiris*, two fiery-hot chile pastes much loved in Sri Lanka, everywhere made by hand with care and attention. It was all such a big treat: hot hoppers, chile-hot *sambols*, a big glass of cold beer, and local news on television read in English!

"You can eat those *sambols*?" I heard a voice suddenly beside me ask. "They are not too hot?"

"I like them," I replied, for the first time seeing Sam, who had walked down the length of the bar to talk to me.

And so we got to be friends, just like that. Now most nights we meet to watch the news together, and then Sam patiently answers all my food questions (he likes food almost as much as he likes numbers). We talk about the world and the Sri Lankan war between the government and the Tamil Tigers, and he tells me the latest hotel gossip, my favorite thing. As the evening gets late, we usually go for a snack, to the Chinese restaurant upstairs for hot-and-sour soup, or to the hotel dining room for more hoppers and *sambol*. We say good night around eleven, which is late by Kandy standards, and head off in our separate directions down the long teak-floored high-ceilinged corridors of the Queen's.

I feel lucky to have a friend like Sam, an eight.

SAM & SAMBOLS

TART MANGO SALSA

· · · · · · · · · · ·

Mangoes can be tart or sweet or a combination, depending on how ripe they are and on their variety (see Glossary). This quick processor chutney is made from fresh herbs and hard green (unripe) mangoes, which are likely to be green on the outside but will usually have flesh that's starting to ripen and so it's pale yellow and slightly sweet. If your mangoes are green-fleshed, they will be more tart, and you will want to add another teaspoon of sugar. PHOTOGRAPH ON PAGE 237

1 large unripe mango, peeled, pitted, and chopped (1 to 1½ cups)

½ cup packed coriander leaves and stems

¼ cup packed mint leaves

2 green cayenne chiles, seeded and coarsely chopped

1 teaspoon coriander seeds, toasted and ground

½ teaspoon jaggery (palm or crude sugar) or brown sugar, or to taste

¼ teaspoon salt, or to taste

Place all the ingredients in a food processor or blender and process or blend very briefly, until finely chopped. If you go on too long, or if your mango is soft, you'll have a green pureed sauce. Taste and add extra sugar or salt, if you wish.

Transfer to one or more small bowls to serve.

MAKES 1 TO 1½ CUPS; SERVES 4

Serve as a sweet-tart dip for flatbreads or as a chutney to accompany kebabs or slices of roast meat or grilled vegetables.

HOT CHILE OIL PASTE

· · · · · · · · · · ·

I first tasted this condiment at the Saturday market in Kalimpong, a town near the Bhutan–Sikkim border, as a red chile paste coating hard-cooked eggs. Each egg was wrapped in a green leaf, a beautiful presentation. The combination of egg and sauce was delicious, for the sauce had a surprising depth of flavor. I had expected just chile heat, but found out when I tasted the egg I'd bought that the chile oil paste was flavored with ginger, scallions, and garlic. We don't eat many hard-cooked eggs in our house, but we do make this paste, called *tsu la-tse*, quite often. We serve it as a condiment to add a little heat and flavor to soups, rice meals, and grills of all kinds. It keeps well in the refrigerator.

2 tablespoons chopped ginger

2 tablespoons chopped garlic

¾ cup stemmed dried red chiles

½ teaspoon salt

½ cup minced scallions

½ cup peanut oil

Place the ginger, garlic, chiles, and salt in a food processor or mini-chopper. Process or chop to a paste; the chile seeds will be spattered up the sides of the bowl. Sometimes grinding dried chiles can put a lot of chile dust in the air, so take care not to breathe in too deeply when you remove the processor lid. Transfer to a heatproof bowl and stir in the minced scallions. Set aside.

Heat the oil in a small heavy skillet until almost smoking. Pour it into the bowl of chopped ingredients and stir to blend thoroughly. Let it cool a little, then transfer it to a glass jar with a good lid.

Once cooled, store it in the refrigerator for up to 1 month.

MAKES ABOUT ¾ CUP

We like to set this out as a condiment for those who want to add a dose of chile heat and to add sparkle to mild-tasting dishes such as Coconut-Rice Soup (page 89). It's also a treat with Darjeeling Market Tibetan Breads (page 136).

ANDHRA SPICED EGGPLANT

. . . .

In the Subcontinent, eggplant (known as *brinjal* in Hindi, *begun* in Bengali, and *bengan* in Urdu) is sometimes roasted, then flavored, a technique that perhaps traveled there from Central Asia. The tender mashed flesh has an inviting smoky taste all on its own (even when the eggplant is oven-roasted, not grilled over a fire).

In this condiment from Andhra Pradesh, roasted eggplant is mashed, then briefly stir-fried with soft-cooked onion and spices. At the last minute, a little minced raw shallot is added for freshness and bite. The flavors are rounded and the textures lush; there's a little cayenne and green-chile heat, and some sweetness from the slow-cooked onion.

4 medium-long purple Asian eggplant (about 1¹/₂ pounds)

About ¹/₃ cup raw sesame oil or vegetable oil

1 large onion, thinly sliced

1 teaspoon minced garlic or garlic mashed to a paste

¹/₂ teaspoon cayenne

¹/₂ teaspoon turmeric

¹/₂ teaspoon cumin seeds, crushed or coarsely ground

2 tablespoons minced green cayenne chiles, or to taste

1 teaspoon salt

2 tablespoons minced shallots

About ¹/₄ cup coriander leaves for garnish (optional)

Preheat the oven to 450°F, or heat a charcoal or gas grill.

Lightly rub the eggplant all over with oil and prick each one about ten times all over with a fork. *If using an oven,* place the eggplant on a rimmed baking sheet or roasting pan and bake in the center of the oven until the skin is brown and the flesh is softened, about 45 minutes. *If using a grill,* grill, turning often, until thoroughly softened. Don't worry if the skin is charred. Set the eggplant aside to cool.

Heat ¹/₄ cup oil in a wok or karhai (see Glossary) or a heavy skillet over medium-high heat. Toss in the onion, garlic, cayenne, turmeric, and cumin and stir to mix well. Lower the heat to medium and cook, stirring frequently, until the onion is well softened and translucent but not browned, about 10 minutes.

Meanwhile, cut the eggplant in half and scrape the pulp from the skin. Place it in a bowl (discard the skin) and mash well with a fork. Set aside by your stove top.

Add the chiles to the onion mixture and stir-fry for about a minute, then add the eggplant pulp and salt and stir-fry for several minutes more, using your spatula to blend ingredients together. (The turmeric-tinted oil will coat the eggplant and the pan.)

Just before serving, stir in the minced shallots and stir-fry for about 1 minute. Turn out into a bowl and sprinkle on some coriander leaves, if you wish. **MAKES ABOUT 2 CUPS; SERVES 6 AS A DIP, 4 AS A SIDE DISH**

Serve hot as a dip for Chapatis (page 110) or pitas, or as a topping for rice.

SALADS,
FRESH & COOKED

the Subcontinent and salads aren't always the world's best

partners. Throughout the region, there are unique and delicious

salads full of good fresh flavors and textures, but fresh can

also mean uncooked, and uncooked breaks a traveler's rule:

If you can't cook it or peel it, you shouldn't eat it. This can

be a predicament, because we've come to see salads as an essential part of a great South Asian meal. A fresh

Sawtooth herb

salad, even one as simple as a plate of fresh cucumbers, chopped shallots, and lime juice, can be all it takes to make an ordinary meal absolutely perfect. Like a fresh herb plate in Lebanon, Armenia, or Vietnam, or the salad greens and scallions served alongside a Thai meal, the flavor-heightening freshness in taste and texture that a salad brings to a curry-centered meal is all-important.

But we still take precautions when we travel. Sometimes we eat fresh salads, sometimes not, depending on how we feel and where we are. We'll eat salads in someone's home, but skip them in most restaurants. Does our caution make a difference? We don't know. When as young budget travelers we first traveled to the Subcontinent thirty years ago, we used to get sick at least once a trip, but nowadays we don't, nor do our children. Anyway, on the salad front, though we're constantly on the lookout for salads when we're traveling in the Subcontinent because they can be so interesting and because we love them, it's at home that we enjoy them most freely.

We decided to include lightly cooked dishes in this chapter as well as "raw" salads and yogurt-sauced raw vegetables. All are dishes we find ourselves turning to as we would to a European or North American green salad, for bright taste and often a little crunch or crisp texture. In Sri Lanka, there is a kind of lightly cooked dish called *mallum,* sometimes transcribed *mallung.* *Mallums* are mostly vegetable dishes that remind us a little of Thai salads, so we've put them here. Other cooked salads include a Nepali green bean salad and a lightly cooked spicy banana *pachadi.*

Fresh salads here include a cucumber raita, a yogurt-sauced salad from Sri Lanka, and a classic chopped salad called *cachoombar.* Simplest of all are the fresh accompaniments to a meal, such as the Bangla salads or the equivalent salad plates found in many parts of the Subcontinent, especially in the north: sliced white radishes or onions or cucumbers, often sprinkled just with salt.

Piles of curry leaves, mint leaves, and other fresh herbs at a Sri Lankan market

BANGLA SALAD PLATE

· · · · · · · · · · ·

The tradition of salad plates is found all around the world. In Vietnam, a salad plate includes fresh herbs, tender salad greens, and crisp mung bean sprouts; in Armenia, it consists of piles of fresh tarragon, mint, and scallions. And in Bangladesh, a salad plate comes with wedges of lime, fresh green cayenne chiles, and usually some coriander leaves.

I was surprised the first time I was served this simple salad plate in Bangladesh, then came to realize that it was a normal part of a meal, a way of adding freshness and last-minute flavorings. A squeeze of lime juice onto a beef curry or a dal lifts flavors, and can be transforming, and the same goes for a sprinkling of fresh coriander leaves.

When I came home from Bangladesh, I found I missed that chance to adjust flavors at the table. So now we often put out a plate with wedges of lime, some coriander leaves (or chopped mint leaves), a sliced chile, and perhaps some chopped chives or scallion greens.

A handful of coriander sprigs

1 to 2 limes, cut into wedges

1 to 2 green cayenne chiles, or substitute jalapeños,

    cut crosswise into thin rounds

Put the coriander, limes, and chiles on a small plate. Serve with the meal, encouraging your guests to help themselves and to use the greens and lime juice as a condiment and way of fine-tuning flavors.

SERVES 4 TO 6

Serve to accompany any meal.

FRESH WHITE RADISH SLICES WITH SALT

· · · · · · · · · · ·

White radishes, called *mooli* in Urdu and Hindi, grow easily in temperate climates (in North America, they're often known by their Japanese name, daikon). In summertime they have a hot taste; in winter they're milder and sweeter.

We learned this pleasing approach to salad from our neighbors Amin and Zinet, whose standby it is. They are Ismaeli Muslims (followers of the Aga Khan) who grew up in East Africa, but their ancestors originally came from Gujarat. They serve white radish to accompany meat dishes or rich vegetarian fare. The simplest version of this casual salad calls for the radish slices to be dressed only with good salt. For alternatives, see below.

About a 4-inch length of white radish (daikon)

Sea salt or kosher salt

Peel the thick outer skin from the radish, then thinly slice. Arrange the slices on a plate, overlapping them. Sprinkle on salt and serve.

SERVES 3 TO 4

Serve whenever fresh crispness would be welcome. This works particularly well with rich, soft-textured dishes such as Chicken Biryani, Dum Style (page 102), Pakistani Lamb Pulao (page 104), or Slow-Cooked Wheat Berries and Lamb with Fresh Mint (page 266).

HERBED RADISH SLICES: Sprinkle on chopped mint or coarsely torn coriander leaves just before serving.

HOT AND TART RADISH SLICES: Squeeze lime juice generously onto the radish slices before sprinkling them with salt and a light dusting of cayenne (or substitute smoky Spanish *pimentón*). This version is very like a radish salad we ate in Assam some years ago. There the radish was coarsely grated rather than sliced.

WATERCRESS AND SHALLOT SALAD

· · · · · · · · · · ·

This cross between a salad and a chutney is a quick way to bring color and bright refreshing flavors and textures to a meal.

Watercress is now fairly widely available. Just make sure you wash it thoroughly in a sink full of water (in the same way that spinach needs a good rinsing), so any sand and soil get washed away, then trim off any roots or coarse stems. Watercress has a slightly tart taste, very agreeable. You can substitute arugula (as we often do) or peppercress, if you prefer. PHOTOGRAPH ON PAGE 101

1 cup packed coarsely chopped watercress (see headnote)
¼ cup thinly sliced shallots
About 1 tablespoon fresh lime juice
About ½ teaspoon salt, preferably coarse salt

Toss the watercress and shallots together in a small shallow bowl. Just before serving, drizzle on the lime juice and toss, then add salt to taste and toss. SERVES 2 AS A SALAD, 4 AS A SMALL EXTRA TASTE HIT

Serve to accompany kebabs of all kinds or simmered meat curries such as Bangla Slow-Cooked Beef with Onion (page 273) or Duck Vindaloo (page 251), or just as an extra bit of sparkle with any meal.

FRESH BEAN SPROUT SALAD

· · · · · · · · · · ·

Although this Sri Lankan dish is another *sambol* (see page 30), we serve it like a salad. It has fiery heat from fresh green chiles, but the shredded coconut and cool crisp sprouts balance it out. A great little dish.

Buy fresh sprouts at an Asian grocery or produce market, and rinse them well. To chop them, hold a bunch in your hand on the cutting board and cut crosswise. PHOTOGRAPH ON PAGE 190

3 to 4 green cayenne chiles, stemmed
½ cup fresh or frozen grated coconut
⅓ cup finely chopped shallots or red onion
½ teaspoon salt
1 tablespoon water
1 tablespoon fresh lime juice
¼ pound (about 2 cups) fresh mung bean sprouts,
    rinsed and cut into 1-inch lengths

Place the chiles, coconut, shallots or onion, salt, water, and lime juice in a food processor and process briefly, just until the chiles and shallots are finely chopped but not pureed. *Alternatively,* use a stone mortar and a pestle to grind the chiles, coconut, and shallots or onion to a coarse paste with the salt and water, then transfer to a bowl and stir in the lime juice.

Turn out into a serving bowl, add the bean sprouts, and toss to mix well. SERVES 4

Serve as part of a rice meal for a hot and fresh flavor, or as a salad with a non-Asian meat-and-potatoes meal.

Women by the Ganges at the bathing ghats in Varanasi

The Ghats

IT WAS HOT SEASON, LATE MARCH. I WAS IN VARANASI (formerly Benares, in northern India, one of the oldest and holiest cities in the Subcontinent), staying in the crowded and intense old town, in a guesthouse that overlooked the Ganges. Before dawn every morning, just below my window, I'd see people in ones and twos walking along the embankment above the river. They were heading to one of the ghats, places where stone steps lead down to the water. I'd hurry over there, too, to watch the action.

By the time the sun came up, the ghats were very lively: There were priests and offering vendors and tea sellers and astrologers, all there because every day hundreds of people come to bathe in the Ganges and pray and make offerings. The Ganges has long been a holy river for Hindus, who believe that the river water has cleansing and curative powers and that bathing in the river—or being cremated and having one's ashes tossed into the river—is a religious act that can help free one from the cycle of suffering and rebirth. The bathers make their way down to the water, leaving a bundle of dry clothes on the steps, then stand waist-deep in the river in their saris or sarongs, splashing water on themselves, alone or with friends and family, praying and making offerings. Then they come back up the steps to dry off and change, always staying modest and covered, before climbing the steps to the top of the embankment and back to the world.

By noon the embankment, baking hot and bleached of color by the sun's harsh light, was bare of life except for the odd water buffalo and the dhobi wallahs, the men and women who earn their living doing laundry, carefully gathering up and folding the clean sheets and shirts and trousers and saris that they had washed at dawn and laid out on the riverbank to dry.

In the evening the air cooled a little and the ghats came alive with people praying, chatting, or just enjoying the gentle breezes off the river.

CACHOOMBAR

. . . .

I first tasted this simple chopped salad in Varanasi. It was very refreshing in the heat. *Cachoombar* is one version of a salad that is found all the way from the Mediterranean through West and Central Asia, combining ripe tomatoes and crisp cucumber. But while it's simple and straightforward to prepare, what it brings to a meal is hugely important. Flavors in the Subcontinent are often complex and intense; when a highly spiced curry or marinated grilled meat is served, it's a fresh salad like this one that helps complement the big flavors, and in some way gives them more impact. The proportions here are just a suggestion. You may find, after you try it once, that you prefer more lime juice, or a little more green chile, or even the addition of finely chopped white radish (daikon).

PHOTOGRAPH ON PAGE 132

1 cup diced tomatoes (peeled if the skin is tough)

1 cup peeled, seeded, and diced English cucumber

1 cup diced red onion, shallots, or mild onion such as Vidalia or Bermuda

1 green cayenne chile, seeded and minced, or to taste

About 1½ teaspoons salt

2 teaspoons cumin seeds, toasted and ground

¼ teaspoon cayenne

¼ teaspoon freshly ground black pepper, or to taste

About 2 tablespoons fresh lime juice

¼ cup packed chopped coriander leaves

Just before serving, combine the tomatoes, cucumber, and onion in a wide bowl. Sprinkle on the chile and 1 teaspoon of the salt and toss gently. Sprinkle on the cumin, cayenne, and black pepper and toss. Add the lime juice and coriander leaves, then toss gently. Taste for seasoning (you will probably want to add a little more salt at the last moment), then serve.

SERVES 4

Serve with big-flavored dishes such as Goan Pork Vindaloo (page 280), Grilled Marinated Beef (page 272), Tamarind Potatoes (page 152), or Tilapia Green Curry (page 222).

ANDHRA CHOPPED SALAD: In Andhra Pradesh, a close relative of *cachoombar* has a similar name: *kuchoomar*. To make it, place 1½ cups diced tomatoes; 1 cup peeled, seeded, and diced English cucumber; and 2 or 3 green cayenne chiles, seeded and minced, in a bowl. Sprinkle on about 1 teaspoon salt and toss, then add about 2 tablespoons fresh lime juice, toss, and serve. As with the salad above, you can include some chopped fresh herbs if you wish, and play with the proportions to suit your taste.

SERVES 3 TO 4

BABY PICTURE

A man I met as I was walking up the trail to Namche Bazaar (a Sherpa market village in the Mount Everest region of Nepal that is perched on a steep hillside about twelve thousand feet above sea level) took me to a one-room stone house near the entrance to the village. "My friend is away with a climbing expedition. His wife, Dolma, has just had a baby. You can stay with her." And so I did. The baby was very, very new, three days old. The fireplace was near the center of the room, the chimney a blackened air hole in the ceiling. A large high double bed stood in the corner, covered with comforters. A bank of multipaned south-facing windows gave light. An extra bed was wedged into another corner; this would be mine. There was no electricity, and the pump for water was down the lane outside.

It was early March, a cold time of year in the Everest region. Without a fire, the house would have been very cold. How did Dolma manage? Well, her mother was there a lot to help. While Dolma rested, or nursed the baby in bed, the grandmother made meals of rice and dal and a little meat. She rinsed out the flannel cloths that the baby was wrapped in, hauled water, and generally kept things going. After the baby nursed, she'd take him from Dolma and sit with him, loosely wrapped, by the fire. She'd pump his legs, holding him above a scrap of paper on the floor, going "Shhh, shhhh, shhh," to get him to have a bowel movement. Each time she was soon rewarded; it was a great way of lessening the laundry burden. Meanwhile, she'd have water heating over the fire. She'd fill a basin with warm water and then gently bathe the baby, chatting and singing to him as she did. He seemed so small to me, scrawny and fragile. Then she'd rub him with oil and massage him all over, tenderly kneading his little limbs, his chest and back. The clean blankets were dried and aired by the fire, so they were warm and welcoming when it came time to wrap him up and return him to his mother.

After several days, I headed out of Namche to walk farther up into the mountains. When I returned nearly two weeks later, the baby was almost unrecognizable. He was rounded and solid, alert, and gleaming with good health. I exclaimed over him. Dolma was pleased. She was up and about, managing the fire and the chores while he slept, carrying him next to her when he was awake. She let me hold the baby and sometimes asked me to mind the fire.

Many years later, when I had a baby of my own, I appreciated even more the ease and grace, and the hard work, that went into keeping this precious newborn alive, clean and comfortable and thriving. Unlike Dolma, I had a washing machine and dryer, and central heating, not to mention running water—and my husband was not off working on some dangerous expedition in the high Himalaya. It was easier, but not necessarily better. I wondered about all that Dolma did have, all that mothering wisdom, the easy touch and care and focus, that made her baby flourish.

Ladakhi baby sitting in the sunshine in the Zanskar area of Ladakh

On the crowded narrow cobbled streets of Kathmandu there are Newars, Thakalis, Tibetans, Gurungs, Magars, Tamangs, Sherpas, Rai—all the people of Nepal. And there are cobblers, jewelers, potters, pilgrims, and men who spin wool for hire. Kathmandu is a living museum, Hindu and Buddhist, but a museum in desperate decay. The street kids speak well in English, Japanese, German, and French, but there's little chance they will go to school. To see an Indian movie at the cinema, they split the cost of a ticket, a nickel, and then share a seat.

CUCUMBER SALAD
WITH HOT SPICED MUSTARD DRESSING

· · · · · · · · · · · ·

This fresh salad, a cousin of Nepali Green Bean–Sesame Salad (page 76), has a semi-cooked dressing: The cucumber sticks are rubbed with a spice paste of yogurt, sesame, and cumin, then dressed with hot spice-infused mustard oil and fresh lemon juice.

As with many dishes from Nepal, traditionally a flavoring called *timbur* seed is used to give a tart edge, but it's not yet available in North America. We have tried substituting ground *anardana* (dried pomegranate seeds; see Glossary), but we find the easiest solution is to use a little yogurt and lemon in the spice paste, as described below. PHOTOGRAPH ON PAGE 62

½ pound cucumbers, preferably a small English cucumber, peeled

Kosher salt

1 tablespoon sesame seeds

½ teaspoon cumin seeds

2 tablespoons plain (full- or reduced-fat) yogurt or water
   (see headnote)

1½ teaspoons mustard oil

⅛ teaspoon fenugreek seeds

⅛ teaspoon nigella seeds

1 green cayenne chile, slit lengthwise and seeded

¼ teaspoon cayenne

⅛ teaspoon turmeric

1 tablespoon fresh lemon juice

2 to 3 tablespoons minced coriander leaves

Cut the cucumber lengthwise in quarters. Slice off the seeds (unless the cucumbers are very small and tender) and discard, then cut into 1½-inch lengths. Cut lengthwise in half again if the pieces are fat. Place in a colander, sprinkle on about 2 tablespoons kosher salt, and set over a bowl or in the sink to drain for 15 minutes.

Meanwhile, in a heavy skillet, dry roast the sesame seeds until golden. Transfer to a plate and set aside. Dry roast the cumin seeds until touched with color and aromatic, then transfer to a spice/coffee grinder, add the sesame seeds, and grind to a powder. Place in a small bowl and stir in the yogurt or water to make a paste. Set aside.

Rinse the cucumbers thoroughly with cold water. Squeeze them gently to squeeze out excess water and place them in a bowl. Add the spice paste and rub the cucumbers all over to coat them. Set aside.

Heat the oil in a small skillet over medium heat. Add the fenugreek, nigella, and chile and cook for about a minute, stirring occasionally, until the spices are aromatic. Add the cayenne and turmeric, stir, and pour the flavored oil over the cucumbers; toss gently. Add the lemon juice and toss, then set aside for 10 to 20 minutes to allow the flavors to blend.

Just before serving, add the coriander leaves and ½ teaspoon salt, or more to taste, and toss gently to mix. SERVES 3 TO 4

The warming flavors in this cucumber salad pair well with mild-tasting dishes such as New Potatoes with Fresh Greens (page 154) or Chickpea Pulao (page 105) or with a simple meal of Chapatis (page 110) or Gita's Luchis (page 115) and Mountain Dal (page 182) or Easy Karnataka Chana (page 196).

Cucumber Salad with Hot Spiced Mustard Dressing (page 61). ABOVE LEFT: *A young Nepali girl eating a round fried bread on a Kathmandu winter morning.*
RIGHT: *A Hindu pilgrim, a follower of Shiva, making the pilgrimage to sacred Mount Kailash in western Tibet.*

Village Lunch

Rice cultivation on the hills by Jayantha's village

JAYANTHA KUMARA, who worked in the hotel where I was staying in south-central Sri Lanka, asked one day if I would like to come as a guest to his village in western Katchh, and when I said that I'd be delighted, plans were made. Very early the following Sunday morning, he arranged for a cycle rickshaw, driven by his friend, and off we went. In terms of miles, his village was not very far away, but on a three-wheeled scooter, it took us three or four hours to get there through the mountains.

Perched on the steep slope of a lush green mountain, the village was absolutely beautiful—quiet and remarkable. He and his sisters, and friends and others who joined in along the way, showed me the entire village in detail: the rice fields, the irrigation system, the school, the temple, the village banyan tree, the areca palms, the betel. . . . Just when the heat and the sun were starting to get intense, Jayantha announced that it was time for lunch, and off to his house we went, taking refuge in the shade of big trees as we walked.

We ate in the cool of his sixty-year-old plastered-brick house. Lunch was beyond good, in part because it was relatively simple. It was village food, straightforward dishes full of flavor, made of ingredients picked fresh from the earth. After lunch we walked down through a canopy of trees and had a yogurt at a tiny village shop, sitting still in the shade and looking out over a huge mountain landscape. And then we got into the cycle rickshaw and rode the long winding road home.

ONE YEAR LATER I was back with Jayantha in his village, again for lunch. The village was just as beautiful as it had been my first time there, and Jayantha's family just as lovely. For lunch we had dishes not unlike before, simple and delicious. The salad that was served was again particularly special, this time made with very thinly sliced banana flower that had been soaked in salted water and then drained.

LEFT: *Sri Lankan Village Salad
(page 66); Cucumber Raita (page 67).*
RIGHT: *Woman walks along the railway
track in southern Goa, not far from
Margao; she brings food to her husband,
who's standing up to his calves in water,
transplanting rice plants.*

Children riding to school on a bicycle, among the tea plantations of mountainous south-central Sri Lanka

SRI LANKAN VILLAGE SALAD

· · · · · · · · · · ·

This salad is our version of the salad in Jayantha's village (see page 64). It has a good fresh taste, with a little heat from fresh chiles. The coconut milk in the dressing blends and rounds flavors beautifully.

The variation here has only one ingredient added, Maldive fish, but that addition transforms it into an entirely different dish, a little wild tasting and equally good. The Maldive fish is quite a dominant flavor; it gives the salad almost the taste of cheese, like a Caesar salad with Parmesan.

PHOTOGRAPH ON PAGE 65

1 small English cucumber, peeled and thinly sliced
Salt
About ⅓ cup thinly sliced shallots
1 green cayenne chile, finely chopped
1 red cayenne chile, finely chopped
½ teaspoon fine sea salt
½ teaspoon freshly ground black pepper
2 tablespoons rice vinegar or fresh lime juice
2 tablespoons canned or fresh coconut milk

Place the cucumber slices in a colander, sprinkle on 1 tablespoon salt, and set aside for 30 minutes. Rinse and gently squeeze dry.

Place the cucumber in a shallow bowl, add the shallots, chiles, sea salt, and black pepper and toss. Pour the vinegar or lime juice and coconut milk over, toss gently, and serve.   **SERVES 3 TO 4**

A good complement to Spicy Bitter Melon (page 159), Stir-fried Rice and Dal (page 96), or Semolina Uppuma (page 92), or grilled meat or fish.

VILLAGE SALAD WITH MALDIVE FISH: Maldive fish is an indispensable Sri Lankan pantry item; it is very small chunks of dried tuna. (You can substitute Japanese bonito flakes.) Mince 1 tablespoon (or grind it in a spice grinder), then add along with the shallots and seasonings (you may want to reduce the amount of salt slightly).

CUCUMBER RAITA

· · · · · · · · · · · ·

We love the yogurt-based dishes, a cross between sauces and salads, that are called *raita* in Hindi and Urdu. They're found in the northwestern part of the Subcontinent, from Pakistan and the Punjab to Rajasthan. They make great dipping sauces for bread or condiments for grilled meat, and they add a cooling balance to a hot or intensely spiced meal.

Draining the yogurt briefly, then whisking in a little water, eliminates much of its tart acidity, leaving it almost sweet tasting. It's worth the small extra effort. PHOTOGRAPH ON PAGE 65

1 cup plain (full- or reduced-fat) yogurt

About ¹/₂ English cucumber (1 cup chopped)

³/₄ teaspoon salt, or to taste

2 tablespoons water

About ¹/₄ cup coriander leaves or 2 tablespoons mint leaves (optional)

Coarsely ground black pepper (optional)

Line a sieve or colander with cheesecloth or a cotton cloth and place in the sink or over a bowl. Place the yogurt in the cloth-lined sieve and let drain for about 20 minutes.

Meanwhile, peel the cucumber and slice lengthwise in half. Scrape off the seeds (unless the cucumber is very young and tender), then finely chop. Place in a bowl and sprinkle on ¹/₂ teaspoon of the salt. Toss and set aside.

Transfer the drained yogurt to a medium bowl. Whisk briefly with a whisk or a fork, then add the water and whisk again. Add the cucumber, but not the juices, to the yogurt. Whisk again. Taste and add more salt, if you wish.

If using the herbs, coarsely chop the coriander or mince the mint leaves, and stir into the raita just before serving. Coarsely grind black pepper over, if you wish. MAKES ABOUT 1¹/₄ CUPS; SERVES 4 TO 6

Serve as a dipping sauce with plain or flavored breads—Potato-Stuffed Parathas (page 130) go particularly well, or simple Chapatis (page 110); or put out as a sauce to accompany a meal of rice with side dishes.

THE RAITA FAMILY: You can take this approach to salad using other ingredients. Just set the yogurt to drain, then prepare, for example, the ingredients in Cachoombar (page 57) and stir them into the yogurt. Or add 2 or 3 tablespoons of Fresh Coriander-Peanut Chutney (page 28) or Mint-Coriander Chutney (page 298) to chopped cucumber before stirring it into the yogurt.

Kolkata's (formerly Calcutta) main train station, Howrah Station, can be intimidating, especially at night. There are people waiting for trains, sleeping on the ground, or leaning on their bags; others hurrying purposefully; announcements that are impossible to decipher; and always that little anxiety about whether you'll find your train, and your compartment and seat, in time.

Late one November evening, we went to the station with our kids to catch the Thiruvananthapuram Express, a train that in two and a half days makes the full diagonal crossing of India from Kolkata in the northeast corner to Thiruvananthapuram (formerly Trivandrum) at the country's far southern tip. We had tickets, but we were not sure about whether we had confirmed berths. First we found our train, then finally, with the help of a porter, our compartment, and there were our names carefully printed on a card outside. It was a great relief. We stowed our bags under the lower berth, next to some huge bags that the people in the next compartment had shoved into our space, nodded gratefully at the attendant who came to make up the berths with sheets and blankets, and then we lay down happily. The train rolled out of the station, past dim lights and into the darkness. Yes! We were headed south!

At dawn we were passing through devastated coastal areas of Orissa, the state south of Bengal and Bihar; a cyclone had hit the previous week, and the platforms in the small stations we clicked past were loaded with sacks of relief supplies. Out in the countryside, we saw palm trees standing at a tilt or uprooted, and great flooded areas near the rivers. On and on we click-clacked our way, stopping occasionally to let passengers on and off. One station platform looked very like the next, with tea stalls, people hawking fresh fruit, and small stands selling biscuits and other snacks, but each time we stopped, the air seemed to be warmer, heavier, more tropical.

Forty-eight hours after we pulled out of Howrah Station, we stood by the open door at the end of our train car as the train lumbered slowly into Ernaculam, the station for Kochi (Cochin), in Kerala. We'd traveled from the Bay of Bengal all the way to the Indian Ocean. We clambered down the steep metal steps, hauled down our bags, and went looking for a place to stay.

I spotted this young boy traveling with his mother on a local passenger train that had paused in the station of a small mountain town in Orissa.

JOURNEY

SPICY BANANA-YOGURT PACHADI

Pachadis are like a South Indian version of raita, a cross between salad and sauce. The ingredients are usually cooked a little, then the yogurt is added and heated until the flavors blend well. We think they're dynamite side dishes in a rice meal, refreshing and intense at the same time.

This is another version of a favorite *pachadi* from Kerala, called *pazham pachadi*, flavored with banana, coconut, and chile, that we included in *Seductions of Rice*. Use a sweet ripe banana and make the *pachadi* at least half an hour ahead, so it has time to cool to room temperature before you serve it.

$1/2$ teaspoon black mustard seeds, ground, plus a pinch of whole seeds
2 tablespoons minced seeded green cayenne chiles
2 tablespoons fresh or frozen grated coconut, chopped
$1/2$ teaspoon salt, or to taste
1 tablespoon raw sesame oil or vegetable oil
3 to 4 fresh or frozen curry leaves, coarsely chopped
1 tablespoon minced ginger or ginger mashed to a paste
Pinch of turmeric
1 large ripe banana, coarsely chopped (about $1/2$ cups)
$1/2$ cups plain yogurt, preferably full fat

In a mortar or a small bowl, mix together the ground mustard, chile, coconut, and salt and pound or mash with the back of a spoon to make a rough paste. Set aside.

Heat the oil in a small heavy skillet over medium heat. Toss in the pinch of mustard seeds and cover briefly while they pop, then add the curry leaves, the reserved flavor paste, and the ginger. Cook, stirring constantly, for about 2 minutes. Add the turmeric and stir in, then add the chopped banana and stir-fry for another 30 seconds or so. Turn the heat to very low, add the yogurt, and stir to blend it in; you want to heat it through, but not so much that it boils. Remove from the heat, and set aside to cool to room temperature before serving. The sauce, which seems very liquid when warm, thickens as it cools.

Store the sauce in the refrigerator, in a well-sealed glass container, for up to 4 days. Stir before serving.   SERVES 5 TO 6

Serve to moisten a pulao *or* biryani, *or to accompany a rice meal, especially a meal where the sweetness of the banana will be a welcome balance to tart flavors, such as those of Bangla Dal with a Hit of Lime (page 178) or Goan Pork Vindaloo (page 280).*

A load of sweet bananas, still on the stalk, being unloaded from a truck at the huge wholesale market in Chennai (Madras), capital of the state of Tamil Nadu, in southern India

TOMATO, RED ONION, AND YELLOW PEPPER SALAD WITH YOGURT DRESSING

· · · · · · · · · · · ·

We're happy to eat this mellow salad in great quantity whenever it's around. Unlike many Sri Lankan dishes, it has only minimal chile heat. If you make it in the heart of tomato season, the combination of yogurt, fresh tomato, red onion, and yellow bell pepper is as distinctive and good as it is colorful.

1 medium-small red onion, thinly sliced (about 1 cup)

Scant 2 tablespoons fresh lime juice, or to taste

1 teaspoon salt

1 banana chile or Hungarian wax chile, seeds and pith removed

1 medium yellow bell pepper, seeds and pith removed

2 to 3 medium tomatoes, cut into 1/2-inch pieces

3/4 cup plain (full- or reduced-fat) yogurt

Freshly ground black pepper

Place the onion in a salad bowl, sprinkle on the lime juice and salt, and mix well. Set aside for 30 minutes.

Slice the chile into matchsticks and add to the onion. Cut the bell pepper into 1/2-inch-wide strips about 1 inch long and toss with the onion and chile. Just before serving, add the tomatoes and yogurt and toss gently to mix. Taste for salt and adjust, if you wish.

Though it's not traditional as far as we know, we also like to include a generous grinding of black pepper. SERVES 4

Serve as a cooling side salad with grills such as Grilled Fish Steaks with Black Pepper Rub (page 210), or with a simple meal of dal with rice or flatbreads.

PEA TENDRILS WITH COCONUT

· · · · · · · · · · · ·

This is a *mallum* (sometimes transcribed *mallung*), a traditional dish from Sri Lanka that is often made with wild greens. The variety of greens used to make *mallums* in Sri Lanka is staggering, a testimony to the tropical lushness of the island.

We're such big fans of *mallums* that back home in North America we started to experiment with a variety of greens. This recipe, using fresh pea tendrils, or pea shoots, is a favorite. Notice that everything is simply put into a pot and cooked together. There's no oil for frying, no water for boiling other than the water clinging to the washed greens. Just follow the recipe and see what happens.

1/2 pound pea tendrils (about 8 cups chopped, loosely packed)

1/2 cup fresh or frozen grated coconut

2 green cayenne chiles, finely chopped

1/3 to 1/2 cup shallots, finely chopped

1/2 teaspoon salt

1/4 teaspoon turmeric

Wash the pea tendrils and drain. Gather them into a tight bundle and finely slice crosswise.

Combine with all the other ingredients in a medium heavy pot and mix well. Place over high heat and cook, stirring frequently, for about 1 minute. Then cover tightly and cook for about 3 minutes, until the pea tendrils have wilted and the shallots are tender. Serve on a flat plate.

SERVES 4

This makes an easy and welcome green vegetable side with a meal of roast or grilled chicken, Potato White Curry (page 155), and rice.

The hotel I am in as I write this is in Chennai (formerly Madras) and costs 550 rupees a night, which is slightly more than twelve U.S. dollars at the current exchange. I have a big bright room with a double bed with a thick foam mattress and a color television with cable. There's a telephone, a large bath towel, and even hot water in the shower, though it's not really necessary in Chennai (the pipes can get so hot in the day that the water runs hot whether you want it to or not). I also have a big ceiling fan. I prefer fan rooms to AC rooms, which is handy, because they're less expensive.

Last night I was in Kamman, a district center in the northern part of Andhra Pradesh, the neighboring state. I stayed in an inexpensive hotel (two dollars a night) next to the bus stand, the only hotel I could find. The room wasn't especially nice, but it was adequate. There was a bar of soap, a little container of shampoo, and a color TV with cable. The thing that made me laugh was that in the morning, right at dawn, after a horrendous night of incredibly loud airhorns from buses and trucks right under my window, I heard the luxurious sound of a newspaper slipping under the door of my room. It was an English-language *Hindi Times*, and it even had my room number written on top.

For us, a good room is 90 percent of traveling happily in the Sub-continent. Take the room where I currently sit. It's loud with the noise of trucks and buses (it's on the ring road around the perimeter of the city), but I'm on the third floor, and with my fan going, I can tune out the traffic. What makes the room good (besides the very reasonable price, for a big city in India) is that the people who work here are very nice, the room is clean, I have a good view, and there's lots of action on the street to pop out into.

But there's something more, and I think it's something that has more to do with me than with the room. I have to *let* the room be nice, and do what I can to make it better. When I'm traveling place to place, not infrequently I have no choice in hotel and maybe find myself in a hotel that feels sort of grungy. The light bulbs are dim, the room a bit musty. But rooms are almost always better than they first appear. I turn on the fan, open a window, unpack a little, and take a shower. I lay out my own bedspread on the bed. (The Subcontinent has the best and most beautiful bedspreads, so I buy a new one first thing every trip, and that way every hotel I stay in becomes special.) If I'm staying a few days, sometimes I even wash the windows to give myself a better view. Anyway, after a good night's sleep, a grungy room usually starts looking lots better.

Oh, and I just had a masala *dosa* and a big pot of coffee. There's room service!

Some hotels and guest houses are in beautiful locations. This was the view, looking across the lake, from our hotel in Pushkar, a town in the Rajasthan desert. In November the town is crowded with visitors to the annual camel fair.

HOTEL ROOMS

OPPOSITE: *Shredded Green Bean Mallum (page 76) with Udaipur Urad Dal (page 189).* ABOVE: *A tethered chicken for sale at a rural market in southern Orissa (see "Orissa," page 274).*

NEPALI GREEN BEAN–SESAME SALAD

. . . .

Salads, fresh chutneys, and some sauces are all called *achar* in Nepali. Here, in *simi achar*, green beans are cooked until just tender, then dressed in hot spiced oil and lemon juice and tossed with toasted sesame seeds, an approach very like that of the Nepali cucumber salad on page 61, and just as dazzling.

1 pound green beans or yard-long beans

3 tablespoons sesame seeds

2 tablespoons peanut oil or vegetable oil

2 green cayenne chiles, seeded and sliced into rings

½ teaspoon salt

2 to 3 tablespoons fresh lemon juice, to taste

Chopped coriander leaves or several mint leaves, minced (optional)

Cook the beans in a large pot of boiling salted water until just tender and still firm. Drain, refresh in cold water for a moment, and then drain again. Trim the beans and slice on a diagonal into ½-inch lengths. Set aside in a bowl.

Heat a dry heavy skillet over medium-high heat. Add the sesame seeds, lower the heat to medium, and dry roast, stirring constantly with a wooden spoon, until lightly touched with gold and aromatic. Transfer to a spice/coffee grinder and grind to a coarse powder, then set aside.

Heat the oil in a small heavy skillet, a wok, or a karhai (see Glossary) over medium-high heat. Toss in the chopped chiles and stir-fry for about 30 seconds, or until lightly touched with brown. Pour the chiles and hot oil over the beans and toss. Sprinkle on the ground sesame seeds and salt and toss. Add the lemon juice and toss.

Serve warm or at room temperature. If you wish, add chopped coriander or mint to the salad just before serving. SERVES 4

Serve warm or at room temperature to accompany a South Asian or Western-style meal.

SHREDDED GREEN BEAN MALLUM

. . . .

We like to make this simple Sri Lankan *mallum* if only for the incredible fresh green color of the finely shredded green beans. It really glows on the table (especially when served on a bright pink or yellow plate!). Like all *mallums* (see Pea Tendrils with Coconut, page 71), it's a cinch to prepare, and when served in the long dark days of winter, when the only green beans available are often well-traveled and tough, it brings a good fresh taste to the table. PHOTOGRAPH ON PAGE 74

¾ pound green beans or yard-long beans

⅓ cup finely chopped red onion or shallots

4 to 5 green cayenne chiles, finely chopped

¼ teaspoon turmeric

1 teaspoon salt

1 teaspoon Maldive fish, or substitute bonito flakes,
**   ground to a powder (optional)**

1 cup chopped fresh or frozen grated coconut

Finely shred the beans (either by hand on a grater or in a food processor using the shredding blade). Place the beans and all the other ingredients in a medium heavy pot over medium-high heat and stir to mix well, then lower the heat to medium, cover, and cook for about 10 minutes, stirring occasionally, until the beans are tender but not dry. Serve hot.

SERVES 4 TO 5

Put out as a green vegetable or salad to accompany a dal such as Udaipur Urad Dal (page 189) or Sri Lankan Fenugreek Dal (page 179), along with plain rice. Or serve with a non–South Asian meat-and-potatoes meal.

SPICED CABBAGE SALAD

. . . .

If you live in a wintry climate as we do, then you know that a cook can never have too many good recipes for cabbage and/or potatoes: It's just an age-old fact of life. This simple and tasty recipe called *gova mallung* comes from tropical Sri Lanka. It makes a mound of tender, pale green, and mildly chile-spiced shredded cabbage, aromatic with curry leaves and cumin, and bright tasting with lime juice.

The curry leaves we buy fresh all winter from a Sri Lankan grocery in our neighorhood. We also keep a stash in our freezer, in a tightly sealed plastic bag (the same way we store wild lime leaves). And with the addition of grated coconut (we use frozen, also always on hand), shredded cabbage takes on a whole new look.

4 cups shredded green or Savoy cabbage

1/3 cup finely chopped shallots

2 to 3 green cayenne chiles, seeded and minced

About 6 fresh or frozen curry leaves

1 teaspoon salt

1/4 teaspoon turmeric

1 teaspoon ground cumin

2 tablespoons fresh lime juice

2 tablespoons fresh or frozen grated coconut

Wash the cabbage, then put it in a medium heavy pot with the shallots, chiles, curry leaves, salt, turmeric, and cumin. Place over medium-high heat, cover, and cook for 2 to 3 minutes (the cabbage will cook in the water that clings to the leaves from washing). Give the pot a quick stir, cover again, and lower the heat to medium. Simmer until the cabbage is cooked and tender, about another 10 minutes, depending on your cabbage and how finely it is shredded.

Add the lime juice and coconut and stir to mix well. Let cook for a minute or two, uncovered, then turn out and serve, mounded on a plate.

SERVES 4

This makes a good accompaniment, with rice, to hearty dishes such as Chile-Hot Bhutanese Cheese Curry (page 173) or Aromatic Slow-Cooked Chicken (page 242), or Fish Bolle Curry (page 219).

NOTE: Adding the grated coconut at the end softens the flavors; also, it absorbs any extra liquid, leaving the dish soft and moist, but with no sauce.

RICE

about, and rice is definitely one of them. We love rice. We find it

infinitely satisfying, day after day, year after year. And we also

find it infinitely interesting, The Subcontinent is a rice-eater's

paradise, with countless varieties and styles of rice, depending

on where you are or what style of food you're eating, from the

mountain rices in Nepal to tiny *kalijira* rice in Bengal and Bangladesh to large fat red rices in southern India

and parboiled rices in Sri Lanka and elsewhere.

And then there is also basmati rice. When we're traveling from place to place in the Subcontinent, one of our pleasures is to taste the local rices, and these days basmati rice sometimes gets in the way. In the last decade or so, with the rise of tourism (both international and domestic), we've noticed the beginnings of a pan-Indian (if not pan-subcontinental) cuisine. In Kerala, for example, which has seen a dramatic rise in international tourism, restaurants in tourist destinations will often have, instead of Kerala dishes and good red South Indian rice, a menu of tandoori breads (from North India) and Punjabi dishes served with basmati rice, something almost unheard of before. We won't lose any sleep over it, because there's always a local restaurant just around the corner serving South Indian rice, but we have to register our concern.

A number of distinctive varieties of rice from South Asia are now available in North America. They're well worth shopping for and trying out. Six of the recipes that follow are for cooking a specific variety of rice, and each results in what's known as *plain rice*. Of course, the flavor of good rice is anything but plain (it's no more so than a glass of wine is plain because it doesn't have anything added to it!).

Plain rice is eaten every day in the rice-eating parts of the Subcontinent, from Gujarat, Bengal, Nepal, and Bangladesh to the southern Indian states and Sri Lanka, especially for the main meal (usually at midday). It's accompanied by curries, flavored dishes of vegetables or meat, some very sauced, others drier, and by dal. One or more chutneys or salsas are served alongside. Breads may also be served, but rice is at the heart of the meal.

Out in the country not far from the town of Jeypore, in southern Orissa, a number of men and women are winnowing rice, separating the grain from the chaff.

Plain-cooked basmati rice (page 82) with its final steaming equipment

We cook our plain rice in a heavy pot with a tight-fitting lid, or in a rice cooker. Instructions for both are in these recipes. During the twenty to thirty minutes the rice takes to cook, we prepare the dishes that will accompany it. With rice as an anchor, weeknight meals come together easily. We store leftover rice, once cooled, in a sealed container in the refrigerator, so we can use it to make fried rice, or rice soup, the next day. Leftover rice should not be kept for more than three days.

You'll also find flavored rice dishes here, as well as several savory dishes made from other grains. Rice is so easy to eat and to digest that it is a frequent breakfast food from Sri Lanka to Assam. We have included a breakfast dish made with rice flakes, as well as a dish called *uppuma,* made of steamed and spiced semolina, that is one of our favorite South Indian breakfasts. There's a coconut-rice soup from Sri Lanka and a Nepali polenta that's eaten with a smoky-tasting sauce of grilled tomatoes.

Finally, we've included some recipes from the rich and interesting *pulao*-biryani tradition. *Pulao, pilau, polo, pullao,* they're all words that denote rice cooked with flavorings (they're cousins of Spanish paella and Italian risotto). Both *pulaos* and biryanis combine rice with spices and flavors that blend Moghul tradition with local ingredients. The simplest are made with dal or vegetables and rice and can be served as main dishes or in place of plain rice. The more elaborate rice creations, such as lamb pulao and chicken biryani, are dishes for a feast or a party.

PLAIN BASMATI, SEVERAL WAYS

· · · · · · · · · · · ·

The subcontinental rice most widely known in North America is basmati. It's long grain and often described as needle-shaped because it's so narrow. The most prized basmati is grown in the Himalayan foothills in northern India and Pakistan.

Basmati is the ideal rice for pilafs and biryanis, since it can absorb flavored liquids while keeping its good texture and not getting mushy. You can also cook it as plain rice, as described here. Basmati is generally soaked in cold water for at least half an hour before cooking. This gives the grains a chance to absorb a little water, which helps them to cook more evenly, and to soften so that they are less brittle.

Basmati can be cooked in lots of water, like pasta, then drained and steamed; or it can be cooked in a measured amount of liquid that gets fully absorbed as the rice cooks. PHOTOGRAPH ON PAGE 81

LOTS-OF-WATER METHOD: Wash 2 cups basmati rice thoroughly in several changes of cold water and drain. Place the rice in a bowl, add cold water to cover by at least 2 inches, and let soak for 30 minutes or more; drain.

Meanwhile, bring a large heavy pot of water to a rolling boil. Sprinkle in the rice, bring back to the boil, and cook, uncovered, until the rice is just tender right through but still firm, 3 to 5 minutes. Drain thoroughly in a sieve.

Place the rice back in the pot over the very lowest heat, drizzle on 2 or 3 tablespoons melted ghee or butter, and cover tightly (place a cotton cloth under the lid to help seal it and to absorb any condensation). Let steam for 20 minutes, or until tender.

ABSORPTION METHOD: Wash 2 cups basmati rice thoroughly in several changes of water and drain.

To cook the rice on the stove top, soak the washed rice in 2½ cups cold water in the rice cooking pot for at least 30 minutes, or for up to 3 hours, if more convenient.

About 40 minutes before you wish to serve it, stir the rice gently with your fingers or a wooden spoon (this loosens it if it has compacted). Place the pot over high heat and bring to a vigorous boil. Stir gently, cover tightly, and turn the heat to low. Cook for 15 minutes. Turn off the heat and let the rice stand, covered, for 10 minutes so it can finish cooking and the starches can firm up.

To cook the rice in a rice cooker, place the washed rice in the cooker with 2¼ cups water and let soak, covered, for at least 30 minutes, or for as long as 3 hours, if more convenient.

About 40 minutes before you wish to serve the rice, gently stir it with your fingers or a wooden spoon (this loosens it if it has compacted as it soaked). Cover and turn on the rice cooker. Once the heat clicks off, let the rice stand, covered and untouched, for 10 minutes, so it can finish cooking and the starches can firm up.

For either of the two methods, lift the lid of the pot (or rice cooker) and pour off any condensation, or wipe it off with a cotton cloth. Wet a rice paddle or wooden spoon with water and slide it down the side of the pot. Lift the rice and turn it over gently, working all around the pot, to fluff the rice and air it. Serve mounded on a platter, with a little melted ghee or butter drizzled over.

Basmati is especially appropriate with a kebab—for example, Tikka Kebabs (page 256) or Yogurt-Marinated Chicken Kebabs (page 239), or with Simmered Kashmiri Paneer (page 171).

MAKES NEARLY 6 CUPS; SERVES 4 TO 5

BROWN BASMATI: Basmati is also available unmilled, as brown rice. To cook 2 cups brown basmati, follow the directions given above, with these adaptations: In the lots-of-water method, the boiling rice will take about twice as long to be tender; it should then steam for 30 minutes. For the absorption method, double the water quantity and the cooking time. MAKES ABOUT 5 CUPS; SERVES 5 TO 6

BHUTANESE RED RICE

· · · · · · · · · · · ·

Rice is the staple grain in much of Bhutan, and the local rice, called *eue chum*, has a reddish bran. Bhutanese red rice is now available in North America. It's partially milled, so it takes a little longer to cook than white rice but is faster than brown rice. The cooked rice is an attractive pale pink, with a slightly clinging texture.

To cook 2 cups rice, first wash the rice well in several changes of water. Place in a pot with 3 cups cold water, bring to a boil, and skim off the foam. Cover tightly, reduce the heat to low, and cook for 25 minutes. Remove from the heat and let stand for 10 minutes, with the lid on. (If using a rice cooker, use the same amount of water. Once the rice is boiling, remove the lid and skim off the foam, then cover again and let the cooker complete its cycle. Let stand for 10 minutes once done.) Turn gently with a rice paddle and serve. **MAKES ABOUT 5 CUPS; SERVES 5 TO 6**

Serve as an accompaniment to hearty side dishes such as any of the dals, or with Bhutanese or Nepalese dishes such as Chile-Hot Bhutanese Cheese Curry (page 173) or Simmered Spiced Soybeans (page 143).

TINY KALIJIRA RICE

· · · · · · · · · · · ·

In Calcutta ten years ago, we were introduced to a princely rice known as *govindabhog*. In Bangladesh it's known as *kalijira*, and it's now sold under that name in North America. It is a polished white long-grain rice, but on a miniature scale, like a baby basmati. It has a delicate slightly sweet flavor. In Calcutta we only ever had it cooked the lots-of-water way with a little salt in the water.

Follow the lots-of-water method set out under Plain Basmati, Several Ways (page 82), but don't soak the rice first. Boiling time will be about 6 minutes.

2 CUPS RAW KALIJIRA MAKES NEARLY 6 CUPS COOKED RICE; SERVES 5 TO 6

Woman transplanting rice in Bangladesh, north of the town of Rajshahi

Boy eating dal bhat *(rice and dal) in the village of Marfa, in the Annapurna region of Nepal*

THERE'S A SHARED SENSIBILITY in the Subcontinent when it comes to matters of eating. People almost always eat using one hand (the right hand), and they very seldom use utensils. This may not sound like a big deal, but we think it is. Time after time we watch foreigners come to the Subcontinent and have a very difficult time at first, eating without utensils and using only one hand. But interestingly, almost everyone breaks through, and when they do, they are entirely converted. Eating by hand influences how food tastes and how we relate to it. It's so sensual, so direct. But when we go back home, no matter how hard we try to resist, out come the utensils. Eating is a very culture-bound tradition.

One of the great pleasures of eating in the Subcontinent is that styles of eating by hand differ from place to place. When northerners eat rice, they pick it up with the tips of their fingers and then use their thumb to push the small amount of rice into their mouth. In southern regions, people eat rice using the entire hand, forming a ball of rice (approximately the size of a golf ball) by gathering the rice into their palm, flicking the wrist sideways to shape it into a mass, and finally tossing the entire ball into their mouth.

As a foreigner, it's fun to watch and learn, to try to imitate (though a style doesn't come quickly). After a while, when you think you've got it down, the style itself feels somehow crucial to the food, as if that particular food has to be eaten in that particular way. And if you eat by hand, when you're finished with your meal, you still have tasty little bits on your fingers, and then later, even after you've washed your hands, there's a delicious aroma that lingers. As foreigners we find all this wonderfully addictive, and so we can only imagine how important it would feel if we'd been eating this same food in this same way all our lives, and how unsatisfying it would feel to eat with utensils.

At a wedding in Ladakh, chang (see page 311) is poured into the bridegroom's bowl.

Parboiling is an ingenious technique for increasing both the nutritional value and the keeping qualities of polished rice. It dates back many centuries and seems to have been developed in southern India. Many people in Bengal, Bangladesh, South India, and Sri Lanka eat parboiled rice as their staple plain rice.

Parboiling is done at both the village and the industrial level in the Subcontinent. Rice still in the husk is soaked, then boiled, then cooled. This has the effect of driving vitamins from the bran into the center of the rice. The rice is then husked (the hulls are removed) and milled (polished) to white. Though milled, it retains much of the nutritional value of unpolished (brown) rice. Parboiled rice takes a little longer to cook than "unboiled" rice (because the starches, once heated, become glassy and hard when they cool), and when cooked the grains stay very separate, with a slightly bouncy texture.

Weighing rice at the weekly market in Savar, near Dhaka, in Bangladesh

This parboiled rice from southern India is now being imported into the United States. It has slightly fat, long grains colored with reddish flecks of bran. During cooking, the rice has an almost meaty smell, and the taste of the cooked rice is somewhat smoky-meaty. As a result, rosematta goes best with distinctive flavors, such as Cashew-Coconut Meatballs (page 262). You can cook it using the lots-of-water method, as described under Plain Basmati, page 82 (no need to presoak it; boiling time will be 10 or 11 minutes), or in a measured amount of water as follows.

To cook 2 cups rosematta, wash well and drain. Place in a pot with 3 cups cold water or in a rice cooker with 2¾ cups cold water.

If using a pot, bring to a vigorous boil, stir briefly, and boil, uncovered, for 3 to 4 minutes. Stir again, cover, and reduce the heat to medium-low. Simmer for 5 minutes, then reduce the heat to very low and cook, still covered, for another 12 to 15 minutes. Without lifting the lid, let stand for 10 to 15 minutes to steam.

If using a rice cooker, turn it on, cover, and let cook automatically. When the cooker turns off, let stand, covered, for 10 to 15 minutes.

Stir the rice gently with a rice paddle or wooden spoon. It will feel firm, with separate grains. **MAKES ABOUT 6 CUPS**

Serve with dishes from Kerala or Tamil Nadu such as Pomfret in Coconut Milk Sauce (page 208) or Tilapia Green Curry (page 222) or Cashew-Coconut Meatballs (page 262). We also think it's beautiful served with colorful bright greens.

BASH FUL RICE

. . . .

We have seen this tasty parboiled Bangladeshi rice for sale only at Kalustyan's in New York City (see page 18). You may come across it in other specialty stores or Indian groceries. It is an overall beige cream in color and looks like a blend of rices, with some grains having small flecks of red bran on them and others translucent with an opaque white strip. The rice should be cooked in plenty of boiling water, with no soaking, no steaming. The cooked grains are separate, soft, and tender.

To cook 2 cups bash ful, first wash thoroughly and drain. Bring a large pot of water to a boil. Sprinkle in the rice, bring back to a boil, and cook for about 11 minutes, or until tender.

Drain the rice in a sieve, then place back in the pot. Drizzle on several tablespoons of ghee or melted butter, if you wish. Cover and let the rice stand for at least 5 minutes before serving. Turn out onto a platter or into a serving bowl. **MAKES ABOUT 6 1/2 CUPS**

Serve with Bengali dishes such as Tiger Shrimp with Onions (page 211) or Classic Bengali Fish in Broth (page 223) or as a plain rice with any meal.

SRI LANKAN SAMBA RICE (WHITE OR RED)

. . . .

These are the parboiled rices you'll find for sale in Sri Lankan groceries. The white samba is more common, with golden white, fairly small grains, and the red rice is reddish brown. Instructions are the same for both.

To cook 2 cups samba rice, wash well and drain. Pick over and discard any stones or discolored grains. Place in a pot with 3¼ cups water, bring to a vigorous boil, uncovered, and stir gently with a fork. Boil for about 2 minutes, then cover tightly, lower the heat, and simmer gently for 25 minutes. Turn gently with a wooden spoon, then cover again. Serve hot or warm. Note that this rice, like most parboiled rices, has a fairly strong aroma when cooking. If you don't like the smell, add a bay leaf to the pot before putting it on to boil. Once cooked, the red rice has a pleasant grainy smell, while the white rice stays pungent. **MAKES ABOUT 6 1/2 CUPS**

Serve to anchor a Sri Lankan meal: Put out a well-sauced dish such as Prawn White Curry (page 217) or a mallum—*Shredded Green Bean Mallum (page 76), for example—and a* sambol.

MOHAN'S MORNING RICE

. . . .

Every morning, from before dawn, Mohan's tea stall by the big Hindu temple in Udaipur (in southern Rajasthan) is busy. Taxi drivers and schoolchildren, laborers and office workers stop in for a quick glass of hot tea or milky coffee, or for a plate of *poha*, aromatic rice flakes cooked like an easy pilaf. It's wonderful morning food, slightly sweet, soft textured, easy to digest. If you don't like hot chiles in the morning (these give a mild heat), then simply omit them.

2 cups rice flakes (see headnote, page 89)

3 tablespoons raw sesame oil or vegetable oil

$\frac{1}{2}$ teaspoon black mustard seeds

1 teaspoon fennel seeds

$\frac{1}{2}$ teaspoon cumin seeds

$\frac{1}{2}$ cup minced onion

$\frac{1}{4}$ teaspoon turmeric

1 green or red cayenne chile, or substitute 1 or 2 jalapeños,
     seeded and coarsely chopped (optional)

$\frac{1}{4}$ cup water

2 teaspoons salt

2 teaspoons sugar

$\frac{1}{4}$ cup or more coarsely torn coriander leaves and stems

Place the rice flakes in a bowl, cover with cold water, and swirl around with your hand, then drain. Repeat two more times. Place the rice flakes in a sieve to drain, and set aside.

Heat the oil in a wok or karhai (see Glossary) or a heavy skillet over medium-high heat. When it is hot, add the mustard seeds; when they have finished popping, about 20 seconds, add the fennel and cumin seeds. Wait 10 seconds, then add the onion, stir well to coat with oil, lower the heat slightly, and cook for 2 to 3 minutes. Add the turmeric and chiles, if using, and cook, stirring frequently, until the onion and chiles are well softened, about 5 minutes more.

Add the rice flakes and cook for a minute, turning and stirring, then add the water. Stir-fry for 2 to 3 minutes: Press the flakes against the pan, then lift and turn them, and press again, so they cook while staying separated. Lower the heat a little more, cover, and let cook for 1 minute. The rice should be cooked through and tender.

Add the salt and sugar and stir-fry for another minute. Remove from the heat and mound on a platter. Top with plenty of coriander leaves.

MAKES JUST MORE THAN 2 CUPS; SERVES 2 TO 3

Serve for breakfast or as a comforting snack anytime. To serve as a light lunch, accompany with a fresh green vegetable dish or a fresh chutney, say, Tart Mango Salsa (page 48), Watercress and Shallot Salad (page 55), or Quick Asparagus Stir-fry (page 158).

COCONUT-RICE SOUP

. . . .

I first learned to make this inviting rice soup while living with the Munasinghes in 1978 (see page 332). It's a traditional breakfast congee, but we serve it as a soup at any time of day. It's a little sweet with coconut milk and sugar and warm with ginger and fresh shallots. We love it as a way of using rice left over from the day before, but originally it was freshly cooked, then immediately made into congee. Use any rice you like, from Sri Lankan samba to basmati.

4 cups cooked rice

3 cups water

1 teaspoon salt

1 tablespoon raw sesame oil or vegetable oil

1 tablespoon thinly sliced garlic

1 tablespoon thinly sliced ginger

2 tablespoons thinly sliced shallots

1 cup canned or fresh coconut milk

1 tablespoon chopped jaggery (palm or crude sugar) or brown sugar

In a food processor, combine the cooked rice, 1½ cups of the water, and the salt. Process long enough to break down the rice, not puree it.

Heat a large heavy pot or a large wok over medium-high heat. When it is hot, add the oil, and when the oil is hot, add the garlic, ginger, and shallots. Stir-fry for 1 to 2 minutes (the shallots and ginger will still be firm to crunchy), then add the coconut milk, jaggery or brown sugar, and the remaining 1½ cups water. Immediately add the rice mixture and stir. Bring just to a boil, then remove from the heat and serve.

MAKES ABOUT 6 CUPS; SERVES 4 TO 6

Serve for breakfast, with a little fresh fruit on the side, or for lunch, accompanied by wilted greens.

NOTE: The Tamil word *kanji* is the origin of the word *congee* that is used by English-speakers as the name for many kinds of Asian rice porridge and rice soup.

MORNING RICE AND YOGURT WITH FRESH FRUIT

. . . .

Flattened rice, also known as *rice flakes*, is called *chira* or *poha* in northern India, *aval* in southern India. It's rice that's been cooked and then run through rollers and flattened into flakes. The flakes are a pale grayish white and fairly soft, rather than crisp. Sold in clear plastic bags, they keep well. *Chira* is very quick to reconstitute and requires no boiling, so it's a godsend for cooks in very hot weather or in a big hurry.

We ate a version of this morning rice flake treat in Assam, the Indian state that straddles the Brahmaputra River, in the far northeast of the country. In Assam, many people eat rice three times a day. The Assamese and Bengali name for the dish is *phalahar*. It's like a tropical granola, the rice flakes stirred into yogurt and then the whole mixture sweetened with honey and perfumed with fresh fruit. PHOTOGRAPH ON PAGE 91

½ cup rice flakes

1 cup plain (full- or reduced-fat) yogurt

Pinch of salt

1 banana, chopped, or about 1 cup chopped mango

1 tablespoon honey or sugar

Place the rice flakes in a larger bowl and wash by adding cold water to cover generously. Swirl around with your hand, then drain in a sieve over a sink. Repeat once or twice. Place the flakes back in the bowl and add ½ cup very hot water. Stir and set aside for 10 minutes, then drain off any excess water.

Add the yogurt and salt and stir to blend. Add the fruit and stir in. Add the honey or sugar and stir. Serve in cereal bowls, or put out the large bowl so guests can serve themselves. MAKES ABOUT 4 CUPS; SERVES 4

Serve for breakfast or a snack.

COOLING FRUIT-YOGURT DESSERT: Serve this in small bowls for dessert, topped with an extra swirl of honey and a sprinkling of toasted almonds, and perhaps a sprig of mint, and accompanied by a crisp sweet cookie for a contrast in texture. SERVES 6

Rice flakes (also called flattened rice; *see headnote, page 89) at a street market in Rajshahi, Bangladesh.* OPPOSITE, LEFT: *Morning Rice and Yogurt (page 89) topped with bananas panfried with butter and honey, and the juices poured over.* RIGHT: *Bananas for sale at a Bangladeshi market.*

SEMOLINA UPPUMA

· · · · · · · · · · · ·

We had many different treats while staying in Goa (see "Prawns by the Kilo," page 214), the famous and much visited string of beaches on India's west coast, for three weeks one Christmas. One of my favorites was going for a swim each morning, then walking down the beach to a small eatery run by a cook from Kerala who served southern Indian specialties. Every day, I'd order coffee and *uppuma,* then sit and slowly savor them.

Uppuma is a South Indian breakfast, and it's also a method of cooking in flavored oil and hot water. This is a classic version, starting with lightly toasted semolina and stirring it into hot water flavored with spiced oil until it becomes a tender aromatic mass, rather like a semolina *pulao.* The whole dish takes about ten minutes, fifteen at most, to prepare. Serve it for breakfast, as described here, or at any time in place of rice or rice *pulao.*

The *uppuma* comes to the table like a savory bulgur pilaf, scented with seasonings, a little fluffy and moist. It invites other flavors, say, some soupy dal (Udaipur Urad Dal, page 189, for example) with a raita (page 67), or the more traditional Shallot Sambhar (page 187), along with Coconut Chutney (page 39). These are delicious options, but in truth the simple combination suggested here is my favorite way to eat *uppuma:* with a little sweetened yogurt, some ripe banana, and a squeeze of lime to balance it all. Eat with a spoon or, my preference, with your hand, South Indian style.

2 cups coarse semolina (not fine) flour

3 to 4 tablespoons vegetable oil or raw sesame oil

About 1 tablespoon ghee or butter

1 teaspoon black mustard seeds

2 teaspoons urad dal

About 10 unsalted cashews, whole or coarsely chopped

2 dried red chiles, stemmed and roughly crushed

Pinch of asafoetida powder (optional)

1 tablespoon minced ginger or ginger mashed to a paste

2 to 3 green cayenne chiles (optional)

About 10 fresh or frozen curry leaves

About 3 cups hot water

1 teaspoon salt, or to taste

FLAVORINGS AND ACCOMPANIMENTS

1 lime, cut into wedges

About 2 cups plain (full- or reduced-fat) yogurt, sweetened with 2 tablespoons honey

4 ripe bananas, chopped

About ½ cup cashews, lightly fried in a little ghee, butter, or oil until golden (optional)

Place a wide heavy skillet over medium-high heat; add the semolina and dry roast it, stirring frequently with a wooden spatula or spoon to prevent burning: The grains at the center, underneath, will start to turn brown first, so every minute or so, run your spatula under the center and move the golden grains to the side to let others take their place. After 2 to 3 minutes, lower the heat to medium, and continue to cook for another 4 minutes or so, until all the semolina is lightly touched with gold. Pour into a bowl and set aside.

Place a wide heavy pot over high heat and add the oil with the ghee or butter. When the ghee or butter is hot, toss in the mustard seeds. Once they splutter, lower the heat to medium, add the dal, cashews, dried chiles, and asafoetida, if using, and stir-fry briefly. Add the ginger, green chiles, and curry leaves and stir-fry briefly, then add 3 cups hot water.

Bring to a boil, add the salt, and let the water come back to a boil, then add the semolina gradually, in a trickle. Keep stirring with a wooden spoon as you add the grain to get it all mixed well and to prevent lumps from forming, just as you would do with porridge or polenta. Continue stirring and turning for another minute to break up lumps and moisten all the semolina. It will absorb all the water very quickly, and if the mixture seems dry (if there are lumps of semolina that have not been fully moistened), add a little more hot water and stir. The semolina should be tender and all the water should be absorbed. Remove from the heat.

Serve softly heaped on individual plates, with the lime wedges on the side. Put a small bowl of yogurt beside the semolina on each plate. Place some chopped banana on each mound, and sprinkle on the fried cashews, if you wish.

To eat, pour some yogurt onto the banana-topped *uppuma* and squeeze on a little lime juice. Use your hand or a spoon to mix and blend flavors, mouthful by mouthful, as you wish.

MAKES A LITTLE MORE THAN 4 CUPS; SERVES 4

Serve for breakfast or brunch.

MIXED FRUIT BREAKFAST: If you are not a banana lover, substitute other sweet, sliced tender fruits: chopped ripe mango or papaya or peaches, or small sweet berries, such as chopped strawberries or ripe raspberries or blueberries, alone or in combination.

SAVORY UPPUMA WITH DAL AND SAUCE: Instead of the flavorings suggested above, serve about 2 cups Shallot Sambhar (page 187) or other cooked dal and 1 cup Coconut Chutney (page 39). Put the *sambhar* out in individual small bowls, allowing about ½ cup per person. Show your guests how to pour it over the *uppuma* to flavor it and moisten it as they eat.

NEPALI POLENTA
WITH HIMALAYAN GRILLED TOMATO SAUCE

· · · · · · · · · · · ·

In Nepal, corn grows in the hills at low and middle elevations. We've had it grilled on the cob in mountain villages, and simmered in soup, but it's also eaten as a grain, coarsely ground and then cooked slowly in a heavy pot, like grits or polenta. The dish is known as *dero*. We like to add a little oil and flavor to the *dero* by tempering it with ghee and mustard seed, as described here.

The classic accompaniment for the polenta is a simple grilled tomato *achar*. It is a spicy sauce or salad that reminds us of the delicious and inventive salsas of Laos that are known as *jaew*. It is smoky tasting and medium-hot to hot, depending on the number and intensity of the chiles we use, and has become a must-make salsa almost anytime we're grilling, whether or not we're making the polenta. We just put some tomatoes and chiles on the side of the grill and turn them occasionally until they're scorched. (If you have no grill, you can scorch the vegetables in a heavy skillet instead.) All the other work is done by the food processor (or in a mortar).

Traditionally the sauce is flavored and enriched with small river fish known as *sidra*, which are grilled and then crumbled or chopped and stirred in. In Nepal, *sidra* are dried for long keeping; we substitute Japanese dried anchovies. From one to three inches long and very slender, they're not salted, just dried, and are sold in plastic packages in Japanese and Korean groceries. We love the grilled tomato sauce both ways, with or without the addition of the fish.

POLENTA

1 cup polenta or cornmeal

4 cups water

1 teaspoon salt

2 tablespoons ghee, butter, or vegetable oil

2 teaspoons black mustard seeds

SAUCE

4 to 5 large ripe tomatoes (about 2 pounds) or
    10 to 12 plum tomatoes

4 to 6 green cayenne chiles

1/2 cup small whole Japanese dried anchovies (see headnote; optional)

Scant 2 tablespoons minced ginger or ginger mashed to a paste

1 tablespoon minced garlic or garlic mashed to a paste

1 1/2 teaspoons salt, or to taste

1/2 teaspoon turmeric

1 1/2 teaspoons mustard oil or vegetable oil

1 cup chopped coriander leaves, chives, or mint leaves, or a blend

Corn, native to the Americas, has become a useful staple in many places in the Subcontinent. On the left, cobs of corn being grilled in a rural market in the state of Orissa. On the right, a nearby fabric vendor sits thoughtfully eating corn, kernel by kernel.

Place the polenta, water, and salt in a small heavy pot and bring to a boil, stirring occasionally, then lower the heat to maintain a simmer. Stir fairly constantly until the polenta is cooked and very tender, 25 to 40 minutes. (Timing varies with the grind of the polenta, we've found.) Remove from the heat.

In a small skillet, heat the ghee, butter, or oil over medium-high heat. Toss in the mustard seeds and cook just until they pop. Drizzle onto the polenta, then stir in. Set aside, covered, while you prepare the sauce.

Meanwhile heat a gas or charcoal grill, or preheat a cast-iron skillet, over medium-high heat. Grill or scorch the tomatoes, turning them to expose all sides to the heat. Use tongs to lift them off the grill or out of the skillet and set them aside to cool. Use the same method to scorch the chiles, then set aside to cool. If using the anchovies, grill or scorch them until touched with golden brown and aromatic, then set aside to cool.

Pull off and discard any very scorched pieces of tomato skin, then cut the tomatoes in half, removing the wedges of core at the stem end. Place them in a food processor, a large mortar, or a food mill set over a bowl.

Peel the scorched skin off the chiles and chop off the stems; discard. Cut a slit in each chile, scrape out the seeds, and discard. Add the chiles to the tomatoes.

Add the ginger, garlic, and salt. If using the fish, crumble them and add. Process or grind to a chunky salsa. Turn out into a serving bowl. Stir in the turmeric and mustard oil. (If you used large tomatoes rather than plum tomatoes, the sauce will be quite liquid.)

Just before serving, taste for salt and adjust if necessary. Stir in the green herbs. Serve warm or at room temperature, spooning the sauce over the polenta.

When asparagus is in season, Quick Asparagus Stir-fry (page 158) makes a good accompaniment to this dish. We often serve the sauce as a condiment for grilled meats and as a sauce for rice.

MAKES ABOUT 4 CUPS POLENTA AND 3 TO 4 CUPS SAUCE; SERVES 4

NOTE: If the sauce is served separately as a condiment or salsa, it will serve 6 to 8. To make a half recipe of the salsa, halve all ingredients except the mustard oil; reduce it to 1 teaspoon.

STIR-FRIED RICE AND DAL

. . . .

Rice and dal combined together make an easy comfortable dish that can be served on its own, perhaps with a salad, or used in place of plain rice, with a substantial curry of some kind alongside. The rice and dal combo is known as *khichadi* in many parts of the Subcontinent. In Bangladesh the name is *kichuri*. (The British, or those who cooked for them, added other flavors to make the hearty breakfast dish known as *kedgeree:* rice and dal with smoked fish and an egg.)

The first time I ate *kichuri* in Bangladesh, it came in what I later learned was a typical combination, together with beef *bhoona* (Bangla Slow-Cooked Beef with Onion, page 273). It was mild, with no chiles, because it was served like a plain rice dish, as a foil for the spiciness of the beef. The *kichuri* was topped with soft-cooked onions (given as an option here), and I used the coriander leaves and lime wedges on the salad plate to season and freshen it mouthful by mouthful.

The trick with *kichuri*, as with other *khichadis*, is to end up with a good blend of tender moist cooked rice and dal, with no mushiness and no lumps. The easiest way to achieve this is to cook the rice and dal separately, then toss them together, lightly stir-frying them with flavorings. Cook rice and dal fresh for the purpose, or use this recipe as a simple way of transforming leftovers.

¼ cup ghee or vegetable oil (plus 1 tablespoon if making the optional onion garnish)

2 cups thinly sliced onions (optional), for garnish

1 teaspoon Bengali Five-Spice Mixture (page 340) or ¼ teaspoon each fenugreek, cumin, black mustard, fennel, and nigella seeds

1 teaspoon minced garlic or garlic mashed to a paste, or to taste

1 cup minced onion

1 to 2 green or red cayenne chiles, chopped (optional)

¼ teaspoon garam masala (page 342 or store-bought; optional)

¼ teaspoon turmeric

4 cups cooled cooked rice

1½ to 2 cups cooked dal (see Note)

1 teaspoon salt, or to taste

About ¼ cup coriander leaves

ACCOMPANIMENTS

2 limes, cut into wedges

Bangla Salad Plate (page 54; optional)

Heat the ghee or oil in a wok or karhai (see Glossary) or a large skillet over medium-high heat. If making the optional onion garnish, toss in the sliced onions and stir-fry until softened and well touched with brown, about 12 minutes. Remove from the heat, lift the onions out of the pan with a slotted spoon, pausing to allow as much ghee or oil as possible to drain off, and set them aside on a plate. Return the pan to medium-high heat and add another 1 tablespoon ghee or oil.

Toss in the whole spices if using (do not add the spice powder at this point), and stir-fry for a moment, until the mustard seeds have popped. Add the garlic and stir-fry briefly. Toss in the minced onion and cook for 5 minutes, stirring frequently, then add the chiles, if using. Continue to cook until the onion is very soft, about 8 minutes altogether. Add the spice powder, if using, and the turmeric, and stir. Add the rice and stir-fry to mix it and to break up any lumps. Add the dal. Stir-fry gently, turning the mixture with your spatula, pressing it against the sides of the hot pan and tossing it to prevent the rice from clumping, until all the ingredients are blended and any liquid from the dal has been absorbed by the rice. Add the salt (the amount will depend on whether your rice was at all seasoned and on which dal you used, so be cautious), then turn the mixture onto a platter or into a wide shallow bowl. Taste and add extra salt if needed.

Top with the reserved browned onions, if you made them, and the coriander leaves. Serve with a plate of lime wedges or a Bangladeshi Salad Plate alongside.

SERVES 2 TO 3 AS A MAIN DISH, 4 TO 5 WITH A NUMBER OF DISHES

For a simple meal, serve as a main dish with just a salad or with Hasna Begum's Mixed Vegetable Curry (page 164) or Bangla-Flavored Fried Zucchini (page 144), a classic accompaniment for kichuri. For a more elaborate meal, serve as the rice dish to accompany Bangla Slow-Cooked Beef with Onion (page 273) or Classic Bengali Fish in Broth (page 223).

NOTE ON COOKING DAL FOR KICHURI: Use any cooked dal from the Dals chapter; the classic dal for this dish in most of the Subcontinent is mung dal. If you don't have dal already cooked, begin with $1/2$ cup uncooked mung dal or masur dal. Rinse well, place in a pot with 4 cups water, a pinch of turmeric, a cinnamon or cassia stick, and a bay leaf, and bring to a boil. Reduce the heat and simmer until tender, about 20 minutes for the masur, 35 for the mung, adding extra water if necessary to prevent the pot from boiling dry. When the dal is tender, stir in about $1/2$ teaspoon salt. Taste and adjust the seasonings if necessary.

GUJARATI KHICHADI: In a Gujarati *thali* meal (see Glossary), rice is served toward the end of the meal. It may be plain, or it may come as *khichadi*, fairly plain and slightly sweetened. To make Gujarati *khichadi*, use the same proportions of rice and dal as above, but use a very simple unspiced dal. Omit the spice blend, and omit the onion, garlic, and chiles. Instead, flavor the hot ghee or oil with a generous pinch of asafoetida, 1 teaspoon black mustard seeds, $1/4$ teaspoon turmeric, and 6 to 8 fresh or frozen curry leaves (optional). Stir-fry the flavorings very briefly, then add the cooked rice and dal and stir-fry as above. Season with 1 teaspoon salt, or to taste, and 1 teaspoon sugar, then turn out and serve plain or topped with coriander leaves.

QUICK TAMARIND PULAO
WITH CURRY LEAVES

· · · · · · · · · · · ·

If we want to put a flavored rice on the table and are working in "last-minute" mode, this inviting tamarind-flavored *pulao* from Tamil Nadu, made with leftover plain rice, is a good place to turn. The yellow-tinted mound of rice is dotted with curry leaves and chopped green chile. We like to serve it with an intensely colored vegetable dish, say, a Shredded Green Bean Mallum (page 76) or Pea Shoots for a Crowd (page 161), perhaps with some grilled yogurt-marinated meat alongside and a sweet or fresh chutney. It also makes a good meal-in-one for two or three people, topped, if you wish, with a fried or poached egg each, and accompanied by a fresh salad.

Traditionally this quick *pulao* has a fair amount of heat from the combination of crumbled dried chiles and chopped fresh green chiles. Somehow the tamarind makes the chiles' heat a little more intense; it's a wonderful combination. Textures are soft, with a little crisp bite from the toasted dal used as a seasoning.

Scant 2 tablespoons tamarind pulp

¼ cup hot water

1 tablespoon urad dal (optional)

3 tablespoons vegetable oil or raw sesame oil

1 teaspoon black mustard seeds

2 pinches asafoetida powder

4 dried red chiles, stemmed and crumbled

2 green cayenne chiles, or substitute 3 jalapeños, coarsely chopped

¼ teaspoon turmeric

8 to 10 fresh or frozen curry leaves

About 4 cups cooked rice, chilled or at room temperature

1 teaspoon salt, or to taste

¼ cup coriander leaves or 2 tablespoons dry-roasted cashews for garnish

Cut the tamarind pulp into pieces, place in a bowl, and pour over the hot water. Use a fork to mash the tamarind into the water, then set aside for several minutes to soak. If using the urad dal, wash it well, drain it, and set it aside.

Place a sieve or strainer over a bowl. Use your fingers or a fork to mash and squeeze the tamarind again, helping loosen the pulp in the water. Pour the mixture into the strainer. Use the back of a spoon to press and mash the pulp against the strainer to extract as much flavor as possible. Discard the tamarind pulp and set the tamarind liquid aside.

Place a wok or karhai (see Glossary) or a wide pot over medium-high heat. Add the oil, and when it is hot, add the mustard seeds. Cover loosely until the seeds have sputtered and popped for 10 to 15 seconds, then toss in the drained urad dal, if using, the asafoetida, and crumbled dried chiles. Lower the heat to medium and stir-fry for about a minute.

Add the green chiles and turmeric. Stir-fry for about 2 minutes, until the chiles are starting to soften, then toss in the curry leaves and give them a stir. Add the rice, crumbling it into the pan to break up lumps. Add the salt, raise heat to high, and stir-fry for several minutes, until the rice is softened, then pour in the tamarind liquid. Continue to stir-fry for a few minutes, tossing the mixture to keep it from clumping, until the liquid is absorbed and flavors are blended.

Turn out into a shallow bowl or onto a platter, and serve topped with the coriander leaves or dry-roasted cashews. SERVES 3 TO 4

Serve accompanied by a fresh salad or a sweet chutney such as Fresh Bean Sprout Salad (page 55) or Hot Sweet Date-Onion Chutney (page 28), and see headnote.

SUMMER VEGETABLE PULAO: You can add 1 cup of tender vegetables to this, if you wish. We like to include corn cut from the cob or green beans chopped into small pieces. Their sweetness is nicely set off by the tamarind. Increase the oil by 1 tablespoon. Add the vegetables after the dried chiles have been briefly stir-fried, and stir-fry them for about 1 minute before you add the fresh green chiles.

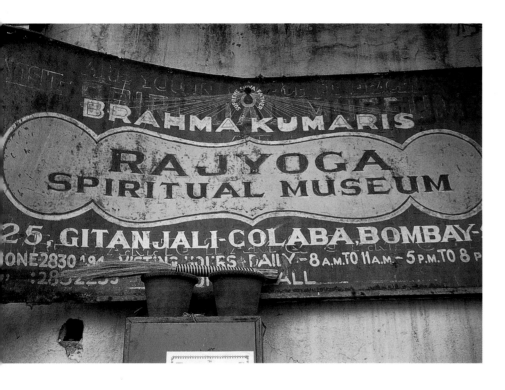

Street sign in the Mumbai (Bombay) neighborhood of Colaba. OPPOSITE: *Chicken Biryani, Dum Style (page 102) served with Watercress and Shallot Salad (page 55) made with arugula.*

CHICKEN BIRYANI, DUM STYLE

. . . .

We were in Delhi in late November. Days were short and evenings cool. One evening we sat outside on the terrace at a restaurant, in layers of sweaters, not wanting to go inside; the stars were beautiful, the sky a midnight blue. All the other diners were safely indoors. We ordered *dum biryani murgh* from the very patient waiter, along with a chopped salad and a raita. The biryani came baked in its own small clay pot, aromatic, hot, tender, inviting. This is our take on that dish.

Biryani is associated with the culinary legacy of the Moghuls; the word *biryani* is from the Persian word for rice, *birinj*. Based in Iran and Afghanistan, the Moghuls began to make incursions into what is now Pakistan and the Punjab about one thousand years ago. By the early sixteenth century, they had conquered much of northern India and had established their capital near Agra (later it was moved to Delhi). With the conquest came Moghul culture, with its highly developed Iranian–central Asian architecture, music, and cuisine. The cooking traditions of the Moghul court, since adapted to local ingredients, are still associated with the wealthy classes in many regions, from Hyderabad to Delhi and Lucknow.

Biryani is a close cousin of the Iranian rice and meat dishes called *polo*, in which partly cooked rice is layered with flavorings, then slow cooked, though over the centuries the spicing has taken on a distinctively subcontinental personality. It's like a meal-in-one casserole, a delicious dish to serve on a cold night or any time you feel like celebrating. It cooks for an hour in a moderate oven, giving you time to prepare salads and other accompaniments, so it's a good dish for a dinner party.

Here boneless chicken is chopped into large bite-size pieces and marinated in a blend of yogurt and flavorings. Flavors include a little cayenne, just enough to give a mild heat, as well as coriander seed, garlic, and ginger. Traditionally the garlic and ginger are ground in a mortar to make a paste. If you have a mortar, do use it; otherwise, mince the ginger and garlic, then place them in a small bowl and use the back of a spoon to mash them a little.

The chicken is layered with almost-cooked basmati and some cooked onions, then baked in a tightly sealed casserole. This technique is called *dum* (also used for Cauliflower Dum, page 148), a shortening of the Farsi word *dampunkt,* meaning "air (or steam) cooked." We use a very heavy cast-iron pot, with a heavy lid that seals well. Traditional *dum* cooking requires that the lid and pot be sealed together with a strip of dough; instructions for the classic method are included here. It's simple and ingenious, very like the technique traditionally used to seal the top and bottom of the *couscoussière* together tightly when making couscous. You can instead cover the pot tightly with aluminum foil before putting the lid on, so no steam can escape while the biryani is cooking.

PHOTOGRAPH ON PAGE 101

About 1 pound boneless chicken breasts or thighs, or a mixture

2 teaspoons minced garlic or garlic mashed to a paste (see headnote)

1 teaspoon minced ginger or ginger mashed to a paste (see headnote)

1½ teaspoons ground coriander

½ teaspoon cayenne

¼ teaspoon turmeric

¼ teaspoon garam masala (page 342 or store-bought), or substitute a generous pinch each of ground cinnamon, freshly ground black pepper, and ground cumin

½ cup plain (full- or reduced-fat) yogurt

2 teaspoons salt

2 cups basmati rice

OPTIONAL DOUGH FOR SEALING THE POT

1¼ cups atta, whole wheat, or all-purpose flour

About ½ cup lukewarm water

3 medium-large onions (about 1 pound)

Scant ¾ cup vegetable oil or ghee, or a blend

1 cup minced coriander leaves

About 2 tablespoons water

Rinse the chicken, then chop it into large bite-size pieces, about 1-inch cubes. Place in a bowl. Add the garlic, ginger, coriander, cayenne, turmeric, garam masala or spices, yogurt, and 1 teaspoon of the salt and stir to mix until all the chicken is well coated with marinade. Cover and set aside in a cool place or the refrigerator for 2 to 4 hours, whatever is most convenient.

Meanwhile, wash the rice thoroughly in several changes of cool water. Place in a bowl, add cold water to cover, and set aside to soak for half an hour or so.

About 1½ hours before you wish to serve the dish, place a rack in the center of the oven and preheat the oven to 375°F.

If you want to make the quick dough to seal the pot you will be using to bake the biryani (see headnote), place the flour in a bowl and add enough lukewarm water to make a moist dough, about ½ cup. Knead briefly, then turn the dough out and cut it in half. On a lightly floured surface, roll each half out under your palms to a rope a little longer than half the circumference of your pot. Set aside, loosely covered with plastic wrap.

Slice the onions as fine as possible (if your onions are large, cut them in half before slicing them); you should have about 3 cups sliced onions. Place a large heavy ovenproof pot with a heavy tight-fitting lid over medium-high heat. Add the oil and/or ghee, and when it is hot, add the onions. Lower the heat to medium. Cook until the onions are very soft, wilted, and touched with golden brown, 12 to 15 minutes. Lift the onions out of the hot oil and set aside. There should be about ½ cup oil left in the pot; leave ¼ cup in the pot, and pour the remaining ¼ cup into a heatproof bowl or small pan, and set aside.

While the onions are cooking, precook the soaked rice: Place about 8 cups water in a large pot and bring to a boil. Add the remaining 1 teaspoon salt, and when the water returns to a boil, sprinkle in the rice. Bring the water back to a boil, then cook at a vigorous boil for 4 to 6 minutes, or until the rice is no longer brittle but still firm to the bite. Drain in a colander and set aside.

Place the pot containing the oil over medium-high heat. Lightly grease the rim of the pot. Distribute half the chicken pieces over the bottom of the pot, then sprinkle on half the precooked rice. Strew half the cooked onions over the top, then sprinkle on about half the coriander leaves. Repeat with the remaining chicken, rice, onion, and coriander. Sprinkle on about 2 tablespoons water, and drizzle on the reserved ¼ cup oil. Place the dough strips on the rim of the pot to make a full circle, sealing the seams. Put the lid on, pressing down firmly to seal. *Alternatively,* lay a sheet of aluminum foil over the top of the pot to cover it completely, then top with the lid.

Transfer the pot to the oven and bake for 1 hour.

Remove the lid (and dough seal). Turn out the biryani onto a platter, mounding it in the center. There will be a little crusted rice and chicken on the bottom of the pot, a real treat. Scrape it out and lay the crusty pieces on top of the biryani. Serve hot or warm.   SERVES 6

Accompany with a salad such as Cachoombar (page 57) and a sauce or fresh chutney such as Cucumber Raita (page 67) or Star Fruit Chutney (page 34).

CLAY POT BIRYANI: You can also make this dish in a clay pot, the traditional way; the pot bakes at a lower temperature, so the cooking time is a little longer. The clay pot must be well seasoned and about 10 inches in diameter. Preheat the oven to 350°F. Fry the onions in a skillet, then drain the onions, reserving the cooking oil (there should be about ½ cup), and set them aside. Pour about ¼ cup of the oil into the bottom of the clay pot and swirl it around to coat the bottom and sides with oil, then layer in the chicken, rice, onions, and coriander as described above. Drizzle the remaining ¼ cup oil over the top. Cover tightly and seal with the dough strips or with foil. Bake for 1½ hours.

BIRYANI FOR TWO OR THREE: To halve the recipe, halve all the ingredients but use 2 onions (to make about 2 cups sliced). Use a small heavy ovenproof pot about 6 inches in diameter. The baking time will be only 45 minutes.

PAKISTANI LAMB PULAO

· · · · · · · · · · · ·

In Pakistan, bread is generally for everyday meals and rice is for special occasions. This lamb *pulao* from Pakistan is a special-occasion dish of lamb and rice that is like the *pulaos* of Central Asia—Afghanistan, Uzbekistan, and Xinjiang, for example. Lamb or goat are traditional, but in Pakistan these days, beef might be substituted. The *pulao* has the blend of flavors that we associate with Moghul dishes: cinnamon, cardamom, cloves, all subtly blended.

The list of ingredients may look long, but they're mostly spices, so all it takes is measuring them out. You will need a wide heavy ovenproof pot with a tight-fitting lid. Techniques are not complicated: The lamb is cooked in oil that is flavored with onion and spices, then the liquids (tomatoes and water) are added. The meat, tomatoes, and rice simmer together until the liquid is absorbed, flavors are blended and aromatic, and textures are tender. Traditionally *pulaos* are cooked over a fire and then simmered over the coals, or finished in the waning heat of a tandoor oven. We start the cooking on our stove top, then finish it in a slow oven, but you can also slow cook the rice over low heat on the stove. Both methods are given here.

Serve as the centerpiece of a special meal.

1½ pounds boneless lamb (preferably shoulder), cut into ¾-inch cubes
About 1½ teaspoons salt
½ teaspoon freshly ground black pepper (optional)

RICE

2 cups basmati rice, washed and soaked in 6 cups water for 1 to 3 hours
6 tablespoons ghee or vegetable oil
One 2-inch piece cinnamon or cassia stick
6 cloves
5 brown cardamom pods, or substitute 5 green cardamom pods
2 bay leaves
2 tablespoons minced garlic or garlic mashed to a paste
3 tablespoons minced ginger or ginger mashed to a paste
6 cups thinly sliced onions
2 teaspoons ground coriander seed
1½ teaspoons ground black cumin or 2 teaspoons regular ground cumin
½ teaspoon mace, preferably freshly ground
½ teaspoon freshly grated nutmeg
½ teaspoon cayenne
1 teaspoon freshly ground black pepper
1 cup diced or crushed canned or fresh tomatoes
1 teaspoon turmeric
1½ teaspoons salt
2 cups water

GARNISHES

About 3 tablespoons melted ghee or butter, or to taste (optional)
¾ cup coarsely chopped almonds (optional)
Generous ½ cup coriander leaves, coarsely chopped

Place the lamb in a bowl, add the salt and pepper, and toss to coat all the meat with the seasonings. Set aside, loosely covered, for 30 minutes.

If you will be baking the *pulao*, place a rack in the center of the oven and preheat the oven to 325°F. Drain the rice and set aside.

In a wide heavy ovenproof pot with a tight-fitting lid, heat the ghee or oil over medium-high heat. Add the cinnamon, cloves, cardamom, and bay leaves and stir. Add the garlic and ginger and stir-fry for several minutes, until aromatic. Add the onions and cook, stirring frequently, until very soft, 10 to 15 minutes; lower the heat to medium if they start to brown before they are well softened. Add the ground coriander, cumin, mace, nutmeg, cayenne, and black pepper and stir-fry for a moment. Add the lamb and cook, turning and stirring it to expose all its surfaces to the heat, until browned. Add the tomato, turmeric, and salt and stir, then add the water and bring to a boil.

Sprinkle the rice into the boiling liquid and bring back to a vigorous boil. Cover tightly (wrap the pot lid with foil if necessary to make a better seal) and place in the oven for 45 minutes. Or, cover the pot tightly, lower the heat to medium-low, and simmer for 40 minutes, reducing the heat to low after the first 5 minutes.

Remove from the oven or the heat and let stand for 15 minutes, still covered. The rice will have absorbed all the liquid and be expanded with flavor.

Turn the rice out onto a platter. Drizzle on the melted ghee if you wish and garnish with the almonds, if using, and chopped coriander.

SERVES 6 TO 8

Accompany with a yogurt salad such as Cucumber Raita (page 67) and several quick-to-assemble chutneys, perhaps Sweet Hot Date-Onion Chutney (page 28) and Tart Mango Salsa (page 48).

NOTE: It doesn't seem to be traditional practice to preseason the meat, but we find it adds good flavor.

CHICKPEA PULAO: For a more everyday *pulao*, using chickpeas instead of meat, substitute 4 cups cooked (or drained canned) chickpeas for the lamb. If the chickpeas aren't seasoned, stir in 1½ teaspoons salt before you begin. Alter the spicing as follows: Reduce the cloves to 2, and the cardamom to 2 pods. Substitute 1 teaspoon ground cumin for the black cumin and omit the mace and nutmeg. Increase the tomatoes to 2 cups crushed or diced. Add the chickpeas to the flavored onions and oil and stir-fry for several minutes, then proceed as above.

Serve as a vegetarian main dish with a sweet chutney, Zinet's Young Ginger Pickle (page 346), a raita (see "The Raita Family," page 67), and stir-fried greens, such as Pea Shoots for a Crowd (page 161). It also makes a great accompaniment to a well-sauced meat dish, such as Aromatic Slow-Cooked Chicken (page 242) or Classic Bengali Fish in Broth (page 223).

NOTE: We often make a half recipe of this chickpea *pulao*. It's a good weeknight-supper dish, for once it's simmering, the cook is free to make a salad or other side dishes. To halve the recipe, just halve the ingredients. Cooking times will remain the same.

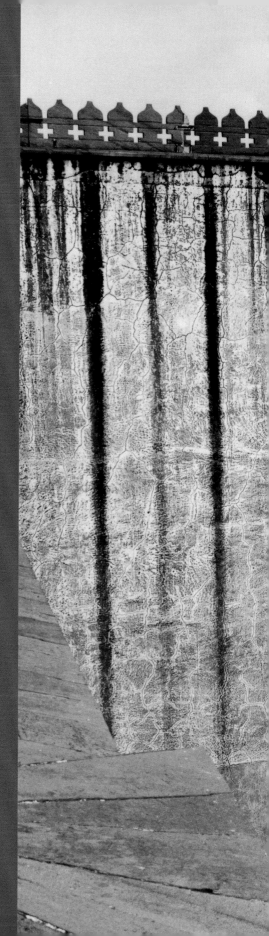

BREADS

has been on trips through Pakistan, in the Punjab, and in Rajasthan and Nepal. Naans made in tandoor ovens and fresh whole-grain chapatis made on simple griddles are some of the most satisfying breads we know of, breads filled with the straightforward taste of wheat. Millet and sorghum griddle breads made in Rajasthan and Gujarat are as undeniably good

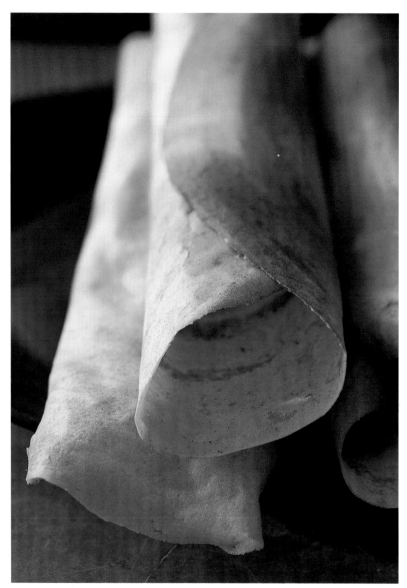

Home-Style Dosas (page 112)

or oven baked. They're all in the flatbread family, but they're wonderfully diverse.

Though it's not entirely accurate to say that the culinary regions of the Subcontinent divide themselves between rice-based and bread-based cuisines, the rice versus bread distinction can explain a lot about the food. It's a question of emphasis. Even though in South India, Sri Lanka, Bangladesh, or Bengal—all classic rice-rich areas—we can almost always find a roti with dal for breakfast or a light supper, and in homes and occasionally in restaurants there will be ingenious rice-based breads, for great bread we will always head north and west, to Rajasthan, the Punjab, and Pakistan.

There the wheat breads, leavened and oven-baked naan, as well as skillet breads—roti, chapati, and *phulka,* and all their close relatives—are simple and oh-so-good. Sometimes they're flavored with yogurt and herbs blended into the dough, or they may be filled with a cooked flavoring of dal or spiced potato. Always the subtle, enticing taste of wheat flour cooked on the griddle makes them irresistible. In the desert, wheat often gives way to hardier crops—sorghum or millet or corn—and then the hand-patted rotis are baked on an unglazed clay griddle, slowly and carefully, as corn tortillas are baked in southern Mexico.

In the rice-eating parts of the region, bread is more of an accompaniment, a snack or side dish, than one of the foundations of the diet. Breads are inventive, often made of rice or dal rather than wheat, and often made of a batter instead of a kneaded dough. A *dosa* in the south of India is like a crepe, made from a fermented batter most often composed of ground rice and dal; a similar batter is used to make the steamed round disks called *idlis*.

Baker's Notes: Each of the recipes in this chapter is self-explanatory. Still, over time we've learned a few general truths about flatbreads, specifically about doughs and shaping and cooking, that you might find useful.

All nonbatter breads are best if the dough is very thoroughly kneaded. Unleavened wheat flour doughs are much easier to roll out and cook if they've been left to rest for an hour or more (or as long as an overnight rest in a cool place).

Skillet-top baking may be an art, but even a beginner can make good bread on the first try. All you need is a heavy cast-iron skillet or *tava* (a flat iron pan; see Glossary), a rolling pin (we prefer a tapered pin), and a smooth surface to work on.

Wheat flour breads can generally be cooked at higher temperatures than breads made from other flours, such as corn or sorghum or rice, but even a wheat flour roti should be cooked only on medium-high. A too-hot skillet can result in hot or scorched spots on your breads. If the bread has scorched patches, lower the heat. (For breads made of any of the nonwheat flours, the ideal cooking surface is unglazed clay, which gives a gentler, more even heat.)

Breads that have a little oil or melted butter in them will be more tender and flaky. Breads cooked in an oiled skillet will cook more evenly, for the oil helps transmit the heat.

Two Dard women at the Hemis mela, *an annual festival at a Buddhist temple in Ladakh, not far from the Indus River valley and the Tibet border (see "Rebirth," page 185)*

CHAPATIS

· · · · · · · · · · · ·

Chapatis are one of the world's simplest breads to make and one of the best to eat. A dough is made with flour, salt, and water, then balls of the dough are rolled out thin and cooked on a griddle or a skillet. Once you get the hang of making chapatis, you can turn out eight breads for breakfast or for dinner in the time it takes to brew a pot of coffee (well, almost).

Chapatis, sometimes called rotis in the north of India and in Pakistan, are quintessential Subcontinent. Village people make them over a simple fire of dung, while people living on the street in Delhi, or herdsmen in the desert, cook them on a makeshift fire of scrap wood and brush. They are a true staple food (like rice) because they not only feed and nourish, but they also taste good day after day, meal after meal. Some of the best simple meals we have ever had have revolved around chapatis: chapatis and dal, chapatis and a curry.

If you're making chapatis for the first time, try to find atta flour in a South Asian grocery. Atta is a special kind of whole wheat flour, made from hard durum wheat that is very finely ground. An attractive pale yellow brown in color, it makes the best chapatis because it is strong and makes a dough that rolls out very smoothly. The cooled breads have an inviting warm-grain flavor and fine texture.

About 2 cups atta flour, or substitute whole wheat flour, sifted,
plus extra for rolling
1 teaspoon salt
About 1 cup warm water

To make the dough by hand, in a medium bowl, mix together the 2 cups flour and the salt. Make a well in the middle and add 1 cup warm water. Mix with your hand or with a spoon until you can gather the mixture together into a dough (depending on your flour, you may need a little extra water or a little extra flour to make a kneadable dough). Turn out onto a lightly floured surface and knead for 8 to 10 minutes.

To make the dough in a food processor, place the 2 cups flour and the salt in the processor and pulse to blend. With the machine going, slowly pour the water through the feed tube and continue to process for about 15 seconds after a ball of dough forms. Turn the dough out onto a lightly floured surface and knead briefly.

Cover the dough with plastic wrap and let stand for at least 30 minutes and up to 12 hours. (The longer the dough stands, the easier the breads are to shape and the more digestible they are.)

Divide the dough into eight pieces. Roll each one into a ball under your lightly cupped palm. Place some flour on your work surface, dust your palm with flour, and flatten each ball in the flour, pressing both sides into the flour in turn.

To shape the breads, work with one piece at a time, leaving the others lightly covered. Working on a lightly floured surface, flatten the dough with a rolling pin, without turning it over, rolling from the center outward with light strokes and rotating the bread slightly between each stroke, until it is 7 to 8 inches in diameter. Set aside and repeat with the remaining breads. Do not stack the rolled-out breads; if you don't have enough counter space for them all, roll out just a few and begin cooking, then roll out the others as the breads cook.

Heat a cast-iron griddle or skillet over medium-high heat. Rub the surface with a well-oiled cotton cloth or paper towel. When the griddle is hot, place a chapati top side down on the griddle and let it cook for only 10 to 15 seconds, then gently flip to the second side. Cook on the second side until small bubbles begin to form in the dough, approximately 1 minute. Turn the chapati back over and finish cooking, about another minute. At this stage, a perfect chapati will start to balloon. The process can be helped along by gently pressing on the bread. Because the bread is hot, we find the easiest method is to use a small cotton cloth or a paper towel wadded up to protect your fingertips. Gently press down on a large bubble, forcing the bubble to widen. If the bread starts to burn on the bottom before it has ballooned, move the bread (with the help of your paper towel) across the skillet, dislodging it from the point at which it is beginning to burn. When you are satisfied with your chapati, remove it and wrap in a clean towel.

Cook the other breads, stacking each as it is finished on top of the others and wrapping the stack in cloth to keep the breads soft and warm.

MAKES 8 BREADS; SERVES 3 TO 4

Serve with any meal, or for breakfast or a snack. Use to scoop up salsa or to lift pieces of kebab, or wrap them around sandwich fillings.

VARIATIONS: You can include 1 to 2 tablespoons vegetable oil or ghee or melted butter to make more tender breads. Add it to the flour and mix it in before adding the warm water; you will need a little less water. To make smaller breads, which are easier to handle, divide the dough into twelve pieces; the breads will be about 5 to 6 inches in diameter. And you can also cook the chapatis in oil or ghee: Put about ½ teaspoon oil or ghee on the hot skillet and spread it over the surface before you lay down each bread to cook.

MAKES 12 BREADS

PHULKA: If you cook the breads over a gas burner or a wood fire, you can make the version of chapati known as *phulka* or *phulka roti*. You need heatproof fingers (as most experienced chapati makers have), or a light touch with tongs, to do this successfully. Proceed as above, cooking the bread in a skillet. Once you have turned the bread back over onto the first side, cook it for a minute, then hold it vertically directly above the flame and turn it slowly to expose the edges to the heat. The bread will puff out as the air in it expands, and the edges will get evenly cooked. You can also try doing this using the skillet as your heat source: Lift the chapati out of the skillet, place the edge on the hot surface, and then turn it slowly, as if you were rolling it on the skillet, so the whole outside edge gets exposed to the hot surface; the chapati should puff.

TANDOOR ROTI: Chapatis are sometimes baked in tandoor ovens. To bake your chapatis, set up the oven as described in Home-Style Tandoor Naan (page 116) and preheat it to 500°F before you start rolling out the breads. Place as many breads as will fit directly on the preheated stone or tiles and bake until done, about 2 minutes. They will usually puff up while baking and become touched with color. Use a long-handled spatula to remove them from the oven. Brush the top of each with a little ghee or melted butter, if you wish, then stack them and wrap them in a cotton cloth to keep warm while you bake the remaining breads.

HOME-STYLE DOSAS

. . . .

If chapati is the staple bread of North India and Pakistan, then *dosa* is the bread of the south. Unlike chapati, it's not the simplest bread in the world to make (though it isn't difficult), but it's one of the most inventive breads we know. A basic home-style *dosa* is prepared with a batter made from rice flour and soaked ground urad dal. The batter is left to ferment, then poured out onto a griddle to make breads that range in size from an eight-inch pancake (as in this recipe) to an enormous thin crepe (from twenty-four to thirty-six inches in diameter) that only a professional with a large griddle can make. *Dosas* may be served plain or wrapped around a filling; they are traditionally accompanied by a *sambhar* (page 186 or 187), a dal dish, and by Coconut Chutney (page 39). No matter what the size, *dosas* are great to eat, and in predominantly vegetarian South India, they have the added benefit of combining complementary amino acids, from the grain and the dal.

We recommend making the batter the day before you wish to make the *dosas*. For a full-on treat, prepare a pot of the *sambhar* and the chutney before you start cooking your first *dosa*, and ask some good friends over to eat with you. PHOTOGRAPH ALSO ON PAGE 108

³/₄ cup urad dal, soaked overnight in cold water

3¹/₂ cups water

2 cups rice flour

1 teaspoon salt

1 tablespoon vegetable oil

Drain the dal and place it in a blender. Add 1 cup cold water and blend until smooth. Depending on your blender, this may require stopping and giving the dal a stir manually at intervals.

In a small saucepan, heat ¹/₂ cup of the water over low heat, stir in 1 tablespoon of the rice flour, and continue to stir until the paste begins to thicken. Set aside.

In a large bowl, mix together the ground dal, the salt, and the remaining rice flour and 2 cups water. Stir well to make a thin batter. Add the thickened rice paste and stir again to mix well. Cover the bowl and let stand for 5 to 6 hours at room temperature, or as long as 12 hours.

Just before you begin cooking, lift up a spoonful of batter and pour it. The batter should resemble a thin crepe batter; add more water to thin it if necessary.

Heat a large (11- to 12-inch) griddle over medium-high heat (you want a griddle with low sides, for the *dosa* will spread to the edges of the pan, and if it has high sides, you'll find it very difficult to lift the *dosa* off the pan). With a paper towel (or, the traditional way, with the cut side of a potato), lightly oil the surface of the griddle. When it's hot, pour on ¹/₂ cup batter, starting at the center and moving out in a spiral. Use a spatula or the back of a wooden spoon to help spread the batter as far as possible to the edge of the griddle, making the *dosa* as thin as possible. Cook for approximately 2 minutes on the first side, then flip over and cook for 1 minute on the other side. Timing will depend on how hot the griddle is; don't be afraid to let the *dosa* cook longer—it is better to have a slightly crispy bread than an undercooked one. Transfer the *dosa* to a plate and cover with a clean cloth to keep warm. Repeat with the remaining batter, stacking the finished *dosas* and covering them to keep warm. MAKES ABOUT 15 BREADS; SERVES 6 TO 8

Serve with Sambhar with Drumsticks (page 186) or Shallot Sambhar (page 187) and Coconut Chutney (page 39) (see headnote), or as breads to accompany any meal. Show guests how to tear pieces off the breads and use them to scoop up pieces of meat or vegetable.

MASALA DOSA: You can make a version of masala *dosa* by placing about ¹/₃ cup Tamarind Potatoes (page 152) or Spicy Potato Filling (page 131) on each *dosa* and then folding it over. Serve as above.

Home-Style Dosas with Shallot Sambhar (page 187)

SPICED RICE-POTATO DOSAS

· · · · · · · · · · · ·

Dosas (or *dosai*, as it is sometimes written) are like crepes, fine-textured flatbreads made of batter poured onto a lightly oiled skillet or griddle. They're most often savory and plain, made to be eaten with a curry or a dal and a chutney. The classic *dosa* (page 112) is made of dal and rice that are soaked, then ground to a batter that is allowed to ferment a little to leaven it. This *dosa* is different, quicker to prepare, because the batter needs no fermentation. It's made of cooked potato, rice flour, and yogurt, and flavored with coriander leaves and green chiles, for a mild heat. The *dosas* are beautiful as they come off the pan, very supple and all lacy and golden and speckled with green flavorings.

There are a few tricks to making these: The batter must be perfectly free of lumps and quite runny, so that it flows quickly over the hot pan; the pan surface must be nonstick or very well seasoned, and must also be oiled; the pan must be hot, over medium-high to high heat. If all these conditions are met, when the batter is poured onto the pan, it will spread out and bubble to create a lacy texture, the bread will be desirably thin, and because of the high temperature, it will be crispy at the edges.

We recommend using two skillets or a large rectangular griddle that sits on the stove so you have a larger surface and can make more *dosas* at one time. We also recommend making them relatively small—four inches or so in diameter—so they're easier to handle.

Place the potato and the rice flour in a food processor and process to an even mealy texture. Add the yogurt, salt, coriander, and chiles and process to mix. With the processor running, add 2 cups lukewarm water and process until you have a smooth batter.

Transfer the batter to a bowl. Add a little extra water if necessary to get a thin, runny batter.

Place a large nonstick skillet or a very well seasoned cast-iron skillet or griddle over high heat. Pour on about 1 teaspoon of the oil, then use a spatula to spread it over the surface of the pan. Lower the heat slightly, then scoop up a scant ¼ cup batter and pour it onto the center of the hot oiled pan. It should spread out on the oil to a 4- to 5-inch round, bubbling and creating a lacy pattern at the edges. Drizzle several drops of oil around the edges of the *dosa* and cook for 2 to 3 minutes, until the underside is a strong golden brown, then carefully flip and cook the second side for another 2 minutes, or until well colored. Transfer to a plate.

Oil the pan with about ½ teaspoon oil before starting to cook the next *dosa*. As you make the remaining *dosas*, you may find that there is actually room in your pan to cook two at a time; you can scoop up a little less batter to make *dosas* just under 4 inches in diameter. The smaller breads are easier to flip over. **MAKES 16 SMALL BREADS; SERVES 4 TO 5**

Serve as a bread to accompany a meal. These are also good dipped into yogurt or salsa, or used nontraditionally as wrappers for cheese or sliced meat and greens.

---

1 cup crumbled cooked potato (from 2 medium baking potatoes,
    boiled until tender and peeled)

1 cup rice flour

½ cup plain (full- or reduced-fat) yogurt

1 teaspoon salt

1 cup loosely packed coriander leaves and stems, minced

2 green cayenne chiles, seeded and minced

About 2 cups lukewarm water

About ¼ cup raw sesame oil or vegetable oil

GITA'S LUCHIS

. . . .

When our children were about to turn seven and four years old, now more than ten years ago, we spent a month living in a friend's mother's apartment (she was away at the time) in Kolkata (Calcutta), in a neighborhood called Ballygunge. In that month we had a very good time exploring the city and the region. Our kids also had a very good time because of the extra attention that came their way from the three other adults—Joy, Gita, and Shanatan—with whom we shared the house. The kids were kings-of-the-castle, treated like royalty.

One day Gita, a fabulous cook who prepared two meals each day for everyone, said she'd make *luchis*, deep-fried puffed Bengali breads (much like *puris* but made with white flour rather than with atta flour). She kneaded the dough and then, after it had rested a while, she poured oil into the karhai and began heating it. We stepped out of the apartment to do a brief errand and when we came back, there was our son Tashi, aged almost four, deep-frying. He was standing on a stool by the small gas stove, proudly using a spatula to press the *luchis* gently and very carefully down into the hot oil so they'd puff up as they fried. He was happy, and Gita looked relaxed, so we suppressed our impulse to fuss about the dangers of hot oil. The *luchis* were delicious, and Tashi was thrilled.

Luchis aren't very oily, and they're a treat to eat.

2¹/₂ cups all-purpose flour, plus extra for rolling

1 teaspoon salt

1 tablespoon ghee or vegetable oil

About 1 cup lukewarm water

About 2 cups peanut oil for deep-frying

To make the dough using a food processor, place the flour and salt in the processor, add the ghee or oil, and process to blend in. With the machine running, slowly pour the water through the feed tube: A ball of dough will form. Process for another 15 seconds, then turn the dough out onto a lightly floured surface and knead briefly until smooth and silky.

To make the dough by hand, mix the flour and salt together in a bowl, then add the ghee or oil and blend in with your fingertips or a spoon. Slowly pour in the water, stirring to moisten all the flour. Turn out onto a lightly floured surface and knead for about 8 minutes, until the dough is very smooth and elastic.

Cover the dough and let rest for 30 minutes, or as long as 2 hours, whatever is most convenient.

Working on a lightly floured surface, cut the dough in half, then cut each half into eight pieces. Roll each one under your palm into a ball. Keep the remainder covered as you flatten two of the balls and then roll them out to thin rounds about 4 inches in diameter. Place on a lightly floured baking sheet or counter and cover with plastic wrap. Repeat with the remaining dough, until you have sixteen shaped breads.

Set out two paper towel–lined plates and a slotted spoon by your stove top. Set up a stable wok or karhai (see Glossary) or other deep-frying arrangement on the stove. Add enough peanut oil to fill it 2 inches deep, and heat until almost smoking. Gently slide in one bread: It will sink, then immediately rise to the surface. Use the slotted spoon to press down on it lightly several times. It will puff up and turn golden. Lift it out of the oil onto a paper towel–lined plate and repeat, cooking two or three breads at a time in the hot oil. **MAKES 16 BREADS; SERVES 5 TO 6**

Serve hot and puffed as a snack with a raita (page 67) or a simple sauce such as Himalayan Grilled Tomato Sauce (page 94), or for a light lunch paired with a dal such as Easy Karnataka Chana (page 196) or a vegetable such as Aromatic Pumpkin and Coconut (page 160). These are also classic with Sweet Yogurt Sundae with Saffron and Pistachios (page 323).

HOME-STYLE TANDOOR NAAN

· · · · · · · · · · · ·

Tandoor ovens are traditionally associated with the northern and western regions of the Subcontinent, from Rajasthan and the Punjab in India to north-central to northern Pakistan (and beyond into Central Asia, where they originated). Over the last decade or so, they've also become a popular restaurant fixture in almost all tourist areas and in truck stops throughout the region, from Bangladesh to southern India. A tandoor oven is a large vertical clay oven shaped like a barrel. Breads made in a tandoor are baked by slapping flat rounds of dough against the very hot curved inside walls of the oven, where they immediately stick. Tandoors are heated to anywhere from 500°F to 800°F, so the breads cook quickly (under 3 minutes). Once cooked, they release from the oven wall and can then be lifted out (with a hooked stick) and served. The taste is delicious, like food fresh off a grill.

To make these tender home-style naans, assuming you don't have a handy tandoor in your kitchen, we suggest you improvise as we do, by putting unglazed quarry tiles or a large baking stone in your oven and cooking the breads directly on the clay surface. It works well, and it's fun.

2 cups lukewarm water

1 teaspoon active dry yeast

1 cup milk

5 to 6 cups all-purpose flour

1 tablespoon plus ½ teaspoon salt

About 2 tablespoons butter or ghee, melted

OPTIONAL TOPPING

1 teaspoon nigella seeds, or about 1 tablespoon sesame seeds

About 4½ hours, or as long as 10 hours, before you wish to serve the breads, begin preparing the dough: Place ½ cup of the warm water in a cup or glass and stir in the yeast.

Place the milk in a saucepan and heat to lukewarm, about 100°F. Add the remaining 1½ cups warm water and transfer to a large heavy bowl. Stir in the yeast mixture. Stir in 2 cups of the flour, stirring always in the same direction. Sprinkle on the salt, then continue adding flour ½ cup at a time until you have a soft dough. Generously flour a work surface, turn the dough out onto the floured surface, and knead for 4 to 5 minutes, incorporating just enough flour to prevent the dough from sticking (it is important to have a dough that is soft and not too tight).

Rinse out your bowl and wipe it dry, then lightly oil with a little melted butter or vegetable oil and place the dough in it. Cover with plastic wrap and let stand for about 3 hours, to rise until more than doubled in volume. If you want to serve warm breads with a meal, leave the risen dough until 1 to 1½ hours before you wish to serve them. The dough can be kept waiting for as long as 6 hours if kept in a relatively cool place, not more than 70°F.

When you are ready to proceed, place a rack in the upper third of your oven and place a baking stone or quarry tiles on it, leaving ½ inch or more between the oven walls and the tiles to allow air to circulate. Preheat the oven to 500°F.

Pull the dough away from the sides of the bowl and transfer it to a lightly floured surface. Use a sharp knife or dough scraper to cut the dough in half. Place half back in the bowl and cover with plastic wrap while you shape the first four breads.

OPPOSITE, LEFT: *At the annual Pushkar camel fair in Rajasthan, the animals all need to be fed. Here a woman carries a load of fodder across the desert sand to her encampment.* RIGHT: *A camel drover moving his herd along a small road in rural Rajasthan, west of Jaipur.*

Cut the dough in half and then in half again. Shape each piece into a round ball, using both hands to round it and smooth it. Place the balls at the side or toward the back of a floured surface, and brush each one with melted butter, then cover them with plastic wrap and let stand for 20 minutes. Just before beginning to shape and bake these four breads, repeat with the second half of the dough.

Dust one end of a peel, or the back of a baking sheet that you will use as a peel, very lightly with flour or semolina or cornmeal. Place one risen ball of dough on your work surface and press and push it out with your fingertips to a round about 6 to 7 inches in diameter (do not turn it over). Set it aside and repeat with a second ball of dough. Go back to the first and push it out with your fingertips to a larger oval, nearly 9 inches by 8 inches; you can also pick it up, drape it on the back of your hands, and stretch it gently by pulling your hands apart slightly.

Place the bread near the end of the peel (or baking sheet) and pull on the edge of the bread nearest the end of the peel to make a more pointed oval or teardrop shape. If you wish, sprinkle 8 to 10 nigella seeds or a scant ½ teaspoon sesame seeds over the top. Transfer the bread onto the hot baking stone or tiles, as close to one side of the oven as possible. Close the oven door quickly, then repeat with the second bread, laying it beside the first.

Bake for 5 to 6 minutes, or until there are light golden spots on the top of the breads. Use a long-handled spatula or your peel to remove the breads from the oven. The breads will have a golden bottom crust and a rippled top surface with golden spots on it. If you want an extra taste of butter, brush the breads again with melted butter just as they come out of the oven. Repeat with the remaining two risen balls of dough.

Stack the baked breads and wrap them in a cotton cloth to stay warm and soft while you bake the remaining four breads. Serve warm or at room temperature. (The breads will stay warm for almost an hour after baking.) MAKES 8 BREADS; SERVES 4 TO 5

Serve with grilled meat, such as Tikka Kebabs (page 256) or Yogurt-Marinated Chicken Kebabs (page 239), Grilled Marinated Beef (page 272) or Cumin-Coriander Beef Patties (page 268), or to accompany Chicken Biryani, Dum Style (page 102) or Simmered Kashmiri Paneer (page 171).

Full Moon at Kanyakumari

Sunset in Goa, on the west coast of India

AT THE SOUTHERN TIP OF INDIA is Kanyakumari, the rocky tip of the country, pointing due south. It's a place of temples and of pilgrims from all over India who flock there, especially at the full moon. We were staying in southern Kerala in late December, along with several friends, and we decided to travel to Kanyakumari for the full moon, which that year fell on the same day as the winter solstice.

The place was packed with pilgrims. We wandered around, looking at the fishing boats, the stalls selling souvenirs, and the temples and shrines, along with crowds of black-clad Shiva worshipers, other pilgrims dressed all in white, and families with children and grandchildren. Then we went to eat *dosas* and *idlis* at a little restaurant. Each order came with a serving of *sambhar* and another of coconut chutney. Our son Dom's *dosa* was a huge one, called a family *dosa,* about three feet long and beautifully lacy. By the time we had eaten, there was a golden late-afternoon glow in the sky.

As the sun moved lower, we found a wall to stand on that overlooked the shore. Pilgrims had gathered down by the water, facing the sunset to the west, some praying, some splashing in the water, some just raptly watching the setting sun. They were all touched with orange-gold light. The sun became a persimmon-colored ball, sinking into the dark sapphire sea, then finally it was gone, and the crowd clapped with pleasure. We turned to our left, toward the east, and there, gleaming, outsized and golden yellow, was the full moon, rising up out of the sea into the midnight blue sky.

LEFT: *A woman praying.* RIGHT: *The crowd at Kanyakumari, watching and waiting as the sun goes down and the full moon rises.*

IDLIS

. . . .

Idlis are round flying saucer–shaped breads about three inches in diameter, made from batter and steam cooked. They're firm but not heavy. They cook in a special pan, which can be found at southern Asian grocery stores (alongside boxes of *idli* mix). The pan is a steamer with three metal layers, each of them with seven small hollows in it, in which the batter steams, so that you can cook twenty-one *idlis* at once. Cooking time is very short, about thirty minutes.

Start soaking the rice and dal in the afternoon, then let the batter ferment overnight so you can make *idlis* for breakfast.

1¹/₂ cups parboiled rice
¹/₂ cup urad dal
About 1 cup warm water
1 teaspoon salt
Oil or ghee for greasing the molds
1¹/₄ teaspoons baking soda

Separately wash and then drain the rice and the urad dal. Put them in separate bowls, add 4 cups water to each bowl, and leave to soak for 4 to 5 hours.

Drain the rice in a sieve, rinse well with cold water, drain again, and set aside. Do the same with the dal.

Place the soaked rice in a food processor and process until the rice is well broken down. Add approximately ¹/₂ cup warm water and process until you have a smooth batter, adding a little more water if necessary. Transfer to a large ceramic or glass bowl. Put the soaked dal into the processor and process until well broken down. Add the remaining ¹/₂ cup warm water and process until smooth but still a little gritty. Add the dal batter to the rice batter and mix. You will have 3 cups batter. Add the salt and mix well. Cover with plastic wrap and set aside to ferment for 8 to 12 hours or overnight. The fermentation should smell sour but not extreme, and the batter should rise in the bowl and have bubbles on the top.

To make the *idlis*, put water in the *idli* steamer and place it over high heat. Grease the *idli* molds thoroughly. Lightly and gently fold the baking soda into the batter, disturbing the batter as little as possible. Put a scant 2 tablespoons batter into each mold (they should be only three-quarters full), stack the steamer layers, then cover and let steam for 30 minutes. To test for doneness, stick in a toothpick; it should come out clean. Remove the steaming trays and use a rubber spatula to remove the *idlis*. Transfer them to a basket or bowl lined with a cotton cloth and cover to keep warm and soft.

If making a double batch, wash and dry the trays thoroughly and re-oil before cooking the next batch. **MAKES 21 BREADS; ALLOW 2 OR 3 PER PERSON**

Serve warm or at room temperature with Shallot Sambhar (page 187) or Sambhar with Drumsticks (page 186) or another dal, and with Coconut Chutney (page 39). Idlis can also be eaten as a snack, dipped into a salsa or chutney such as Andhra Spiced Eggplant (page 49) or Sri Lankan Seeni Sambol (page 33).

HOPPERS

· · · · · · · · · · · ·

Hoppers are soft, leavened stove-top flatbreads, a kind of cross between pancakes and bread, that cook in a wok-shaped pan (hopper maker) to make bowl-shaped bread. The middle area of the "bowl" is thick, with thin, almost frilly edges all round. The bottom of the bread is lightly browned, the top tender and steam cooked. The unusual name is an English adaptation of the Tamil word for rice breads, *appa* or *appam*, that is commonly used in Sri Lanka. (In Sri Lanka, there is another kind of hopper, called a *string hopper*, that is a bundle of steamed noodles made from a similar batter.)

We have a little nonstick wok that works beautifully for hoppers. They're easy to make for three or four people, but unless you are an expert hopper maker (which we aren't), they're not the most practical food to prepare when you're cooking for a crowd. Hoppers are at their best when served fresh and hot; when you can make only one at a time, it's hard to produce a lot quickly. This being said, they're a ton of fun to make: If you're just home from a trip to Sri Lanka, you won't believe that you're actually turning out hoppers in your own kitchen.

Hoppers are made with all-purpose flour or rice flour, or a blend; this recipe uses all-purpose flour. The flour is mixed with coconut milk to make a thick batter that we leaven with yeast; in Sri Lanka, the batter is often soured instead with toddy, a local liquor (see page 310).

Hoppers are an important food in Sri Lanka, commonly served for breakfast or late-afternoon snack. Little restaurants specialize in hoppers, and even a pub will often have a hopper maker turning them out for late-night snackers. They're typically eaten with a variety of spicy *sambols* (Sri Lankan salsas). PHOTOGRAPH ON PAGE 122

1 teaspoon active dry yeast
¼ cup warm water
½ teaspoon sugar
1½ cups all-purpose flour
¼ teaspoon salt
1¾ cups canned or fresh coconut milk
Vegetable oil for cooking

In a small bowl, dissolve the yeast in the warm water, then sprinkle on the sugar and stir to mix well.

In a medium bowl, mix the flour and salt. When the yeast is dissolved, add the mixture to the flour, along with the coconut milk, and stir to mix until smooth. Cover the batter and leave to rise for 2 to 3 hours.

Grease a small wok (or hopper pan), nonstick if possible, and put out a lid for it. Heat it over medium to low heat. Stir the batter; if it has thickened and is too thick to pour, stir in 1 to 2 tablespoons water.

Pour ¼ cup batter into the hot wok and immediately lift and tilt the pan to get the batter to flow outward and form a wide circle. Place the pan back on the heat, cover, and cook for 2 to 3 minutes, until the bottom of the bread is lightly browned (the top will be smooth and steam cooked). Ease it out of the pan with a flat wooden spoon.

Serve the hoppers hot, as they come off the pan, and lightly oil the pan with an oiled paper towel between each hopper.

MAKES 12 TO 15 BREADS; SERVES 5 TO 6

Accompany with a sambol *or two: Try Sri Lankan Seeni Sambol (page 33) and Coconut Sambol (page 30) for starters.*

Hoppers (page 121). ABOVE, LEFT: *Coconuts and beet greens for sale at a street market in Sri Lanka.* RIGHT: *Rose petals as far as the eye can see, at the wholesale market in Chennai (Madras), the capital of Tamil Nadu.*

ONION SKILLET BREADS

· · · · · · · · · · · ·

These skillet breads from Andhra Pradesh are like a lot of breads from southern India. Whether they are made from rice, or rice and dal (such as *dosas* or *idlis*; see pages 112 and 120), or from only dal, as these are, the breads tend to be tender and soft, and are generally best eaten hot. They're more like pancakes than like bread, because they most often start with a batter, not a dough.

We first came across these in the south, in Andhra Pradesh. Naomi later saw a man making very similar breads on the street in Varanasi, in northern India (see page 56). When they talked, she learned that he was from Andhra Pradesh, not a local. Many of his customers were pilgrims from Andhra Pradesh, hungry for a taste of home. In Andhra, the bread is called *pesarattu*.

1¼ cups urad dal

1 cup water

1 teaspoon salt

1 tablespoon minced green cayenne chile

1 teaspoon minced ginger or ginger mashed to a paste

About 3 tablespoons raw sesame oil or vegetable oil

1 cup finely chopped onion or shallots

½ teaspoon finely ground cumin

About 1 cup loosely packed coriander leaves

Wash the dal, and put it in a bowl with 4 cups of water to soak for 2 to 3 hours.

Drain the dal, put it into a food processor with the 1 cup water, salt, chile, and ginger, and process until well pulverized. The batter will feel a little gritty, but process it long enough to break the dal down as much as possible.

Put a griddle or large skillet over medium-high heat (or use two griddles or skillets and cook the breads two at a time). Add 1 teaspoon of oil to the skillet and tilt to coat the pan. When it is hot, pour ⅓ cup of the dal mixture into the skillet. Using a rubber spatula, quickly spread the mixture out into a circle about 7 inches in diameter. Immediately sprinkle 2 tablespoons of the chopped onions, a pinch of ground cumin, and about 1 tablespoon chopped coriander leaves over the batter.

Cook the bread on this first side for 3 minutes; after a minute or two, loosen the bread around the edges with a spatula. Flip the bread over and continue to cook for another 3 minutes. (It may seem like a long time, but the bread needs this time to cook through.) Turn the bread out onto a plate and serve immediately, or cover to keep warm.

Repeat with the remaining batter and toppings, adding 1 teaspoon of oil to the skillet before making each bread. As with all pancake sorts of bread, the first one might seem tricky and awkward, but as you adjust for a perfect heat, and as the skillet gets seasoned, the cooking will go quite easily. Serve hot. **MAKES 8 BREADS; SERVES 4**

These are great as part of a meal, served with a sambhar *(see pages 186 and 187), but they also make a good snack or breakfast served with a simple chutney such as Tomato Chutney (page 44) or Andhra Spiced Eggplant (page 49).*

DHOKLA

. . . .

Dhokla is a Gujarati specialty. It's made of a batter that steams to a moist corn bread texture, and then is tempered with a little flavored oil. *Dhokla* is always served with fresh chutney, sometimes as a snack, sometimes to accompany a meal. The amazing thing about *dhokla* is its versatility: It can be made of cornmeal (as we saw it in Udaipur) or, more commonly, as here, a blend of dal and white rice that is soaked, then ground into a batter. The batter often contains yogurt.

Dhokla is one of a category of Gujarati dishes known as *farshan*. They are traditionally part of the meal, but they are eaten a little apart, as either an appetizer or a break from the meal, in the same way as in France and Italy you might eat a little bread during the main course—as a pause.

The dal and rice need to soak for six hours (you can leave them for twenty-four hours if it's more convenient), then they are ground in the food processor with yogurt and a little water to make a batter. In Ahmadabad, when Riku (see Gujarati Mango Chutney, page 40) showed me her way of making *dhokla*, she used baking soda to help it rise, and that's what we do, too, to guarantee a light and well-risen bread. Traditionally the batter would be left to ferment for twelve hours to gain natural leavening before being cooked.

NOTE: You'll need an 8-inch round cake pan and a steamer or other steaming arrangement that can hold the cake pan. We use a large (12-inch) pot and put into it a heavy domed lid turned upside down that the cake pan can stand on above the water. We add 1 inch of water to the pot.

½ cup toovar dal, well washed and picked over

¾ cup raw white rice, washed and drained

¼ cup water

½ cup plain (full- or reduced-fat) yogurt

½ teaspoon salt

½ teaspoon baking powder

TEMPERING

2 teaspoons peanut oil or raw sesame oil

½ teaspoon black mustard seeds

½ teaspoon sesame seeds

About 6 fresh or frozen curry leaves

Seven to 24 hours before you wish to serve the *dhokla*, start soaking the dal and the rice: Wash them separately. Place the dal in a bowl and add water to cover by 1 inch. Place the rice in another bowl and add water to cover by 1 inch. Cover both bowls and set aside to soak for at least 6 hours, or overnight.

Drain the dal, measure out 1 cup, and place it in the food processor. Drain the rice, measure out 1 cup, and transfer it to the processor. Add the ¼ cup water and process for about a minute, until the dal and rice are well ground. Add the yogurt and process until smooth. The batter should be thick but pourable. Leave the batter in the processor bowl.

Organize your steaming arrangement (see Note) and bring the water to a boil. Lightly grease an 8-inch round cake pan.

Add the salt and baking soda to the batter and process briefly to mix well. Pour the batter into the cake pan to a depth of between ½ and ¾ of an inch (the length of your thumbnail is a good measure).

continued

Use oven mitts to protect your hands and arms as you set the pan in the steamer. Cover the pan and bring the water to a vigorous boil, then lower the heat just slightly to maintain a strong boil. After 5 minutes, remove the lid and wipe the underside dry, then replace it. Continue cooking until the top of the *dhokla* is shiny and the sides are pulling away slightly from the pan, about 15 minutes total. (The *dhokla* will rise and puff after about 5 minutes, but it needs more time to cook through.)

Use oven mitts again to protect yourself from the steam when you remove the pan from the steamer: Set the pan aside for 10 minutes to set.

Use a sharp knife to slice the *dhokla* into about 1-inch-diameter diamonds or squares; if the *dhokla* sticks to the knife as you slice, wipe the knife clean and lightly oil the blade before proceeding. Set the pan of sliced *dhokla* by your stovetop.

Heat the oil in a small heavy skillet over medium-high heat. Add the mustard seeds, and when they start popping, add the sesame seeds. Once the seeds have popped, about 20 seconds, toss in the curry leaves, and then pour the oil and flavorings over the *dhokla*.

You can serve it right away or leave it in the pan for an hour before serving. We think this gives it more time to gain flavor from the oil and allows the texture to firm up more.

Serve warm or at room temperature. Use a spatula to lift the diamonds or squares out of the pan and onto a serving plate, or else serve from the pan.   SERVES 6

Serve as a bread to accompany a meal, with one or more fresh chutneys, such as Fresh Coriander–Peanut Chutney (page 28), Mint-Coriander Chutney (page 298), and/or Tamarind Sauce (page 45).

CUMIN-FLECKED SKILLET BREADS
· · · · · · · · · · ·

These flavored rotis are slightly thicker than chapatis. They are a big favorite in our house: quick and forgiving to make, and delicious to eat on their own as a snack or for breakfast. We also use them to make sandwiches for our kids' lunch boxes. Because there's a little ghee or oil in the dough, and more used on the skillet for cooking, they stay soft and fresh for longer than chapatis do.

The breads are just one take on the flavored skillet bread idea (see Gujarati Flavored Breads, page 127, for another). For a very mild, almost imperceptible heat, use the amount of cayenne called for. If you want a little more punch (if, say, you plan to serve these with cream cheese or a fresh goat cheese), double the cayenne.

1 teaspoon cumin seeds

2 cups atta flour, plus extra for rolling

1/2 teaspoon cayenne, or to taste (optional)

1 teaspoon salt

1 tablespoon hot melted ghee or butter

1 cup hot water

2 to 3 tablespoons butter, ghee, or vegetable oil

Heat a small skillet over medium-high heat. Add the cumin seeds and dry roast, stirring to prevent burning, until just fragrant, about 2 minutes. Remove from the heat and coarsely grind in a spice/coffee grinder or use a mortar and pestle.

Mix together the flour, cumin, cayenne, salt, and hot ghee or butter in a bowl or combine in a food processor. *If working by hand*, add the hot water and mix well, then turn out onto a lightly floured surface and knead for about 5 minutes, until very smooth. *If using the food processor*, with the machine running, pour the hot water through the feed tube and continue to process for 15 or 20 seconds after a ball of dough forms. Turn out onto a lightly floured surface and knead briefly.

Wrap the dough tightly in plastic wrap to prevent it from drying out, and let rest for half an hour, or as long as overnight if more convenient.

To shape the dough, cut it in half and set one half aside, well covered with plastic. Use a dough scraper or sharp knife to cut the other half into eight equal pieces. (If we're making these to be used for sandwiches, we divide the dough into six, instead of eight, to make larger breads, about $4\frac{1}{2}$ inches across.) Roll each piece into a ball on your work surface, then, working on a very lightly floured surface, flatten each into a disk about 2 inches across. Set aside for a moment, loosely covered with plastic.

Work with two heavy skillets if possible, to cook the breads more quickly. Put about 2 teaspoons butter, ghee, or oil in each pan and heat over high heat until sizzling, then lower the heat to medium-high. Use a spatula to spread the grease around the pan.

Using the palm of your hand and your fingertips (or a rolling pin if you wish), flatten one ball of dough into a disk less than $\frac{1}{4}$ inch thick and just over $3\frac{1}{2}$ inches across ($4\frac{1}{2}$ inches if you divided the dough into six rather than eight pieces). Place the bread top side down in the hot pan for 10 seconds, then flip over. Continue shaping breads and placing them in the pan(s) until there is no more room (you should be able to fit two or three in each pan). Cook each flipped bread over medium-high to medium heat for 2 to 3 minutes, moving them around after about a minute to cook evenly. Then flip each bread back over and cook for about 2 minutes, until cooked through. Transfer to a cotton cloth and wrap to keep warm. Repeat with remaining dough, regreasing the pan(s) with about 1 teaspoon ghee, butter, or oil after each batch.

MAKES 16 BREADS ABOUT 3½ INCHES ACROSS
OR 12 BREADS ABOUT 4½ INCHES ACROSS; SERVES 4 TO 5

Serve with a meal or as a snack with a dip of Cucumber Raita (page 67) or Tart Mango Salsa (page 48). We like them for sandwiches because they stay fresh and keep their texture in a lunch box for 4 hours; hard cheese is an especially good filling, but our kids love them with peanut butter.

GUJARATI FLAVORED BREADS: We learned another version of these breads from a woman named Ragini in Ahmadabad, in Gujarat. The flour she used was a half-and-half blend of atta and *bajra* (millet) flour, but she said we could use all atta. Place 2 cups flour in a bowl or in the food processor and add a generous teaspoon each minced garlic and green chile, $\frac{1}{4}$ cup chopped coriander, a dash of turmeric, $\frac{1}{2}$ teaspoon ground coriander, 1 teaspoon sugar, and 1 teaspoon salt. Add about $\frac{1}{2}$ cup yogurt and stir or process to blend, then add enough water (about $\frac{3}{4}$ cup) to make a dough. Knead, or process and knead, as above. Divide the dough into eight balls and roll out to larger thinner breads, about 7 or 8 inches in diameter. Bake as above, but note that the breads will cook through a little more quickly because they're thinner. Drizzle a little oil or melted ghee onto the breads after you've flipped them over for the second time. MAKES 8 BREADS

FOLLOWING PAGE: *Framed by the color of her sari, Sangana Bai smoothes the clay mixture on the side of an unfinished tandoor oven (see page 129).*

MY FIRST TANDOOR

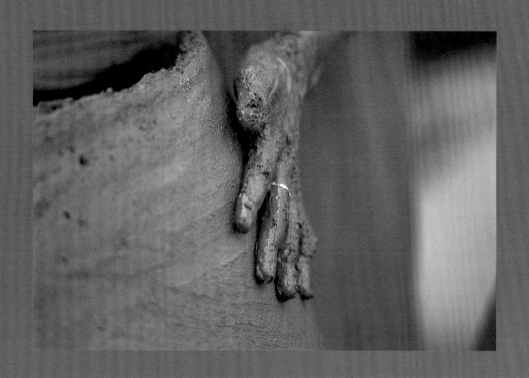

her living by shaping mud and clay into low hearths (*chula*) and tall barrel-shaped tandoor ovens. I met her outside her house; she was working in her front yard, smoothing wet mud onto the walls of a half-built tandoor, and I stopped to watch. She worked with skill and grace; she was beautiful, with good bones and large, alert eyes. I guessed that she was in her forties, but it was hard to tell, for age, sun, and hard work had left wrinkles and lines, a map of her life, on her face.

She nodded a yes when I asked if I could photograph her as she worked. I took a series of shots of her hands as they moved, smoothing the wet clay, constantly shaping the curve of the tandoor. Her daughters came out of the house and asked if I'd come in and drink tea. We climbed up a steep flight of stairs to a cement terrace that overlooked the street. Here was the outdoor kitchen: a clay hearth and several pots and spoons hanging from hooks on the wall in the December sun.

The daughters, Lalita, twenty-one, and Jamna, eighteen, were both confident young women. Lalita was at university, studying Hindi and politics, but Jamna had no plans for university. They immediately engaged with me, asking me questions and insisting that I correct their English. After we'd talked for a while, Sangana Bai came up the stairs to have tea and a break. We smiled at each other, but shared no language.

I asked Jamna and Lalita if they would ask her if she'd teach me how to make a clay tandoor. I would come by every day for however long it would take. . . . I waited as they translated and then watched as Sangana Bai's face broke into a warm smile. "Tomorrow," said Jamna. "She says to come at eleven tomorrow morning. It will take about nine days."

To have a picture of my lessons, you need to know that the ovens and hearths are built of a heavy mud blend that must be made up fresh each day. I found it hard work. I'd crouch on my haunches as Sangana Bai used a mattock—a digging tool like a slant-handled hoe—to pull clay soil and a mix of dried straw and horse manure from two piles. She'd pour on water to wet the mixture, and then we'd knead to blend and moisten it evenly, squeezing large handfuls of it through our fingers to blend it.

Each day we needed to make up a large batch, for Sangana Bai was working on several tandoors and hearths as I was slowly working on my one oven. The kneading and mixing took a good half hour. Passersby would stop and make jokes when they saw me working with the mud. Then we'd carry large lumps of the heavy mixture, load by load, up the steps to the terrace, a sunnier and more private place to work.

The tandoors, like the hearths, are made of pieces of the mud that are smoothed with wet hands and built up in layers. The first day, Sangana Bai helped me make a curved wall of the mud mixture that eventually formed a full circle on the ground. She showed me how to shape it between my palms, finally pinching off little bits of mud from the top to make a jagged edge. It would dry out overnight. So each day I returned to add another layer, smoothing it onto the existing dried wall of oven and thinning it upward, then pinching the top edge. Each day I learned, too, about food and daily life in a loving household. It was a great privilege.

Then, one day my oven was done, a four-foot-tall barrel of clay with a rounded rim. It was time to say good-bye.

Thank you, Sangana Bai.

POTATO-STUFFED PARATHAS

· · · · · · · · · · · ·

A Rajasthani version of *aloo paratha*, this bread, called *alookar roti* in Udaipur, is delicious and not hard to make. I learned it from Sangana Bai's daughters (see "My First Tandoor," page 128) in Udaipur, in southern Rajasthan. It's one of many simple and inventive stove-top dishes they taught me. A basic chapati dough is rolled out into rounds, then each is spread with some cooked potato filling, folded over it, and rolled out again. The breads are very tender but without any oiliness. The flavors of the potato filling and the bread wrapper blend beautifully. Unlike chapatis, these breads can be made an hour ahead; they'll stay tender and soft, even if reheated on a griddle. PHOTOGRAPH ON PAGE 132

2 cups atta flour, plus extra for rolling

1 teaspoon salt

Scant 1 cup lukewarm water

About 2 cups Spicy Potato Filling (page 131), at room temperature

About 2 tablespoons vegetable oil

Place the flour and salt in a food processor and pulse to blend. With the machine running, add the water through the feed tube and process until a ball of dough forms. Process for another 30 seconds, then turn the dough out onto a lightly floured surface and knead for 2 to 3 minutes. *Alternatively,* combine the flour and salt in a bowl. Add the water and stir, then turn out onto a floured surface and knead for about 5 minutes, or until very smooth.

Cover the dough with plastic wrap and let stand for at least 30 minutes or, preferably, for 2 hours (the longer wait makes the dough easier to handle).

Meanwhile, if you have not done so already, prepare the potato filling and let it cool. Mash any larger lumps with the back of a spoon.

Cut the dough in half and set one half aside, covered. Cut the other half into four pieces. Flatten each one into a disk with the palm of your hand, and press both sides of each disk onto a floured surface to flour it. Working on a lightly floured surface, using a rolling pin, roll out one

disk to an approximately 8-inch round, rotating the dough after each stroke of the pin and rolling with light strokes; do not turn the bread over. Set aside, loosely covered, and repeat with the remaining pieces of dough.

Spread 3 to 4 tablespoons of the potato filling over one half of one of the dough rounds, then fold the bare half over to make a half-moon shape. Fold in half again to make a quarter-round (wedge) shape; use a lightly floured hand to flatten this out a little, and then roll it out to a rough round 8 to 9 inches in diameter. Don't worry if the edges are a little uneven, or if a little potato leaks out. Shape the remaining breads the same way.

Begin cooking these first breads while you start to divide, fill, and roll out the other half of the dough: Place a heavy cast-iron skillet over high heat. When it is hot, add about 2 teaspoons vegetable oil and use a wadded-up cloth or paper towel to spread it all over the pan to grease it well. Place a pastry brush and a small bowl of oil near your stove top. Lower the heat to medium-high or medium, and place the first bread top side down in the hot skillet. Cook for about 45 seconds, then turn over. The top should have lightly browned patches; brush all over with a little oil. Cook on the second side for about 1½ minutes, then turn over again and cook for another 30 seconds, or until well browned in patches. Lift out onto a plate, and cover to keep warm. Repeat with the remaining breads, re-oiling the skillet each time with about 1 teaspoon oil.

Once you become practiced, you will be able to roll out and shape breads easily while you are cooking others. MAKES 8 BREADS; SERVES 4 TO 6

Serve for a snack on their own or with a raita (see "The Raita Family," page 67) or a fresh chutney such as Fresh Coriander–Peanut Chutney (page 28) or Tart Mango Salsa (page 48). Served with a dal such as Udaipur Urad Dal (page 189) or a Western-style soup or stew and perhaps a simple salad such as Pea Tendrils with Coconut (page 71), these make a satisfying meal.

SPICY POTATO FILLING

· · · · · · · · · · · ·

Potatoes are used in wonderfully imaginative and satisfying ways all over the Subcontinent. Many simple potato dishes begin, as this recipe does, with potatoes boiled in their skins, which are then peeled, chopped or crumbled, and cooked with some oil and spices or herbs in an infinite number of variants (see Tamarind Potatoes, page 152, and Parsi Potatoes and Snow Peas, page 153, for example). You can begin with potatoes you boiled a day or two earlier or just boil up potatoes half an hour before you wish to make the filling. If you use floury baking potatoes, they'll crumble nicely; if you use waxy potatoes, you'll need to cut them into small cubes.

This spicy filling is very versatile. Flavors are distinct, and medium hot chile-wise, but you can tone down the heat if you wish. The filling can be made up to forty-eight hours ahead and refrigerated, covered, until you are ready to use it. In addition to the *parathas*, we also use it to stuff samosas (see page 296), one of the classics of the North Indian repertoire. Any leftovers can be stirred into dal or eaten as is.

The coriander leaves are an Udaipur-style touch, and we love them, but you may prefer to use chopped flat-leaf parsley or finely chopped mint leaves, or to do without herbs at all.

Generous 1 pound potatoes, preferably baking potatoes or 3 cups chopped peeled boiled potatoes

2 tablespoons vegetable oil

1/2 teaspoon black mustard seeds

1/2 teaspoon turmeric

2 teaspoons minced garlic or garlic mashed to a paste

1 cup finely chopped onion

2 green cayenne chiles, or substitute jalapeños, seeded and minced

1/4 teaspoon cayenne (optional)

1 teaspoon salt, or to taste

About 1/4 cup packed minced coriander leaves and stems, or mint or flat-leaf parsley (optional)

Place the potatoes in a large pot with cold water to cover. Bring to a boil and cook until just tender. Drain, return the potatoes to the pot, cover tightly, and let stand for 20 minutes.

Peel the potatoes and place in a large bowl. Use a fork or masher to break the potatoes into small pieces; if using waxy potatoes, it may be easier to chop them into small cubes. You will have about 3 cups potatoes. Set aside.

Place a wok or karhai (see Glossary) or a large heavy skillet over high heat. When it is hot, add the oil and swirl it around to coat the pan. Toss in the mustard seeds and cook for 20 seconds, or until they have mostly stopped spluttering. Lower the heat to medium-high, add the turmeric and garlic, and stir-fry for about 30 seconds, then toss in the onion. Cook, stirring frequently, for about 8 minutes, until the onion is tender and starting to brown. Add the chiles and cayenne, if using, and stir, then add the potatoes and the salt and cook, mixing the ingredients and pressing the mixture against the hot pan, then turning and stirring, until flavors are well blended and the chiles soft. Turn out into a large bowl to cool to room temperature.

Before using, taste for salt and adjust if necessary, then stir in the herbs, if using.   MAKES ABOUT 2 1/2 CUPS; SERVES 3 TO 4 AS A VEGETABLE

Use as a filling for parathas *(page 130) or samosas (page 296) or for* dosas *(page 112).*

SPICY POTATO AND GREEN PEA FILLING: If you like, include about 1 cup fresh or frozen green peas in the filling; add them about 2 minutes before you remove the filling from the heat. Peas are very commonly included in samosa fillings to add a bright touch and fresh taste.

Both of these images are from Rajasthan, where wheat, millet, and sorghum are the staple grains; they are ground into flour and used to make flatbreads. On the left, a man is winnowing wheat in the market in Jodhpur. On the right, a woman is winnowing millet by the side of the road. The wind catches any chaff or dust and blows it away, leaving the heavier grains to fall to the ground. OPPOSITE: *Potato-Stuffed Parathas (page 130) with Cachoombar (page 57).*

SAVORY DEEP-FRIED STREET-SIDE BREADS

· · · · · · · · · · · ·

Known as *kachoris*, these are like small filled *luchis* (see page 115), deep-fried breads that are filled with a savory, enticing cooked dal mixture. It seems as if there's a *kachori* maker every hundred yards or so on the main bazaar streets in Rajasthani cities like Jaipur and Jodhpur. It's fascinating to watch them deep-fry. The *kachoris* look like small flying saucers as they bubble in the hot oil, then emerge all brown-gold, with small bubbles on their surface. I love to split a hot *kachori* in half just after it's cooked and breathe in the aroma of the mint and the mustard seed and fennel spicing of the dal filling: essence of northern India.

The dough for these breads is made from all-purpose flour rather than the tougher, pale yellow atta flour that is used for *puris* and for chapatis. Because the dough has a little oil in it, the breads are tender and slightly flaky.

You can make the dough and the filling a day ahead, then shape and cook close to the time you wish to serve them. Otherwise, start two hours ahead: First put the dal on to boil, then make the dough. Set the dough aside, covered, while you finish making the filling, then shape and cook the breads. You'll be surprised at how easy they are, and at how they please everyone.

FILLING

1 cup urad dal

3 tablespoons vegetable oil

¹/₄ teaspoon black mustard seeds

¹/₄ teaspoon cumin seeds

¹/₄ teaspoon turmeric

¹/₄ teaspoon cayenne

1 teaspoon salt

About ¹/₄ cup minced mint leaves (optional)

DOUGH

2 cups all-purpose flour

³/₄ teaspoon salt

2 tablespoons ghee or vegetable oil, plus extra for shaping

About ³/₄ cup lukewarm water

Peanut oil for deep-frying

Wash the dal thoroughly in several rinses of warm water. Place in a saucepan with 3 cups water and bring to a boil. Cook at a medium boil, partially covered, for 1 hour. The dal will be very soft, but not completely cooked. Transfer the dal to a food processor and process to a smooth puree. Set aside in a bowl. (The dal can be prepared up to 3 days ahead. Store in a covered container in the refrigerator.)

Heat the oil in a wok or karhai (see Glossary) or in a large heavy skillet over medium-high heat. Add the mustard seeds and let them pop in the hot oil, then toss in the cumin seeds and cook for 10 seconds. Add the pureed dal and stir, then stir in the turmeric, cayenne, and salt. Cook, using a wooden spoon or wide metal spatula to smear the dal against the surface of the pan to expose it to the heat, then to lift it off to prevent sticking, for about 5 minutes. Lower the heat and cook for another minute or two, until the dal has firmed to a smooth paste. Turn out of the pan into a bowl and set aside to cool to room temperature. (If you will not be using the dal within an hour, refrigerate, tightly covered.)

To make the dough, place the flour and salt in the food processor. With the machine running, add the ghee or oil through the feed tube, then add water until a ball of dough forms. Process for another 15 seconds or so, then turn out onto a lightly floured surface and knead until very smooth, about 4 minutes. Set aside, well covered with plastic, for at least 30 minutes, or as long as 3 hours, whatever is most convenient. (The dough can be refrigerated for up to a day. Bring to room temperature before using.)

Place the bowl of filling by your work surface together with a large plate and a small bowl of ghee or vegetable oil. Add the mint, if using. Lightly oil the palms of your hands. Scoop up a scant 1 tablespoon filling, roll it between your oiled palms into a ball, and place it on the plate. Repeat with the remaining filling, until you have sixteen balls. Set aside.

Place the dough on a lightly floured surface and cut into sixteen equal pieces by cutting in half and then half again, and so on. Flatten each piece into a 3-inch disk and set aside.

Place a disk on one palm and make a dent in the center with your thumbs. Place a ball of filling in the dent, then pull up the dough to cover the filling, pinching to seal it closed. Lightly flour both your palms and flatten the dough between your palms to a disk about 4 inches across. Set aside on a lightly floured surface. Repeat with the remaining breads, and cover loosely with plastic wrap.

Place a large stable wok or karhai (see Glossary) or a wide heavy pot or other stable deep-frying equipment over high heat. Add peanut oil to come to a depth of 2 inches. Place a slotted spoon near your stove top, and set a wire rack over a baking sheet or large plate. Test the oil temperature by dipping a chopstick or the handle of a wooden spoon vertically into the oil: If bubbles come bubbling up along it, the oil is at the right temperature; if there are no bubbles, wait until the oil has heated more and test again. (A deep-fry thermometer in the oil should read 325° to 350°F.)

Slide in one and then a second *kachori*. (If your pot is large, you may be able to cook more than two at a time.) The oil will bubble around them as they sink to the bottom. They should then slowly start to rise to the surface; if they rise immediately or seem to be darkening very quickly, lower the heat slightly. Use the back of your slotted spoon to press down lightly on them several times. Use the spoon to turn them over so that they brown evenly. Once they are a medium brown on both sides, use the spoon to lift each one out, pausing at the edge of the pan to let oil drain off, then transfer to the wire rack. Repeat with the remaining breads.

Serve hot or warm. **MAKES 16 BREADS; SERVES 6 TO 8**

Serve as a snack, on their own or with Tamarind Sauce (page 45), Fresh Coriander–Peanut Chutney (page 28), Mint-Coriander Chutney (page 298), or (less traditionally) a tomato salsa.

NOTE: *Kachoris* are made street side in many places in northern India, and sometimes they're much smaller, less than 3 inches in diameter. To make smaller ones, perhaps to serve as an appetizer or with drinks, divide the dough into twenty-four pieces and use a scant 2 teaspoons filling for each.

DARJEELING MARKET TIBETAN BREADS

· · · · · · · · · · ·

Phale (pronounced "pah-lay," and sometimes written *pali*) is the Tibetan word for "bread." These round empanadalike filled breads are called *shaphale* (*sha* is the Tibetan word for "meat"; the filling on its own is called *shapka*). They're made from two flatbread dough rounds pinched together around a cooked meat filling, then skillet baked in a little oil. The edges are attractively fluted, the breads pale golden brown. We first tasted them on a damp, cold March evening in the market in Darjeeling, a hill town near the borders of Sikkim and Bhutan that has a large Tibetan population. The *shaphale* makers' wooden stalls were lined up in a row, each lit by several small oil lamps. They looked warm and welcoming and were doing a steady business. The breads were wonderful, a satisfying blend of warm grain taste and aromatic succulent meat filling.

Make up the dough, then let it rest while you cook the simple filling. Serve hot, either in hand or tidily on a plate.

DOUGH

3 cups all-purpose flour, plus extra for rolling

1 teaspoon salt

About 1 tablespoon melted ghee or butter

1 cup lukewarm water, or a little more

About ¼ cup ghee or vegetable oil for frying

FILLING

2 tablespoons vegetable oil

1 cup minced onion

1 tablespoon minced ginger or ginger mashed to a paste

1 cup (about ½ pound) coarsely chopped (¼-inch pieces)
   boneless chicken thighs, beef, or pork

1 dried red chile or ¼ teaspoon cayenne

½ teaspoon ground coriander

½ teaspoon salt, or to taste

Generous grinding of black pepper

A Sherpa man with a traditional carrying basket stands on the trail that leads to the villages of Kunde and Khumjung, above Namche Bazaar, in the Everest region of the Nepal Himalaya.

Place the flour and salt in a bowl or in a food processor. *If working by hand,* add the melted ghee or butter and blend into the flour, then add 1 cup lukewarm water. Stir with your hand or with a wooden spoon to blend the water into the flour; if the dough seems stiff, add a little more water. Turn out onto a lightly floured surface and knead for 5 minutes, or until very smooth and elastic. *If using the food processor,* with the machine running, add the ghee or butter through the feed tube, then add 1 cup water. A ball of dough should form; if it doesn't, add up to another ¼ cup water. When a ball of dough forms, process for another 15 or 20 seconds, then turn the dough out onto a lightly floured surface and knead for about a minute, until smooth.

Cover the dough with plastic wrap and let rest for 30 minutes to 2 hours, whatever is more convenient.

Meanwhile, prepare the filling: Heat the oil in a wok or karhai (see Glossary) or a large heavy skillet over medium-high heat. Add the onion and ginger and cook, stirring frequently, until the onion is well softened, 6 to 8 minutes. Add the meat, the chile or cayenne, coriander, salt, and pepper and stir-fry, breaking up any lumps in the meat, until it is browned and cooked through. Taste and adjust the seasoning if necessary. Remove and discard the chile if you used one. Set aside to cool to room temperature.

On a lightly floured surface, divide the dough into sixteen pieces. Flatten each piece a little, turning it over to flour it on both sides. Leaving the other pieces lightly covered, roll two pieces out to 7-inch rounds. Spread a generous 2 tablespoons filling on one bread, leaving a 1-inch margin all round. Place the other bread on top and pinch and roll the edges closed all around between your thumb and forefinger, to make a sealed fluted edge. Flatten gently under the palm of your hand.

Place a heavy skillet or griddle over medium-high heat. (You can speed up the cooking if you use a large griddle or two skillets.) Add about 2 teaspoons ghee or oil and spread it over the surface with a spatula. Lower the heat a little. Place the bread top side down in the skillet, and cook for 1 minute. Turn over and cook on the second side until golden brown, then turn back to the first side to cook until well browned (if you get dark patches before the bread has cooked through, lower the heat slightly). While the first bread is cooking, roll out two more rounds, fill, and shape.

Remove the first bread from the skillet and serve hot, or wrap in a cotton cloth to keep warm. Grease the skillet again with about 1 teaspoon ghee or oil and cook the next bread. Continue to shape and bake the remaining breads. **MAKES 8 BREADS; SERVES 4**

Serve for lunch, with a bowl of soup or dal (Mountain Dal, page 182, for example), and accompanied by salad or wilted greens.

NOTE: The filling makes a good topping for egg noodles or for rice.

VEGETABLES

THERE ARE VERY FEW FRUITS AND VEGETABLES

that aren't available at least somewhere in the great Subcontinent.

From the wintry snow-capped Himalaya all the way down to

hot, humid tropical Sri Lanka, there's a perfect place for almost

everything to grow. A regional cook's repertoire of vegetable

dishes can be mind-boggling, from mushrooms and asparagus

Sword beans

of life's joys, treated with great respect, almost reverence.

Visitors to the Subcontinent are sometimes a bit perplexed when they see so many different kinds of vegetables in a local market, but then when it comes time to eat in a local restaurant, to find such a predominance of very familiar vegetables such as potatoes, cauliflower, and onions. Though the potato is the king of vegetables in the Subcontinent, it's also true that potatoes make up a much higher percentage of a local restaurant menu than they do of a home-cooked meal (which, come to think of it, is probably true here in North America, too, at least in fast-food places).

If you're on a trip to the Subcontinent, one good way to taste local vegetable dishes is to search out neighborhood restaurants that come highly recommended for serving the main meal of the day, which is most often served at noontime. In the north of India, the main meal is called *thali*; in Sri Lanka, it's "rice and curry"; and in the south of India, it's "meals." These main meals of the day are the ones most likely to include local vegetables, from beets to yard-long beans to seasonal greens, for they generally consist of at least three vegetable dishes, as well as chutneys and dal, and often more. When you find a good place to eat, go back every day and don't be afraid to ask when there's something unfamiliar.

Back home in North America, it might seem that all of these newly discovered vegetables are impossible to find, but a little intrepid shopping can yield great surprises. In this chapter, we've included a few dishes that call for ingredients that may be unfamiliar to many people, such as bitter melon, pointed gourd, and fenugreek greens. In most cases we've also included ideas for substitutions, but those recipes are here as a way of introducing ingredients that may soon become more available, and also, of course, because they're good. If you have access to a well-stocked South Asian grocery, you'll find everything you need. Even a large general grocery store will have most of the ingredients called for. Also look in the produce section of African and Caribbean groceries.

The vegetable dishes of the Subcontinent have clean, clear flavors and distinctive personalities. Some are simmered, others stir-fried, and many are a blend of the two. Vegetables are generally cooked until very tender, rather than being left al dente. When we come across a cook in India or Bangladesh or Nepal or Pakistan preparing vegetables, she's apt to be cooking them in a *karhai,* a wok-shaped pan, and stirring them with a flat metal spatula. Many travelers to the Subcontinent are surprised that stir-frying is such a common technique. Food historians believe that the wok of China and Southeast Asia descends from the *karhai,* so stir-frying, which we in the West associate so exclusively with East Asia, is perhaps originally a southern Asian technique.

We gravitate to dishes with bright flavors and easy technique, and we love greens and potatoes. As a result, this chapter has many stir-fried vegetable dishes and several variations on the flavored potato theme. We've included some dairy recipes at the end of the chapter. One uses buttermilk or yogurt; another simmers fresh pressed cheese (*paneer*) in tomato sauce; and the third is a Bhutanese curry made of *churpi,* fresh Bhutanese cheese (for which we substitute feta), simmered with onions and tomatoes.

Photographing below the village of Karimabad, in Pakistan's Hunza Valley, we came upon these Hunzakot men wearing their distinctive caps.

GREEN TOMATO CURRY

· · · · · · · · · · · ·

We're forever looking for recipes that use green tomatoes, and this is one of our favorites. When autumn arrives, instead of lamenting the fact that all our carefully cared-for tomato plants in the backyard are soon to perish, we can at least look forward to this green tomato curry. As with so many recipes from Sri Lanka, a fresh supply of green chiles and curry leaves (even fresh from the freezer) is almost all you need. The Maldive fish, that other distinctively Sri Lankan ingredient, can be omitted, or you can substitute dried bonito flakes. Either gives an agreeable, slightly smoky layer of flavor.

The recipe takes less than half an hour to cook; it can be made ahead, set aside for an hour, and then reheated. The tartness of the green tomatoes is mellowed by the sweetness of the coconut milk and onion.

2 tablespoons vegetable oil

¼ to ½ cup chopped onion

2 green cayenne chiles, seeded and chopped

6 to 8 fresh or frozen curry leaves

1 teaspoon Maldive fish, or substitute bonito flakes,
    finely ground (optional)

¼ teaspoon ground fenugreek

Pinch of turmeric

1 pound green or semi-ripe tomatoes, coarsely chopped (about 2 cups)

2 teaspoons salt

¾ cup canned or fresh coconut milk

Heat the oil in a medium heavy pot over medium-high heat. When the oil is hot, add the onion, chiles, and curry leaves and cook until the onion is light brown, 8 to 10 minutes. Add the Maldive fish or bonito flakes, if using, the fenugreek, turmeric, tomatoes, and salt. Cook for about 15 minutes, or until the tomatoes are very soft.

Add the coconut milk and bring to boil, then reduce the heat and simmer until the sauce has thickened, about 5 minutes. Serve hot or at room temperature.   SERVES 4

Serve as a side dish with simple grilled kebabs of pork or lamb or beef (see Cumin-Coriander Beef Patties, page 268, or Lamb Slipper Kebabs, page 257, for example).

SIMMERED SPICED SOYBEANS

· · · · · · · · · · ·

This Nepalese dish made with fresh green soybeans is as yummy as it is bright and beautiful. You can also use frozen soybeans, out of their shells (now widely available and labeled "edamame").

1 tablespoon mustard oil

1 medium onion, chopped

1 tablespoon minced garlic or garlic mashed to a paste

1 tablespoon minced ginger or ginger mashed to a paste

1 red cayenne chile, minced

$^1\!/_2$ teaspoon turmeric

1 teaspoon ground cumin

$^1\!/_2$ teaspoon salt

1 large tomato (about $^1\!/_2$ pound), chopped into $^1\!/_2$-inch chunks

2 cups shelled fresh or frozen soybeans (edamame)

1 cup water

About $^1\!/_2$ cup coriander leaves

Heat the oil in a large heavy saucepan over high heat. Add the onion, garlic, ginger, and chile and stir-fry for 2 minutes, or until the onion is well softened. Stir in the turmeric, cumin, and salt, then toss in the tomato. Stir-fry for 1 minute, or until the tomato starts to soften and give off liquid.

Add the soybeans and mix well. Add the water and bring to a boil, then lower the heat and simmer, uncovered, for about 10 minutes, or until the beans are softened but still firm to the bite. (Frozen or fresh should take about the same time.) Serve garnished with the coriander leaves.   SERVES 3 TO 4

Serve with plenty of rice to soak up the sauce, along with a mild dish such as Stir-fried Greens, Bangla Style (page 165) and a simple grill.

SIMMERED SPICED OKRA: The acid of tomatoes balances okra's sweetness beautifully. Substitute okra for the soybeans; use about $^1\!/_2$ pound tender small okra. Leave them whole and cook them in the tomato broth until just tender.

SPICED GRATED CARROTS, KERALA STYLE

· · · · · · · · · · ·

The small side dishes that are arranged around a mound of white rice at the noontime main meal in Kerala are infinitely varied. They fall into a number of categories: wet or dry, with or without grated coconut, mild or chile-hot, sweet or tart. This dish is an *oleete*, a category of vegetable dish that is stir-fried, then moistened with yogurt as it finishes cooking. *Oleetes* are moist and soft-textured but have little sauce. This carrot version has a mild heat, as well as a little sweetness, and is very attractive when served mounded on a dark plate.

2 tablespoons raw sesame oil or vegetable oil

1 teaspoon black mustard seeds

About $^1\!/_2$ cup minced onion

$^1\!/_4$ teaspoon turmeric

1 tablespoon minced ginger or ginger mashed to a paste

2 green cayenne chiles, slit lengthwise and seeded

About 10 fresh or frozen curry leaves

3 to 4 medium carrots, coarsely grated (about 1$^1\!/_2$ cups)

$^1\!/_2$ teaspoon salt, or more to taste

Coarsely ground black pepper (optional)

About $^1\!/_2$ cup plain yogurt, preferably full-fat

Heat the oil in a medium heavy skillet or a wok or karhai (see Glossary) over medium-high heat. Add the mustard seeds and partially cover until they pop, then add the onion and turmeric and stir-fry for 2 minutes. Add the ginger, chiles, and curry leaves and stir-fry until the onion is very soft, about another 5 minutes. Toss in the carrots, salt, and pepper, if using. Stir-fry for about 5 minutes, or until the carrots are very soft.

Turn the heat to very low. Add the yogurt and stir for a minute or so to warm the yogurt through and blend flavors; do not allow it to boil.

Serve in a shallow bowl.   SERVES 4

Serve as a side vegetable with rice and Tilapia Green Curry (page 222), Pomfret in Coconut Milk Sauce (page 208), or Grilled Marinated Beef (page 272).

BANGLA-FLAVORED FRIED ZUCCHINI

· · · · · · · · · · · ·

One of our favorite dishes from Bangladesh is *potol jal*, Bengali for "fried potol." *Potols* are called "pointed gourds" in English, *patol* in Hindi. They're shaped like small fat cucumbers, with pointed ends, light and dark green lengthwise stripes, and large flat seeds. Since *potols* can be hard to find here in North America, we usually substitute zucchini; if you can find *potols*, do try them.

The cooking technique here is shallow frying, which gives the slices of zucchini or *potol* a wonderful crisped outer surface, leaving the center creamy and tender-textured.

4 or 5 small (4 to 5 inches) zucchini or *potols* or

    2 longer (8 to 10 inches) slender zucchini

2 tablespoons mustard oil

2 tablespoons vegetable oil

¼ teaspoon turmeric

¼ teaspoon black mustard seeds, ground

¼ teaspoon cayenne

1 teaspoon sugar

About ½ teaspoon salt

Slice small zucchini or *potols* lengthwise into barely ½-inch-thick slices (you should get 3 or 4 slices from each). Or, if using long zucchini, cut them crosswise in half, then slice lengthwise.

Heat the oils in a large wok or karhai (see Glossary) or a heavy skillet over medium-high heat. Add the turmeric, mustard, cayenne, and sugar and fry for about 10 seconds. Add the zucchini or *potol* and cook, turning and moving them, for about 3 minutes if using zucchini, 5 minutes if using *potol*, until softened through but not mushy.

Use a slotted spoon to remove the slices, holding them for a moment against the side of the pan to allow excess oil to drain off. Blot briefly with a paper towel if you wish, and place on a platter or in a shallow bowl. Sprinkle with the salt, toss, and serve. (The seeds in the *potol* may be a bit chewy-crispy, a real treat.)

Let the flavored oil cool, then pour it into a clean glass jar and store, covered, in the refrigerator. Use for stir-fries or other frying. SERVES 4

Serve as a vegetable side in a meat-and-potatoes meal, or to accompany a meal of Mountain Dal (page 182) with rice, or Stir-fried Rice and Dal (page 96) and Bangla Slow-Cooked Beef with Onion (page 273).

BANGLA-FLAVORED GRILLED ZUCCHINI: This recipe transforms easily from frying to grilling. Heat the oils in a skillet or wok and fry the spices and sugar for about 10 seconds, as described above, then remove from the heat and set aside. (You can flavor the oil a day ahead if more convenient, then store it, once cooled, in a clean glass container until ready to use. Stir before using.) Preheat a charcoal or gas grill. Brush the zucchini or *potol* slices with the flavored oil, then grill over moderate heat until well softened and touched with color. Sprinkle on a little chopped mint or coriander leaves before serving, if you wish. You can also use this technique with slices of Asian eggplant; they will take a little longer to cook through.

SUCCULENT MOUNTAIN MUSHROOMS

· · · · · · · · · · · ·

We haven't come across mushrooms much in the Subcontinent, so we were happy to discover this dish, called *chiayou*, a cross between a simmer and a stir-fry. It's from the mountainous Darjeeling area of northern India, near Sikkim.

The mushrooms are stir-fried in mustard oil, very characteristic of the region, with onions and whole spices, then flavored with powdered spices. It all comes together easily in about fifteen minutes. The sauce is thickened with yogurt, then chopped tomatoes are added to simmer until tender. This version of the dish is mild; for a forceful chile heat, increase the cayenne to 1 teaspoon.

½ pound white button or portobello mushrooms
   (about 3 cups coarsely chopped)
3 tablespoons mustard oil or vegetable oil
Pinch of asafoetida powder
¼ teaspoon fenugreek seeds
¼ teaspoon nigella seeds
2 teaspoons minced garlic or garlic mashed to a paste
1 medium-large onion, thinly sliced
1 teaspoon minced ginger or ginger mashed to a paste
1 teaspoon ground coriander
½ teaspoon ground cumin
½ teaspoon turmeric
¼ teaspoon cayenne, or more to taste
⅓ cup plain (full-fat or reduced-fat) yogurt
About 1 cup finely diced tomatoes (fresh or canned)
¼ cup chopped coriander leaves (optional)

Brush off the mushrooms, or rinse them briefly under cold water, then coarsely chop and set aside.

In a large wok or karhai (see Glossary) or a wide heavy pot, heat the oil over medium-high heat. Toss in the asafoetida, and once it has "fizzed," toss in the fenugreek and nigella seeds. Lower the heat to medium, add the garlic and stir-fry for about 30 seconds, until it starts to change color, then add the onion. Raise the heat back to medium-high and stir-fry for about 8 minutes, or until the onion is starting to change color.

Raise the heat to high and add the mushrooms. Stir-fry for about 3 minutes, until touched with color all over and starting to release their liquid, then lower the heat to medium. Toss in the ginger, coriander, cumin, turmeric, and cayenne and stir-fry to blend. Pour the yogurt onto the center of the cooking mushrooms. Stir to blend in, then simmer gently for about 3 minutes. Add the tomatoes and stir to blend in, then continue to simmer, stirring occasionally, until the tomatoes are very soft and a film of oil has risen to the surface, about 5 more minutes.

Stir in the chopped coriander, if you wish, and serve hot.

SERVES 3 TO 4 AS A MAIN COURSE, 5 TO 6 AS A SIDE DISH OR A SAUCE

We like this as a vegetarian main course with rice, accompanied by a green salad or freshly stir-fried green vegetables such as Pea Shoots for a Crowd (page 161) or Quick Asparagus Stir-fry (page 158). It is also very successful as a (nontraditional) sauce for rice noodles.

It's hard to generalize about the restaurants here in the town of Kandy, in the hills of tropical Sri Lanka, because there are so many different kinds. The one where I'm sitting as I write this, for example, the Winchester Café, serves mostly South Indian Tamil food. Just up the street there's a Muslim halal restaurant, and a little farther along, another Tamil restaurant, only this one serving Sri Lankan Tamil food, not South Indian Tamil food.

An island at the southern tip of India, Sri Lanka is roughly the size of Ireland but with a population of nearly twenty million people. Seventy-four percent of Sri Lankans are Sinhalese (and primarily Buddhist in religion), 18 percent are Tamil (and primarily Hindu), and 8 percent are Muslims, mostly descendants of Arab and Indian traders.

Here at the Winchester, I usually order hoppers (soft steamed skillet breads). They're served on a wide green banana leaf. A waiter comes and pours the hot tamarind-based soupy lentil stew called *sambhar* over the hoppers, and then I eat it all, holding the hoppers with the fingers of my right hand. When I finish eating, I take my leaf to the back of the restaurant and throw it into a large container (the leaf is later fed to animals—simple recycling). I wash my hands, come back to my chair, and it's time for tea.

Most people in Sri Lanka, whether Tamil, Sinhalese, or Muslim, eat their main meal of the day, fondly referred to in English as "rice and curry," at lunchtime. Sometimes if I'm feeling particularly hungry, I go to the Old Empire Hotel for rice and curry. The hotel is well over one hundred years old. The restaurant has high ceiling fans that *whoosh* the humid tropical air around in circles, giving the impression, at least, of cool. At lunchtime, businessmen file into the dining room dressed in pressed white shirts and ties, and they sit at tables covered with starched white tablecloths, eating rice and curry ever so skillfully with their fingers, while the very professional waiters move across the polished wood floor, as I imagine they always have, in bare feet.

The only problem with rice and curry, at least for me, is that in tropical 95-degree weather, I'm seldom hugely hungry at lunch. So on most days I eat at the Winchester, because meals here are smaller. When I first started coming to the Winchester, it had me fooled. Usually in Sri Lanka I can read a restaurant the minute I walk in. In a Hindu restaurant, there will be a calendar or a poster with Lord Shiva hanging in a prominent location. In a Muslim restaurant, there will be a large framed photograph of Mecca, and in a Buddhist restaurant, an altar with a statue of Lord Buddha.

But in the Winchester, I somehow didn't notice the little statue of Buddha standing near the cash register, and the food had me fooled. The place had a Sinhalese feel, but the food was Tamil, and so was most of the staff. Then I was told that the owner is Sinhalese. When I finally got to meet her, I learned that she had visited Tamil Nadu, in South India, a few years back. She liked the food so much that she had learned to make it, and soon she started serving it in the restaurant, along with Tamil dishes from Sri Lanka.

This may not sound like a big deal, but here in Sri Lanka, after two decades of civil war, it is a big deal.

THE WINCHESTER

CAULIFLOWER DUM

· · · · · · · · · · · ·

This North Indian dish of cauliflower coated with a thick, mellow tomato-onion sauce is really a treasure. *Dum* cooking means slow cooking in a tightly sealed heavy pot, a form of steaming. Flavors intensify during the slow cooking, and the cauliflower is transformed into a meltingly tender vegetable. You can *dum* cook on the stove top, but we usually prefer to bake this so that the stove top is left free for other cooking, and so we can forget about it until it's ready.

To *dum* cook over a wood or charcoal fire—the traditional way—the pot is buried in the ashes or coals, making a kind of Dutch oven. Like its close relative, clay-pot cooking, it's a way of producing moist and tender dishes using little heat. The method is rather like the *oop* style of cooking in the Mekong region, or the "beggar's chicken" tradition of Chinese cuisine, both of which rely on slow cooking in a tightly sealed container. *Dum* cooking seems to have come to the Subcontinent with the Moghuls and it's still associated with Moghul cuisine.

Traditionally the lid is sealed by wrapping a strip of dough around the seam, so no steam can escape during cooking, but we've found that if we use a heavy pot with a tight-fitting heavy lid—cast-iron or Le Creuset—there's no need to seal the lid. To make sure of a good seal, though, cover the pot with aluminum foil before you put the lid on. If you want to take the traditional route and make the dough, see Chicken Biryani, Dum Style (page 102), for details.

1 medium cauliflower (about 1½ pounds)

¼ cup ghee, vegetable oil, or peanut oil

1 teaspoon cumin seeds

1 or 2 bay leaves

1 teaspoon minced garlic or garlic mashed to a paste

2 teaspoons minced ginger or ginger mashed to a paste

About 1 cup grated onion

Scant 1 cup diced tomatoes (fresh or canned)

1 teaspoon salt

1 tablespoon coriander, preferably freshly ground

½ teaspoon garam masala (page 342 or store-bought)

¼ teaspoon cayenne

½ teaspoon turmeric

2 green cayenne chiles, stemmed and slit lengthwise

Scant 1 cup water

2 to 3 tablespoons coriander leaves (optional)

PRECEDING PAGE: *A rice meal in a village in southern Orissa, a more rural setting than the Winchester. The rice is mounded on a plate made of stitched-together leaves of the sal tree; the curries and condiments come in small bowls alongside.*

Trim off the cauliflower leaves and the tough core. Cut into large florets, wash well, and set aside.

Place a rack in the center of the oven and preheat the oven to 350°F.

Place a deep heavy ovenproof pot with a tight-fitting lid over medium heat. Add the ghee or oil, then add the cauliflower and cook (if it doesn't all fit comfortably, fry it in two batches), turning the cauliflower florets every 2 to 3 minutes to brown them evenly, until they are touched all over with brown, 7 to 8 minutes. To keep the oil from spattering, keep the pot partially covered as the florets fry. Remove the cauliflower (tongs are the easiest way) and set aside.

Place the pot back over medium heat and toss in the cumin seeds and bay leaves. As soon as the seeds start to splutter, about a minute or less, add the garlic and ginger and stir-fry briefly. Add the onions and cook, stirring frequently, until the onions soften and turn light brown all through, 8 to 10 minutes.

Add the tomatoes, salt, ground coriander, garam masala, cayenne, and turmeric and stir to blend in. Cook, stirring frequently, until you see the oil rise (you'll notice a gleam on the surface of the flavor paste), 6 to 7 minutes. Add the chiles and cook for another 2 to 3 minutes, until they shine bright green with oil.

Add the water, stir well, and raise the heat to bring it to a boil. Lower the heat and simmer, uncovered, for 5 minutes, stirring occasionally. The flavor paste will be thick and wet. Add the cauliflower to the pot and gently stir and turn until well coated with the spice paste.

Place a sheet of aluminum foil over the pot to seal and then put the lid on top (or seal it with dough; see headnote). Transfer the pot to the oven and bake for 20 minutes.

Release the steam by lifting off the lid, opening it away from you to avoid the hot steam. Taste for salt and adjust if necessary.

Spoon the cauliflower and sauce into a shallow bowl and garnish with the coriander leaves, if you wish.   SERVES 4 TO 5

Serve to accompany Chickpea Pulao (page 105) or a meal of rice, Tikka Kebabs (page 256) or Yogurt-Marinated Chicken Kebabs (page 239), and lightly cooked greens or a green salad.

KATCHHI VILLAGE POTATO CURRY

. . . .

In a tiny hamlet called Luria, near the Pakistan border in the desert of western Gujarat, I watched and took photographs as my hostess, Sona Bai, washed and peeled potatoes and then lit a small fire indoors. Her twelve-year-old daughter, Liku, chopped shallots and tomatoes and minced garlic. Sona Bai fried the potatoes in oil, then added the other ingredients and cooked them together into a simple curry (the spices, even the mustard seed, went in after the initial cooking of the onion and potato). As it simmered, she mixed up a dough of flour and water, using *bajra* (Indian millet flour) stored in a large square tin. She shaped one bread, then set the potato curry to the side of the fire and cooked the bread on a clay griddle. She brushed it with ghee as it came off the griddle, then wrapped it in a cotton cloth to keep warm. She went on to knead, shape, and bake five more flatbreads. She said the Katchhi word for bread was *mani*, so these were *bajra mani*.

When the breads were done, we ate together, she and I and her daughter. Along with the breads and curry, there were slices of onion, some green chiles that she'd fried whole, and chunks of chopped jaggery (palm or crude sugar), as a kind of condiment to accompany the bread. It was a surprising and delicious combination. This recipe, with its suggested accompaniments, re-creates that welcome, made-from-scratch lunch. PHOTOGRAPH ALSO ON PAGE 12

2 tablespoons raw sesame oil, vegetable oil, or ghee

2 teaspoons minced garlic or garlic mashed to a paste

1 pound potatoes, peeled and cut into 1/2-inch cubes

1 cup finely chopped shallots

1 cup chopped tomatoes

2 green cayenne chiles, seeded and chopped

1/2 teaspoon turmeric

1/2 teaspoon black mustard seeds

1 teaspoon ground cumin

1 teaspoon ground coriander

1/4 cup water

1 teaspoon salt, or to taste

OPTIONAL ACCOMPANIMENTS

2 shallots or 1 mild onion, thinly sliced

3 or 4 green cayenne chiles, fried whole in oil

About 2 tablespoons chopped jaggery (palm or crude sugar)

About 6 chapatis (page 110), made of atta

Heat the oil or ghee in a wok or karhai (see Glossary) or wide pot over medium heat. Add 1 teaspoon garlic and cook for a minute, then add the potatoes and shallots. Stir-fry for several minutes, until the shallots have softened, pressing the potato cubes against the surface of the hot pan, then add the chopped tomatoes and chiles and stir to blend.

Add the turmeric, mustard seeds, cumin, coriander, and the remaining 1 teaspoon garlic and stir. Add the water and salt and bring to a boil. Cover tightly and simmer vigorously until the potatoes are just tender, about 20 minutes. Check after 10 or 12 minutes to make sure there is enough liquid and that nothing is sticking; add a little more water if necessary.

Serve hot, with any or all of the optional accompaniments.

SERVES 3 TO 4

Serve with the listed accompaniments or as part of a meal with rice and a green vegetable and perhaps a kebab such as Tikka Kebabs (page 256) or Cumin-Coriander Beef Patties (page 268).

Katchhi Village Potato Curry with accompaniments: Chapatis (page 110), sliced onions, fried green cayenne chiles, and jaggery

TAMARIND POTATOES

. . . .

This is a great dish to serve when you have eight or ten at the dinner table. Like Parsi Potatoes and Snow Peas (page 153), it starts with plain boiled potatoes that are peeled and chopped, then cooked with flavorings in a combination of stir-frying and simmering. The name says it all: *alur dam*, meaning "tart potatoes." There seem to be as many versions of it as there are cooks in the Subcontinent; this one comes from Bengal.

2¹⁄₂ to 3 pounds waxy potatoes, preferably new potatoes, washed

3 tablespoons tamarind pulp

1 cup boiling water

About 1¹⁄₂ cups water

¹⁄₄ cup mustard oil

3 cinnamon or cassia sticks

5 cloves

3 bay leaves

2 cups grated onions

¹⁄₄ cup minced garlic or garlic mashed to a paste

2 tablespoons minced ginger or ginger mashed to a paste

1 teaspoon cayenne, or to taste

1 teaspoon turmeric

1 tablespoon sugar, or to taste

2 to 3 teaspoons salt

Place the potatoes in a large pot with cold water to cover, bring to a boil, and cook the potatoes until just cooked through but still firm (test the largest potato in the pot; it should be firm but cooked at the center). Drain and immediately place back in the pot, covered, to firm up.

(The potatoes can be cooked up to a day ahead. If you will not be using them for more than 3 hours, once they have cooled to room temperature, place in a well-sealed container and refrigerate.)

Slide off the potato skins. Cut the potatoes into 1-inch cubes, or into halves or quarters, depending on their size. Set aside.

Place the tamarind pulp in a bowl, pour over the boiling water, and use a fork to break up the pulp in the water. Set aside for about 15 minutes.

Once the tamarind water has cooled enough, use your fingers to rub the paste off the pulp. Place a sieve over a bowl and pour the mixture into the sieve. Use the back of a spoon to rub and mash the pulp against the mesh of the sieve to extract as much flavor as possible. Scrape the paste that clings to the underside of the sieve into the bowl. Measure the tamarind liquid, and add enough water to give you 2 cups (discard the pulp). Set aside.

In a large heavy pot, heat the oil over medium-high heat. Add the cinnamon, cloves, and bay leaves and stir for a moment. Add the onions, garlic, and ginger and stir-fry until well softened and the onions are starting to brown, about 8 minutes. Stir in the cayenne and turmeric, then add the potatoes and stir-fry, stirring and turning them gently so they don't break up. After 3 to 5 minutes, depending on the size of your pot, the potatoes should have some browned patches.

Pour in the tamarind liquid, add the sugar and 2 teaspoons salt, and stir to coat the potatoes. Bring to a boil, then reduce the heat and simmer, stirring occasionally, for 3 to 4 minutes. Taste for salt and sugar: There should be a good balance of tart and sweet in the sauce; stir in a little more salt if needed, and more sugar if it seems too tart to you.

Serve warm or at room temperature; we like these both ways. Leftovers are delicious the next day.   SERVES 8 TO 10

Serve with a simple grill of lamb or pork, green vegetables such as Stir-fried Greens, Bangla Style (page 165), and a fresh salad. You can also use tamarind potatoes as a filling for dosas (page 112).

PARSI POTATOES AND SNOW PEAS

. . . .

One cool November night as we were being driven into Delhi from the airport, we talked to our taxi driver about food. It was late, almost midnight, so the highway into town was full of truck traffic, which is banned during the day. The air was thick with exhaust; we could see it eddying in the beams from the headlights and in the pools of light below the street lamps. But we were transported elsewhere by the driver's conversation, as he told us about growing up in the hills, eating fresh vegetables and breathing clean air. And of all the vegetables, his favorite was the potato: "We call the potato the king of vegetables. You can mix it with many foods, with beans, pumpkin, pulses, cauliflower. . . ."

This is one of the most attractive potato dishes we know, and one of the quickest to make. The potatoes are boiled whole, then easily stripped of their peel, chopped, and stir-fried with chopped, lightly cooked snow peas (or green beans) in a sauce flavored with tomato, cumin, and minced green chile.

About 2 pounds (8 medium) waxy potatoes, washed

About $\frac{1}{2}$ pound snow peas, green beans, or yard-long beans

About 3 tablespoons vegetable oil or ghee

1 tablespoon black mustard seeds

1 tablespoon cumin seeds

1 teaspoon turmeric

2 medium tomatoes, coarsely chopped

2 teaspoons salt, or to taste

2 green cayenne chiles, seeded and minced,
    or substitute 3 scallions, minced

3 tablespoons chopped coriander or mint leaves

Place the potatoes in a large pot with cold water to cover, bring to a boil, and cook until just cooked through but still very firm (test the largest potato in the pot; it should be firm but cooked at the center). Drain and immediately place back in the pot, covered, to firm up. Set aside to cool.

Meanwhile, pour about an inch of water into a medium pot and bring to a boil. Toss in the snow peas or the beans, and cook until bright green and just tender, a brief minute or two for the snow peas, up to 10 minutes for the beans, depending on size. Drain, rinse under cold water to cool, and then drain again. Trim, cut into $\frac{1}{2}$-inch lengths, and set aside.

Peel the potatoes and chop them into large bite-size pieces. Set them aside.

Heat the oil or ghee in a wok or karhai (see Glossary) or a wide heavy pot over medium-high heat. When the oil is hot, toss in the mustard seeds. When they stop popping, add the cumin seeds and turmeric, stir briefly, and then stir in the tomatoes and salt. Stir-fry for about 1 minute. Add the potatoes and stir-fry until they are tender, 3 to 5 minutes. Stir in the chiles or scallions, the reserved peas or beans, and the coriander or mint. Remove from the heat; taste for salt and adjust if necessary. Serve hot.

SERVES 6

Serve with a simmered dish: Fish Bolle Curry (page 219), for example, or a meat dish such as Ginger-Lamb Coconut Milk Curry (page 261) or Roadside Café Chicken (page 250).

NEW POTATOES WITH FRESH GREENS

. . . .

This cross between potato salad and a simmered vegetable dish is another example of the creative ways in which subcontinental cooks work with potatoes. It's great hot from the pan, perhaps even better at room temperature. There's a mild heat from the touch of cayenne and from the ginger.

The recipe calls for small, thin-skinned new potatoes. If yours are under one inch across, leave them whole. The smallest we can find are usually about an inch and a half across; we cut them in half. Any larger, and they should be quartered.

The potatoes are first fried with cumin and ginger, then boiled in a little water until tender. They're finished off in the same pot with ground spices plus fenugreek greens (*methi* in northern India, Pakistan, Bangladesh, and Nepal). If you can't find fenugreek greens, substitute well-washed and chopped arugula or sorrel, or instead use a handful of fresh coriander or mint leaves, a nice summer option.

2 pounds small thin-skinned new potatoes

$1/4$ cup raw sesame oil or vegetable oil

1 teaspoon cumin seeds

$1/2$ teaspoon turmeric

2 tablespoons minced ginger or ginger mashed to a paste

$3/4$ cup water

$1^1/2$ teaspoons salt, or to taste

1 tablespoon ground coriander

Pinch of ground cinnamon

$1/2$ teaspoon cayenne

1 cup packed finely chopped fenugreek greens, arugula or sorrel, or substitute $1/2$ cup packed chopped coriander sprigs or mint leaves

1 lime, cut into wedges

Two views of Rajasthan: On the left, Rajasthani men make morning tea over a small fire, at the annual camel fair in Pushkar. On the right, a tailor works in the entryway of his small shop in Udaipur.

Wash the potatoes and halve or quarter if necessary (see headnote).

Heat the oil in a large heavy pot or large wok or karhai (see Glossary) over medium-high heat. Toss in the cumin and stir, then add the turmeric and stir. Add the ginger and stir-fry for 1 minute, then add the potatoes and stir-fry for 2 to 3 minutes. Add the water and 1 teaspoon salt, raise the heat, and bring to a vigorous boil, then cover tightly and cook until the potatoes are tender, 10 to 15 minutes (lower the heat slightly after the first 5 minutes). The water should be almost gone.

Uncover and add another ½ teaspoon salt, the ground coriander, cinnamon, and cayenne. Stir, then add the greens or herbs and stir-fry until tender, about 3 minutes if using greens, less than a minute if using herbs.

Serve hot or at room temperature. Put out lime wedges so guests can, if they wish, squeeze lime juice over generously as they eat.

SERVES 5 TO 6

We like to make this dish to serve with meat from the grill, say Nepali Grilled Chicken (page 238) or Grilled Marinated Beef (page 272), with perhaps some lightly salted sliced cucumbers or white radish (daikon) for crisp contrast.

POTATO WHITE CURRY

. . . .

This is a typical Sri Lankan "white curry" (coconut milk curry), but in fact the color is pale yellow from the turmeric. There are two approaches to white curries in Sri Lanka. One kind is flavored with Maldive fish and fenugreek seeds, as this potato curry is. The other style uses ground coriander and cinnamon.

Like many Sri Lankan simmered dishes, white curries are traditionally cooked in clay pots. There's no preliminary frying of spices. Instead, all the ingredients simmer together until the vegetables are tender, and the flavors are mellow and well blended, then the dish is brought together and enriched with coconut milk.

1 pound waxy potatoes, peeled and cut into 1-inch cubes

½ teaspoon turmeric

¼ teaspoon fenugreek seeds

1 teaspoon Maldive fish, or substitute bonito flakes, finely ground

⅓ cup chopped shallots

2 green cayenne chiles, thinly sliced

8 to 10 fresh or frozen curry leaves

1 teaspoon salt

1½ cups water

½ cup canned or fresh coconut milk

1 teaspoon fresh lime juice

In a medium heavy pot, combine the potatoes, turmeric, fenugreek seeds, Maldive fish or bonito, chopped shallots, green chiles, curry leaves, and salt. Pour in the water and bring to a boil, then reduce the heat to a simmer. Cook for 15 minutes or until the potatoes are just tender.

Stir in the coconut milk. When the curry starts to gently boil, remove from the heat and stir in the lime juice. Serve immediately, in a bowl.

SERVES 4 TO 5

Serve as part of a meal with plain rice, a simple grill such as Grilled Fish Steaks with Black Pepper Rub (page 210) or Grilled Marinated Beef (page 272), and a sambol such as Mint Sambol (page 32).

THE BANJARA

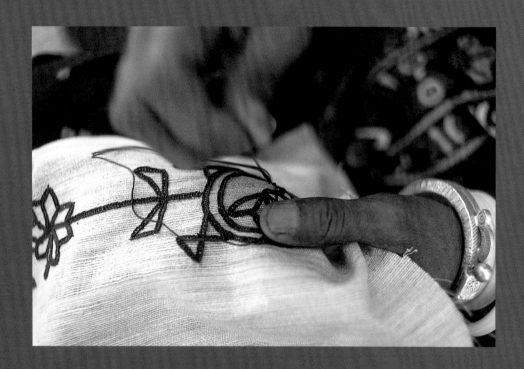

We're used to a certain level of personal befuddlement when we're in the Subcontinent, because there is, and always will be, so much that we know nothing about. Take, for instance, a group of people called the Banjara. We remember first being aware of the Banjara when traveling in Rajasthan, in northwestern India. We would see them walking quickly and confidently through busy city centers, the women, often with tattooed patterns on their faces, wearing complicated embroidered clothing and heavy jewelry. They were usually shepherding goats laden with rocks bundled in woven straw, but we could never figure out where they were going with the goats, or why.

A few years later, we bought embroidery from a similarly attired woman far in the south of India, in Kerala. The embroidery was beautiful, and we were thrilled to be able to buy it, but when we asked the woman where she came from, she said that she came from Karnataka, the state to the north. A few days later, though, we bought a few more pieces, and again we talked, but this time she said that she was from Rajasthan. It seemed strange.

The following year, in Goa, we bought more Banjara embroidery. But just like the women in Kerala, the women selling the embroidery were always evasive. "We are from Gujarat," they would say, or on another day, "We are from Karnataka." We'd laugh, but there was no way they would give us a straight answer.

So finally we ended up in the library and found a wonderful book called *Mud, Mirror, and Thread: Folk Traditions of Rural India*. Two chapters of the book, written by textile historian Nora Fisher, are about the Banjara and they discuss in detail the embroidery, the people, and their extraordinary way of life. According to Fisher, there are anywhere from three million to twenty million Banjara in the Subcontinent. A more exact figure is almost impossible to arrive at because the Banjara are nomadic, and they are also deeply secretive and protective of their culture.

For several hundred years, they flourished by transporting goods with bullocks, covering long distances. But with the arrival of trains and roadways, they lost their primary occupation and turned to other trades, though they always lived on the outside of the mainstream culture. Banjara men and women now often work on road-building crews, or on construction projects in towns and cities. Sometimes they sell ironwork or jewelry on the street; we've noticed that city folk try to avoid dealing with them. At night, they always return to Banjara camps located in the surrounding countryside. They are a Subcontinent version of gypsies, a part of the social fabric, but for centuries their own people.

And now, thanks to Nora Fisher, there is for us at least one mystery cleared up. But when we come to think about it, the Banjara seem more mysterious than ever.

Woman from rural Katchh embroidering, photographed in a village north of Bhuj, in western Gujarat

QUICK ASPARAGUS STIR-FRY

. . . .

Asparagus in season is one of life's great pleasures. In this Nepali stir-fry, it cooks in a simple flavor paste of cooked onion, garlic, and ginger. Rather than being masked, the asparagus comes through loud and strong and delicious against the background flavors.

¾ pound asparagus (25 to 30 medium-thin spears)

1 teaspoon minced ginger or ginger mashed to a paste

2 teaspoons minced garlic or garlic mashed to a paste

½ teaspoon ground coriander

2 tablespoons vegetable oil

¼ teaspoon fenugreek seeds

1 cup thinly sliced onion

¼ teaspoon turmeric

½ teaspoon salt, or to taste

½ cup water

Wash and drain the asparagus, then cut into approximately 1-inch lengths, discarding the tough thick bottom ends. Set aside.

In a small bowl, mix together the ginger, garlic, and ground coriander. Set aside.

Heat a wide heavy skillet or a wok or karhai (see Glossary) over medium-high heat. Add the oil and swirl to coat the pan, then add the fenugreek and stir. After about 20 seconds, add the sliced onion and stir-fry until softened and starting to brown, about 7 minutes. Stir in the reserved flavor paste. Add the asparagus and sprinkle on the turmeric and salt. Stir-fry for a minute to expose all the surfaces of the asparagus to the hot pan, then add the water. Bring to a boil, cover, and cook for 2 to 3 minutes.

Remove the lid and cook for a few minutes more (timing will vary depending on the thickness and freshness of the asparagus), until the asparagus is just tender. Taste and adjust the salt if necessary. Serve hot.

SERVES 3 TO 4

We like this as one of several dishes in a casual meal, say, with Mountain Dal (page 182), Himalayan Grilled Tomato Sauce (page 94), and rice.

FLOWERING CHIVE STIR-FRY: Chinese chives (also called flowering chives) also make a quick and attractive stir-fry. Begin with 3 bunches, cut into 1-inch lengths, to yield 3 cups. Heat 3 tablespoons oil, toss in ½ teaspoon fenugreek and 2 red cayenne chiles slit lengthwise, and stir-fry briefly. Add 1 teaspoon each minced garlic and ginger and ½ teaspoon turmeric, and stir-fry for 30 seconds. Toss in the chives and ½ teaspoon each ground coriander, cumin, and salt, and stir-fry until softened (3 minutes or so).

SPICY BITTER MELON

· · · · · · · · · · · · ·

In Bangladesh, I discovered the pleasures of bitter melon, or *korola* as it's known there, where it's available in both the hot season and the rainy season. Also referred to as bitter gourd, bitter melon is a bumpy, pale green cucumber-shaped vegetable; it's widely available in Asian markets in North America. It is eaten in China and Southeast Asia, as well as in the Subcontinent. It's thought to be cleansing for the blood and very good for the health. Bitter melon is usually, as here, thinly sliced, then salted to draw out excessive bitterness (as Mediterranean eggplant sometimes is); it needs to sit for about 45 minutes, so the dish requires a little thinking ahead, but not much work.

This is a simple Bangladeshi stir-fry, known as *korola jal*. The dish comes to the table as a dry curry (moist-textured, but without lots of sauce or gravy), dark in color, and with a seductive "have another bite" flavor.

3 medium (about 8 inches) or 6 small (4 to 5 inches) bitter melons

Salt

2 tablespoons vegetable oil

1 tablespoon mustard oil

1/2 teaspoon cayenne

2 teaspoons minced garlic or garlic mashed to a paste

2 green cayenne chiles, thinly sliced

1 cup thinly sliced onion

1 teaspoon sugar

An hour before you wish to serve the dish, salt the bitter melon: Cut the melons lengthwise in half, scoop out and discard the seeds, and then slice very thinly crosswise. Place in a bowl, sprinkle on about 3 tablespoons salt, toss, and let stand for 45 minutes or so.

Rinse the bitter melon thoroughly, drain, squeeze out excess water, and set aside.

Heat the oils in a wok or karhai (see Glossary) or a large heavy skillet over medium-high heat. Add the cayenne and garlic and stir-fry for about 15 seconds. Add the chiles and onion and stir-fry until very soft, about 10 minutes. Add the sliced bitter melon, reduce the heat to medium, and cook for about 15 minutes, stirring frequently, until tender. Add the sugar and 1/2 teaspoon salt and stir-fry for another few minutes until very tender. Serve hot. SERVES 4

Serve with a mild to sweet dal such as Udaipur Urad Dal (page 189), or with carrots (Carrots with Tropical Flavors, page 166, for example), or with lamb, any of them pleasing, slightly sweet foils for the bitter edge of this surprising vegetable.

AROMATIC PUMPKIN AND COCONUT

. . . .

This intriguing Bengali dish is an ingenious and delicious way to serve pumpkin. The pumpkin and coconut are both grated, then cooked together with savory and aromatic spices to a tender mass, with no extra liquid, no sauce or gravy. Flavors are subtle, with a hint of sweet and a touch of heat. We serve it as a cross between a vegetable dish and a condiment.

NOTE: Use a wedge of any kind of pumpkin for this, from orange pie pumpkin to darker orange Caribbean pumpkin (and see the variation for squash options). A 6- to 7-inch-diameter pie pumpkin yields 6 to 8 cups grated pumpkin. Scrape off the seeds, cut off the skin and discard, then grate on a box grater.

Scant 2 tablespoons vegetable oil

1/4 teaspoon nigella seeds

1/2 teaspoon cumin seeds

About 1 cup chopped onion

About 4 cups coarsely grated pumpkin (see Note)

1 teaspoon ground coriander

1 teaspoon sugar

1 teaspoon salt

1 cup fresh or frozen grated coconut

1/4 cup water

2 dried red chiles, stemmed

One 1-inch piece cinnamon or cassia stick

1 large or 2 small bay leaves

About 1/4 cup small coriander sprigs (optional)

Heat the oil in a large heavy skillet over medium-high heat. Add the nigella and cumin seeds and fry briefly, then add the onion and cook, stirring frequently, until it is starting to brown, about 8 minutes. Add the pumpkin, lower the heat to medium, and cook, stirring constantly to prevent sticking, for 2 to 3 minutes. Add the ground coriander, sugar, and salt and cook for 2 minutes or so, until the pumpkin is well softened.

Add the coconut and stir to break up lumps and blend it into the pumpkin. Cook, stirring, for about 2 minutes, then stir in the water. Add the dried red chiles, cinnamon, and bay leaf, reduce the heat to medium, and cook for 2 to 3 minutes, stirring to prevent sticking. Taste for seasonings, and adjust if necessary.

Serve mounded on a plate or in a shallow bowl, topped with sprigs of coriander, if you wish.   MAKES ABOUT 2 1/2 CUPS; SERVES 4 TO 6

Serve alongside simple grilled or roasted chicken and a soupy dal such as Bangla Dal with a Hit of Lime (page 178), with rice.

SAVORY SQUASH AND COCONUT: You can substitute kabocha, acorn, or other winter squash for the pumpkin. Some squashes will give off more moisture as they cook than pumpkin does, so you may need to add a little less water. Your finished dish will then be a pale yellow mound rather than pale tangerine colored, but just as aromatic and pleasing.

RICH PUMPKIN AND COCONUT: Instead of moistening the dish with water, use a generous 1/4 cup canned or fresh coconut milk.

PEA SHOOTS FOR A CROWD

. . . .

In the Hindu calendar there are three lunar months each year that are particularly auspicious for marriage, and one of those months falls more or less in November. This means that if you're traveling in Nepal or India during November (which is a nice time of the year, cool and dry), there's a great likelihood that you'll encounter a wedding (or two or three) several times a week.

From a food point of view, weddings in Nepal are especially fun to observe. A wedding crowd will sit on the ground, in rows, and food will be served on leaves set out in front of each person. It's a lovely scene, and if you can catch a glimpse of the cooks, it's even better. Using huge woks and giant pots, they cook the wedding feast so it's ready to serve all at once, an enormous task.

Last summer, inspired by Nepalese weddings, we bought a giant wok at a Chinese kitchen store here in Toronto. It's more than three feet in diameter, and strong and sturdy, yet it cost less than thirty-five dollars. We set it up over a campfire at our farm and fired it with a roaring wood fire. And just as if it had been a wedding in Nepal, we found ourselves cooking effortlessly in huge quantities, whenever the occasion arose. It's a lot of fun, and it's easy.

But you don't need a giant wok to make this recipe. The quantity called for may seem enormous, but greens shrink a lot during cooking, so it's important to start with enough. We use pea shoots, also known as pea tendrils, because we love them, but you could use spinach or amaranth or beet greens instead.

10 to 12 loosely packed cups pea shoots or spinach, or 8 cups chopped amaranth or beet greens

2 tablespoons mustard oil

3 dried red chiles, stemmed

2 garlic cloves, crushed or minced

1 teaspoon turmeric

1 teaspoon salt, or to taste

About ½ cup water or light broth, if using amaranth or beet greens

About ½ cup coriander leaves, coarsely chopped (optional)

Wash the greens thoroughly in a sink full of cold water, swishing them around to get all the dirt and sand dislodged. Lift them out of the water, then rinse again with water. Hold the greens a bundle at a time on your cutting board and chop them crosswise into 2-inch lengths; discard any coarse stems. Set aside.

Place a large wok over high heat. Add the oil and swirl it around a little. Toss in the dried chiles, garlic, and turmeric. Stir-fry for about 15 seconds, then add the greens; the water drops on them will sizzle nicely as they hit the hot pan. Sprinkle on the salt, then stir-fry, turning and tossing until all the greens have been exposed to the hot surface of the wok. Or, if using the tougher greens, add the ½ cup water or broth, bring to a boil, cover, and cook for about 1 minute; then remove the lid and continue to stir-fry until done.

Stir in the chopped coriander, if you wish, then turn out onto a platter and serve. These are also delicious at room temperature.   SERVES 8

Serve as the vegetable side dish in a meal of Yogurt-Marinated Chicken Kebabs (page 239) with Chickpea Pulao (page 105) or Stir-fried Rice and Dal (page 96), or with Roadside Café Chicken (page 250) and Gita's Luchis (page 115).

SERVES 4

NOTE: If your wok is not large enough to handle the volume of greens, then cook this in two batches, starting with 1 generous tablespoon oil each time; use 2 dried red chiles for each batch. To make this for 4 people, use 1 generous tablespoon oil and 2 chiles and halve the quantity of all the other ingredients. Cooking times will be a little faster with the smaller quantities.

Remarkable Women

When you're trekking in Ladakh or really anywhere in the mountains of the Subcontinent, you have encounters with all kinds of people. This Ladakhi man lives in a small hamlet about three days' walk from the town of Padum, in the Zanskar region.

IT FELT LIKE THE BEST KIND OF LUCK, to meet Lala and her mother, Hasna Begum (see Note, below), on my second day in Dhaka. I'd dropped by to deliver a message to Lala from a mutual friend, and then found myself sitting eating a wonderful lunch in Hasna Begum's light airy kitchen with two very unusual and accomplished women.

"This is all leftovers, I'm afraid," said Hasna Begum. Several dishes were placed on the table, and each of us had a plate of rice. "We eat one dish at a time," she explained as she placed several serving-spoonfuls of the first dish, *niramish* (mixed vegetable curry), on one area of my rice. Once I'd eaten my portion, she carefully spooned some of the next dish onto a fresh portion of my rice.

After the mixed vegetables, we ate a dal, then a green vegetable stir-fried with a little dried fish, before continuing with two heavier dishes, a simple *jhol* (simmered curry) made with carp, called *rui* in Bengal, and a spicy beef curry. All the flavors were distinct eaten this way, one dish at a time.

And as we ate, we talked. Hasna Begum is a retired philosophy professor, now widowed, who taught at the university in Dhaka. She has such intellectual energy and confidence that I might have been intimidated had she not been so warm and engaging. Lala is an artist who teaches fine art at the university and publishes an art magazine. As we walked to my car, there was a gorgeous, liquid bird call from a rosy-throated bird in a tree in the yard.

"That's a bulbul," said Lala (see Note).

NOTE: *Begum,* like "Madame" in English, is a polite title for a woman of importance. A *bulbul* has the same magic aura in folktales from Iran to Bangladesh as nightingales do in Europe.

Hasna Begum's Mixed Vegetable Curry (page 164) over Plain Basmati Rice (page 82)

HASNA BEGUM'S MIXED VEGETABLE CURRY

· · · · · · · · · · · ·

This simple Bangladeshi mixed vegetable dish is called *niramish*, meaning "no protein." It contains no meat—and no onion or garlic either. It cooks in about ten minutes, a real bonus when you're in a rush. Chopping takes a little time, but not more than ten minutes.

The main thing is to use an equal amount of a number of vegetables, all cut small. This recipe calls for about one cup (from about a quarter pound) of five different vegetables. If you want to omit one, increase the others a little. You could use different vegetables, substituting fresh corn cut from the cob, for example, or green peas, for one of the squashes. Chop all the vegetables into small cubes, the harder vegetables into the smallest cubes so they will all cook in the same time. PHOTOGRAPH ON PAGE 163

3 tablespoons mustard oil or vegetable oil or a blend of the two

1/2 teaspoon turmeric

1/2 teaspoon cayenne

1 teaspoon ground coriander

1 teaspoon Bengali Five-Spice Mixture (page 340),
 or a scant 1/4 teaspoon each black mustard, cumin,
 fennel, fenugreek, and nigella seeds

2 bay leaves

1 scant cup cubed (1/4-inch dice) carrots

1 scant cup cubed (1/2-inch dice) potatoes

1 cup seeded, peeled, and cubed (1/2-inch dice) squash,
 such as delicata or pumpkin

A generous handful of green beans, trimmed and
 cut into 1/2-inch lengths (1 cup)

1 cup peeled and cubed (1/2-inch dice) zucchini or
 other summer squash

2 green cayenne chiles, cut into 1/2-inch-wide rings

1 1/4 cups water

About 1 1/2 teaspoons salt

2 teaspoons sugar

About 1 tablespoon fresh lime juice, or to taste

Coriander sprigs (optional)

Lime wedges

Heat the oil in a heavy pot or a large wok or karhai (see Glossary) over medium-high heat. Add the turmeric, cayenne, ground coriander, and spice mixture and stir-fry briefly, keeping the spices moving in the hot oil. Add the bay leaves and stir. Add the vegetables one at a time, starting with the hardest ones (carrots, then potatoes, then squash, and so on), stir-frying briefly after each addition. (If using fresh corn or green peas, do not add yet.) Then cook for several minutes after the last addition.

Add the chopped chiles, then add the water and bring to a strong boil. Add 1 teaspoon of the salt (and corn or peas, if using) and cook for 5 to 7 minutes, or until all the vegetables are cooked, stirring occasionally. Stir in the sugar, then taste for salt and adjust if necessary. Add the lime juice and stir in just before serving.

Top with coriander sprigs, if you wish, and serve with lime wedges.

SERVES 4 TO 5

Serve with rice, as part of a vegetarian meal with a dal and several other vegetable dishes, or as a mild-tasting complement to the oniony intensity of Tiger Shrimp with Onions (page 211).

MIXED VEGETABLE CURRY WITH DAL: Several cooks in Bangladesh told me that sometimes *niramish* includes lentils, especially in wintertime, when people need more sustenance. Use 1 cup cooked lentils, either leftover dal or lentils cooked ahead for the purpose, say masur dal or mung dal. Stir them in once the water has come to a boil.

STIR-FRIED GREENS, BANGLA STYLE

· · · · · · · · · · · ·

During the monsoon, the beautifully arranged stacks of greens at vegetable stands in Bangladesh are evidence that in rainy season there, greens rule the vegetable world. Many leafy greens that are common in Bangladesh are available only in South Asia, but other greens can be cooked using the same techniques and flavorings.

One common monsoon green is succulent-stemmed *puishak* (*shak* means "green leafy vegetable"). The closest equivalent is that staple of the Thai-Chinese-Vietnamese repertoire, morning glory stems and leaves (*pak bung* in Thai, *rau muong* in Vietnamese). Another Bengali green is *patsag*, the tender green tips of the jute plant. They have an agreeable, slightly bitter taste.

A good substitute in springtime would be leafy endive or dandelion greens, which also have a bitter edge. In summer, chard leaves or spinach can be substituted, and in cooler months, the smaller members of the cabbage family, such as baby bok choi, cook up beautifully when stir-fried Bangla style.

Cooking times will vary depending on the tenderness and fineness of the greens. Baby bok choi, with its small tight knots of leaves, will take about five minutes of simmering, while spinach will take much less time.

About 1 pound leafy greens (such as amaranth leaves, baby bok choi, or dandelion greens)

3 tablespoons vegetable oil

1 teaspoon Bengali Five-Spice Mixture (page 340), or a scant ¼ teaspoon each black mustard, cumin, fennel, fenugreek, and nigella seeds

½ teaspoon cayenne or red pepper flakes

2 teaspoons minced garlic or garlic mashed to a paste

1½ cups finely chopped onions

½ teaspoon sugar, if using bitter greens (such as dandelion)

1 teaspoon salt

Wash the greens thoroughly in several changes of water, then drain. Coarsely chop and set aside.

Heat the oil in a large wok or karhai (see Glossary) or a large deep heavy skillet over medium-high heat. Add the spice mixture and cayenne (or pepper flakes) and stir briefly, then add the garlic and stir-fry for just 10 seconds. Add the onions and stir-fry, lowering the heat to medium after 2 minutes, until very tender and soft, about 10 minutes. If using bitter greens, add the sugar.

Raise the heat to high, add the greens, and stir-fry until they turn bright green—1 to 5 minutes, depending on the greens. Add the salt and continue to stir-fry until the greens give off their liquid, then cover and steam for 1 minute. Remove the lid and continue to stir-fry until tender and cooked through; timing will depend on the greens you use (see headnote).

Transfer to a serving bowl and serve hot.   SERVES 6

Serve with rice and a fish dish such as Classic Bengali Fish in Broth (page 223), or a simmered meat dish such as Sri Lankan Beef Curry (page 278), or a dal.

BANGLA PEA SHOOTS: Pea shoots are known as *matar shak*, meaning "pea greens," in Bangladesh. For about 6 cups pea shoots, washed and chopped, follow the recipe above, changing the spice blend to 1 teaspoon each cumin seeds and white poppy seeds and ¼ teaspoon *ajowan* (lovage seed), if available. Omit the sugar.   SERVES 4

BEETS WITH TROPICAL FLAVORS

· · · · · · · · · · · ·

Beets are a common Sri Lankan vegetable, which always catches us a little by surprise. They seem like such hearty, cold-weather root vegetables, unlikely candidates for the cuisine of a tropical island in the Indian Ocean. But the mountains are high, more than five thousand feet, and in the towns in the center of the island, like Nuwara Eliya, temperatures can get cool. We assume beets were brought by the European colonizers—the Dutch or the British seem the most likely candidates—but we don't know. In any case, they do pop up regularly, both in restaurant fare and in home cooking.

Here beets are peeled and chopped into julienne, then simmered with a blend of minced shallots, green chiles, curry leaves, vinegar, and, of course, a little coconut milk to round out the flavors. The green chiles disappear into the sauce as they cook, leaving only a hint of heat. Because the beets are cut into strips, they cook in only twenty minutes or so (and see the variation made with precooked beets). Leftovers are delicious the next day, served cold or rewarmed.

³⁄₄ to 1 pound beets (3 to 4 medium), washed

Generous 1 tablespoon raw sesame oil or vegetable oil

About 8 fresh or frozen curry leaves

Scant 2 tablespoons minced seeded green cayenne chiles,
  or substitute jalapeños

2 to 3 tablespoons minced shallots

1 tablespoon rice vinegar

1 teaspoon salt

³⁄₄ teaspoon sugar

¹⁄₂ cup canned or fresh coconut milk

¹⁄₄ cup water

About ¹⁄₂ teaspoon coarse salt (optional)

Peel the beets. (Beets will stain your hands as you peel and slice them unless you wear rubber gloves. The stain can take a day to wear off completely.)

Cut them into julienne strips by first thinly slicing them, then cutting into strips about ¹⁄₄ inch wide. Set aside.

Place a heavy pot with a tight-fitting lid over medium-high heat. Add the oil, and when it is hot, add 4 of the curry leaves, the minced chiles, and shallots. Cook for 2 to 3 minutes, stirring occasionally. Add the beets and stir, then add the vinegar, salt, and sugar and stir and turn to mix well. Raise the heat to high and stir-fry for 2 to 3 minutes. The beets will give off a little liquid as they cook.

Mix half the coconut milk with the water, then add to the pot and bring to a vigorous boil. Stir well, cover tightly, reduce the heat, and cook at a strong simmer until the beets are just tender, about 20 minutes or so. Check the water level after 10 minutes of cooking and add a little more if it is almost dry.

Add the remaining ¹⁄₄ cup coconut milk and remaining curry leaves. Bring to a boil, then reduce the heat and simmer for another 2 to 3 minutes. Remove from the heat and taste for seasoning. Sprinkle on coarse salt, if you wish. Transfer to a serving dish, and serve hot or at room temperature.   SERVES 4

Serve as a vegetable dish with any meal, South Asian or not.

CARROTS WITH TROPICAL FLAVORS: The same method and flavorings can be used to cook carrots. Peel the carrots and cut them into julienne. Follow the instructions above, but decrease the vinegar to 2 teaspoons and the sugar to ¹⁄₄ teaspoon. Top the cooked carrots with chopped coriander leaves.

PRECOOKED BEETS WITH TROPICAL FLAVORS: You can make a quick (10- to 15-minute) version of this dish using 2¹⁄₂ to 3 cups chopped, already cooked and peeled beets, now available in many grocery stores. (Canned beets are not a substitute.) Chop the beets into bite-size cubes. All the other ingredients remain the same, except that the coconut milk should be reduced to ¹⁄₄ cup. Follow the instructions above, but add all the curry leaves with the chiles. Stir-fry the beets for only a minute, and after you add the liquid, simmer the beets for only 5 to 10 minutes, partly covered. Transfer to a shallow bowl, taste for seasoning, and adjust, if you wish. Let cool to room temperature before serving.

SPICED TENDER CHOPPED BINDI

· · · · · · · · · · · ·

Bindi is the Hindi name for "okra." In South Asia, okra is rarely cooked in water. Instead it is deep-fried or fried in a spiced oil–based sauce. This dish is a rather magical transformation of dull green okra into nuggets of flavor, with no sliminess, just good bite.

In Udaipur we stayed at the Jagat Niwas Hotel, family owned and very pleasant, right by the lake and just beside the imposing palace of the maharaja of Udaipur. The food at the restaurant tended to the elaborate. But the staff ate simpler Rajasthani village-style food, for that was where they came from, villages in the western part of Rajasthan. We tasted a version of this dish at the hotel on a day when the dish had been made for the staff meal. We loved it, then later were told how to make it by the family of Sangana Bai, the tandoor oven maker (see "My First Tandoor," page 128).

As you must with all quickly cooked stir-fried dishes, you should prepare all your ingredients ahead and place them by your stove top. The heat is medium, the spicing easy to assemble, yet complex tasting.

½ pound okra (2 cups trimmed and chopped)
3 tablespoons raw sesame oil or vegetable oil
½ teaspoon black mustard seeds
1 teaspoon cumin seeds, whole or ground
½ teaspoon ground coriander
½ teaspoon turmeric
½ cup finely chopped onion
1 tablespoon minced garlic or garlic mashed to a paste
1 tablespoon minced ginger or ginger mashed to a paste
½ teaspoon garam masala (page 342 or store-bought)
½ teaspoon salt
1 green cayenne chile, minced

Wash the okra, then cut into ¼-inch slices, discarding the stems and any tough spots. Set aside.

Heat a wok or karhai (see Glossary) or a wide heavy skillet over medium-high heat. When it is hot, add the oil. Toss in the mustard seeds, then cover briefly while they pop. Add the cumin, coriander, and turmeric and stir into the oil. Add the onion, garlic, and ginger and cook, stirring frequently, until the onion has softened, about 5 minutes. Add the okra, garam masala, and salt and stir-fry for 6 to 8 minutes, or until the okra is nearly tender. Add the minced chile and stir-fry for another 2 minutes.

Turn out into a shallow serving bowl and serve hot or at room temperature.

/ SERVES 4

Serve as a dry curry, alongside rice and a simmered dish such as Udaipur Urad Dal (page 189) or Cashew-Coconut Meatballs (page 262) or Simmered Kashmiri Paneer (page 171).

A monk waiting at Ringdom Gompa, a monastery in Ladakh, in northern Kashmir, not far from the Pakistani–Indian line of control

LADIES' FINGERS CURRY

. . . .

In Sri Lanka, as in many other places that were colonized by the English, okra is known in English as *ladies' fingers,* and it is usually chopped crosswise into short lengths before being cooked. Even though the sauce has the deep flavor of a long-simmered dish, this curry is very quick to make.

1 tablespoon coconut oil or sunflower oil

5 or 6 fresh or frozen curry leaves

1 teaspoon cumin seeds

¹/₃ cup chopped shallots

2 green cayenne chiles, thinly sliced

¹/₂ pound okra, washed, trimmed, and cut into 1-inch pieces (2 cups)

¹/₂ teaspoon turmeric

1 tablespoon Maldive fish, or substitute 1 teaspoon bonito flakes,
    finely ground (optional)

1 teaspoon salt

¹/₂ cup water

¹/₂ cup canned or fresh coconut milk

Heat a medium heavy pot over medium heat, then add the oil. When the oil is hot, add the curry leaves, then the cumin, shallots, and chiles, and cook for 1 minute, stirring occasionally. Add the okra, turmeric, Maldive fish or bonito, if using, salt, and water. Stir briefly to mix, then cover and simmer for 5 to 6 minutes, until the okra is just tender.

Add the coconut milk and heat almost to a boil, then pour into a serving dish and serve.   SERVES 4

The coconut milk sauce makes this a good dish to pair with rice, Sri Lankan or another, and a simple grill such as Grilled Marinated Beef (page 272) or Bangla-Flavored Grilled Zucchini (page 144). For extra heat, put out Red Onion Sambol (page 32) or Fresh Bean Sprout Salad (page 55).

SIMMERED KASHMIRI PANEER

. . . .

We learned this home-style dish from an Australian named Kate, whom we met in Rajasthan. She had learned the dish from her Kashmiri husband's family. A slow-simmered tomato sauce bathes slices of golden fried *paneer* (fresh pressed cheese). The dish is vegetarian, with the rich and subtle spicing that is characteristic of the Kashmiri kitchen, and easy to make ahead. It's worth taking the time to first fry the slices of *paneer*, and to let the sauce simmer down to a thick rich flavor.

The chiles used in Kashmir are milder than the ones in most other parts of the Subcontinent, and the dried chile powder tastes more like Spanish *pimentón*, slightly smoky and sweet and less hot than regular cayenne. If you have *pimentón*, do use it here.

2 pounds very ripe tomatoes, or substitute 3 cups crushed
    good-quality canned tomatoes
About 1 pound *paneer* (page 345 or store-bought)
About ²/₃ cup ghee, peanut or safflower oil, or raw sesame oil for frying
¹/₂ cup minced garlic or garlic mashed to a paste
3 tablespoons minced ginger or ginger mashed to a paste
3 cups chopped onions (¹/₂-inch dice)
3 to 4 cups water
2 tablespoons minced seeded green cayenne chile
3 brown cardamom pods, smashed, or substitute
    5 green cardamom pods, smashed
2 cloves (optional)
1 teaspoon turmeric
¹/₂ to 1 teaspoon Spanish *pimentón* (see headnote) or
    ¹/₂ teaspoon cayenne
1¹/₂ teaspoons salt, or to taste

If using fresh tomatoes, bring a large pot of water to a boil. To peel the tomatoes, immerse them in the water for 30 seconds, then lift out and refresh in a bowl of cold water. Peel the tomatoes and remove and discard the cores. Crush the tomatoes between your fingers into a bowl and set aside, loosely covered.

Slice the *paneer* into rectangles ¹/₂ inch thick and about 1 by 2 inches, and set aside.

Fill a wide heavy skillet or wok or a karhai (see Glossary) with just over ¹/₄ inch ghee or oil. Heat over medium-low heat, then add only as many *paneer* slices as will fit in the pan without overlapping and cook, turning once, until lightly browned on both sides, 4 to 5 minutes per batch. Lift out, letting the oil drain off, and place on a plate. Repeat with the remaining *paneer*.

Measure out ¹/₃ cup ghee or oil from the pan and pour into a large heavy-bottomed nonreactive saucepan (reserve the remaining ghee or oil for another purpose). Heat over medium-high heat, then add the garlic and ginger, lower the heat to medium, and stir-fry for about a minute. Add the onions and cook, stirring frequently, until very soft and pale honey in color but not caramelized to brown, 10 to 12 minutes.

Add the tomatoes and stir in, then add 3 cups water. The mixture should be very liquid; if your tomatoes are not very juicy, add up to another cup of water. Bring to a boil over high heat. Add the green chile, cardamom, cloves, if using, turmeric, *pimentón* or cayenne, and salt. Lower the heat to maintain a steady simmer and simmer for about an hour, stirring occasionally to prevent sticking. You may need to lower the heat a little more partway through the cooking as the mixture thickens.

Add the *paneer* to the sauce and simmer for another 45 minutes. Taste and adjust the seasoning if necessary. (We like to add a generous, untraditional, grinding of black pepper to the sauce just before serving.)

SERVES 6

Serve as a main dish with basmati rice, accompanied by an easy green such as Pea Tendrils with Coconut (page 71) and by Fresh White Radish Slices with Salt (page 54) or Zinet's Young Ginger Pickle (page 346).

NOTE: Kate's instructions included placing the fried slices of *paneer* in cold water to soak until you are ready to add them to the sauce. We've found that if they're slow fried until a little browned and crisping at the edges, they're not oily, and we like the crispy texture, so we don't soak them. If you prefer a chewy texture, place the fried *paneer* in a pan of cold water until ready to add it into the sauce.

RAJASTHANI "BUTTERMILK" CURRY

· · · · · · · · · · · ·

This is one of the family of buttermilk curries found in the northwestern parts of India, places where dairy products such as yogurt and buttermilk play a large role in the kitchen. I learned the curry from Pushpa, who comes from a small village near Barmer in the desert of Rajasthan but lives most of the year in the city of Udaipur, where her husband, Indra, works.

The curry is beautiful, with strands of scallion and bits of green chile floating in the pale yellow broth. Traditionally it is eaten with *bajra roti* (millet flatbread). The bread is dipped, mouthful by mouthful, into the curry, as you might dip bread into soup to moisten and flavor it. But we also love to serve this as a sauce for rice. It's mild-tasting, flavored with cumin and mustard seed—very enticing.

Though the curry is called a buttermilk curry, we more often have yogurt on hand, so that's what we use. If you have buttermilk, the curry will be smoother and more velvety. The whole dish takes only about ten minutes to prepare.

1 tablespoon vegetable oil

1½ teaspoons black mustard seeds

½ teaspoon cumin seeds

½ teaspoon turmeric

1 large or 2 medium scallions, trimmed, sliced lengthwise in half
   and then crosswise into 1-inch lengths

1 green cayenne chile, minced

¼ cup water, if using yogurt

1 cup plain (full- or reduced-fat) yogurt or 1¼ cups buttermilk

½ teaspoon salt, or to taste

2 to 3 tablespoons chopped coriander leaves

Heat the oil in a wok or karhai (see Glossary) or a medium heavy pot over medium-high heat. When it is hot, toss in the mustard seeds. When most of them have popped, add the cumin and turmeric and stir. Lower the heat to medium, add the scallions and chile, and stir-fry for about 3 minutes, until softened. If using yogurt, stir in the water. Reduce the heat to low, pour in the yogurt or buttermilk, and stir until warmed through; do not allow to boil. Stir in the salt.

Transfer to a serving bowl and top with the coriander. Serve hot.

SERVES 2 TO 3

This makes a wonderful sauce to accompany flatbreads, such as Potato-Stuffed Parathas (page 130) or Cumin-Flecked Skillet Breads (page 126), or to drizzle over rice.

CHILE-HOT BHUTANESE CHEESE CURRY

. . . .

I'd heard of this simmered dish before I traveled to the Bhutanese border area, but I could never quite picture it. It's called *ema daji*, and it's often made very chile hot. The version here is quite hot; to make it more extreme, increase the number of cayenne chiles to twelve or add some crushed dried red chiles.

I saw Bhutanese cheese being sold in large fresh balls in the Kalimpang market. There it's called *churpi*. It's like a cross between feta and farmer's cheese, fresh and not very salty, and it doesn't melt when it's heated. We substitute feta, and because the one we use is salty, we don't add extra salt to the curry. Tomatoes give the dish color and balance the cheese nicely.

Cheese curry is rich and warming on a cool day, soupy and generous, an ideal vegetarian main dish. Leftovers are great reheated.

8 green cayenne chiles, seeded and coarsely chopped (about ⅓ cup)

1 large onion, sliced lengthwise (about 1½ cups)

1½ cups water

2 teaspoons vegetable oil

1½ cups chopped tomatoes

2 scant tablespoons coarsely chopped garlic or garlic mashed to a paste

⅓ pound feta, chopped into ½-inch cubes

Salt, if needed

3 or 4 tablespoons chopped coriander leaves

Freshly ground black pepper (optional)

Put the chiles, onion, water, and oil in a medium pot and bring to a boil. Cover, reduce the heat slightly and cook at a strong simmer for 15 minutes.

Add the tomatoes and garlic and bring back to a boil, then simmer uncovered for 10 minutes, or until the tomatoes are melting into the liquid and the garlic has softened.

Add the cheese and simmer for another 3 to 4 minutes. Stir, remove from the heat, cover, and let sit for 10 minutes before serving. (This is best served warm, not hot.)

Taste and add a little salt if you need it. Stir in the coriander and black pepper, if using, and serve.   SERVES 5 TO 6

Serve with Bhutanese Red Rice (page 83) or another plain rice and accompany with a stir-fried green vegetable.

DALS

you know what dal is, and if you've spent time cooking Indian, Nepali, Bangladeshi, or Pakistani food at home, learning recipes from cookbooks, you probably know what it is. But if you are coming across the word for the first time, explanation is in order, because it can be a little confusing.

First of all, dal (sometimes written as *dhal*) is the common name in the northern part of the Subcontinent for a dish that is made of split beans, peas, or lentils. Dal may be like a thin soup, or it can be a very thick puree. Often its texture is

Dongria woman and child at the large weekly market in Khati Kona, in southern Orissa

between the two, so that it's a little like split pea soup. In most parts of the Subcontinent, the main meal includes dal, bread or rice, and a vegetable, so dal is one of the essential culinary categories. It's a very flexible and creative one, too.

Dal dishes are very easy to cook, nutritious, and incredibly versatile and inexpensive, like the easiest of soups. For travelers in the Subcontinent, dal, like bread in Europe, can feel like a great friend, always available, sustaining.

"Dal" also refers to dried legumes (beans, peas, or lentils) that have been split into a lentillike shape. We call for only five dals in this book: mung (bright yellow and quick cooking, from split hulled mung beans); chana (split chickpeas/garbanzos, dull brown or pale off-white); urad (grayish white and small like pebbles); toovar (dark golden, split, hulled pigeon peas); plus an orange-red lentil called masur dal. (More detailed descriptions of all these dals are given in the Glossary under Dal.)

Cook's Notes: Dal cooks in plenty of unsalted water, sometimes with whole or ground spices. We put a pot of dal on to cook and then leave it, unattended, while we prepare other elements of the meal. Cooking time for masur and mung dal is only 25 to 40 minutes, so they're the ones we turn to most often. We make up large batches of the slower-cooked dals, then freeze them in 2-cup containers. They defrost quickly, like a frozen soup, and can then be flavored as we please. Many cooks in the Subcontinent use a pressure cooker to shorten cooking times and save fuel. It's a very practical approach, reducing the cooking time for urad dal, for example, from 1½ hours to 15 minutes. If you have a pressure cooker, do use it to cook the dals in this chapter; use a little less water than called for.

This brings us to the question of consistency: Dal can be very thin and soupy or it can be thick; the legumes can be mashed or left whole. In any given recipe, you can choose to serve it thin or thick. Thick dal becomes thin with the addition of water (and salt to taste), and thin dal can be made thick by simply cooking it down uncovered.

Once cooked, dal is *tempered* (flavored). The tempering enriches and flavors the dal and gives it character. Spices are heated in oil, and then aromatics, such as onion, garlic, ginger, tomatoes, and chopped vegetables, are added and cooked together before being stirred into the pot of hot cooked dal.

BANGLA DAL WITH A HIT OF LIME

· · · · · · · · · · · ·

The name of this Bangladeshi classic is *tok dal*, and it's become one of our favorite versions of simple dal. *Tok* means "sour" in Bengali, sour from lime or green tomato or an acidic fruit or, as here, from tamarind.

Masur (red dal) is cooked until soft, then tempered with simmered onions, tamarind, and spices. The combination is given a fresh finish with a squeeze of lime juice from the lime wedges that are served alongside. We serve this often as part of a weeknight supper, with plain rice, a stir-fried green, and perhaps a green salad or a fresh chutney.

1 cup masur dal, washed and drained

5 cups water

1 heaping tablespoon tamarind pulp, chopped

¼ cup vegetable oil or 2 tablespoons each vegetable oil and mustard oil

½ teaspoon ground coriander

½ teaspoon ground cumin

½ teaspoon cayenne

½ teaspoon turmeric

1 tablespoon minced garlic or garlic mashed to a paste

1½ cups thinly sliced onions

½ teaspoon salt, or to taste

ACCOMPANIMENTS

Lime wedges

About ½ cup coriander sprigs (optional)

In a large heavy saucepan, combine the dal and water and bring to a boil. Skim off the foam for the first few minutes of boiling, then lower the heat to medium and simmer for 20 minutes.

Meanwhile, place the tamarind pulp in a small bowl. Scoop out about ¼ cup of the water from the pan of dal, add it to the tamarind pulp, and stir well; then set aside for several minutes to soak.

Place a fine sieve or strainer over a small bowl and press the tamarind through the strainer. Discard the pulp; set the tamarind liquid aside.

Partially cover the dal and lower the heat to medium-low. Cook until it is completely soft and soupy, 10 to 15 minutes. Keep warm over low heat.

Heat the oil in a wok or karhai (see Glossary) or a heavy skillet over medium heat. Add the coriander, cumin, and cayenne and stir-fry for about 15 seconds, or until a little fragrant, then add the turmeric, garlic, and onions and stir-fry until the onions are very soft and tender, about 10 minutes.

Add the reserved tamarind liquid to the dal, then add the onion mixture and stir well. If you want a thinner, soupier texture, add another cup or more of water. Add the salt, and cook for 5 minutes or so to allow the flavors to blend. Taste and adjust the seasonings, if you wish.

Serve hot, accompanied by lime wedges and perhaps a small plate of coriander sprigs. Instruct your guests to squeeze on lime juice generously and to sprinkle on the coriander sprigs, if they wish.

MAKES ABOUT 4 CUPS; SERVES 4

Serve with rice, a fresh salad, and a stir-fried vegetable dish or a simple grill such as Cumin-Coriander Beef Patties (page 268).

SRI LANKAN FENUGREEK DAL

. . . .

In Sri Lankan English-language terms, this curious and appealing dish is sometimes referred to as a "gravy," and that's a good description. It has a gravylike consistency, like a sauce for pasta, and a taste of familiarity, of comfort food, even to someone who didn't grow up in Sri Lanka. This is an old-style version of the dish called *kirihodi*, made with a relatively large proportion of fenugreek that simmers in a sauce flavored with curry leaves and smoothed with coconut milk. More modern recipes reduce the amount of fenugreek, but we like the uniqueness of the traditional dish. Though we most commonly think of fenugreek as a spice, it is actually a legume, and it is eaten as a legume in a few other parts of the world (Ethiopia, for example), as well as in Sri Lanka.

Kirihodi is usually served as the sauce for a vermicellilike steamed pasta called *string hoppers*, but it also makes a flavorful dish when eaten over plain rice, with a fresh salad. It's popular with children, and then later in life is regarded as comfort food.

4 teaspoons fenugreek seeds, soaked in water for 30 minutes

1 tablespoon raw white rice

1¹/₂ cups water

¹/₂ cup finely chopped shallots

5 or 6 fresh or frozen curry leaves

One 1-inch piece cinnamon or cassia stick

1 to 2 green cayenne chiles, finely chopped

2 green cardamom pods

¹/₄ teaspoon turmeric

1 teaspoon salt

1¹/₂ cups canned or fresh coconut milk

About 2 tablespoons fresh lime juice, or to taste

Drain the fenugreek seeds and set aside. Dry roast the rice in a small dry skillet until lightly golden, then grind to a powder in a spice/coffee grinder.

Place the water in a small saucepan, add the fenugreek, rice powder, shallots, curry leaves, cinnamon, chiles, cardamom, and turmeric, and bring to boil over medium heat. Turn the heat down to very low and cook slowly for 30 minutes, stirring occasionally. The fenugreek should be tender and the onions very soft.

Add the salt and increase the heat to medium, then add the coconut milk a little at a time, stirring steadily as you mix it in. Bring almost to a boil, then remove from the heat and pour into a serving bowl.

When the dal has cooled a little, approximately 10 minutes, stir in the lime juice. Serve warm. MAKES ABOUT 4 CUPS; SERVES 6 AS A DAL, 8 AS A SAUCE

Serve as a warming dal in a winter meal with Grilled Marinated Beef (page 272) and Spiced Cabbage Salad (page 77). Or in hotter weather, serve as a sauce for noodles or rice, with a salad on the side.

NOTE: If you'd like some color in the dish, add 1 small tomato, finely chopped, along with the shallots.

Arugam Bay

Hopper shops are easy to spot in Sri Lanka because the cook who makes the Hoppers (page 121) stands at the front of the shop, turning them out one by one.

THE REASON I ENDED UP IN ARUGAM BAY was because of a tip from a traveler I'd met in a train station in India. One of her favorite places was a small village in southeastern Sri Lanka, near Lahugala National Park. She'd spent almost a month there, she told me, but she had no memory of nearly ten days of that time! She'd been bitten by a snake and had fallen unconscious. The villagers had taken her in and given her local treatments for the snake bite, and she'd survived. Still, it was one of her favorite places in the world. Must be pretty good, I thought.

Several months later, I found my way to Arugam Bay. The only accommodation was in bamboo bungalows just outside the village, which was called Pottuvil. There were a dozen or so other foreigners, all from Australia, all there for long stays with their surfboards (the bay is on the ocean). Living was simple. A bungalow cost one rupee a night (twenty-five to a dollar at that time), and food was nine rupees a day. The only other things to buy were bananas and peanuts.

The big attraction came late afternoon almost every day. If I walked down the beach a ways, and then looked over a group of small sand dunes, there I could watch wild elephants coming down to a freshwater tank to drink and to bathe. Heaven.

LEFT: *Eggs are less breakable than we think, and heavier. Here, crate after crate of eggs is being carried past a bus and into the morning market in Kandy, Sri Lanka.*

RIGHT: *Stalks of ripe bananas are a common sight in tropical southern India and Sri Lanka.*

MOUNTAIN DAL

· · · · · · · · · · · ·

In Nepal, even more than in South India, rice and lentils rule. *Dal bhat* (lentils and rice) is eaten every day, several times a day, over and over again. It commonly comes served with a vegetable dish (known as *takari* or *sabzi*), but it's the rice and lentils that are essential. The rice is generally good, and there are hundreds of different versions of dal. Most, like the recipe here, are relatively simple and not overly spiced.

Most foreigners first encounter *dal bhat* when they go trekking, or go for a stay in a smaller town or village, for in Kathmandu there are lots of European-style food places geared for tourists. There are bakeries, and pizzas baked in wood-fired ovens, not to mention well-stocked supermarkets, with row after row of treats imported from abroad. Almost everyone likes *dal bhat* (there is nothing not to like), but the thought of eating rice and dal over and over again doesn't sound so appealing. Then time goes by, and with every day that passes, *dal bhat* tastes better and better. After a while, just as for Nepalis, *dal bhat* becomes the meal of choice.

And then back in Kathmandu: "Where can I find *dal bhat*?"

This Nepali dal has a good deep taste. We call for split mung (yellow) dal, but you could instead use masur (red) dal, which cooks even more quickly. The dish smells clovey when cooking, but the cloves back off in the final taste and blend happily into the cinnamon, coriander, cumin, and cardamom. If made with split mung, it has an appealing creamy texture.

1 cup mung dal (see headnote), washed and drained

5 to 6 cups water

½ teaspoon turmeric

1 teaspoon salt

TEMPERING

2 to 3 dried red chiles, stemmed

1 teaspoon coriander seeds

½ teaspoon cumin seeds

3 cloves

One 1-inch piece cinnamon or cassia stick

Seeds from 2 green cardamom pods

5 or 6 black peppercorns

1 tablespoon mustard oil or vegetable oil

1 cup finely chopped onion

Put the dal into a large pot with 5 cups water and the turmeric and bring to a boil. Reduce the heat to maintain a strong simmer, partially cover, and cook for 30 to 40 minutes, until the dal is almost mushy. For a more liquid texture, add another ½ to 1 cup water.

Meanwhile, using a mortar and a pestle or a spice/coffee grinder, grind together the chiles, coriander, cumin, cloves, cinnamon, cardamom, and pepper. Set aside.

When the dal has finished cooking, add the salt and stir, then lower the heat to very low to keep it warm.

Heat a wok or karhai (see Glossary) or a cast-iron skillet over medium-high heat. Add the oil, then the finely chopped onion, and stir-fry for 5 minutes. Add the ground spice blend and stir-fry for 1 to 2 more minutes, then transfer to the pot of dal.

Stir the dal well and cook for about 10 minutes, then serve hot.

SERVES 4

Serve with rice or Chapatis (page 110), or both. Accompany with Nepali Green Bean–Sesame Salad (page 76) or another vegetable side dish.

REBIRTH

I turned twenty-seven the year my mother died, at home, of cancer. She died in November as the year was turning gray and cold, and that winter was a long, numb one for me. Spring came at last, and in early May I traveled to India, first to Delhi and then on to Srinagar.

I was heading to the dry mountain valleys of Ladakh, also known as "Little Tibet," north of the Himalaya, in those days newly opened to foreign travelers. I reached Leh, the Ladakhi capital, in early June, after a two-day bus ride from Srinagar. A week later, I headed farther east along the Indus Valley to Hemis *gompa* (*gompa* means "monastery"), where the big annual *mela*, or "festival," was about to start. Buses and trucks loaded with pilgrims made their way up the rocky road to the *gompa*. People found places to camp on the hillsides, by the streams, wherever they could find a piece of open ground. I set up my tent not far from the *gompa*, then went to look around. Small tea stalls, and stands selling *momos* (boiled meat-filled dumplings) and simple noodle stews called *thugpa*, were doing good business near the entrance, feeding the throng. Butter lamps (small bowls filled with melted butter, with a wick in the center) were lit inside the Tibetan-style temple, and the smoke from offerings of dried juniper perfumed the air. It's the closest I've ever been to a medieval religious festival, both a holiday and a pilgrimage.

Every afternoon and evening, standing shoulder to shoulder with Ladakhis and a small assortment of foreigners, I watched the monks perform, in dance and mime, the story of the coming of Buddhism to Tibet. One day a Dard woman was standing next to me on the flat roof, looking down over a low wall into the courtyard where the performances were about to start. She was wearing a goatskin cape over her jacket and skirt, and a complicated headdress adorned with coins and needles on her braided hair (see photograph, page 109). She and her husband and sister had traveled to the festival on foot and by bus from an area that was off-limits to foreigners, in the disputed territory (disputed by India and Pakistan) west of the Indus River in Ladakh. I was as unusual a sight to her as she was to me. She offered me a handful of dried apricots that she carried in a pouch at her waist. After I'd eaten the fruit, sucking its tart flesh off the pit, she showed me how to crack the pit and extract the "almond" within. Later, during a break, we walked together to one of the tea stands and had tea and bread, dunking the bread in our tea as we watched the passing scene.

And ever since, whenever I bite into a tart dried apricot, that encounter comes back: the sharp bright sun, the shy alert smile of the Dard woman, the scents of dust and goatskin and hot tea.

A Hindu shrine near Darbar Square in Kathmandu. People come at all hours to pray and make offerings; they ring the bell when the offering is made.

SAMBHAR WITH DRUMSTICKS

· · · · · · · · · · · ·

Sambhar is probably the most famous dish of southern India. It originally comes from Tamil Nadu, but it's now found throughout the four states of the South, and virtually all across India, for that matter. It's a form of dal, the most common accompaniment to *dosas* (crepelike flatbreads; see page 112) and *idlis* (steamed breads; see page 120), and also a big part of a southern rice meal.

There are many different kinds of *sambhar*, but all are made with toovar dal (split dried pigeon peas) and are characterized by tamarind-based acidity as a dominant flavor. *Sambhar* can be thin and soupy, or thick and rich, but it almost always has a distinctive dark butterscotch color and a tamarind tang. There are two different methods for making it. The first, as in this recipe, includes the spicing (using mostly whole spices) in the early stages of cooking, while the second, like Shallot Sambhar (page 187), adds a spice blend at the end of cooking to flavor the dish.

We've called for drumsticks (the vegetable version, no chicken involved) in this version of *sambhar*, but realize that they aren't always the easiest vegetable to find. If you have a South Asian grocery nearby, then there's a good chance of finding them: long slender green pods, eighteen inches to three feet in length. If you've never eaten or cooked with drumsticks, the thing to know about them is that, as with artichokes, only a portion of the vegetable is edible: You don't eat the outside tube; rather you pull it between your teeth, sucking out all the tender pulp.

If you can't find drumsticks, substitute cubes of Asian eggplant. Add it to the hot pan with the curry leaves and stir-fry for several minutes to expose all surfaces to the heat before adding the tamarind liquid and water.

²/₃ cup toovar dal, washed and picked over

6 cups water

¹/₂ teaspoon turmeric

2 tablespoons tamarind pulp, cut into pieces

1 cup hot water

About ¹/₂ pound drumsticks, or substitute Asian eggplant (see headnote)

1 tablespoon raw sesame oil or vegetable oil

¹/₂ teaspoon black mustard seeds

¹/₂ teaspoon fenugreek seeds

Pinch of asafoetida powder

5 dried red chiles, stemmed

15 to 20 fresh or frozen curry leaves

1¹/₂ teaspoons salt

¹/₄ cup coriander leaves

Place the dal in a large pot with 4 cups of the water and the turmeric. Bring to a vigorous boil, then reduce the heat to maintain a strong simmer, partially cover, and simmer for approximately 1 hour, stirring occasionally.

Meanwhile, soak the tamarind in the hot water for 10 minutes. Strain it through a sieve set over a bowl and use the back of a wooden spoon to press it against the mesh of the sieve. Set the tamarind liquid aside and discard the pulp. Wash the drumsticks and cut them into 2-inch lengths.

When the dal is cooked and starting to disintegrate, transfer it to a bowl and puree, using a potato masher or whisk. Set aside.

Rinse out and dry the pot and put it back on the stove over medium-high heat. Add the oil, and when the oil is hot, add the mustard seeds, fenugreek seeds, and asafoetida. Cook for approximately 30 seconds, or until the mustard seeds have popped. Lower the heat to medium, add the red chiles, curry leaves, and salt, and stir-fry for 1 minute, then add the reserved tamarind liquid and the remaining 2 cups water. Bring to a boil, then add the drumsticks and simmer for 20 minutes, or until the drumsticks can be squeezed easily between your teeth.

Add the mashed dal, reduce the heat to low, and cook for another 10 minutes or so to blend the flavors. Just before serving, garnish with the coriander leaves.   SERVES 4

Serve to accompany plain rice such as Rosematta (page 86) or Home-Style Dosas (page 112), Idlis (page 120), or Semolina Uppuma (page 92). Like many dals, this also makes a delicious and unusual soup course in a non–South Asian meal.

NOTE: Tastes vary widely in how thick or thin a *sambhar* should be served. If we are eating it with rice, we like it fairly thin; if we are serving it with *dosas* or *idlis*, we like it thick. Add extra water to this or the next *sambhar* to thin it, if desired, then taste and adjust the seasoning if necessary.

SHALLOT SAMBHAR

· · · · · · · · · · · ·

Unlike Sambhar with Drumsticks (page 186), this *sambhar* is flavored in the more usual way, with a *sambhar* powder that's added toward the end of the cooking period, just as garam masala may be added to a northern dal, such as Udaipur Urad Dal (page 189). This particular dish is a very typical Tamil *sambhar,* recognizable to anyone who has traveled through southern India. It smells great when it's cooking, and the taste transports you immediately. It's easy to prepare, and once you have a good quantity of *sambhar* powder (the recipe follows) on hand, you're rolling. If you can't find small Asian shallots (purplish under their reddish-brown papery skins), substitute European shallots and cut them into approximately 1-inch chunks. PHOTOGRAPH ON PAGE 113

1 heaping tablespoon tamarind pulp

1 cup hot water

1 cup toovar dal, washed and picked over

6 cups water

¹/₂ teaspoon turmeric

TEMPERING

2 tablespoons raw sesame oil or vegetable oil

¹/₂ pound small Asian shallots, trimmed and left whole (see headnote)

3 to 4 green cayenne chiles, finely chopped

10 to 12 fresh or frozen curry leaves

Generous 1 cup finely diced tomatoes

2 tablespoons *sambhar* powder (page 188 or store-bought)

1 teaspoon salt

¹/₂ cup coriander leaves

continued

Coarsely chop the tamarind, then place in a bowl and add the hot water. Mash with a spoon or a fork to help the pulp dissolve in the water. Set aside to soak for 10 minutes.

Place the dal in a large pot with the water, add the turmeric, and bring to a boil, then reduce the heat to maintain a strong simmer. Cook for 45 minutes to 1 hour, stirring occasionally, until the dal is starting to break down.

Meanwhile, place a sieve over a bowl. Pour in the tamarind mixture and use the back of a wooden spoon to press it against the mesh of the sieve. Discard the pulp and set the tamarind liquid aside.

When the dal is cooked, pulverize and mash it with a potato masher or heavy whisk so that it has the consistency of split pea soup, then set it over very low heat to keep warm.

Place a medium heavy skillet over medium-high heat. Add the oil, and when it is hot, add the shallots, chiles, and curry leaves. Cook for 1 minute, then add the tomatoes. Cook for 2 to 3 minutes, until the tomatoes start to break down, then stir in the *sambhar* powder and salt. Add the reserved tamarind liquid and mix again. Bring to a boil, then add the mixture to the dal.

Bring the dal to a boil, reduce the heat to low, and let cook at a gentle simmer for 10 to 15 minutes, until the shallots are very soft. Adjust the consistency of the dal with more water, if you wish. Mix in the coriander leaves; serve hot.   SERVES 6

Serve with Home-Style Dosas (page 112) or Semolina Uppuma (page 92) or as a dal with rice, along with a vegetable such as Spiced Grated Carrots, Kerala Style (page 143) or a stir-fried green (say, Pea Shoots for a Crowd, page 161), and a chutney or sambol.

SAMBHAR POWDER

The spice blend used to flavor *sambhar,* this is fun to make. There's the great smell of all the seeds roasting, and then they smell doubly good when you grind them. If you like *sambhar* as much as we do, you'll be making this often.

1/2 cup coriander seeds
1/2 cup dried red chiles
1 teaspoon black peppercorns
1 teaspoon cumin seeds
One 1-inch piece cinnamon or cassia stick
1 tablespoon toovar dal, or substitute masur dal

Heat a small cast-iron skillet over medium-high heat. Toast each ingredient separately (because they cook at different rates), until well browned and aromatic, then transfer to a medium bowl. When all are toasted, use a spice/coffee grinder (you will probably have to work in batches) or a mortar and a pestle to grind them fine. Let the powder cool completely before storing it in a well-sealed glass jar.   MAKES 3/4 CUP

UDAIPUR URAD DAL

· · · · · · · · · · · ·

Sangana Bai's family in Udaipur (see "My First Tandoor," page 128) showed me this simple and pleasing way to flavor dal. Their staple was urad dal, which they cooked quickly in a pressure cooker, without added flavorings, then spiced later in this easy way. You can begin with 1 cup raw urad dal, as here, or with 3 to 4 cups cooked urad dal (or any dal or lentil you prefer), and flavor it as in the variation.

1 cup urad dal, washed

7 cups water

¼ cup raw sesame oil or vegetable oil

1 teaspoon black mustard seeds

5 black peppercorns

½ cup minced onion

1 green cayenne chile, minced

½ teaspoon turmeric

½ to 1 teaspoon cayenne

1½ teaspoons salt

½ teaspoon garam masala (page 342 or store-bought)

About ¼ cup coarsely chopped coriander leaves

Place the dal in a heavy pot with 6 cups of the water and bring to a vigorous boil. Skim off the foam. Cover almost completely, lower the heat to maintain a strong boil without causing it to boil over, and cook until the dal is very tender and broken down, 1¼ to 1½ hours. (You will have 3 to 4 cups cooked dal.) Set aside.

Heat the oil in a medium heavy pot over medium-high heat. When it is hot, add the mustard seeds and cover until they pop, then toss in the peppercorns, onion, and chile. Lower the heat to medium and cook gently, stirring occasionally, for 10 minutes, or until the onion is tender and starting to brown.

Add the turmeric, cayenne, and salt, and stir in. Pour in the cooked dal and the remaining 1 cup water. Raise the heat and bring to a boil. Stir in the garam masala, then lower the heat and simmer for a few minutes to blend the flavors.

Transfer to a serving bowl, stir in the coriander, and serve hot.

SERVES 4 TO 5

Serve with Chapatis (page 110) or other flatbreads, and accompany with a salad such as Fresh White Radish Slices with Salt (page 54) or Cachoombar (page 57). We also like serving this dal as part of a rice meal with several vegetable side dishes.

GUJARATI DAL: In Ahmadabad, Riku (see page 40) showed me her basic home-style dal. Like many Gujarati foods, it has a subtle balance of hot, sweet, and tart, with flavors mild rather than punchy, and it contains no garlic or onion. Start with about 4 cups cooked urad dal (as above) or toovar dal. Mash to a loose puree with a potato masher, or use a food processor. Transfer to a medium pot and add ½ teaspoon cayenne, ½ teaspoon turmeric, 1 teaspoon ground coriander, 2 teaspoons chopped jaggery (palm or crude sugar) or brown sugar, 1 teaspoon salt, and ½ cup unsalted boiled peanuts (see Glossary). Stir and bring just to a simmer over low heat.

Meanwhile, heat 2 tablespoons vegetable oil in a small heavy skillet over medium-high heat. When it is hot, add 1 teaspoon black mustard seeds. Let them pop, then add ½ teaspoon fenugreek seeds, ¼ teaspoon ground cinnamon, a pinch of ground cloves, a pinch of asafoetida powder, 2 pieces fish tamarind (see Glossary, or substitute the liquid from 1 teaspoon softened and strained tamarind pulp), 2 dried red chiles, and 1 cup chopped tomatoes. Cook for several minutes, stirring frequently, until the tomatoes are starting to soften, then add ½ cup chopped coriander and pour into the dal. Add another 1 cup water to thin it a little, then simmer until the flavors have blended, another 5 minutes or so. Taste for salt and adjust if necessary.

Serve with Cumin-Flecked Skillet Breads (page 126) or Chapatis (page 110), as well as with plain rice. Put out Gujarati Mango Chutney (page 40) as an accompaniment if you have some on hand, or mix up a batch of Tart Mango Salsa (page 48).

DAL WITH COCONUT MILK

· · · · · · · · · · · ·

Masur dal (the little red-orange one that cooks quickly) is the most common dal used in Sri Lanka, popular with everyone. While there is a wide variety of dals and legumes for sale in the market, the others don't have as big a role in the cuisine here as they do in India.

This particular version of masur dal is modeled after one that I used to eat almost every day, long ago in a little Tamil restaurant in Kandy. For a light lunch I would stop in and order dal and bread (a not-so-bad loaf of crusty white wheat bread), and then I would dunk pieces of bread in my dal as if it were split pea soup. Even late in the afternoon, or midmorning, I could always count on this particular restaurant to have bread and dal, simple and good.

The only drawback to the restaurant was that it had wooden benches, so early on I learned to always carry a newspaper, and before I sat down, I would first put down my newspaper. Wooden benches in Sri Lanka, like wicker chairs, were often home to a tiny little ant (so tiny I never even managed to see one) that would bite my thighs (sarongs are easy to bite through), and then the bites would swell and swell until three-quarters of the back of my thigh was inflamed. The first time it happened I thought some terrible disaster had befallen me, but everyone around me started to laugh, and then someone told me not to worry. The swelling soon goes down, but it itches. A newspaper works well as prevention.

1 cup masur dal, washed
5 cups water

TEMPERING
1 tablespoon vegetable oil
1 tablespoon minced garlic or garlic mashed to a paste
2 tablespoons minced shallots or red onion
6 to 8 fresh or frozen curry leaves
2 to 3 dried red chiles
1 teaspoon ground coriander
1 teaspoon salt
1 cup canned or fresh coconut milk

Put the dal in a medium pot with the water. Bring to a boil, reduce the heat to a low simmer, and cook for 20 minutes. Keep warm over low heat.

Heat a wok or karhai (see Glossary) or a heavy skillet over medium-high heat, then add the oil. Toss in the garlic and shallots or onion and stir-fry for 2 minutes. Add the curry leaves, red chiles, and ground coriander, mix well, and cook for another 2 minutes. Stir in the salt and coconut milk, then lower the heat and simmer for 5 minutes.

Add the tempering mixture to the hot dal and simmer for a few minutes to blend the flavors. If you prefer a thicker texture, allow the dal to cook for a little longer. Serve hot.   SERVES 4

Serve with rice and Fresh Bean Sprout Salad (page 55) or a green salad or simple cooked green vegetable.

Dal with Coconut Milk alongside Fresh Bean Sprout Salad (page 55)

We weren't able to get back to Pakistan in the last three years, while we were working on this book. Naomi was set to go to Lahore, but as time got close for going, people whose opinions we trust said no, don't go—it's not safe or smart for a foreigner to be out with a camera, wandering around, not now. We kept thinking that maybe things would change, and they have, but very slowly.

Relations between India and Pakistan have improved dramatically, though. We were in India in March 2004, when Pakistan hosted the first series of cricket matches between India and Pakistan to be played in the Subcontinent in fifteen years. The papers were full of it. Everyone was delighted. The matches were televised, and every other day for more than a week, millions of pairs of eyes in both countries watched intently and appreciatively as India and Pakistan squared off. It seemed so silly not to go, just across the border. It probably would be safe, we thought. But we might not *feel* safe, and we always feel safe in the Subcontinent.

Years before, in 1986, we'd traveled into Pakistan by bicycle from China, through Hunza and the northern territories. On the road we'd bicycled across large letters painted in red, USA DEAD, but we'd never felt afraid, not at all. Northern Pakistan was one of the most beautiful and amazing places we'd ever seen, a place where we could touch with our hands rocks that had crashed into each other when the two continents had collided (see page 8), stone against stone, in all directions. Northern Pakistan was a bit of a dream, with its precious patches of irrigated green against the gravel and rock walls of the valleys, its stone water mills, its tenacious villagers. We watched the full moon rise over Mount Rakaposhi, we waded through glacial streams, we breathed in dry mountain air that was perfumed with the scents of wild roses and Russian olive trees in bloom.

When we got out of the mountains, life was more complicated, as it usually is. The Afghan war in the 1980s had destabilized life in Pakistan. America had put in billions of dollars, and once the war was over, the money disappeared overnight. There were millions of Afghan refugees living inside Pakistan, and the international community mostly looked in other directions. People were angry, with cause. But we never felt fearful. People engaged with us—it's the Subcontinent. We were invited into people's homes, into people's lives. We took photographs, we ate great food, we laughed, listened, we drank chai and smoked *chillums*, and we left with a very big soft spot for Pakistan, a remarkable country.

In Pakistan's Hunza Valley, the hillsides of the Karakoram Mountains are bare stone and sand, the peaks topped with snow. Wherever there is a stream coming down from the glaciers above, people have created irrigation channels and built terraces on which they cultivate wheat and apricots and vegetables, turning the barrenness green.

PAKISTAN

In the mountains of the Subcontinent, people walk or use pack animals. This small boy is in Ladakh, just two mountain passes away from northern Pakistan.
OPPOSITE: *Easy Karnataka Chana (page 196).*

This simple dal, called *bele potole*, can be served as a soup, or else as a dal to accompany rice or flatbreads. You can use large North American–style pale chickpeas (garbanzos, known in the Subcontinent as *kabuli chana*) or the smaller brown split chickpeas sold in South Asian groceries.

If you grind the soaked chickpeas to a coarse paste in a food processor, they will cook much more quickly than whole chickpeas do. In contrast to most dal recipes, here the dal is tempered with flavored oil before it is cooked (similar to the European tradition in which a soup begins with aromatic flavorings cooked in broth or olive oil). Then the water is added and the whole dish comes together as a simmered pale yellow soup. It contains no onion or garlic, just asafoetida powder, chiles, and cumin.

PHOTOGRAPH ON PAGE 195

1 cup chickpeas (see headnote), soaked overnight,
    or for at least 4 hours, in 4 cups water and drained
4¼ cups water (plus up to 3 cups if serving as a soup)
1 teaspoon ground cumin
4 green cayenne chiles, minced
3 tablespoons vegetable oil
1 teaspoon black mustard seeds
Pinch of asafoetida powder
½ teaspoon turmeric
½ to 1 teaspoon cayenne
About 1½ teaspoons salt
About ½ cup chopped coriander leaves

Place the chickpeas in a food processor with about ¼ cup water and process to a coarse paste; stop the processor after about 20 seconds and use a rubber spatula to wipe down the sides of the bowl, then replace the lid and continue to process until the texture is even, another 10 to 20 seconds. Add the cumin and chiles and pulse several times to blend, then turn into a bowl and set aside.

In a deep heavy pot, heat the oil over medium-high heat. When the oil is hot, add the mustard seeds and cover until they stop popping. Quickly add the asafoetida, turmeric, and cayenne and stir, then pour in the dal mixture; it will spatter a little as it hits the hot pan. Stir-fry for a moment to expose all the dal to the hot oil.

Add the remaining 4 cups water and stir to blend to an even consistency until the mixture comes to a boil. Lower the heat, cover, and simmer for about 45 minutes, or until the dal is cooked through, stirring from time to time to prevent it from sticking. If serving as a soup, add up to 3 cups more water, as you like, and bring to a boil.

Stir in the salt and simmer for a few minutes longer. Taste and adjust the seasonings (if you added the extra water, you will probably need to add salt). The dish can be set aside, covered, at this point for up to 4 hours. Reheat just before serving—stir in a little water and bring to a boil, stirring occasionally.

Stir in the coriander and serve.   MAKES 4 CUPS THICK DAL
OR 7 CUPS SOUP; SERVES 4 AS A DAL, 6 AS A SOUP

Serve as a dal with rice and a green vegetable or salad, or as a soup with any tender flatbread, perhaps followed by a substantial salad or a vegetable dish such as Aromatic Pumpkin and Coconut (page 160) or Hasna Begum's Mixed Vegetable Curry (page 164).

TOOVAR DAL WITH GREEN MANGO

. . . .

This is a close approximation of a toovar dal dish I first tasted in a small village restaurant in mountainous Orissa, in the eastern part of India. The restaurant had two or three wooden tables and a thatched roof, and there was no choice about what to eat for lunch, only lunch itself. All I had to do was to sit down and lunch arrived, served on a beautiful "plate" made of round *sal* leaves knitted together with tiny slivers of wood. My meal was rice, a green mango dal, a mutton curry, and a lime pickle. Everything was full of flavor, but not fussy. It was no surprise to see mangoes in the dal, because in the lush subtropical mountains of Orissa in late February, giant mango trees are everywhere, and green mangoes are beyond abundant.

The first time we made this dal at home, we used mangoes that were half ripe, and they were perfect. The mangoes' tart taste complements the dal beautifully.

³/₄ cup toovar dal, washed and picked over

6 to 7 cups water

¹/₂ teaspoon turmeric

1 large green mango (³/₄ to 1 pound), peeled, pitted,
   and cut into ¹/₂-inch dice

1 teaspoon salt

TEMPERING

2 tablespoons raw sesame oil or vegetable oil

1 tablespoon minced garlic or garlic mashed to a paste

1 teaspoon minced ginger or ginger mashed to a paste

1 cup finely chopped onion

2 to 3 green cayenne chiles, finely chopped

¹/₂ teaspoon cumin seeds

Put the dal in a heavy pot with 6 cups water and the turmeric, and bring to a strong boil. Reduce the heat to maintain a strong simmer, partially cover, and continue to cook the dal for 50 minutes to an hour, looking in on it occasionally while it cooks to make sure there's enough water and adding water if necessary, until the dal is well cooked, almost mushy.

Add the mango and salt, and stir. Raise the heat to medium-high, bring to a boil, and cook for about 10 minutes, stirring frequently, until the mango is tender. Reduce the heat to a low simmer. (The dal can be made ahead to this point and set aside, covered, until you are ready to proceed. If the wait will be more than 2 hours, cool to room temperature, then refrigerate. Place over low heat when you are ready to proceed and bring to a simmer; the dal will have thickened, so you may want to stir in another cup or so of water.)

Heat the oil in a medium heavy skillet over medium-high heat. When it is hot, add the garlic, ginger, onion, chiles, and cumin seeds. Stir-fry for about 7 minutes, until the onions are soft and a little brown, then turn out into the dal.

Stir well, then heat the dal for 2 to 3 minutes to blend the flavors. Serve hot.　　　　SERVES 4 AS A MAIN COURSE, 6 AS A SIDE DISH

Serve as a main course with rice or flatbreads and a vegetable side such as Spiced Tender Chopped Bindi (page 168). Or, for a larger meal, serve with rice, a stir-fried green vegetable, and Tiger Shrimp with Onions (page 211) or Ginger-Lamb Coconut Milk Curry (page 261), the sweetness of which will balance the green mango nicely.

PEPPER-TAMARIND BROTH

. . . .

I remember the first few times I tasted *rasam*, this thin broth from southern India. It was always served at the start of a large fabulous meal, and I remember wondering afterward why, in a meal with so many different tastes and textures, did we start by drinking this rather acidic pepper water? Compared to all the other great tastes in the meal, it seemed a little unimportant.

But after a while it started to grow on me, as I think it grows on everyone. Now I love it, and if it is not included in a South Indian meal, I miss it. In southern India, it is said to be important in aiding digestion, and while I'm sure that's right, it also makes for a pleasurable and distinctive start to a meal.

1/4 cup toovar dal, washed and picked over

3 1/2 cups water

2 tablespoons tamarind pulp, cut into pieces

1/2 cup hot water

1 1/2 cups diced tomatoes

1/4 teaspoon asafoetida powder

2 1/2 teaspoons Rasam Powder (page 199 or store-bought)

1/2 teaspoon salt

TEMPERING

2 teaspoons raw sesame oil or vegetable oil

1 teaspoon black mustard seeds

1/2 teaspoon cumin seeds

4 to 5 fresh or frozen curry leaves

1 red cayenne chile, stemmed and slit lengthwise

About 1/4 cup chopped coriander leaves

Place the dal in a heavy pot with 2 cups of the water and bring to a boil, then partially cover and lower the heat to maintain a strong simmer. Simmer for an hour or a little more, until very soft, stirring occasionally.

Meanwhile, place the tamarind pulp in a small bowl with the hot water. Stir, then let stand for 15 minutes.

Rub the tamarind to help it dissolve in the water, place a sieve over a wide medium pot, and press the tamarind liquid through it into the pot; discard the pulp. Add the tomatoes, asafoetida, *rasam* powder, salt, and the remaining 1 1/2 cups water and bring to a boil, then reduce the heat to medium and simmer for about 15 minutes. The tomatoes should have dissolved into the liquid; mash with a spoon or potato masher to help pulverize them if necessary. Remove from the heat.

Add the dal and cooking liquid to the tomato mixture. Bring to a boil, then reduce the heat to low and let simmer while you prepare the tempering.

Heat a small heavy skillet over medium-high heat. Add the oil, and when it is hot, add the mustard seeds, cumin, curry leaves, and chile. Once the mustard seeds have popped, lower the heat to medium and stir-fry for another 15 seconds or so. Pour the oil and flavorings into the hot *rasam*, stir well, taste for salt, and adjust if necessary. Simmer for another few minutes. Serve hot in small soup bowls, sprinkled with coriander leaves.   SERVES 4 TO 6

Serve as a soup before a rich main course of meat or a coconut milk–based curry such as Pomfret in Coconut Milk Sauce (page 208). Or put it out as one of several dishes in a vegetarian rice meal. Because rasam *is tart and peppery, you'll want a balancing mild to sweet dish such as Spicy Banana-Yogurt Pachadi (page 70) or Carrots with Tropical Flavors (page 166).*

RASAM POWDER

1/2 cup dried red chiles, stemmed

1/2 cup coriander seeds

2 tablespoons cumin seeds

2 tablespoons black mustard seeds

1 1/2 teaspoons black peppercorns

1 tablespoon urad dal

In a small heavy cast-iron skillet dry roast each ingredient in turn (since times will vary), over medium-high heat, stirring frequently to prevent burning, until fragrant and starting to brown. Turn out into a small bowl. Transfer the spices to a spice/coffee grinder or a large stone mortar (you may have to work in batches) and grind to a fine powder. Let cool completely before storing in a well-sealed glass jar.

MAKES ABOUT 1 CUP

Street vendor on a crowded street in Kolkata (Calcutta)

FISH & SHELLFISH

of coastline, not to mention island nations like Sri Lanka and the

Maldives, so seafood is locally available to many people. The Indian

Ocean, Bay of Bengal, and Andaman Sea all provide seafood, while

the rivers large and small that drain the Subcontinent are also

Large shrimp from Sri Lanka

In 1977, I lived for five months in Thiruvananthapuram (then called Trivandrum), the capital city of the southern state of Kerala in India. I was not far from Palayam Market, the city's second-largest outdoor food market and quite a beautiful one. On my side of the market was the fish section. When I walked to the market, I would deliberately take a longer route that circled around and missed the fish. In the very hot, humid Kerala weather, the fish section had an unbelievably difficult smell, at least for me, the uninitiated. Almost the entire section was made up of individual stalls selling dried and salted fish, and because there was a lot of fish, it was a big smell!

Eighteen years later, when I first went back for a visit, I went for a walk through Palayam Market and felt that something was very different. The market was as beautiful as ever, even more beautiful. The tons and tons of green bananas, the fresh coconuts, the huge hunks of manioc, and the stacks of fresh okra, they were all still there. But then I realized what was different:

The smell of dried fish was gone. I walked into the fish section and there discovered fresh fish, fish on ice, and local refrigerated transport trucks. The dried fish market had become a fresh fish market.

For now, the biggest eaters of fish and shellfish in the Subcontinent are those who live near an ample year-round source and who are not vegetarians: Keralans; Goans; Bengalis, both those in Bangladesh and from Indian Bengal; and Sri Lankans. Consequently, the dishes in this chapter come from Bangladesh and Bengal, Kerala, Goa, and Sri Lanka.

There's a whole baked fish from Goa flavored with a fresh herb chutney and a Kerala specialty that simmers whole pomfret in a coconut milk–enriched sauce. There are stir-fries, grills, and simmered curries. Some call for whole fish, others begin with fish steaks or fillets. Fish steaks may be rubbed with spices and then grilled, or fried with spices and then simmered. Other dishes include a quick shrimp and green chile stir-fry, and a lush shrimp and coconut milk curry from Sri Lanka.

One day when we were in Rawalpindi, in Pakistan, all the shops were closed because there was a political demonstration in support of Benazir Bhutto. This man had found a place to sit and watch the action.

BAKED GOAN FISH
WITH FRESH GREEN CHILE CHUTNEY

. . . .

This is a great way of cooking a whole fish. It's flavored with a fresh green chutney, wrapped in foil, and baked. Start with a cleaned whole firm-fleshed fish, about two pounds, preferably with the head on (it's more attractive, and also helps keep the stuffing inside). In Goa we ate small kingfish prepared this way. We make it with pickerel or with red snapper (the pink skin is always so beautiful next to green herbs).

Make up a quick batch of the chutney, then cut a slit along either side of the backbone and push the stuffing in there, as well as in the fish's cavity. The fish is wrapped in foil, placed on a rimmed baking sheet (to catch any leaks), and oven baked; in Goa, the fish is usually wrapped in banana leaves and baked in the ashes of a fire.

The hot pan juices are delicious drizzled over rice, or you can serve the whole dish at room temperature after chilling it for some hours. Leftovers are a bonus; the pan juices jell in the refrigerator and then both fish and jelled sauce make a great topping for hot rice or for bread.

PHOTOGRAPH ON PAGE 207

One 1³/₄- to 2-pound firm-fleshed fish, such as pickerel, trout,
or red snapper (see headnote), cleaned and scaled
About ¹/₄ cup vegetable oil
About 2 tablespoons fresh lime or lemon juice
About 1 tablespoon fine sea salt
About ¹/₂ cup Fresh Green Chile Chutney (page 205),
plus extra to serve as a condiment

Place a rack in the center of the oven and preheat the oven to 400°F.

Wash and dry the fish. Cut a slit along each side of the backbone down the length of the fish. Place a large sheet of foil on a rimmed baking sheet (or in a large roasting pan). Pour about 3 tablespoons oil on the part of the sheet where the fish will lie, and set near your work surface.

Rub the fish all over with the lime or lemon juice, then with the salt. Stuff some of the chutney into the slits and put the remainder in the fish's cavity. Lay the fish on the foil. Pour on the remaining 1 tablespoon oil and spread it over the top of the fish. Wrap the foil fairly tightly around the fish; use another piece of foil if necessary to ensure that the package is well sealed.

Bake for about 30 minutes; time will depend on the size and thickness of the fish. To test, peel back the foil a little and press on the flesh at the thickest part of the fish. It should yield a little and feel soft. The other test is to unwrap more of the fish and test the texture of the flesh: If the flesh flakes with a fork, it is cooked.

Serve the fish warm or at room temperature, with extra chutney alongside as a condiment. Serve by lifting sections of the top fillet off the bone; when the first side is finished, flip the fish over to serve the second fillet.

To serve the fish warm, open the foil and let stand for 10 minutes, then transfer the fish to a platter (flip it off the foil). Pour the pan juices into a small jug, so they can be drizzled onto each serving. *Alternatively, let the fish cool to room temperature* with the foil open, then wrap again tightly in the foil and refrigerate overnight, or for at least 4 hours. When it is chilled, the pan juices around the fish thicken to a jelly, beautiful bright green in color and with a wonderful flavor blend; the fish is firm and holds its shape well. Bring back just to room temperature before serving.   SERVES 4

Serve hot as the centerpiece of a rice meal (rice soaks up the pan juices beautifully), accompanied by a vegetable such as Spiced Grated Carrots, Kerala Style (page 143) or Spiced Cabbage Salad (page 77), as well as some simple sliced tomatoes. Or serve after chilling, accompanied by hot rice—or, less traditionally, serve the fish on toast or on sections of warm Home-Style Tandoor Naan (page 116).

FRESH GREEN CHILE CHUTNEY

The fresh flavors in this chutney are a treat. Use it to stuff a whole fish, or as a condiment for grilled fish or grilled chicken, or as a simple topping for rice. If you use the six green chiles called for, the sauce is quite hot, though the coconut softens the impact of the chiles. Traditionally the chutney is made using a mortar and a pestle, but this is one case where a food processor is not only easier, but also does just as good a job of reducing the ingredients to a salsa texture.

About 2 cups coriander leaves and stems

6 green cayenne chiles, coarsely chopped (see headnote)

6 to 10 medium garlic cloves, chopped

2 teaspoons minced ginger or ginger mashed to a paste

About 1 cup fresh or frozen grated coconut

1 teaspoon cumin seeds

About 3 tablespoons fresh lime juice, or substitute lemon juice

1 teaspoon sugar

1 teaspoon salt, or to taste

Place the coriander, chiles, garlic, and ginger in a food processor and process to a paste. Add the coconut and process to incorporate. Transfer to a bowl.

Briefly grind the cumin seeds with a mortar and a pestle or a spice/coffee grinder, not to a powder but to crush them a little, then add to the chile mixture. Stir in the lime (or lemon) juice, sugar, and salt, then taste for salt and adjust as necessary. Serve or use immediately, or refrigerate, covered, until ready to serve. The chutney will keep for about 4 days in a well-sealed container in the refrigerator.

MAKES A GENEROUS 1 CUP

With practice, you can carry large or heavy loads on your head, using your neck and spine to support the weight. Both these images are from Udaipur, in southern Rajasthan: On the left, a woman carries a stack of brass pots full of water from a neighborhood tap to her house. On the right, men unload a truck at the market.

Women carrying firewood from where they gathered it, near Palolem beach in Goa, to their village several miles away. RIGHT: *Baked Goan Fish with Fresh Green Chile Chutney (page 204), using red snapper, ready to be wrapped in a banana leaf and baked.*

POMFRET IN COCONUT MILK SAUCE

. . . .

I spent time hanging around in Mrs. Asha Abraham's kitchen in Kochi (formerly Cochin) in Kerala. She ran the guesthouse on Lily Street where we stayed, and she was a good cook. Because she and her husband had worked in the Gulf, they'd earned enough money to come back and open the guesthouse in Mr. Abraham's family home. His widowed sister lived with them. The kitchen was equipped with a blender and several other labor-saving tools, as well as a traditional coconut scraper.

In the rest of India, people in Kerala are known as fish eaters. And because India has a strong vegetarian tradition, it's not unusual to come across articles in the newspaper that talk about how bad or unhealthy it is that Keralans eat so much fish. Most Keralans would disagree. In any case, the tradition has resulted in a large number of inventive fish dishes, among them this coconut milk curry that is known there, in English, as *fish malli*.

Pomfret, a thick-bodied sea fish with firm rich flesh, is one of the most highly prized fishes along the Kerala coast. It looks almost like a child's drawing of a fish, with a nearly circular body that is pointed slightly at the mouth end, its tail a fine arc at the other. It has a flat wide backbone, so the flesh lifts off easily and it is easy to eat, even for those who shy away from fish because they don't like dealing with bones.

Pomfret are now available frozen whole (uncleaned) in Asian grocery stores, clearly labeled. The ones we've found are about a pound and a half each. If you find smaller ones, use two fish. You can substitute pompano, which is easier to find and is also a delicious fish; use two smallish pompano, weighing a total of about two pounds. (You could instead use a whole lake trout or whole snapper.) To defrost the pomfret, bring it out of the freezer and place in the refrigerator twenty-four hours before you wish to serve it. We've been astonished at how long it takes to defrost; the flesh is dense and the fish is rather thick, so it's slow to change temperature. Once the fish has defrosted, it's easy to clean.

Mrs. Abraham's method calls for the fish to be marinated for twenty minutes, then cooked in a richly flavored sauce. We have included her full recipe, but we confess that we generally skip the marinade, for the flavors of the sauce penetrate well during cooking. Cooking time is about 45 minutes total.

FISH AND OPTIONAL MARINADE

One 1¹⁄₂- to 2-pound pomfret, fresh or defrosted (see headnote), cleaned and scaled, or substitute two 1-pound pompano or other firm-fleshed whole fish

1 tablespoon coarsely chopped ginger

1 teaspoon coarsely chopped garlic

Scant ¹⁄₂ cup coarsely chopped shallots

Salt

3 to 4 tablespoons water

SAUCE

3 tablespoons ghee or vegetable oil, or a blend

2 cups coarsely chopped onions

¹⁄₂ cup thinly sliced garlic

¹⁄₄ cup thinly sliced ginger

8 green cayenne chiles, halved lengthwise and seeded

¹⁄₄ teaspoon freshly ground black pepper

About 1 cup coarsely chopped tomatoes

About ¹⁄₄ cup fresh or frozen curry leaves

2 teaspoons turmeric

2 teaspoons ground cumin

1 teaspoon salt, or to taste

2 cups canned coconut milk, divided equally into the thinner and thicker milk, or 1 cup "second pressing" and 1 cup "first pressing" fresh coconut milk (see Note, page 261)

¹⁄₂ to 1 cup water

¹⁄₂ cup coarsely chopped coriander leaves

Scant ¹⁄₂ cup coarsely chopped mint leaves

Wash the fish thoroughly. If it has not been gutted, cut along the belly line from an inch below the mouth all the way back to the tail, cutting in until you reach the abdominal cavity. Scrape out and discard the stomach and intestines, and wash the fish again thoroughly (see Note). Set the fish aside on a plate or platter.

If using the marinade, place the ginger, garlic, shallots, and 1 teaspoon salt in a blender or a mortar. If using a blender, add a generous 1/4 cup water and blend to a smooth paste. If using a mortar and a pestle, pound and grind to a paste, using several tablespoons of water to help make a paste. You will have just over 1/2 cup paste. Rub the paste all over the fish, inside and out. You will have some paste left over; set it aside.

If not using the marinade, rub the fish all over with salt, using a little less than 2 teaspoons.

Set the fish aside, covered, while you make the sauce.

Heat the ghee and/or oil in a wide heavy pot (we use a large Le Creuset pot) over medium-high heat. Add the onions and stir, then add the sliced garlic and ginger, chiles, pepper, and the reserved marinade paste if you made it. Cook over medium-high heat for a minute, stirring, then lower the heat to medium and continue cooking until the smell of the spices rises out of the pot and the onions are very soft, about 10 more minutes. Add the chopped tomatoes and cook for 4 to 5 minutes, until softened. Toss in half the curry leaves, then add the turmeric, ground cumin, and salt and stir in.

Add the 1 cup thinner (or second-pressing) coconut milk and 1/2 cup water and bring to a boil. Stir in the coriander and mint. Lay the fish (and any paste clinging to it) in the pot and bring back to a boil. Add the 1 cup thicker (or first-pressing) coconut milk and the remaining curry leaves and bring back to a boil, then reduce the heat and simmer gently, uncovered, until the fish is cooked through, about 20 minutes; if the fish is not completely immersed in the sauce, you will need to turn it over after about 10 minutes. If the sauce thickens as it simmers, becoming very pastelike, add a little water, up to 1/2 cup additional, to make it more liquid.

Serve the fish on a platter with the sauce poured over. The flesh lifts off the bone easily.   SERVES 3 TO 4

Serve with plenty of rice to soak up the sauce. This is best with a simple accompaniment, such as a fresh green salad or a Sri Lankan mallum, such as Shredded Green Bean Mallum (page 76).

MOGHUL-TASTING MALLI: Mrs. Abraham added about 8 cloves and a 1- to 2-inch cassia stick to the sauce when she added the thicker coconut milk. We have made the dish both ways. The cloves and cassia (or use a cinnamon stick) taste a little sharp to us, and also foreign, like northern additions to a Kerala dish, so we prefer it without them. You may very well disagree, though, so don't hesitate to try it Mrs. Abraham's way.

NOTE: After cleaning the fish, Mrs. Abraham soaked it in a vinegar bath, a traditional way of making sure the fish is clean. If you want to try it, here's the method: Combine 1/2 cup vinegar and 1 1/2 cups water in a wide bowl or deep nonreactive platter. Add 1 tablespoon salt and stir to dissolve, then place the fish in the solution for 5 minutes. Turn over and let stand for another 5 minutes. Remove from the vinegar bath and rinse off, then proceed with the recipe.

Mrs. Abraham keeps her chopped onion, tomato, and herbs in cold water to keep them fresh in the Kerala heat until she's ready to add them to the pot.

A temple priest in Thiruvananthapuram (Trivandrum) giving water to an elephant that is kept on the grounds of the temple complex

GRILLED FISH STEAKS
WITH BLACK PEPPER RUB

. . . .

We think that when grilling fish, simplest is best. Here the fish steaks (use any fish you like, from tuna to cod to salmon) are rubbed with salt and a generous amount of black pepper, then brushed with turmeric-tinted coconut milk. They stay wonderfully moist.

2 pounds fish steaks (see headnote)

1 teaspoon salt

About 1 teaspoon coarsely ground black pepper

1 teaspoon turmeric

About ½ cup canned or fresh coconut milk

Heat a charcoal or gas grill. If using charcoal, wait until you have a good bed of coals. Wash the fish steaks in cold water, then wipe dry.

Mix the salt and pepper together and rub onto the fish. Stir the turmeric into the coconut milk. Brush some of the coconut milk onto the fish. Set the fish and remaining coconut milk aside.

Brush the grill rack with oil and put the fish steaks on to cook. Grill until tender and just cooked through (or leave the center less well done, if you prefer), turning the steaks over once and brushing a little more coconut milk onto the freshly grilled surfaces.　　SERVES 5 TO 6

Serve with rice and a salad or some stir-fried greens.

GRILLED WHOLE FISH WITH BLACK PEPPER RUB: To use this approach with whole fish, start with firm-fleshed fish (we like lake trout), cleaned and scaled. Allow 2 pounds whole fish for 4 people. Wash the fish well and pat it dry. Make several slashes on the flanks of each fish on both sides. Rub all over (inside and out) with the seasoning rub. Brush all over with the coconut milk. Grill over a moderate flame or coals, turning and basting with a little extra coconut milk, as described above, until just cooked through. The fish is done when the flesh flakes when tested with a fork; allow about 10 minutes' cooking per inch of thickness.

TIGER SHRIMP WITH ONIONS

The word for "shrimp" in Bengali is *chingri*, so this is a *chingri jhal*, or stir-fry with shrimp. The base of the dish is mustard oil flavored with whole spices as well as with ginger and garlic. As in many Bangladeshi dishes, this flavored oil is used to stir-fry a generous pile of finely chopped onion. The shrimp go in once the onion has cooked to a softened, aromatic, slightly sweet mass. When cooked, they look like pink jewels dotting the onion. The whole dish takes about twenty minutes' cooking time.

In rainy season in Bangladesh, this would most often be made with freshwater shrimp. During the rest of the year, when the rivers are less swollen and dangerous and the Bay of Bengal is less turbulent, tiger shrimp from the sea, fished in the tidal waters of Bangladesh's great rivers (or, these days, more commonly harvested from fish farms), would be the shrimp of choice. Use any kind of medium-size shrimp.

³/₄ to 1 pound medium shrimp, fresh or frozen

2 tablespoons mustard oil, or substitute vegetable oil

¹/₂ teaspoon fennel seeds

¹/₄ teaspoon nigella seeds

¹/₄ teaspoon cumin seeds

1 stick cinnamon or cassia

1 tablespoon minced garlic or garlic mashed to a paste

1 tablespoon minced ginger or ginger mashed to a paste

1¹/₂ cups packed thinly sliced onions

3 green cayenne chiles, slit lengthwise (for less heat, scrape out the pith and seeds)

¹/₄ cup water

¹/₂ teaspoon salt, or more to taste

Coriander sprigs (optional)

Lime wedges

Rinse, peel, and devein the shrimp. Rinse again and set aside. (If your shrimp are large rather than medium, you may want to cut them in half.) Place the other ingredients near your stove top.

Set a wok or karhai (see Glossary) or a large heavy skillet over medium heat and add the oil. When it is hot, toss in the fennel, nigella, and cumin seeds and the cinnamon stick, and stir-fry for a minute or so, until the spices release their aroma. Toss in the garlic and ginger and stir-fry for about 1 minute. Add the onions and stir-fry for 5 minutes, then lower the heat and cook slowly for another 5 minutes, or until the onions brown a little.

Add the green chiles and stir-fry for about a minute, then raise the heat to high, add the water, and cook, stirring occasionally, until the onions are very soft and most of the liquid has evaporated. (The dish can be made ahead to this point and set aside at room temperature for an hour. Begin again by adding ¹/₄ cup water to the pan, placing it over high heat, and stirring occasionally until the onions are hot, then proceed.)

Add the salt and the shrimp and stir-fry until the shrimp have all changed color, 3 to 8 minutes, depending on the size of your pan, the size of the shrimp, and whether or not you began with hard-frozen shrimp.

Turn out onto a plate, remove the cinnamon stick if you wish, and serve, topped, if you wish, with sprigs of coriander. Put out a plate of lime wedges.

SERVES 2 TO 3

Serve with rice, a small plate of crisp sliced cucumber or white radish (daikon), and a dish to provide a contrast to the sweetness of the shrimp and onion: perhaps Spicy Bitter Melon (page 159), Stir-fried Greens, Bangla Style (page 165), or Bangla Dal with a Hit of Lime (page 178).

LEFT: *Man mending his fishing gear, in Kochi (Cochin), in Kerala, southern India. In the background are the triangular frames that support the Chinese fishing nets so characteristic of Kochi and widely found in Southeast Asia.* RIGHT: *Farther down the Malabar coast, in the fishing village of Vizhinjam, nets are readied for the night's fishing.*

THE DAY THE ELECTRICITY ARRIVED, Felix said, "Tonight we'll have cold drinks!" We'd watched the poles go in, one by one, marching south toward us from Trincomalee. We were staying in one of Felix's small grass-thatched huts on Kalkudah Beach in northeastern Sri Lanka. The communal shower was behind a screen but open to the sky, a lukewarm (warmed by the sun) trickle of fresh water to wash away the day's salt spray. Every night we'd eat fish and rice and vegetables for supper and drink tall glasses of lukewarm juice or water or beer. The fish was always freshly caught, hauled onto the beach in long nets in the morning by gaunt, sun-parched fishermen, and grilled over an open flame by Felix's wife. We never tired of it. We'd sit around talking in the soft light of several candles and a lantern, sharing stories. Sometimes Felix would talk about Sri Lanka, and about his hopes and fears for the future.

Felix was Sinhalese. He'd moved to the mostly Tamil northeast about five years earlier, in 1975, hoping to make a living from his beach huts. He was happy with the life, and his wife and children were also thriving. He was pleased about the electricity, because he was sure it would be good for business.

Felix had already bought a small refrigerator and lightbulbs. He strung some wires in the late afternoon and screwed in the bulbs. When night fell that first night, we sat in the star-dimming brightness of the new electric lights as we drank our cold drinks. We were happy that we still needed to take a candle with us to light the way to bed.

Electricity

Children of Vizhinjam heading home from school along a road lined with coconut palms

PRAWNS BY THE KILO

We are on Palolem Beach in south Goa, a beautiful crescent-shaped beach about a mile long, or maybe closer to two miles. I don't really know how far it is; I've yet to make it to the other end. We like the food here, though we can't say we've tried many restaurants.

I still can't believe we're here. We'd always sworn that we'd never come to Goa, because every traveler to India comes to Goa, it's a cliché of Indian tourism, but here we are. We were in Rajasthan, headed for Nepal, but then a bomb went off in a Kathmandu restaurant, and another in a bank, both in the neighborhood where we intended to stay. The communist insurgency had invaded the city. So we came here instead, a spur-of-the-moment decision.

Already we are big Goa fans. We eat mostly at Rock-it, the restaurant connected to the bungalows where we're staying. It's owned by Clem Fernandes, and the bungalows are owned by his brother Agnel. It doesn't seem polite to stay in Agnel's bungalows and then walk down the beach to eat somewhere else. A lot of other people do, but loyalty seems important here. Anyway, we really like Clem. He's twenty-three years old, full of energy and good humor, and very enterprising. He grew up in the fishing village just beyond the beach. His mother helps keep things running at the restaurant, and his sister and his younger brother too, and there's a teenager named Jai from the village who waits tables with grace and plays Frisbee with the kids in his spare time.

Clem's cook at the restaurant is from Kathmandu, like a lot of cooks in Goa, we're told. He is a good cook, and the food would be much better if Clem would revise the menu. Kathmandu cooks have been cooking "foreigner food" for a long time; they are pros. But don't put Italian, Israeli, German, French, American, South Indian, North Indian, *and* Chinese food on the menu! No cook can do a good job with a menu like that, especially when the kitchen's in the sand and electricity comes and goes like the waves.

Our favorite meal is the tuna, caught fresh every day and grilled. It comes perfectly grilled, moist and delicious. The tuna is so simple and good that we have a hard time ordering anything else. But the other day, by accident, we discovered "staff meal." Staff meal is what everyone in the kitchen eats, and it is different each day, although it is almost always a variety of fish curry, Goan style, served with rice. So now we have a difficult decision every day, deciding between staff meal and tuna.

Yesterday morning Clem arrived from the market with kilos of large fresh prawns. There had been an unusually big catch and the price was way down, so he bought the prawns as a special-occasion treat. For lunch, and again for dinner, everyone at the Rock-it feasted on prawns, grilled or steamed. For staff meal, the cook made a prawn stir-fry. We drank Kingfisher beer, ate staff meal, and had a great day. I wonder what the staff meal will be today.

Boys pulling in a net in Goa. The nets are taken out into the sea, then hauled in by lines of men and boys on the beach, trapping fish as the nets get closer to shore.

CHILE SHRIMP STIR-FRY

· · · · · · · · · · ·

We first tasted these chile-hot shrimps in Goa (see "Prawns by the Kilo," page 214). Later Jeffrey ate a similar chile-hot shrimp dish in Sri Lanka, served as an appetizer with *raksi* (Sri Lankan liquor; see page 311). Back home, we found chile shrimp quick and easy to make, and very tasty (though unfortunately, the *raksi* is nowhere to be found). PHOTOGRAPH ON PAGE 216

1 pound medium shrimp, fresh or frozen

2 tablespoons peanut oil or coconut oil

4 to 6 fresh or frozen curry leaves

1 medium onion, finely chopped

1 tablespoon finely chopped garlic or garlic mashed to a paste

2 to 3 green cayenne chiles, finely chopped, or substitute jalapeños

¼ teaspoon turmeric

1 teaspoon salt

One 1-inch piece cinnamon or cassia stick

1 clove

1 green cardamom pod

About 1 teaspoon lime juice

2 limes cut into wedges

Rinse, peel, and devein the shrimp. Rinse again and set aside.

In a wok or karhai (see Glossary) or a heavy skillet, heat the oil over medium-high heat. Toss in the curry leaves, onion, and garlic and stir-fry until the onion is soft and the garlic has begun to brown, 6 to 7 minutes. Add the chiles, turmeric, salt, cinnamon, clove, and cardamom and stir-fry for 30 seconds. Add the shrimp and stir-fry until they are beautifully pink and just cooked through, 3 to 4 minutes (if they stick as you cook them, add a little water).

Add the lime juice, stir, and serve hot, with the lime wedges on the side. SERVES 4 AS A MAIN DISH, 6 AS AN APPETIZER

Put out as an appetizer or bar snack, or serve as part of a meal with rice, a moist vegetable dish such as Simmered Spiced Soybeans (page 143) or Potato White Curry (page 155), and a salad.

PRAWN WHITE CURRY

· · · · · · · · · · ·

This is a member of the Sri Lankan "white curry" family (see Potato White Curry, page 155). In typical South Asian fashion, food is never wasted, and the heads and shells of the shrimp are traditionally ground and added to the curry for depth of flavor (or they are ground to a paste, then sun dried or dried in an oven, to be added to another dish). We aren't so conscientious (though we should be), but still this prawn curry comes out tasting great. It's an ideal main course served with rice and a vegetable or two. PHOTOGRAPH ON PAGE 17

About 1 pound medium prawns, fresh or frozen

6 to 10 fresh or frozen curry leaves

1 tablespoon minced garlic or garlic mashed to a paste

1 teaspoon salt

¼ teaspoon ground fenugreek

1 cup canned or fresh coconut milk

1 cup water

3 green cayenne chiles, finely chopped

⅓ cup minced shallots

1 teaspoon minced ginger or ginger mashed to a paste

¼ teaspoon turmeric

1 large tomato, cut into ½-inch dice

1 to 2 teaspoons fresh lime juice

Rinse, peel, and devein the shrimp. Rinse again, then set aside.

Put all the ingredients except the shrimp and lime juice in a medium heavy pot and bring to a boil over medium-high heat. Lower the heat to medium-low and simmer for 15 minutes, or until the sauce is a little reduced and thickened.

Add the shrimp and cook for 3 to 4 minutes, until they have changed color. Stir in the lime juice and remove from the heat. Taste and adjust the seasonings if necessary. Serve hot. SERVES 4

LEFT: *Near the main market in Ahmadabad, capital of Gujarat, I came upon this child playing with a line of laundry hung in a side lane.*

RIGHT: *Beside the entryway of a house in the old section of Udaipur, the protective imprint of a pair of hands on the wall.*

FISH BOLLE CURRY

. . . .

This is a popular Sri Lankan dish, made in a great many different ways, depending upon where on the island you are and who is cooking. Fish is an all-important part of the cuisine of Sri Lanka, as one would expect on an island. The fish is quickly processed to a paste with curry leaves and chiles, mixed with garlic, ginger, and onions, and then shaped into flavorful aromatic balls. They simmer in an easy coconut milk sauce and then they're done!

1 pound skinless tilapia, halibut, or other white-fleshed fish fillets

3 green cayenne chiles, coarsely chopped

About 6 fresh or frozen curry leaves

1 tablespoon minced garlic or garlic mashed to a paste

1 teaspoon minced ginger or ginger mashed to a paste

¼ cup finely chopped shallots

1 teaspoon salt

SAUCE

1¾ cups water

1 tablespoon ground coriander

2 teaspoons ground fenugreek

¾ cup finely chopped onion

1 tablespoon minced garlic or garlic mashed to a paste

2 red or green cayenne chiles, finely chopped

2 cloves

Seeds from 2 green cardamom pods

¼ cup canned or fresh coconut milk

About 10 fresh or frozen curry leaves

Wash and dry the fish well, and cut into small pieces. Place in a food processor, along with the chiles and curry leaves, and process to a paste. Add the garlic, ginger, shallots, and salt and pulse briefly to blend. Transfer to a medium bowl.

Divide the mixture into 16 portions, then roll each piece lightly between your palms into a ball. Set the balls on a plate.

To make the sauce, pour the water into a wide pot and add the coriander, fenugreek, onion, garlic, chiles, cloves, cardamom seeds, coconut milk, and curry leaves. Bring to a boil, then reduce the heat and simmer until the onions and garlic are very soft, about 15 minutes.

Add the fish balls and simmer for 10 minutes, or until they are cooked through. Serve hot. SERVES 4 TO 5

Serve over rice and accompany with a lightly cooked unsauced green vegetable, such as Pea Tendrils with Coconut (page 71), or a simple chopped salad.

Fish Passions

TALK TO A BENGALI about food and the conversation always turns, sooner rather than later, to fish. The rivers that flow through Bengal are rich in fish and so is the Bay of Bengal. Bengalis are known as eaters of rice and fish; in Bengal even most Hindus, who elsewhere are largely vegetarian, eat fish. The favorite Bengali fish seem to be mostly freshwater varieties. One of the preferred fish is *rui,* a large carp. Carp is widely available in North America, especially in Chinese markets. It has lots of small bones, and perhaps because of that, many people here avoid it. Another, a huge Bengali favorite, available only seasonally, is a rich-fleshed delicious cousin of herring and shad called *hilsa* (or *illsh* in Bengali), also very bony. Fishermen catch it during the monsoon season as it travels upriver from the sea. Unfortunately, it's hard to find outside the Subcontinent. (If you come across *hilsa,* perhaps flash-frozen, do try it, either in Classsic Bengali Fish in Broth, page 223, or else simply lightly rubbed with salt and turmeric and panfried or grilled.)

In the city of Kolkata (Calcutta), many rickshaws are still the old traditional style, pulled by men who run in front of them in the shafts. A number of attempts have been made to banish the rickshaws, but as the rickshaw men point out, they cannot afford a cycle rickshaw and so would have no way to earn a living. The bell on the shaft handle is there to alert passersby that the rickshaw is available for hire or to ring as a warning in traffic. OPPOSITE, LEFT: *Classic Bengali Fish in Broth (page 223).* RIGHT: *Man on the street in the Kalighat area of Kolkata (Calcutta).*

TILAPIA GREEN CURRY

. . . .

Don't be daunted by the length of the ingredient list in this recipe from Kerala. It all comes together without much fuss into a hot, fresh curry sauce bathing bite-size chunks of fish fillets. Choose any fish you like; we suggest tilapia or any firm fish, such as cod. The tempering is added after the fish cooks, as a final flavoring that rounds things out.

About 1¹⁄₂ pounds tilapia or other fish fillets (see headnote)

¹⁄₄ cup coconut oil or vegetable oil

2 teaspoons black mustard seeds

¹⁄₂ cup fresh or frozen curry leaves

2 cups water (1 cup if using tomato)

4 to 6 pieces fish tamarind (see Glossary), or substitute 1 cup chopped (preferably green) tomatoes

1¹⁄₄ teaspoons salt

MASALA PASTE

3 tablespoons chopped ginger

1 tablespoon chopped garlic

¹⁄₂ cup chopped shallots

6 green cayenne chiles, seeded and coarsely chopped

¹⁄₂ cup packed coriander leaves and stems

¹⁄₂ cup fresh or frozen grated coconut, or substitute dried shredded coconut mixed with 1 tablespoon water

1 teaspoon ground coriander

1 teaspoon turmeric

TEMPERING

About 4 tablespoons ghee or butter

4 to 6 fresh or frozen curry leaves

¹⁄₂ cup sliced shallots

2 tablespoons minced garlic or garlic mashed to a paste

3 green cayenne chiles, stemmed and cut in half

Rinse the fish fillets, cut into 2-inch pieces, and set aside.

To prepare the masala paste, place the ginger, garlic, shallots, chiles, and fresh coriander in a food processor, mini-chopper, or stone mortar and process or grind to a coarse paste. Add the coconut and process or grind to a paste (if the mixture seems dry, add a little water as necessary to make a paste). Transfer to a bowl and stir in the ground coriander and turmeric; set aside.

To prepare the tempering, heat the ghee or butter in a medium heavy skillet over medium-high heat. Toss in the curry leaves, wait a moment, then add the shallots and garlic. Lower the heat to medium and cook until starting to soften, for about 4 minutes, stirring occasionally. Add the chiles and cook until the shallots are very soft and touched with brown, about 5 minutes more. Set aside.

Heat the oil in a wok or karhai (see Glossary) or a heavy pot over medium-high heat. Add the mustard seeds, and when they have popped, add the curry leaves and masala paste. Lower the heat to medium and cook, stirring occasionally, until the oil rises to the surface, about 5 minutes. Add the water and fish tamarind or tomatoes and bring to a boil. Add the salt and the fish and simmer, turning the fish once, for 3 to 5 minutes, until just barely cooked through.

Add the tempering mixture and simmer for a minute, then serve hot.

SERVES 4 TO 5

Serve with rice, a vegetable dish such as Spiced Grated Carrots, Kerala Style (page 143), and a fresh salad.

CLASSIC BENGALI FISH IN BROTH

· · · · · · · · · · · ·

This is a deceptively simple Bengali fish and vegetable stew, called *jhol* (meaning "simmered," or "cooked in water"). *Jhol* is served at the main noon meal in many households in Bengal. There's a lot of broth, and flavors are delicate, with some heat from fresh green chiles and a little cayenne as well as from mustard oil. This is a West Bengali version of *jhol*, an adaptation of one that Gita made when we stayed in Kolkata (Calcutta; see Gita's Luchis, page 115). In Bangladesh it would include onions, and the fish would usually not be first panfried. Gita used *bekti*, a large river fish without many bones, that is sold cut up into sections or steaks in the markets in Bengal. It's hard to find here; use cod (our preference) or halibut or tilapia or even salmon, any fish you prefer that will hold together when fried. The dish includes two vegetables. We suggest zucchini (in place of the Bengali *potol* gourd) and Asian eggplant, but you could use thinly sliced potatoes or cauliflower florets instead of the eggplant. PHOTOGRAPH ON PAGE 221

1 to 1¹⁄₂ pounds cod fillets or steaks, or fillets of another firm-fleshed fish
   (see headnote)

1¹⁄₂ to 2 teaspoons salt

1¹⁄₂ teaspoons turmeric

3 to 4 tablespoons mustard oil

3 tablespoons vegetable oil

1 teaspoon Bengali Five-Spice Mixture (page 340) or scant ¹⁄₄ teaspoon
   each black mustard, nigella, fennel, fenugreek, and cumin seeds

1 teaspoon minced ginger or ginger mashed to a paste

¹⁄₂ cup diced tomato

1 cup cubed zucchini

1 cup cubed Asian eggplant (see headnote)

1 teaspoon ground coriander

1 teaspoon ground cumin

¹⁄₄ to ¹⁄₂ teaspoon cayenne

3 cups water

4 or 5 green cayenne chiles, stemmed, seeded, and cut into large pieces

¹⁄₄ to ¹⁄₂ cup chopped coriander leaves

Wash the fish, dry it, and then cut into approximately ³⁄₄-inch pieces. Set on a large plate. In a small bowl, mix together 1 teaspoon each of the salt and turmeric, then sprinkle onto the fish and toss gently to coat; set aside.

Heat 2 tablespoons of the mustard oil in a wok or karhai (see Glossary) or a large heavy skillet over medium-high heat. Add the fish and panfry until just touched with brown (you will probably have to cook in several batches, adding extra oil for each batch), then lift out, pausing to let the excess oil drain off, and set aside on another plate.

Add the vegetable oil and place the pan back over medium-high heat. When the oil is hot, add the spice mixture and stir-fry briefly, then add the ginger and tomato and stir-fry for about 1 minute, until the tomato starts to break down. Toss in the zucchini and eggplant (or other vegetable), and stir-fry for several minutes, until they begin to soften. Add the remaining ¹⁄₂ teaspoon turmeric and the ground coriander, cumin, and cayenne and stir to blend in, then add the water, cover, and bring to a vigorous boil.

Slide in the fish and the chiles, lower the heat, and simmer until the chiles and vegetables are tender, another 5 minutes or so. Stir in the remaining ¹⁄₂ teaspoon salt, then taste for seasoning and adjust if needed.

Remove from the heat and stir in the coriander leaves. Transfer to a serving bowl and serve hot. SERVES 4 TO 5

Serve with plenty of rice, along with an unsauced vegetable such as Spicy Bitter Melon (page 159), Quick Asparagus Stir-fry (page 158), or Bangla-Flavored Grilled Zucchini (page 144), and a dal.

Ocean fishing in the Subcontinent, like fishing in most places in the world, isn't an easy livelihood. The handmade wooden fishing boats and their beautiful black or ochre-colored sails, blown full with the ocean breezes, are a gorgeous sight to those of us watching from the shore, but life on the water is as hard as can be. In the calmer seas of winter, the fishermen go out at night, spending dusk to dawn laboring in the wet and cold while everyone else is asleep. In the monsoon season, when the sea is turbulent and dangerous, the fishermen work the waters and their enormous nets with great difficulty, often with little to show for the effort.

When traveling in the Subcontinent, especially as parents, we've spent our share of time lodging at the beach, taking time to swim and relax, to read and watch sunsets (see "Prawns by the Kilo," page 214), but beach time in the Subcontinent, unlike beach time in some more "resorty" places around the world, isn't all that different from time spent any other place there. Though there are now a few very fancy resorts remote from daily life, most beaches are still places where people live and work.

If you're staying at Kovalam Beach, for example, a popular place just south of Thiruvananthapuram (formerly Trivandrum) in Kerala, you can watch at dawn every morning as groups of fishermen work together to pull in enormous nets. They stand in the shallows and on the beach in two long lines, each line hauling on a heavy rope. The lines start far apart and then gradually come closer together as the net gets pulled toward the shore, corraling the fish that chance and the tides have brought into the bay. (We've seen the same fishing net technique used in northeastern Sri Lanka.) South of Kovalam, walk to the remarkable village of Vizhinjam on its crescent-shaped cove, with a mosque set high on one promontory and a Hindu temple perched on the other. There the fishermen's boats are chockablock the length of the beach, an incredible sight, and Muslim, Hindu, and Christian fishing communities exist side by side along the shore. (If you walk down into the maze of fishing boats pulled up on the sand, beware, because it's filthy, like most fishing beaches.)

It's a very hard life, the fisherman's, beautiful to see, but not always beautiful from the inside looking out.

Men pushing a fishing boat into the water on Thiruvananthapuram (Trivandrum) Beach, in southern Kerala

FISHERMEN

CHICKEN & EGGS

Subcontinent is to get a car and head out into the wonderful vast

world of village life. Villages, just like cuisines, vary tremendously

from region to region, from country to country. The architecture

is different, the agriculture is different, the feel of a village can be

night-and-day different even from the nearest neighboring village.

But for years we spent very little time in villages when we traveled

here. As young travelers on a tight budget, we traveled on buses and, of course, on trains—fifty-four hours by train from Kolkata (Calcutta) to Chennai (Madras), three days by bus from Kathmandu to Delhi, long overnights from Peshawar to Lahore. We'd stare out the windows and watch as villages came and went, almost like blinks of an eye. But we'd almost never set foot in a village except when we were trekking. We could jump off the bus at a little local stop, but more than likely there'd be no hotel, no restaurant, and we wouldn't know exactly how and when to catch another bus to travel on our way, so we never did.

Then one year I went to India with our friend Lee, another photographer. Knowing we could split the cost, on our first morning in Delhi we set off to hire a car. We asked a taxi driver, and he pointed us to a tourist office and the tourist office people picked up a telephone; by lunchtime we had a car, and a driver! We were on the road for three weeks, driving in a loop west and north through Rajasthan, then back eastward in a loop through to Madhya Pradesh and points in Uttar Pradesh.

Girl carrying water in the early morning in southern Kerala

At one point, when we were staying in the agricultural heartland in Khajuraho, a small town in Madhya Pradesh that is famous for its temple carvings, our driver fell sick for a few days. So he just handed us the car keys and wished us good luck. We felt very lucky, in fact. Each day we would drive slowly across the land, stopping outside villages, walking in, and drawing a crowd every time. We learned a lot and came to see the villages with fresh eyes. People were so nice to us, and it was so okay to be there.

Nowadays we seldom make a trip to the Subcontinent without spending at least a little time driving from village to village. The trick is to take the smallest roads, of course, and not to think of making any great distance. The smallest roads aren't really there for cars, anyway. We drive very slowly, along with the oxcarts carrying mountains of hay and the bicycle riders pedaling; and the people on foot, and cows and goats and chickens.

Watch out for the chickens! Chickens are what this chapter is all about, or mostly all about. . . .

We begin with several inventive and easy egg dishes, variants on the scrambled egg/omelet theme. Then there's a grilled marinated chicken from Nepal and a grilled chicken kebab marinated in yogurt. There are several takes on simmered chicken curry—from rural Bangladesh, northern India, Pakistan, and tropical Colombo in Sri Lanka—as well as a Goan vindaloo made with duck. If you can, use free-range birds for these dishes.

Yard-long beans

PERSIAN-FLAVORED EGGS

· · · · · · · · · · · ·

This combination of sweet golden raisins, lightly fried nuts, minced green chiles, and tender scrambled eggs is as good as it is unique. Like Eggs with Curry Leaves, page 234, it's an *akoori*, a Parsi dish. Not surprisingly, it feels like a distant cousin of the Persian baked egg dishes known as *kukuye*, for the Parsis, Zoroastrians who came to India from Persia (Iran) more than eleven centuries ago as religious refugees, have kept their distinctive style of cooking, with mild spicing, generous use of nuts and raisins in savory dishes, and a large number of interesting egg dishes.

The eggs have a mild to medium heat; for more, double the chile quantity, or put out a spicy chutney such as Hot Chile Oil Paste (page 48) as accompaniment.

4 large or extra-large eggs

½ teaspoon salt

1 teaspoon butter

1 generous tablespoon chopped cashews or slivered almonds

2 teaspoons raw sesame oil or vegetable oil or butter

2 green cayenne chiles, seeded and minced

2 teaspoons golden raisins

1 lime, cut into wedges

Break the eggs into a bowl, then use a fork or a whisk to beat them well until smooth and even. Stir in the salt and set aside.

Melt the butter in a heavy 10-inch skillet over medium heat. Add the nuts and cook, stirring to prevent burning, until just golden, 3 to 4 minutes. Lift the nuts out with a slotted spoon and set aside.

Add the oil or butter to the pan. When it is hot, beat the eggs again briefly, then pour the mixture into the pan. Sprinkle on half the chiles. Lower the heat to medium-low and use a wooden spatula to gently fold the cooked outer edges of egg over toward the center, working your way all round the pan and tilting the pan to encourage the liquid uncooked egg at the center to flow out onto the hot pan. Sprinkle on the raisins, and continue to fold over the edges. Toss on most of the nuts, then run the spatula under the mass of eggs and turn it over. Cook briefly, then turn out onto a small serving plate and sprinkle on the remaining nuts and green chile.

Put out the wedges of lime on the side. SERVES 2

Serve as an easy last-minute lunch or light supper, or for brunch, perhaps with Stir-fried Greens, Bangla Style (page 165) or Fresh Bean Sprout Salad (page 55), and tender breads such as Cumin-Flecked Skillet Breads (page 126) or Home-Style Tandoor Naan (page 116).

NOTE: To serve 4 or 5, double all the ingredients. Cook all the nuts together, then cook the eggs in two batches, to make two *akooris;* set the first on a warm plate to wait until the second is cooked, a matter of minutes.

LEFT: *A shrine in Varanasi, near the ghats (see page 56).* RIGHT: *At a rural weekly market in Orissa, a tribal woman cleans dal.* FOLLOWING PAGE: *Hard-boiled egg coated with chile paste (see Hot Chile Oil Paste, page 48) at the market in Kalimpang, a trading town near the Bhutanese border.*

PENNY & FRED

We'd often eat in five different restaurants in one night, Fred and I, and sometimes Penny. We were all in our twenties, all studying at a small neighborhood yoga ashram in Thiruvananthapuram (formerly Trivandrum) in southern Kerala. All morning we'd do hatha yoga, five or six hours every day, so by late afternoon we'd feel really hungry, and that's when we'd start eating. We'd stop only when it was time to go to bed.

Fred was from a small town in British Columbia. He'd been at the ashram for more than a year by the time I arrived, and he was the star pupil. When Guruji, our teacher, was invited to give a presentation at the All-India Yoga Conference in Kolkata (then known as Calcutta), Fred traveled all the way with him by train, four days and three nights, just to perform the headstand in front of hundreds at the conference. He was really good at the headstand.

One night as we sat in a brightly lit restaurant, Fred pulled out his Canadian driver's license and passed it over. He didn't say anything—he didn't have to. The person on the license looked nothing like the person sitting in front of me. The man on the license looked big and burly, beer-guzzling, bearded, mean and ornery.

"If my father were here," Fred said at last, breaking a silence, looking down at the white homespun *dhoti* wrapped around his waist and the string of prayer beads hanging from his neck, "he'd kill me."

Fred was a quiet guy. We ate dinner together almost every night, but we didn't talk very much. We'd usually watch others in the restaurant. At the Ajanta Bhavan, our favorite place to eat, we'd joke and play games with the kids who served the meals. Most of them were orphans, working in exchange for food and shelter. Occasionally a new kid would arrive, usually a child who'd never seen a foreigner before, and for weeks he'd just stare at us without blinking.

Fred would do tricks with the kids to make them laugh. He knew lots of tricks, magic tricks. Penny would joke that Fred might consider magic as a career instead of yoga, but Fred never found this funny. Penny was from London and had been at the ashram even longer than Fred. She was very good at all those yoga postures that involved bending at the waist, but Fred was better all around.

Once a week or so, Penny would go out to dinner with two handsome Kerala guys who'd come to the ashram to pick her up on their shiny black Enfield motorcycles. This used to drive Fred crazy. He knew that they'd go to the Coffee House downtown, a hip place to be. And at the Coffee House, Fred knew that Penny would sometimes eat an omelet. Omelets aren't vegetarian. But I never understood why it bothered Fred so much, Penny eating an omelet.

Well, after five months I left the ashram, and I never heard from Fred or Penny again. Eighteen years later I was back in Thiruvananthapuram, looking through a scrapbook (Guruji had died, but his wife, Indira, was still there), and suddenly I saw an old photograph of Guruji, in London.

"But who are these other people with him?" I asked.

"That is Penny, and that is Fred," said Indira. "They have an ashram in England. And those are their four children!"

EGGS WITH CURRY LEAVES

. . . .

We love the aroma of curry leaves as they fry in hot oil, and we're very fond of eggs. No wonder then that this is one of our favorite dishes. It's an *akoori* (see Persian-Flavored Eggs, page 230) flavored with curry leaves and ginger, as well as the usual green chiles. With one green chile, the heat is mild; for more heat, double the quantity. PHOTOGRAPH ON PAGE 236

4 large or extra-large eggs

¹/₂ teaspoon salt, or to taste

1 teaspoon butter or ghee

1 teaspoon raw sesame oil or vegetable oil

5 to 8 fresh or frozen curry leaves, coarsely chopped

1 teaspoon minced ginger or ginger mashed to a paste

1 green cayenne chile, seeded and chopped, or substitute a serrano chile

¹/₄ cup finely sliced shallots

2 scallions, minced

Whisk the eggs in a bowl until very smooth, add the salt, and set aside.

Heat a large heavy skillet over medium-high heat. Add the butter or ghee and oil, and when the butter is just melted, add the curry leaves, ginger, and chile and stir-fry briefly. Add the shallots and scallions, reduce the heat to medium, and stir-fry until the shallots are softened, about 4 minutes.

Beat the eggs briefly again, then pour into the hot pan. Lower the heat to medium-low and use a wooden spatula to gently fold the cooked edges of the egg in toward the center of the pan. As the mass of egg starts to set, run the spatula under the central mass of egg and turn it over. Cook a little longer; the eggs should be just set but still soft and tender.

Slide the eggs onto a warm plate, and serve hot. SERVES 2 TO 3

Serve as part of a rice meal, with a vegetable dish such as Hasna Begum's Mixed Vegetable Curry (page 164), or with a salad, Sri Lankan Village Salad (page 66) or Spicy Banana-Yogurt Pachadi (page 70), for example. Or serve with toast or warm flatbread for breakfast or brunch.

CORIANDER EGGS: Another version of *akoori* uses 2 to 3 tablespoons chopped coriander rather than curry leaves, and a little garlic instead of the scallions. Add the garlic with the ginger, and add the coriander to the eggs just before you pour them into the pan.

ANDHRA SCRAMBLED EGGS

. . . .

We eat more eggs, more omelets and scrambled eggs, traveling in the Subcontinent than we do at home. We're not sure why, but part of it probably has to do with having different patterns of eating when we're traveling. At home we can eat whenever we like, simply going to the kitchen and cooking something up or looking for leftovers. But when we're on the road, we have to pay more attention to breakfast, lunch, and supper, to the hours of the day when food in restaurants and tea shops is being freshly made. As good as food can be in the Subcontinent, it's also true it's not always around when we want it to be. That's where eggs come in: A local tea shop will often cook up an omelet at a moment's notice. Eaten with a *chapati* or two and a cup of tea, it tastes so good.

Then after we come back home, we eat more eggs and omelets for a while than usual because we're in the habit. Eggs are so easy, and scrambled eggs and omelets from the Subcontinent are full of flavor. These are like the eggs Jeffrey had at a small tea shop in rural Andhra Pradesh, about a day's drive north of Chennai (Madras).

4 to 5 large or extra-large eggs

1 teaspoon salt

2 tablespoons raw sesame oil or vegetable oil

1 cup chopped shallots

1 tablespoon minced garlic or garlic mashed to a paste

1 teaspoon minced ginger or ginger mashed to a paste

2 green cayenne chiles, seeded and minced

¼ teaspoon turmeric

2 tomatoes, cut into ½-inch dice

½ cup coriander leaves, finely chopped

Beat the eggs lightly in a bowl, and whisk or stir in the salt.

Heat a large cast-iron or other heavy skillet over medium-high heat. Add the oil, and when it is hot, add the shallots, garlic, ginger, chiles, and turmeric and stir-fry for 2 minutes. Add the tomatoes and fry for another 2 to 3 minutes, until they are softened.

Add the eggs and swirl and tilt the skillet to distribute them. Using a flat wooden spoon or spatula, toss the eggs with the shallots and tomatoes, cooking the eggs while getting everything well mixed. Then continue to cook for 2 to 3 minutes more, until the eggs are well cooked. Turn out onto a flat plate to serve, garnished with the fresh coriander.

SERVES 2 TO 3

Serve with a green salad and Chapatis (page 110) or Onion Skillet Breads (page 124), or as part of a casual rice meal.

OPPOSITE: *Eggs with Curry Leaves (page 234).*
LEFT: *Nepali Grilled Chicken (page 238) with Tart Mango Salsa (page 48).*

NEPALI GRILLED CHICKEN

· · · · · · · · · · · ·

Nepali chefs are famous in the Subcontinent, just like Filipino rock musicians in Asia. Nepali chefs have been cooking restaurant food, and particularly "foreigner food," for two, almost three generations. If you go to Goa, the big beach resort destination in high tourist season, there will be Nepali chefs in the kitchens. And it's the same thing in the mountain town of Manali, in Himachal Pradesh, in high tourist season, and in Delhi. Kathmandu has long had a restaurant tradition. Many Nepali chefs have grown up working in those restaurants, and then they take their skills elsewhere during slow times in Kathmandu.

This grilled chicken, marinated in a tomato-based blend of flavorings, may be Nepali (we've eaten a version of it in Kathmandu) or it may be a Nepali chef–inspired invention, but either way it's good. Use a cleaver to cut the chicken into pieces as you wish for grilling (we usually cut legs into two, and breasts into four, for example), or ask the butcher to do it.

PHOTOGRAPH ON PAGE 237

**One 3¹/₂- to 4-pound chicken, cut into 12 to 16 pieces, or 3 to 3¹/₂ pounds
    chicken legs and breasts, cut into smaller serving pieces**

MARINADE
1 cup chopped ripe tomatoes or canned tomatoes
1¹/₂ teaspoons ground cumin
1¹/₂ teaspoons ground coriander
1 tablespoon minced ginger
3 tablespoons chopped garlic
1 tablespoon fresh lime juice
2 teaspoons salt
¹/₄ cup vegetable oil

Wash the chicken well in cold water and set aside.

Place all the marinade ingredients except the oil in a blender or food processor and process to a paste. Transfer to a large bowl and stir in the oil. Place the chicken pieces in the bowl and rub to coat them with marinade. Cover and refrigerate for 4 to 8 hours.

Prepare a charcoal or gas grill or preheat the broiler.

To grill the chicken, place it on a rack about 5 inches from the coals or flame and grill, turning several times (tongs work well), until cooked through, about 20 minutes. *To broil the chicken,* place it on a lightly oiled rack in a broiler pan and put the pan in the oven so the meat is about 5 inches below the broiler element. Prop the door open slightly and broil for about 20 minutes, turning the chicken once after about 7 minutes, and then again after about 15 minutes. Test for doneness with a skewer: The juices should run clear.

Transfer the chicken to a platter and serve hot.   SERVES 6

Serve as the centerpiece of a family meal or a dinner party, with rice or flatbreads, a chutney such as Fresh Green Chile Chutney (page 205), and a salad: Cucumber Salad with Hot Spiced Mustard Dressing (page 61) or Nepali Green Bean–Sesame Salad (page 76), or a tossed green salad.

YOGURT-MARINATED CHICKEN KEBABS

. . . .

This grilled marinated boneless chicken comes from Uttar Pradesh, a heartland state of northern India, just south of Nepal. Uttar Pradesh is famous for a lot of things, including the siege of Lucknow during the Indian Mutiny in 1857, the holy city of Varanasi, and the Taj Mahal, in Agra. The region has a rich Hindu vegetarian culinary culture as well as a reputation, especially in Lucknow, for great Moghul-style cooking. But whenever I think about Uttar Pradesh, I always think of crowded dusty bus stations, horns blowing, and people yelling. Many times I've traveled up from Varanasi to Kathmandu, and down from Kathmandu to Varanasi, always on old tired buses and always through Uttar Pradesh.

Here boneless chicken is cut into bite-size pieces that are marinated in a simple sauce of yogurt flavored with garlic and chopped garlic chives or regular chives or scallions. (In the Subcontinent, where the chickens tend to be free-range and well exercised, the chicken pieces are first beaten with the flat of a knife to tenderize them.)

1 pound boneless skinless chicken breasts

1 tablespoon minced garlic or garlic mashed to a paste

¼ cup finely chopped garlic chives, regular chives, or scallions

1¼ teaspoons salt

½ teaspoon freshly ground black pepper or ¼ to ½ teaspoon cayenne

2 tablespoons vegetable oil

½ cup plain (full- or reduced-fat) yogurt

1 or 2 limes or lemons, cut into wedges

Rinse off the chicken, cut into 1-inch chunks, and place in a wide shallow bowl.

Mix the marinade in a small bowl, whisking the garlic, greens, salt, pepper, and oil into the yogurt. Pour over the chicken and stir. Cover and set aside in the refrigerator to marinate for 1 to 2 hours, whatever is most convenient; turn the pieces after 30 minutes.

Prepare a charcoal or gas grill or preheat the boiler.

Slide the chicken pieces onto metal skewers, without crowding them together. (If you are grilling but don't have skewers, place the chicken on a lightly oiled mesh rack.) Reserve the remaining marinade.

If grilling the chicken, place the skewers (or metal rack) about 5 to 6 inches above the coals or flame. *If broiling the chicken*, place the skewers (or chicken pieces) on a lightly oiled rack in a broiling pan, place the pan 5 to 7 inches below the broiler element, and leave the oven door propped open slightly. Grill or broil, turning the skewers or chicken pieces over once and basting them occasionally with a little of the marinade, for 12 to 15 minutes, until cooked through.

Serve on the skewers or slide them off; mound the chicken on a platter. Put out lime or lemon wedges so your guests can squeeze a little juice onto the chicken as they eat. **SERVES 4**

Serve with plain rice or a pulao *such as Stir-fried Rice and Dal (page 96), and a green salad or simple chopped salad. Put out some Tart Mango Salsa (page 48) or Zinet's Young Ginger Pickle (page 346) to add another layer of flavor to the meal.*

BONE-IN GRILLED CHICKEN: We also use this marinade for bone-in pieces of chicken, which we then grill or broil as described in Nepali Grilled Chicken (page 238).

YOGURT-RUBBED ROAST CHICKEN: The yogurt marinade is a delicious way of preparing roast chicken. Wash and dry a 3- to 4-pound chicken that has been brought to room temperature. Rub the marinade all over the chicken, inside and out. Pierce a (preferably organic) lemon all over with a fork and insert it in the cavity of the chicken. Set the chicken on the lightly oiled rack of a roasting pan, breast side down, and set aside while you preheat the oven to 400°F.

Roast the chicken in the center of the oven for 1 to 1½ hours; the legs should be loose when wiggled and a thermometer inserted into the thigh should register 175°F. Let stand at room temperature for 10 minutes to firm up before carving and serving.

BANGLES

I love the sound of glass bangles. They make a fragile tinkling as they slide on the arm. They're getting hard to find in the cities in India now; you need to be at a village market or festival to find a glass bangle seller with the full array of colors and sizes. Glass bangles cost very little, the equivalent of twenty-five cents for a dozen. They're the least expensive form of ornamentation, worn by village women all over the Subcontinent, and the most fun.

In the busy city of Patna recently (in the state of Bihar, in northern India), on my way to Bodh Gaya (the Buddhist holy place where the Buddha attained enlightenment), I went into a small shop that sold bracelets and bangles, metal and plastic ones of all colors and descriptions. When I asked about glass bangles, the merchant shook his head at me: "Why do you want those?" he asked. "They break." Yes, they do break, but I think that is part of their charm.

The first glass bangles I ever wore were a present, given to me by two teenagers in Udaipur. They'd bought sixteen, alternating colors, in bright blue and iridescent green. They oiled my right hand, then squeezed it tightly as they slid the bangles on carefully, two by two. I loved the look of them, and then I came to love the sound, which kept me company as I walked or as I worked. Later, at a bangle seller's stall in Karnataka, on the west coast south of Goa, I picked out some more, to wear on my other arm. The bangle sellers were sitting in a row on the ground at a weekly market, their clients crouched before them. They were all ruthless. I could hear little gasps of pain, little groans as they slid the tight bangles in pairs over their clients' hands, forcing them over the joints. (If you try to slide them on one at a time, the bangles break with the strain.)

And then, of course, once on, the bangles stay on until they crack: a little ping or a dull clink, and a piece of bangle falls off. "Another gone," I think. Another reminder of life's fragilities. Another small lesson in nonattachment.

At rural fairs (melas) there's a lot to marvel at and inexpensive treats on sale for people of all ages: glass bangles, deep-fried snacks, colorful balloons, cassettes of Bollywood songs, and much more. At a mela in a village west of Ahmadabad, in the state of Gujarat, several henna women were offering to decorate women's hands with henna, using wooden blocks to stamp on the designs. As I waited to have my hands done, a young girl of seven or eight was smiling happily as her hands and arms were gently and firmly stamped with the designs.

AROMATIC SLOW-COOKED CHICKEN

· · · · · · · · · · · ·

There's nothing like simmered chicken for comfort, or to feed hungry guests. We think of this as a North Indian version of a European-style slow-cooked chicken dish such as pot-au-feu, brothy, with wonderful depth of flavor. The chicken pieces simmer in plenty of aromatic sauce that is tempered at the last minute with a little vinegar and sugar. Any leftovers are delicious.

About 2 pounds bone-in chicken breasts and legs or
    one 2¹/₂- to 3-pound chicken

About 3 cups water

¹/₄ cup vegetable oil or ghee

1 teaspoon cumin seeds

¹/₂ teaspoon coarsely ground black pepper

About 1 cup grated onion

1 tablespoon minced garlic or garlic mashed to a paste

1 tablespoon minced ginger or ginger mashed to a paste

1 tablespoon ground coriander

1¹/₂ teaspoons salt

2 green cayenne chiles, minced

2 tablespoons plain (full- or reduced-fat) yogurt

2 teaspoons rice vinegar

1 teaspoon sugar

About ¹/₂ cup chopped coriander leaves and stems

If using chicken pieces, wash them well; remove the skin and discard. With a cleaver, chop breasts into three or four pieces. Separate the thighs and drumsticks (if still attached), and if the drumsticks are large, chop each one in half. If using a whole chicken, cut into ten to twelve pieces. Remove the skin, check the cut surfaces, and remove any bone fragments. Rinse all the chicken pieces well.

Place the chicken in a wide heavy pot and add the water. Bring to a vigorous boil, then lower the heat and simmer partially covered until the chicken is just cooked through, 30 to 40 minutes. Remove the chicken pieces and set aside. Pour out the broth and measure it; add a little water if necessary to bring it to 2 cups. Set aside.

Rinse and dry the pot, then heat the oil or ghee in it over medium heat. Toss in the cumin seeds and pepper, and when the oil splutters a little, after about 30 seconds, immediately add the onion, garlic, and ginger and stir. Cook for 5 to 10 minutes, stirring frequently, until the onion is well softened and translucent, then toss in the ground coriander, salt, and minced chiles. Stir well and cook for several minutes to blend the flavors.

Stir in the yogurt, a spoonful at a time, until well blended in. Pour in the reserved broth and add the chicken pieces. Bring to a boil, then reduce the heat and simmer for several minutes. (The dish can be prepared ahead to this point. If the wait will be longer than 2 hours, let it cool to room temperature, then refrigerate, covered. About 10 minutes before serving, place back over medium heat and bring to a simmer. If the sauce has jelled in the cold, stir as it heats until it is liquid again.)

Add the vinegar and sugar and stir in. Raise the heat and bring to a boil, then reduce the heat slightly and cook at a strong simmer for several minutes. Toss in most of the chopped coriander and simmer for another minute or so.

Serve hot, with the remaining coriander strewn on top for garnish.

SERVES 5 TO 6

Serve with plain rice to soak up the sauce. Accompany with an unsauced vegetable dish, perhaps Spiced Tender Chopped Bindi (page 168) or Aromatic Pumpkin and Coconut (page 160), and a simple salad of crisp sliced white radish for a contrast in texture.

COLOMBO CHICKEN CURRY

· · · · · · · · · · ·

Be sure to make this Sri Lankan curry with bone-in chicken. If you want to make life simpler, buy your chicken already cut up, or buy legs and breasts rather than cutting up a whole chicken. Not only do the bones give the curry more flavor, but it's a pleasure to pick up the pieces with your fingers and to eat the curried meat from the bone.

The chicken pieces are rubbed with a spice paste and left to marinate briefly, then slow simmered with shallots and chiles in a sauce made smooth with coconut milk. Flavors are complex and mellow, even though the dish cooks for less than an hour.

One 2¹/₂- to 3-pound chicken or about 2 pounds bone-in chicken legs and breasts (see headnote)

SPICE MARINADE

1 tablespoon coriander seeds

2 teaspoons cumin seeds

¹/₂ teaspoon fenugreek seeds

3 tablespoons cashew nuts

1 tablespoon raw white rice

2 tablespoons fresh, frozen, or dried grated coconut

One ¹/₂-inch piece cinnamon or cassia stick or ¹/₂ teaspoon ground cinnamon

Seeds from 3 green cardamom pods, or substitute ¹/₂ teaspoon ground cardamom

1 tablespoon minced garlic or garlic mashed to a paste

SAUCE

2 tablespoons coconut oil or vegetable oil

2 green cayenne chiles, finely chopped

¹/₃ cup thinly sliced shallots

1 teaspoon minced ginger or ginger mashed to a paste

1¹/₄ teaspoons salt

2 small tomatoes, chopped

¹/₂ cup canned or fresh coconut milk

¹/₂ cup water, or as needed

Using a sharp cleaver, cut up the chicken or chicken pieces. Chop the whole breast into four pieces and separate the legs into drumstick and thigh (if still attached). Check the cut surfaces and discard any bone fragments. If you began with a whole chicken, include the wings in the curry. Rinse thoroughly with cold water and set aside in a shallow bowl.

Dry roast the coriander, cumin, and fenugreek seeds, the cashews, rice, and coconut, one by one (because they brown at different rates), in a small heavy skillet over medium-high heat until touched with brown, stirring frequently to prevent burning, then turn out into a bowl. Using a spice/coffee grinder or a stone mortar and a pestle, grind the roasted mixture to a powder with the cinnamon and cardamom. Transfer to a bowl and stir in the garlic to make a paste.

Rub the spice paste all over the chicken pieces. Set aside, covered, in the refrigerator to marinate for 15 to 20 minutes, or as long as 2 hours if more convenient.

Heat a wide heavy pot with a tight-fitting lid over medium-high heat. When it is hot, add the oil and swirl to coat the bottom of the pot. Add the chiles, shallots, and ginger and stir-fry for 2 to 3 minutes, then add the chicken and salt. Stir and turn for approximately 5 minutes to expose all sides of the chicken to the heat. When it is touched with color all over, add the tomatoes and cook for another minute or two.

Add the coconut milk and ¹/₂ cup water, cover tightly, lower the heat, and cook at a low simmer for about 40 minutes or until the chicken is cooked through. Check periodically to make sure the pot is not running dry, and add more water if needed. (The dish can be cooked ahead. Refrigerate, once cooled, if prepared more than 2 hours in advance. Reheat just before serving; you may need to add a little water, as the sauce will have thickened.)

Transfer the chicken to a platter, spooning the sauce over; serve hot.

SERVES 6

Serve with plain rice and a simple mallum, *such as Shredded Green Bean Mallum (page 76), and a salad—Fresh Bean Sprout Salad (page 55), for example. Put out Red Onion Sambol (page 32) or Tart Mango Salsa (page 48) as a condiment.*

Gujarat is famous as the place where Gandhi held the Salt March in 1934, a nonviolent protest against the colonial British monopoly on salt (locals were forbidden to gather salt). With its long coastline, Gujarat has a hot dry climate for much of the year, and salt is still an important product. Here a woman is raking salt crystals in one of the collecting ponds at a small saltworks at the edge of the Rann of Katchh, a desert area.

ZINET'S CHICKEN WITH TOMATO AND GREENS

· · · · · · · · · · · ·

One day our neighbor Zinet told me that fenugreek greens were fabulous cooked with chicken, and she described how she prepared them. We were in her photocopy shop in Toronto, talking about the recipe, and a young woman who overheard our conversation said delightedly, "But that's the way my mother prepares it, too!" Turns out her parents are from Pakistan; Zinet's forebears came from the Indian state of Gujarat.

This is our version of Zinet's recipe, which is one of the most attractive curries we know. There's the red of the tomatoes and the bright green of the chopped fenugreek leaves (they keep their bright greenness during cooking). Together they make a very festive-looking dish. The small pieces of browned chicken are bathed in plenty of thickened, well-flavored sauce.

We like the way the sauce soaks into plain rice, but we have to admit that Zinet is right when she says it goes even better with Chapatis (page 110). Somehow the wheaty flavor of the bread is a wonderful match for the flavors of the stew.

Fenugreek greens are a winter vegetable in northern India, as well as in Bangladesh and Pakistan. When they're in season, stacks of green bundles appear in the market and then disappear into every kitchen, for fenugreek is a treat and the greens find their way into many dishes, from dals to vegetables (see New Potatoes with Fresh Greens, page 154) to easy stews such as this.

In North America, you will find fenugreek greens in South Asian groceries and at some farmers' markets, usually sold in large bundles with the roots still on. (Fenugreek grows well in the summer in temperate North America. Just soak the seeds in lukewarm water overnight, then plant in a sunny spot after the danger of frost is past.) Cut off the roots and thickest stem ends, wash thoroughly, and then chop crosswise into 1/4-inch lengths. If necessary, substitute spinach or pea shoots or amaranth greens; trim, wash, and chop in the same way. PHOTOGRAPH ON PAGE 246

1½ pounds bone-in chicken legs or breasts, or a combination

3 tablespoons raw sesame oil or vegetable oil

1½ cups chopped onions

2 teaspoons cumin seeds or ground cumin

2 teaspoons ground coriander

½ teaspoon turmeric

1 tablespoon minced garlic or garlic mashed to a paste

1 tablespoon minced ginger or ginger mashed to a paste

½ teaspoon cayenne, or to taste

About 1½ pounds ripe tomatoes, chopped (2 to 2½ cups),
    or 2 cups canned whole or diced tomatoes

1 teaspoon salt, or to taste

1½ cups packed finely chopped fenugreek leaves and stems,
    or substitute finely chopped spinach or pea shoots

¼ to ½ cup coriander sprigs

Wash the chicken, then pull off the skin and excess fat and discard (or reserve them for another purpose). Use a cleaver to chop the chicken into smaller pieces: the drumsticks into two or three pieces each, the thighs (if still attached) the same, the breasts into four or so. Check the cut surfaces and discard any bone fragments. Rinse thoroughly with cold water and set aside.

In a wok or karhai (see Glossary) or a wide heavy pot, heat the oil over medium-high heat. Add the onions and cook, stirring frequently, until lightly browned, about 10 minutes. Add the cumin, coriander, turmeric, garlic, and ginger, and stir. Add the chicken and raise the heat slightly. Cook, stirring frequently, until the chicken pieces are browned on all sides, about 5 minutes. Add the cayenne, tomatoes (if using canned whole tomatoes, crush them between your fingers), and salt, and stir and turn until the tomatoes start to break down and create more liquid; *do not add any water*. If using canned tomatoes, cook just long enough to incorporate them well.

Once the liquid is simmering well, partially cover the pan and simmer gently over medium-low heat for 15 to 20 minutes, or until the oil rises to the surface. (The dish can be prepared ahead to this point and set aside, covered, for up to an hour. If preparing further ahead, let cool to room temperature, then cover and refrigerate.)

Bring the stew to a strong simmer over medium-high heat. Add the chopped greens and stir until tender, about 5 minutes (less for spinach and a little longer if using pea shoots). Remove from the heat and sprinkle on the coriander sprigs.
SERVES 4

Serve accompanied by fresh flatbreads or over rice. For a little bit of flavor on the side, put out Gujarati Mango Chutney (page 40) or Fresh Coriander–Peanut Chutney (page 28) and a simple salad of Fresh White Radish Slices with Salt (page 54) or a raita (see "The Raita Family," page 67).

Zinet's Chicken with Tomato and Greens (page 244). ABOVE: *A man herding ducks in southern Andhra Pradesh, right beside a new modern superhighway.*

EARLY MORNING can be so tough when we're traveling. It's still dark, and bed is comfortable, but we know that dawn comes quickly and that those first few hours of daylight are best for photographs and for understanding. Early morning is the time to catch glimpses of farmers heading out to their fields, children starting to school, markets setting up, mist on the water, fishermen with their nets at first light. So it was, one morning in the town of Rajshahi, in western Bangladesh. There was a little chill in the air, and the sky was just starting to lighten as we drove through deserted streets and out of town, heading north toward a pre-Moghul mosque called Kosumbra Masjid.

Once we were in the countryside, we were on a raised road, an old trunk road built to stay dry even in monsoon floods. It was lined with trees; in places, these were huge mango trees. Where our road crossed another tree-lined road, it looked as though two columns of giant soldiers were marching in parade drill. Rice fields, brilliantly green with the new monsoon season crop, and with patches of open water in places, stretched out in all directions to the flat horizon.

In one small village, we came on people parboiling rice, heating it in a barrel over a fire fueled by rice bran, then spreading it out on the ground, rich brown and steaming, to dry in the morning sun. When we reached the turnoff to the mosque, we headed slowly up a narrow cobbled lane through a small hamlet, and there it was, stone and peacefulness, by a large manmade pond. The mosque was austere except for the roof, which had many small domes, like bubbles popping up in the gray stone. I walked around and photographed it from outside; then suddenly, it seemed, the sunlight was high and harsh and I realized how tired and hungry I was. It was time to take a break.

Down the road a little way was a village with a roadside café. We stopped in and discovered they had flatbreads and curried chicken, as well as tea, a perfect finish to the morning.

OPPOSITE, LEFT: *In the mist of early morning, a Kutia Kondh woman carries vegetables to a weekly market in Orissa.* RIGHT: *In a village in Madhya Pradesh, thick adobe walls keep the heat of summer at bay.* ABOVE: *As dawn breaks, a bullock cart carries straw on a small road in the large agricultural expanse of northern Andhra Pradesh.*

ROADSIDE CAFÉ CHICKEN

. . . .

This is our approximation of the aromatic simmered chicken we ate one morning in western Bangladesh (see "Dawn," page 249). We like to serve a green salad or cucumber slices on the side, for a contrast in texture and a cooling balance to the medium-hot chile hit of the gravy. Leftovers are delicious.

6 chicken drumsticks

1 tablespoon vegetable oil, raw sesame oil, or peanut oil

2 tablespoons ghee or butter

1 teaspoon Bengali Five-Spice Mixture (page 340) or a scant ¼ teaspoon each black mustard, cumin, fennel, fenugreek, and nigella seeds

2 whole cloves or a generous pinch ground cloves

1 cinnamon or cassia stick

2 bay leaves

1 teaspoon ground coriander

2 teaspoons minced garlic or garlic mashed to a paste

1 tablespoon minced ginger or ginger mashed to a paste

About 1¼ cups packed grated onions

4 dried red chiles

About 1½ cups water

1 teaspoon salt, or more to taste

1 teaspoon sugar

Rinse the drumsticks and peel off the skin if you wish. Use a cleaver to chop each one into three pieces. Check the cut surfaces and discard any bone fragments. Rinse well with cold water and set aside.

Heat the oil and ghee or butter in a wide heavy pot over medium-high heat. When hot, toss in the spice blend, cloves, cinnamon stick, and bay leaves and stir until aromatic, 2 to 3 minutes. Lower the heat to medium, add the ground coriander, and stir, then add the garlic and stir-fry for 30 seconds. Add the ginger and cook until softened, 2 to 3 minutes. Add the onions, raise the heat to medium-high, and stir-fry for about 5 minutes, until the onions start to soften a little. Add the dried chiles and stir briefly, then lower the heat to medium and cook until the onions are very soft, about 5 minutes.

Raise the heat to high and add the chicken pieces. Cook, turning and pressing the chicken pieces against the hot pan until all surfaces are browned a little, about 8 minutes. Add 1 cup of the water and bring to a boil. Add the salt and sugar and stir well, then cover tightly, lower the heat to medium, and cook for about 30 minutes. Check occasionally to make sure nothing is sticking.

Add another ½ cup water to the pot and bring to a boil, then reduce the heat, partially cover, and simmer for 15 to 30 minutes, until the chicken is cooked through.

(The dish can be made up to 2 days ahead. Let cool to room temperature, then cover and refrigerate. To reheat before serving, add a little water and bring to a simmer over medium heat, stirring to prevent sticking. Simmer until the chicken is heated through.)

Taste for salt just before serving and adjust if necessary. Serve hot.

SERVES 4

Serve for a simple lunch or supper, with plain rice or Stir-fried Rice and Dal (page 96), or chunks of tender bread such as luchi *(see Gita's Luchis, page 115) to absorb the spiced gravy.*

DUCK VINDALOO

· · · · · · · · · · · · ·

Duck is not a traditional food in Goa, as far as we know, but we thought it would make a wonderful vindaloo, and so it does. (For more about the vindaloo tradition, see Goan Pork Vindaloo, page 280.) The sake, vodka, or Chinese rice wine are our suggested substitutes for the traditional local liquor called *feni* (see page 310).

This vindaloo has heat, but it's not overwhelming. It makes a great main dish for a dinner party because it can be made ahead, giving the flavors even more time to blend. Start a day ahead—the duck has the most flavor if it marinates for 12 to 24 hours, though you can get away with less (4 to 5 hours) if pressed for time.

1 whole duck or 1¹⁄₂ to 2 pounds bone-in duck breasts

1¹⁄₂ teaspoons salt

5 dried red chiles, stemmed and crumbled

¹⁄₄ teaspoon black peppercorns

¹⁄₂ teaspoon cumin seeds

¹⁄₂ teaspoon black mustard seeds

1 whole clove or a pinch of ground cloves

1 tablespoon minced garlic or garlic mashed to a paste

1 tablespoon minced ginger or ginger mashed to a paste

¹⁄₄ cup rice vinegar

¹⁄₂ teaspoon sugar

¹⁄₄ cup rendered duck fat or raw sesame oil or coconut oil

1 cup minced onion

¹⁄₄ cup medium-dry sake, vodka, or Chinese rice wine

Strip most of the skin and fat off the duck and set aside (for how to render fat, see Oils and Fats in the Glossary). Use a cleaver to cut the duck into pieces, leaving the meat on the bone; we usually cut the thighs as well as drumsticks into two pieces, and we cut the breasts into pieces slightly smaller than 2 inches by 2 inches. Place the duck in a large bowl with the salt and turn to ensure that it is salted all over. Set aside, loosely covered.

To prepare the spice paste using a spice/coffee grinder, place the dried chiles and the whole spices in the grinder and reduce to a powder. Turn out into a small bowl and add the ground cloves, if using. Add the garlic, ginger, and 2 tablespoons of the vinegar. Stir to mix, then use a spoon to smear the mixture against the side of the bowl to blend well. *To use a mortar and a pestle,* start by pounding or grinding the dried chiles and whole spices, then add the garlic and ginger and pound or grind to a paste, moistening the mixture with a little of the vinegar, up to 2 tablespoons. Transfer to a small bowl and stir in the ground cloves, if using. If you didn't add a full 2 tablespoons vinegar as you were grinding, add the balance now.

Stir the sugar into the spice paste. Add the spice paste to the bowl with the duck and turn and stir to coat the meat. Cover and refrigerate for 4 to 12 hours, or as long as 24 hours, whatever is most convenient.

Place 2 tablespoons of the duck fat or oil in a wide heavy skillet over medium heat. When it is hot, add the onion and sauté until tender and lightly browned, about 15 minutes. Turn out into a bowl and set aside.

Heat the remaining 2 tablespoons duck fat or oil in the same pan. Add the duck pieces (reserve any excess marinade) and turn and stir to expose all sides of the duck to the hot surface of the pan. Once the duck is browned on all sides, add the onion, the reserved marinade, if any, the remaining 2 tablespoons vinegar, and the sake, vodka, or wine. Bring to a boil, then cover tightly, lower the heat, and simmer for 45 minutes, or until the duck is tender. Transfer to a platter and serve hot or warm.
SERVES 4 TO 6

Serve with rice and a mild or slightly sweet side dish, such as Pea Shoots for a Crowd (page 161), Cauliflower Dum (page 148), or Aromatic Pumpkin and Coconut (page 160), as well as a plate of crisp sliced cucumbers and some of Zinet's Young Ginger Pickle (page 346).

LAMB, BEEF & PORK

THE CONCEPT EXPRESSED BY THE SANSKRIT

word *ahimsa*, which means "avoidance of harm," is an important

one in Hinduism. It's generally interpreted as forbidding the

taking of life. Consequently, many Hindus are vegetarians.

Others eat fish but not chicken or meat. (All generalizations

invite exceptions, and in this case they include the Rajputs,

a warrior caste in Rajasthan, who are famous hunters and have

a large repertoire of meat dishes. At the other end of the scale are the Jains, who are scrupulously vegetarian,

avoiding even ripe fruit that has fallen from the tree, in case the insect life in it might be harmed.) Because of Hinduism's largely vegetarian tradition, the repertoire of meat dishes in this chapter draws heavily on the cuisines of the other communities of the Subcontinent: the Muslims of Pakistan, India, Sri Lanka, and Bangladesh; the Sinhalese of Sri Lanka; and the Christian communities of Goa and Kerala.

In the deserts and hills of Pakistan and Rajasthan, and in the harsh flat desert of Katchh in western Gujarat, hardy goats forage for the smallest blade of grass. Goats are mostly used for meat (and for wool), as they are across Central Asia; they're much more common than sheep. Substitute goat meat in any of the lamb recipes; it is delicious and is becoming more widely available in North America. (Subcontinental cookbooks written in English have recipes that call for "mutton," by which they mean goat.) The Ladakhis and Gujars who live in the mountains of Kashmir and Himachal Pradesh even use goats as pack animals: Once, on my way up a steep, rocky pass in Ladakh, I saw a herd bobbing and swaying as it moved down the slope toward me. Closer to it, I could see that each adult goat was carrying a full pair of cloth bags, like saddle bags, strapped around its shoulders. The bags were full of salt from Tibet.

There are also lots of cows in India. They hang around in cities and villages—especially in areas near market stalls—with no particular owners, fending for themselves. Their meat is absolutely forbidden to Hindus, and to harm the cows in any way is forbidden. Consequently, in many parts of the Subcontinent, though cows may be milked, they are not butchered for meat, and die instead of old age. In Nepal, it's actually illegal to kill a cow, although water buffaloes are eaten by some people in place of beef. Water buffaloes, in contrast to cows, are valuable property. They give milk and pull plows, and their manure (as well as cow manure) fertilizes the fields or is dried and used as fuel for cookfing. In Bangladesh, Pakistan, and Sri Lanka, both cows and water buffaloes are used for meat.

Pigs roam the streets and back lanes of Kathmandu, foraging, and then they return to their owners at night. You'll also find them in small villages in Goa, rooting around for food and keeping things clean. Pork is eaten by Christians and by nonvegetarian Hindus and Buddists. Because pork is *haram*, "unclean," for Muslims, pigs are a rare sight in Bangladesh, Pakistan, and Muslim areas of India and Sri Lanka.

Though grilled and roasted meat is widely associated with the culinary traditions brought by the Moghul conquerors, in fact, in the Subcontinent dishes of minced meat and roasts grilled over a fire apparently date much further back. The word *kebab* came with the conquerors and generally refers to meat grilled on a skewer, though it can instead be cooked on a rack over a grill or under a broiler.

We've included a number of kebabs from the northern regions of the Subcontinent, mostly lamb kebabs, that can be either grilled or broiled, as well as several simmered lamb dishes, two of them from southern India. The beef recipes also come from far and wide: Apart from a beef patty with Pakistani spicing, there's a Bangladeshi *bhoona* beef curry and, from Sri Lanka, a tropical-flavored beef curry and a grilled kebab of spice-rubbed beef. Pork is simmered with distinctive spicing in two southern curries: a pork vindaloo from Goa and a coconut curry from Sri Lanka.

An itinerant musician playing in the courtyard of a house in Udaipur. Musicians travel to the city from the villages to earn small amounts of money, especially at times when the crops have been poor because of drought.

TIKKA KEBABS

· · · · · · · · · · · ·

This is an easy lamb kebab, made with small chunks of lamb marinated in a garlic-yogurt sauce, then grilled on flat metal skewers. It's a reminder of the nomadic Central Asian roots of many lamb dishes, simple and good. PHOTOGRAPH ON PAGE 271

1½ to 2 pounds boneless lamb shoulder

½ cup plain (full- or reduced-fat) yogurt

2 teaspoons minced garlic or garlic mashed to a paste

2 tablespoons fresh lemon juice

1 teaspoon ground coriander

1 tablespoon vegetable oil

About 2 teaspoons salt

¼ to ½ teaspoon cayenne

¼ to ½ teaspoon freshly ground black pepper (optional)

Lime or lemon wedges

Trim the lamb of excess fat and cut into approximately ¾-inch cubes. Set aside in a large bowl.

In a small bowl, mix together the yogurt, garlic, lemon juice, coriander, oil, 1 teaspoon of the salt, the cayenne, and black pepper, if using. Pour over the lamb, then stir with a spoon or with your hands to get all the meat surfaces coated with marinade. Cover and refrigerate for at least 2 hours, or for as long as 12 hours.

Prepare a charcoal or gas grill.

Slide the lamb cubes onto 6 to 8 flat metal skewers, without pressing them tightly together. Grill over moderate heat, turning occasionally, until browned on the outside and succulent pale pink in the center (or cooked right through, if you prefer).

Just before serving, sprinkle about 1 teaspoon salt over the lamb. Slide the meat off the skewers, or serve on the skewers and allow guests to slide the meat off. Put out lime or lemon wedges so guests can squeeze on fresh juice. SERVES 6 TO 8

Serve with flatbreads or rice, or both. Home-Style Tandoor Naan (page 116) or Chapatis (page 110) are traditional accompaniments. Put out a simple chopped salad, such as Watercress and Shallot Salad (page 55) or Fresh White Radish Slices with Salt (page 54), and a fresh herb chutney, such as Fresh Coriander–Peanut Chutney (page 28) or Mint-Coriander Chutney (page 298). For a feast, serve with basmati rice or a pulao, such as Chickpea Pulao (page 105), along with a chopped salad, Cucumber Raita (page 67), and Tart Mango Salsa (page 48).

LAMB SLIPPER KEBABS

· · · · · · · · · · ·

These kebabs are from Peshawar (see page 258), though they can now be found in many other places in the Subcontinent. Called *chapli kebab*, meaning "slipper kebab," they're made of ground lamb and spices and shaped into an oblong rather like the outline of the sole of a slipper or sandal (*chapple*). They can be grilled or fried. A similar kebab, with the same name, is made on the Afghan side of the Khyber Pass, that ancient passage between Central Asia and the Subcontinent.

1 pound ground lamb

1 cup grated onion or shallots

½ cup chopped tomato

2 teaspoons minced ginger or ginger mashed to a paste

2 green cayenne chiles, minced

About 1½ teaspoons salt

½ teaspoon cayenne

1 teaspoon garam masala (page 342 or store-bought),
   or a pinch each ground cinnamon and cloves plus
     ½ teaspoon each ground cumin and coriander

1 teaspoon coriander seeds, toasted and ground

2 tablespoons *anardana* (dried pomegranate seeds), ground,
   or 1 tablespoon rice vinegar or cider vinegar

½ cup chopped coriander leaves

¼ cup chickpea flour (*besan*) or scant ¼ cup atta flour
   or all-purpose flour

About 1 cup peanut oil, if panfrying the kebabs

Lemon or lime wedges

Place the meat, onion or shallots, tomato, ginger, chiles, 1 teaspoon salt, the cayenne, garam masala or mixed spices, ground coriander, *anardana* or vinegar, chopped coriander, and flour in a food processor and process to blend well, 1 to 2 minutes. Turn the mixture out into a bowl.

Alternatively, combine all the ingredients except the oil and citrus wedges in a bowl and knead thoroughly with your hands to blend all flavors into the meat. Cover and refrigerate for 1 to 12 hours.

If you will be grilling or broiling the kebabs, preheat a charcoal or gas grill or the broiler.

Divide the meat mixture into 16 portions and shape into oblong patties about 3 inches long, 2 inches wide, and less than ½ inch thick.

Grill the patties over a medium flame or broil on a rimmed baking sheet about 5 inches from the heating element, turning once, until well browned on both sides, 8 to 10 minutes; sprinkle on a little salt just before you turn the patties over.

Alternatively, heat about ½ inch oil in a large skillet over medium-high heat. Panfry the patties, in batches, in the hot oil, turning once, until browned and a little crunchy on both sides, 8 to 10 minutes; sprinkle on a little salt when you remove them from the hot oil. Keep the batches warm in a low oven while you cook the rest.

Put out wedges of lemon or lime for squeezing over the kebabs, and serve hot or warm.

SERVES 8

Serve with flatbreads, accompanied by a mixed salad such as Cachoombar (page 57). These are also delicious served alongside a simple flavored rice such as Quick Tamarind Pulao with Curry Leaves (page 98) or Stir-fried Rice and Dal (page 96).

OPTIONS: For a brighter green kebab, use chopped scallions (the white and tender green parts) instead of onion.

BEEF SLIPPER KEBABS: Substitute beef for lamb if you wish. Increase the ginger to 1 tablespoon and add ¼ teaspoon freshly ground black pepper.

PESHAWAR

We were in Peshawar, in northern Pakistan, for a hot, sweaty, exhausting week in late June 1986. I remember spending hours lying under a slowly turning ceiling fan, trying to tune out the heat. The bazaar was full of Afghans, refugees from the war then going on between the mujahideen and the Russian army. I wore long-sleeved *shalwar-kameez* (a long baggy cotton shirt and very loose trousers) and had my head and shoulders draped with a shawl, yet the looks I got from many of the men on the street made me feel as if I were walking around naked. Most women I saw were wearing full-length *burqas* that covered them from head to toe, leaving only a mesh "grill" over their eyes. But some Punjabi women drew stares, as well, because they wore only loose shawls over their hair, leaving their faces bare or half-draped—even though they all had their arms and legs covered in loose, flowing cotton or silk. The local tourist brochure proudly advertised the local Pashtun culture as "the most male-dominated culture in the world."

Things were tough for the Afghan refugees. The locals resented them for taking jobs away from Pakistani citizens and straining the town's resources. Many refugees had started small carpet shops, where they did business, chatted over glasses of tea, and worried about those they'd left behind. We met a young Englishman who had just come back from a short stay in Afghanistan. He had walked in through the mountains with a group of mujahideen, just to see what was happening. He was exhilarated by the adventure, caught up in a romantic idea that seemed remote from the real pain being suffered by the Afghans and the locals.

The mountain peaks that tower above Pakistan's Hunza Valley are sharply etched, so high and far away that they look almost like castles in the sky.

Two very different views of Nepal: On the left, a car at the front of a wedding procession in Kathmandu is garlanded with strings of fresh and paper flowers. On the right, in the village of Marfa, below the Annapurna massif in western Nepal, apple rings strung between wooden poles are set out to dry.

GINGER-LAMB COCONUT MILK CURRY

. . . .

This is a good example of a Muslim curry from southern India. It's flavored with the classic Moghul spicing of cinnamon, cloves, and cardamom, but softened and enriched with coconut milk, a very southern ingredient. Make this with tender lamb or with goat. There's plenty of sauce here, so serve the dish with lots of rice.

1 pound boneless lamb

MARINADE

1 tablespoon minced ginger or ginger mashed to a paste

1/2 teaspoon cayenne

1 teaspoon coriander seeds, toasted and ground

1/2 teaspoon turmeric

1 teaspoon salt

2 tablespoons coconut oil, raw sesame oil, or vegetable oil

One 1-inch piece cinnamon or cassia stick

2 cloves

4 green cardamom pods

2 cups coarsely chopped onions

6 green cayenne chiles, slit lengthwise and seeded

1 teaspoon minced garlic or garlic mashed to a paste

2 teaspoons minced ginger or ginger mashed to a paste

1 1/2 cups canned or fresh coconut milk, with 1/2 cup of the thickest milk set aside (see Note)

1 cup water

About 1/4 cup coriander leaves or minced mint leaves

1 or 2 limes, cut into wedges

Trim the lamb of excess fat, cut into 3/4-inch pieces, and set aside in a large bowl.

Combine all the marinade ingredients in a small bowl, adding a little water as necessary to make a paste. Add to the meat and mix well to coat the meat. Set aside to marinate for an hour or so (if it's more convenient, marinate the meat for up to 12 hours, covered and refrigerated).

Heat the oil in a wide heavy pot over medium-high heat. Toss in the cinnamon, cloves, and cardamom and stir-fry briefly, then add the onions and stir-fry until softened, about 8 minutes, adding the chiles after the first few minutes.

Lower the heat to medium, add the garlic and ginger, and stir-fry for 2 to 3 minutes, until a little softened. Add the meat and any excess marinade and turn and stir over medium to medium-low heat until all the surfaces have been exposed to the heat, about 6 minutes. The meat may stick a little; just loosen it from the bottom of the pan.

Add the 1 cup thinner coconut milk and the water and bring to a boil, then lower the heat and simmer, partially covered, until the meat is tender, 25 to 30 minutes. Add the thicker coconut milk and bring almost to a boil, then lower the heat and simmer for a few more minutes.

Transfer to a serving bowl, sprinkle on the coriander leaves or mint, and serve hot. Put out lime wedges so guests can add a tart note as they eat.   SERVES 5 TO 6

Serve with rice and, to balance the richness of the sauce, a simple chopped salad and a tart condiment such as Star Fruit Chutney (page 34).

NOTE: Traditionally the second pressing, or thinner, coconut milk is used to simmer the dish until the meat is cooked, then the first pressing, the thicker milk, is added to finish the dish. If using canned coconut milk, as we do, you will usually find that some thicker milk has collected at the top or bottom of the can. If, however, your coconut milk is of a uniform thickness, don't worry; just use the remaining 1/2 cup when the thicker milk is called for.

GINGER-LAMB CURRY WITH VEGETABLES: You can extend this dish by including 2 cups or so thinly sliced bitter melon (salted for 10 minutes, then rinsed) or diced Asian eggplant or diced potato. Add them once the meat has browned, and stir-fry for several minutes before adding the thinner coconut milk and proceeding with the recipe. Make sure the vegetables are cooked through before you add the thicker coconut milk. Taste for seasoning as the dish finishes; you may need to add a little salt.

CASHEW-COCONUT MEATBALLS

. . . .

These delectable meatballs from southern India could just as well be placed in the Snacks chapter, because they're so good served simply on their own in the summertime with an ice-cold beer, or in winter with a glass of red wine. The first time we tested them at home, just as we finished, our doorbell rang. It was a couple of friends stopping by unexpectedly. So we put out the meatballs and sauce in a bowl with a serving spoon, and put out small plates and forks and spoons. We poured some wine, and as we talked, we ate. Then simultaneously all of us said, "Yum!"

The combination of cashew nuts, lamb, and coconut is unusual, but the tastes of the three blend beautifully, and the meatballs are mild and delicious. The sauce is a very southern Indian take on tomato sauce, tart with tamarind, a great foil for the lamb.

MEATBALLS

About $3/4$ pound boneless well-trimmed lamb shoulder or leg, chilled

$1/2$ cup cashew nuts

3 or 4 green cayenne chiles, coarsely chopped

1 teaspoon fennel seeds

1 small onion, minced

1 tablespoon finely chopped garlic or garlic mashed to a paste

1 cup fresh or frozen grated coconut

1 large egg

1 teaspoon salt

SAUCE

2 tablespoons tamarind pulp

1 cup hot water

1 tablespoon coriander seeds or ground coriander

1 teaspoon fennel seeds or ground fennel

$1/2$ teaspoon cumin seeds or ground cumin

2 tablespoons raw sesame oil or vegetable oil

1 medium onion, finely chopped

1 tablespoon minced garlic or garlic mashed to a paste

4 red or green cayenne chiles, finely chopped

$1/4$ teaspoon turmeric

$3^1/2$ to 4 cups chopped ripe tomatoes or drained canned tomatoes

$1/2$ teaspoon salt, or to taste

2 cups water

$1/2$ cup coarsely chopped coriander leaves

Thinly slice the lamb, then place in a food processor and process until fairly smooth. Add the remaining meatball ingredients and process until well blended. Transfer to a bowl, cover, and refrigerate until an hour before you wish to serve.

To make the sauce, chop the tamarind into several pieces and place in a bowl. Pour the hot water over it and let soak for 15 minutes.

Mash the tamarind with the back of a spoon or use your fingers to separate the pulp from the seeds. Place a sieve over another bowl and pour the tamarind mixture through, pressing against it to extract as much liquid as possible. Discard the seeds and pulp; set the tamarind liquid aside. If using whole coriander, fennel, or cumin seeds, grind to a powder in a spice/coffee grinder. Set aside.

Heat the oil in a wide heavy nonreactive pot over medium-high heat. Add the onion and garlic and cook until well softened, about 10 minutes, stirring occasionally to prevent sticking. Add the chiles and stir, then add the ground spices and turmeric and stir. Add the tamarind liquid, the tomatoes, salt, and water and bring to a boil. Reduce the heat and simmer, uncovered, for 15 to 20 minutes. Remove from the heat. (The sauce can be prepared ahead to this point and set aside at room temperature for as long as 4 hours.)

Remove the meat from the refrigerator. Place a lightly greased plate by your work surface, and lightly rub your palms with oil or water. Scoop up a heaping tablespoon of the meat mixture and roll it lightly between your palms into a golf ball–size meatball. Set aside on the plate and repeat. You will have 16 to 18 meatballs.

Place the sauce over medium heat and bring to a strong simmer. Gently slide the meatballs into the sauce. The sauce will not cover them completely, so you will need to stir and move them around occasionally as they cook at a medium simmer for 20 minutes, or until cooked through.

Just before serving, stir in the coriander. Transfer the meatballs and sauce to a serving bowl and serve with a ladle or large spoon.

SERVES 6 AS AN APPETIZER, 4 AS A MAIN COURSE

Serve as a main course with rice, a simple green salad or stir-fried greens, and Zinet's Young Ginger Pickle (page 346) or another pickle. Or serve as an appetizer with drinks.

GRILLED OR BROILED CASHEW-COCONUT LAMB PATTIES: You can also cook the meatballs without the sauce, grilling or broiling or panfrying them, as with Lamb Slipper Kebabs (page 257). They will cook more evenly if they are flattened into a patty shape, 2½ to 3 inches across. Shape them as described at left, then flatten each one gently into a disk. Follow the cooking instructions on page 257, and once the patties are cooked, generously grind black pepper over them.

SERVES 6 AS AN APPETIZER, 4 AS A MAIN DISH

Serve with a moist fresh chutney or side salad, such as Tart Mango Salsa (page 48) or Spiced Grated Carrots, Kerala Style (page 143), as well as plenty of lime or lemon wedges.

Bargaining is, of course, very standard practice in the Subcontinent, and it's something that visitors sometimes have a hard time getting used to. If people aren't accustomed to bargaining, or even if they are, it's not always obvious how much bargaining is appropriate, and in what situations. The best thing to do is to ask around first, and then when you're in a bargaining situation, try to have fun with it.

When I was in my late twenties, in the early 1980s, for several years in a row I traveled to Nepal and India to buy jewelry and clothing that I would then sell at summer street fairs in Wyoming. It was my "living" for a while. I'd spend about fifteen hundred dollars each year buying, and make forty-five hundred to five thousand dollars in return. With my profits I would buy another round-trip air ticket and have enough left over to live in Asia the next twelve months.

One of the jewelers I most depended upon was a friend in Kathmandu named Rajendra Singh, "Raju" for short. He had a tiny shop at the bottom of Freak Street (Jochen Tol), where he and two helpers made silver rings and earrings, each one handmade, not cast. I would typically order forty to fifty items, then go trekking for three weeks, and when I returned, the jewelry would be finished. It was enormous fun, in part because Raju was such a nice person. While I was in Kathmandu, I'd usually sit all afternoon in his shop and drink tea and smoke cigarettes (even though I didn't smoke . . .) and talk about jewelry and gemstones and life.

Every so often through the afternoon, foreigners would come into the shop, bending low so as not to bump their heads (Kathmandu doorways have a large ledge at the bottom and the top), and look over the jewelry. Inevitably they'd ask the price of things. Raju, as gracious and polite a shopkeeper as ever existed, would patiently respond, "That ring is one hundred rupees; that one is one hundred twenty." I would sit to one side, barely able to keep a straight face. Sometimes a ring that had been sixty rupees ten minutes ago would suddenly be one hundred rupees. And when the person at last stepped out, I'd ask.

"You see," Raju would explain, "the second person—I could see when he walked through the door—he is from Italy. I know that he will bargain more, so I have to start higher." As simple as that.

No set price. When you think about it, we have a less flexible version of sliding scale prices in North America. If I buy something in a fancy neighborhood, in a fancy shop, it costs more, even though it's the same thing I'd find somewhere else. Even coffee.

At a rural market in southern Orissa, a bangle vendor slides bangles over the hand of a customer and onto her wrist (see "Bangles," page 240).

BARGAINING

SLOW-COOKED WHEAT BERRIES AND LAMB WITH FRESH MINT

· · · · · · · · · · · ·

Known in most of Pakistan, India, and Afghanistan as *haleem*, this warming easy-to-eat combination is a cousin of the meat and grain dish known as *harissa* in Iran and in some Arab countries and as *herissah* in Armenian. *Haleem* is associated with the Muslim communities of the Subcontinent, from Pakistan to southern India. It's a savory main-course dish made of whole grains (usually wheat, as here, or sometimes barley or oats) cooked until tender with lamb (or, in other versions, chicken or beef) and flavorings, then ground. *Haleem* is the best kind of comfort food, satisfying on a cold day or after strenuous activity, or as a way to break a fast: It is a traditional food for the evening meal (after sundown) during the Muslim fasting month of Ramadan.

We like this version of *haleem* very much. Its complex blended flavors are rounded out by the warm taste of wheat and a noticeable chile heat. For less heat, reduce the green chiles or omit the cayenne. *Haleem* has a thick porridge texture, moist but not liquid, easy to spoon up. It's made with wheat berries, which you can find in most natural food stores. They need to be boiled and soaked ahead; then they simmer with the lamb and flavorings until softened, about an hour. *Haleem* can be made well ahead, then reheated at the last minute.

2 cups wheat berries, washed and drained

About 3 quarts water

1 pound boneless lamb shoulder or leg, trimmed of excess fat

¹/₂ cup ghee, rendered lamb fat, peanut oil, or vegetable oil

About 3 cups thinly sliced onions

3 cloves

6 green cardamom pods

One 2-inch piece cinnamon or cassia stick

1 tablespoon minced garlic or garlic mashed to a paste

2 teaspoons minced ginger or ginger mashed to a paste

1 tablespoon coriander seeds, toasted and ground

1 teaspoon cumin seeds, toasted and ground

¹/₂ teaspoon cayenne

3 green cayenne chiles, minced

1¹/₂ teaspoons salt, or to taste

About 1 cup finely chopped mint leaves

2 limes, cut into wedges

Place the wheat berries in a large heavy pot with 6 cups of the water, bring to a boil, partially cover, and boil hard for 30 minutes.

Remove the wheat berries from the heat and let soak, covered, for 3 hours (or as long as overnight, if more convenient; the wheat berries can also be covered and refrigerated for as long as 36 hours). You will have about 6 cups soaked softened wheat.

Cut the lamb into large bite-size pieces and set aside. About 1½ hours before you wish to serve the *haleem*, heat the ghee, fat, or oil in a wide heavy pot over medium-high heat. Add the onions and cook over medium to medium-high heat until softened and lightly browned, 12 to 15 minutes. Lift out the onions, pausing to let as much oil as possible drain off, and set them aside.

Place the pot (with the onion-frying oil still in it) over medium heat. Toss in the cloves, cardamom, and cinnamon stick and fry for a minute, or until aromatic, then add the garlic and ginger and stir-fry for 30 seconds. Toss in the ground coriander, cumin, and cayenne and stir to blend them into the oil. Add the lamb and stir-fry to expose all the surfaces to the hot pan and to brown them a little, 5 to 10 minutes, depending on the size of your pot.

Add the green chiles and stir in, then add the remaining 6 cups water and the soaked wheat and bring to a boil. Add 1 teaspoon of the salt and cook, partially covered, at a medium boil until the wheat is very soft and the meat is tender, about 1 hour. Stir occasionally to make sure that nothing is sticking, and add extra water if needed; lower the heat slightly after about half an hour as the mixture thickens. Taste and add salt to taste.

Transfer the mixture to a food processor (you will have to work in batches), removing and discarding the whole spices as you do so, and process to a porridgelike texture (each batch takes about 1 minute in the processor). Or pass the mixture through a food mill, or mash it with a potato masher or using a large mortar and a pestle until fairly even textured. The grains of wheat will still have a little bite, very agreeable, but most of the dish will be smooth textured.

Place the mixture back in the pot and reheat, stirring in a little water if necessary to prevent sticking.

Serve hot, mounded in a wide shallow serving bowl, topped with the fried onions and a generous sprinkling of mint leaves. *Alternatively*, spoon the *haleem* into individual serving bowls or wide soup plates, allowing about 1 cup per person, then top each with the onions and mint. Put out the lime wedges and squeeze on fresh lime juice if desired.

MAKES 8 CUPS; SERVES 6 TO 8

Haleem is traditionally served with flatbreads, such as Home-Style Tandoor Naan (page 116) or Chapatis (page 110), and perhaps a fresh salad, such as Cucumber Raita (page 67) or Cachoombar (page 57).

BALTI HALEEM: We've come across a recipe for *haleem* from Baltistan, the mountainous area on the upper Indus River in Pakistan. There wheat is a luxury, and perhaps that's why the Balti *haleem* was made with crushed oats and a mixture of chana, masur, and mung dals, all soaked, then cooked together with the aromatics, rather than the wheat and meat of more agriculturally prosperous regions.

CUMIN-CORIANDER BEEF PATTIES

· · · · · · · · · · · · ·

This is the best and easiest way we know to eat ground beef—succulent, delicately scented with cumin and coriander, and pretty with fresh coriander leaves blended into the meat. It's important to start with good beef, preferably organic or grass raised. If you're using defrosted frozen meat, see the Note.

The usual name for these patties is *kebabs*, because originally they were shaped onto metal skewers so they could be easily grilled over a flame. We find ourselves often making them on a rushed weeknight and grilling them or panfrying them. Frying gives them a crunchy crust and succulent aromatic interior.

For very mild heat, use ¼ teaspoon cayenne; for more perceptible heat, use ½ teaspoon or more. PHOTOGRAPH ON PAGE 270

About 1 pound best-quality lean ground beef

½ cup finely chopped or grated onion or shallots

1 teaspoon minced ginger or ginger ground to a paste (optional)

1 teaspoon ground cumin

1 teaspoon ground coriander

¼ to ½ teaspoon cayenne

1 teaspoon salt

¼ cup plain (full- or reduced-fat) yogurt

1 teaspoon rice vinegar

¼ to ½ cup packed chopped coriander leaves or
**   ¼ cup minced mint leaves**

Peanut oil or vegetable oil

Place the meat in a bowl, add the onion or shallots, ginger, if using, cumin, coriander, cayenne, salt, yogurt, and vinegar, and mix well with your hands or a rubber spatula or wooden spoon, turning and mashing and kneading to blend the flavors and to get a smooth texture.

A smooth elastic texture helps the meat hold together during cooking. (The mixture can be refrigerated, covered, for several hours. Remove from the refrigerator half an hour before cooking.)

Add the coriander or mint and mix in. Put out two plates and lightly oil them.

To shape eight medium patties, wet your hands with water, then scoop up about ¼ cup of the mixture. Use your hands to shape and press it into an oval or round ¾ inch thick. Give it several light but firm squeezes so it holds its shape, then place it on an oiled plate and repeat with the remaining meat.

To grill the patties, prepare a charcoal or gas grill. Lightly oil the rack. Transfer the patties to the grill and cook over a medium flame, turning them after 5 minutes or so, until done the way you like them. Do not press and flatten the meat with your spatula.

To broil the patties, preheat the broiler. Place the patties on the lightly oiled rack of the broiler pan and place the pan under the broiler so that the patties are 5 to 7 inches from the heating element. Leave the oven door propped slightly ajar as you broil. Cook until the tops are browned, then turn them over and cook on the second side; you may wish to turn them back over to finish off the first side. Cooking time depends on how well done you like them; we usually allow about 8 minutes total.

To panfry the patties, place a large heavy skillet over high heat. Add 2 tablespoons oil, then lower the heat to medium-high. Put in as many patties as fit comfortably in the pan. If you like a slightly crusty outside, leave the heat at medium-high; if you want a softer outside, lower the heat to medium. Cook for about 3 minutes over medium-high, 4 minutes over medium, then turn the patties over and cook for another 3 or 4 minutes on the second side.

MAKES 8 MEDIUM BEEF PATTIES; SERVES 4

Serve with flatbreads or rice and a fresh salad or with Himalayan Grilled Tomato Sauce (page 94). For an extra vegetable dish, try Succulent Mountain Mushrooms (page 145). You might put out a hot condiment as well, a sambol, such as Sri Lankan Seeni Sambol (page 33), or just Dijon mustard.

NOTE: If you are using frozen ground beef, make sure that the meat has completely defrosted. If there are any little cold lumps left in the meat, they will prevent it from holding together properly, and they will also give off excess water as they cook. Pour off any water that accumulated as the meat defrosted.

SPICED PORK KEBABS: The kebab tradition in the Subcontinent came with the Moghul conquerors, who brought their tandoor ovens and Persian-style tastes about ten centuries ago. The Moghuls were Muslim, so the meat traditions they introduced included lamb or goat and also beef, but not pork, which is *haram*, or "forbidden," to Muslims. Pork does, however, make a great kebab, especially if it's freshly ground. Our friend Cassandra, who helped test many of the recipes in this book, tried this recipe with pork and loved it. (If you are grinding the pork yourself in the food processor, it grinds easily if it's well chilled.) Use 1 tablespoon fresh lime juice in place of the vinegar, and use only 2 tablespoons yogurt; also include a pinch of ground cloves in the mixture. Make the patties thinner, ½ inch at their thickest point, so you can get them cooked through easily.

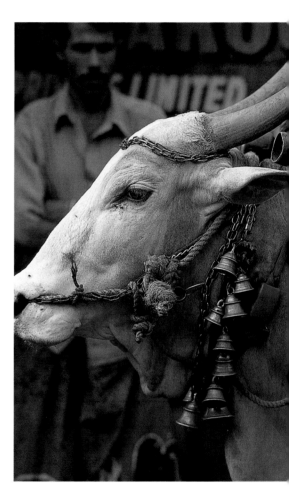

A bullock decorated with bells pulls a cart through the market in Kandy, Sri Lanka.

GRILLED MARINATED BEEF

. . . .

This easy beef grill comes from the Muslim community in Sri Lanka. We make it with organic or grass-raised beef, usually part of a round or rump roast. The meat comes off the grill with a flavored crust and meltingly tender interior. Allow an hour for the beef to marinate, then place it straight onto the preheated charcoal or gas grill.

1 pound boneless beef (see headnote)

MARINADE
1 tablespoon minced garlic or garlic mashed to a paste
3 tablespoons minced shallots
1/2 teaspoon ground ginger
1 tablespoon coriander seeds
2 dried red chiles, stemmed
1/2 teaspoon turmeric
1/2 teaspoon salt
1 tablespoon peanut or vegetable oil
1/2 cup plain (full- or reduced-fat) yogurt
1 tablespoon fresh lime juice

Cut the beef into 1-inch cubes. Set aside.

To make the marinade, place the garlic, shallots, and ginger in a medium bowl. Grind the coriander seeds and chiles in a spice/coffee grinder or with a stone mortar and a pestle. (If you're using a stone mortar, the garlic and shallots can be ground together with these dry ingredients). Add the ground spices to the bowl, along with the turmeric, salt, oil, yogurt, and lime juice, and stir to mix well. Add the beef and mix to ensure that the meat is well coated with marinade. Cover and refrigerate for at least 1 hour, and as long as 4 hours, whatever is most convenient.

Prepare a charcoal or gas grill.

Put the beef onto skewers (see Note), so the pieces are just touching. Cook over a hot fire, turning the skewers frequently so the meat cooks but doesn't burn, until medium-rare or medium, about 6 minutes. The hot fire will give a crisp outer crust to the meat; to test for doneness, cut into one cube to see that the interior is as you wish it to be.

SERVES 4 TO 5

Serve with plain or flavored rice, a green salad, a sambol or chutney, and Ladies' Fingers Curry (page 170) or Green Tomato Curry (page 142) or another well-sauced vegetable dish.

NOTE: We have metal skewers, so that's what we use for all our grilled kebabs. They're especially good here, where the fire called for is hot. If you have only bamboo skewers, be sure to soak them well in water for an hour before using, so they don't burn on the grill.

PRECEDING PAGES, LEFT: *Cumin-Coriander Beef Patties (page 268).* RIGHT: *Tikka Kebabs (page 256) and arugula and shallot salad (see page 55), wrapped in Home-Style Tandoor Naan (page 116).*

BANGLA SLOW-COOKED BEEF WITH ONION

· · · · · · · · · · · ·

We haven't eaten much beef on the Subcontinent, because in Hindu communities there's no beef around. So it was a delicious surprise to be served beef *bhoona,* as this dish is called, when I was in Bangladesh. It was accompanied not by plain rice, but by *kichuri,* a kind of easy pilaf of rice and dal (page 96). In a traditional home-style Bangla meal, if you served plain rice with the beef *bhoona,* you would also serve a simple dal, as well as a green vegetable.

Bhoona is a method of slow cooking spices and meat until tender. It is very suited to beef, for beef is one meat that must be cooked either very briefly or for a good long time. Anything in between results in tough meat. The small pieces of meat in this thick, rich-tasting stew are briefly browned, and then the whole dish simmers for a good hour. At the end of this second cooking, the meat is very tender, and the sauce has reduced to a thick aromatic gravy.

Use stewing beef and look for meat with some marbling, for that will give the best flavor and the tenderest texture. You can substitute round steak or flank steak, but again select meat with some marbling.

1 pound stewing beef (see headnote)

4 tablespoons butter or ¼ cup ghee, or 2 tablespoons each
    mustard oil and vegetable oil

1 teaspoon Bengali Five-Spice Mixture (page 340) or a scant ¼ teaspoon
    each black mustard, cumin, fennel, fenugreek, and nigella seeds

½ teaspoon turmeric

2 teaspoons ground coriander

2 bay leaves

One 2-inch piece cinnamon or cassia stick

1 tablespoon minced garlic or garlic mashed to a paste

1 tablespoon minced ginger or ginger mashed to a paste

1½ to 2 cups thinly sliced onions

4 green cayenne chiles, sliced into ¼-inch-thick rings

½ to 1 cup water

2 tablespoons fresh lime juice

1 teaspoon salt, or to taste

1 teaspoon sugar

About 1 cup loosely packed coriander leaves

½ cup Browned Onions (page 343; optional)

2 limes, cut into wedges

Cut the meat into ½-inch cubes or into narrow strips about 1 inch long. Set aside.

In a wide heavy pot, heat the butter, ghee, or oils over medium-high heat. Add the spice blend and cook for about 30 seconds, or until the mustard seeds have popped. Add the turmeric, coriander, bay leaves, cinnamon, garlic, and ginger and stir-fry for 30 seconds. Add the sliced onions, reduce the heat to medium, and cook, stirring frequently to prevent sticking, until well softened, about 10 minutes.

Add the meat and chiles and cook for a minute or two, stirring frequently, to brown the meat on all sides. Add enough water to moisten the dish well and the lime juice. Raise the heat and bring to a boil. Toss in the salt and sugar, lower the heat to medium, cover loosely, and simmer for 40 minutes to 1 hour, stirring occasionally to prevent sticking, until the meat is very tender and softened. The sauce will be rather thick. (The dish can be set aside, covered, for up to 1 hour, or refrigerated for up to 1 day. Reheat until very hot, stirring to prevent sticking.)

Stir in half the coriander leaves, then transfer to a serving bowl. Top with the browned onions, if using, and the remaining coriander leaves. Serve hot, with the lime wedges on a plate alongside; a squeeze of lime juice brings forward the flavor of the beef.   SERVES 4

Serve with rice, either plain rice or kichuri *(see headnote), and with Bangla Salad Plate (page 54) on the side. A fresh or lightly cooked vegetable dish, such as Pea Shoots for a Crowd (page 161), makes a good accompaniment.*

I wanted to plan a visit to Orissa, a state on the east coast of India, so one night at home I started searching the Internet. I was specifically interested in the tribal mountainous regions of Orissa, and sure enough, there on the Internet I found several different small tourist agencies willing to arrange for a car and driver. One seemed especially good because it was the only one actually located in Orissa, and the language was matter-of-fact, not overblown with adventure.

So I e-mailed them, and the next day I heard back from Gagan, the president of the company, giving me details concerning possible itineraries and costs. Over the next few weeks we e-mailed back and forth, and finally arrangements were settled upon. It was easy.

Six weeks later, in early February, I at last arrived in Bhubaneshwar, the capital city of Orissa, and there was Gagan to meet me at the airport. He took me to his office (located below his and his parents' home), and introduced me to Ranjan, who would be my driver. (Gagan, it turned out, was not only the president of Dove Tours, his company, but in fact he *was* the company and hired drivers as he needed them.)

Next day Ranjan and I headed out. We drove all day long, arriving just after dark at Baliguda, our first destination. The hotel in Baliguda was basic, reminding me of a Tibetan truckstop, so I set up my mosquito net in the dark (the power in town was out), then caught a candlelit meal on the main street and turned in early, knowing we would be back on the road at five, an hour before dawn.

Next morning we headed out on a bumpy dirt road, going about fifteen miles per hour in Ranjan's sparkling white Ambassador sedan. Under a giant canopy of sal trees and mango trees, light began to arrive, illuminating the morning mist in all directions. On the road in front of us we saw a group of women approaching, carrying firewood on their heads to sell in the local market.

"These are Kutia Kondh people," Ranjan said as he stopped the car, and we got out to meet them.

Ten days Ranjan and I traveled together, driving all day every day, at fifteen to twenty-five miles per hour (sometimes even faster). We drove from Baliguda to Rayagada to Gupteswar to Jeypore to Kunduli, meeting Kutia Kondh, Desia Kondh, Dongria, Dhrua, Gadaba, and Bondo people, all tribal peoples living remote lives in the mountains and forests of Orissa. We walked into villages, visited small village markets, shopped at big weekly fairs (at Kunduli, more than five thousand people gather each week). I learned about harvesting turmeric, boiling and drying it; about reducing palm sugar; about distilling liquor from millet and sago palm juice. I had a glimpse of the daily life of Orissan herders and hunters and fishermen.

I had a time I will never ever forget, thanks to the Internet, Ranjan, Gagan, and the amazing indigenous peoples of Orissa.

A group of Bondo women and girls wait at a market in the chill of early morning. The Bondo are one of many distinct cultural groups that live at a subsistence level in the densely jungled hills of southern Orissa.

ORISSA

A typical lovingly and gaudily decorated Bangladeshi rickshaw by a wall in the village of Savar, north of the capital, Dhaka. OPPOSITE: Sri Lankan Beef Curry (page 278) topped with sliced red radish; alongside, Tamarind-Mint Tea (page 313).

SRI LANKAN BEEF CURRY

· · · · · · · · · · · ·

The curry leaves and green chile give this Sri Lankan curry a pretty pale green color. We use either boneless beef or ribs, and you can also use the same method to make lamb curry (see the variation). The dish has plenty of aromatic sauce slightly enriched with coconut milk, and a mild chile heat. Leftovers are delicious. PHOTOGRAPHS ON PAGES 20 AND 276

1 pound boneless beef (such as round steaks or roast) or
    about 1¹/₂ pounds short ribs or cross ribs
1 tablespoon vegetable oil
About 10 fresh or frozen curry leaves
1 green cayenne chile, finely chopped
Generous 1 cup finely chopped onion
1 teaspoon turmeric
1 teaspoon salt
¹/₂ cup canned or fresh coconut milk
1 tablespoon tamarind pulp
¹/₄ cup hot water
3 cups water

DRY SPICE MIXTURE
1 tablespoon raw white rice
1 tablespoon coriander seeds
1 teaspoon cumin seeds
One 1-inch piece cinnamon or cassia stick
5 to 6 cardamom seeds (from 1 to 2 green cardamom pods)

Cut the boneless beef into approximately ¹/₂-inch cubes. Or, if using ribs, cut them apart. Set aside.

In a small dry heavy skillet, roast the dry spice mixture over medium-high heat for 3 to 4 minutes, stirring frequently, until it has a good aroma. Transfer to a spice/coffee grinder and grind to a powder, or grind with a mortar and a pestle. Set aside in a small bowl.

In a wide heavy pot, heat the oil over medium-high heat. When the oil is hot, add the curry leaves, green chile, onion, and turmeric and stir-fry for 3 minutes. Add the beef and salt and cook, stirring occasionally to expose all surfaces of the meat to the hot oil, for 5 minutes, or until the meat is browned.

Add the reserved dry spice mixture and the coconut milk and stir to coat the meat with the coconut milk. Reduce the heat to medium and cook for 10 minutes, stirring occasionally.

Meanwhile, chop the tamarind pulp and soak it in the hot water for about 10 minutes. Press the mixture through a strainer or sieve placed over a bowl. Discard the pulp and combine the tamarind liquid with the 3 cups water.

Add the liquid to the pot and bring to a boil, then lower the heat and cook at a strong simmer for about 1 hour, or until the meat is tender and the flavors well blended.

Taste and adjust the seasoning, if you wish. Serve hot.   SERVES 4 TO 5

Serve with plenty of rice to soak up the sauce and with a sweet chutney, such as Hot Sweet Date-Onion Chutney (page 28). Andhra Spiced Eggplant (page 49) or Fresh Bean Sprout Salad (page 55) would be a good side dish.

SRI LANKAN LAMB CURRY: Lamb makes another wonderful version of this curry. The slight acidity of the sauce complements the sweetness of the lamb. Use 1 pound boneless lamb shoulder, trimmed of fat.

PORK CURRY IN AROMATIC BROTH

· · · · · · · · · · ·

We enjoy dishes that can be put on to simmer, needing no care while they cook and gain flavor, and this easy pork curry from Sri Lanka falls into that category. Like many curries from Sri Lanka, it originated as a clay-pot dish that simmered over a low fire, but it also works well in a heavy pot over medium heat on the stove top.

The traditional recipe is made with a souring agent called *goraka* (fish tamarind; see Glossary). It's hard to find in North America, so we substitute tamarind, an equivalent souring fruit. We chop the other ingredients while the tamarind soaks, and once that's done, the dish takes very little work.

There's no coconut or coconut milk in the curry, just pork simmered with aromatics. Flavors are reminiscent of Southeast Asia, particularly northern and northeast Thailand, with a hint of lemongrass and a touch of sour. Some versions of this dish include cloves and cinnamon, but we find their flavors too intrusive with the mildness of the pork. If you add the optional spice powder at the end, it gives a touch of smokiness and thickens the broth a little. Without the spice powder, the broth is clear and still full of flavor.

1 tablespoon tamarind pulp

¼ cup very hot water

1 tablespoon raw sesame oil or vegetable oil

½ cup finely chopped shallots

1 tablespoon minced garlic or garlic mashed to a paste

1 tablespoon minced ginger or ginger mashed to a paste

2 green cayenne chiles, finely chopped

1 teaspoon minced lemongrass

10 to 12 fresh or frozen curry leaves

1 pound boneless pork butt or shoulder,
   cut into ½-inch cubes (see Note)

1¾ cups water

1 teaspoon salt

1 teaspoon Fragrant Sri Lankan Spice Powder
   (page 341; optional; see headnote)

Chop the tamarind pulp into several pieces and place it in a small bowl with the hot water. Let soak for 10 minutes, then use a fork or your fingers to squeeze and mash the pulp. Place a strainer or sieve over another small bowl, pour the tamarind blend into the strainer, and use the back of a spoon to press it against the mesh. Discard the pulp and set the tamarind liquid aside.

Heat the oil in a wide heavy pot over medium heat. Add the shallots, garlic, ginger, chiles, lemongrass, and curry leaves and stir-fry for 3 to 4 minutes, until the shallots and chiles are starting to soften. Add the pork and cook, turning it to expose all surfaces of the meat to the hot pan, for about 4 minutes, until the pork is touched all over with pale brown.

Add the water, the reserved tamarind liquid, and the salt, stir to mix well, and bring to a boil. Reduce the heat to maintain a medium simmer and cook, uncovered, for about 30 minutes. Add the spice blend, if using, about 5 minutes before the curry is finished.

Taste, adjust the seasonings if you wish, and serve hot. **SERVES 4 TO 5**

Serve with rice, Shredded Green Bean Mallum (page 76) or another lightly cooked green vegetable, and Red Onion Sambol (page 32) or Fresh Bean Sprout Salad (page 55).

NOTE: We use pork butt trimmed of fat because even trimmed it has a little veining of fat that makes the meat tender and smoothes the flavors in the broth. You can use pork shoulder, or any cut that has a little fat in it.

GOAN PORK VINDALOO

. . . .

When I was a student in London in the 1970s, Indian food was an inexpensive treat. The curry houses in those days always had a pork vindaloo on the menu, but only for the brave or foolhardy, we used to think, for it was always made very chile hot.

Since then, we've eaten vindaloo dishes in Goa (where they originated) and elsewhere in India, and we've made them at home. They're easy and most rewarding. Tastes are hot, yes (from a mix of ground mustard seed, dried chiles, ginger, and black pepper), but also clean and direct. There's no coconut milk, no yogurt, just a slightly acidic (from vinegar) spice paste that tenderizes and flavors the meat.

In Goa, the chiles are usually only medium hot, and very bright red, like the chiles of Kashmir. They're hard to find here, so we substitute dried red chiles from Thailand. If you're worried that this dish may be too hot, reduce the number of chiles. Then, if you find the dish is too mild, you can always add a pinch of cayenne powder to up the heat as the dish is simmering.

Traditionally in Goa, the dried spices are ground with a mortar and a pestle, using a little vinegar to moisten the mixture and make a paste. If you use a spice/coffee grinder, add the vinegar after the spices are ground, as directed here.

The meat is rubbed with salt, then with the marinade, and it marinates for 4 to 12 hours. The vinegar-spice paste makes the meat flavorful and tender, and final cooking is very quick. The only rule with vindaloo is, *don't add water*, just liquid flavorings. We add a little more vinegar, for sourness, as Goans do, but in Goa traditionally the sourness would come from *kokum* (fish tamarind; see Glossary). We use medium-dry sake or vodka or rice wine as a substitute for the Goan liquor *feni*, which is made from fermenting cashew apples or coconut (see page 310).

Use a cut of pork with a little fat, such as pork butt or shoulder; the fat gives tenderness and flavor. Because the meat simmers under a tight lid, there is no evaporation, so there's plenty of delicious sauce.

About 1 pound boneless pork butt, shoulder, or belly, trimmed of excess fat and cut into bite-size pieces
1½ teaspoons salt, or to taste
2 tablespoons raw sesame oil, coconut oil, or peanut oil
About ½ cup minced onion
2 tablespoons rice vinegar
¼ cup medium-dry sake, vodka, or Chinese rice wine

SPICE PASTE
5 dried red chiles, stemmed and crumbled, or 1 to 2 teaspoons cayenne (see headnote)
¼ teaspoon black peppercorns
½ teaspoon cumin seeds
½ teaspoon black mustard seeds
1 clove or a pinch of ground cloves
½ teaspoon ground cinnamon
1 tablespoon minced garlic or garlic mashed to a paste
2 teaspoons minced ginger or ginger mashed to a paste
2 tablespoons rice vinegar
½ teaspoon sugar

Place the pork in a bowl and sprinkle on all sides with 1 teaspoon of the salt. Set aside.

Make the spice paste. *To use a spice/coffee grinder,* place the chiles and all the whole spices in the grinder and reduce to a powder. Turn out into a small bowl and add the ground spices. Add the garlic, ginger, and vinegar and stir to mix, using the spoon to smear the mixture against the side of the bowl to blend it well. *To use a mini-chopper,* grind the chiles and whole spices as fine as possible in the chopper and transfer to a small bowl. Place the garlic and ginger in the chopper and chop to a fine paste, then add all the ground spices. Transfer to the small bowl and stir in the vinegar. *To use a mortar and a pestle,* start by pounding or grinding the chiles and whole spices, then add the garlic and ginger and pound or grind to a paste, moistening the mixture with some or all of the vinegar. Transfer to a small bowl. If you didn't add the full 2 tablespoons vinegar as you were grinding, add the balance now.

Stir the sugar into the spice blend and then add to the meat, turning and stirring to coat the meat. Cover and refrigerate for 4 to 12 hours, whatever is most convenient.

Place a large wok or karhai (see Glossary) or a wide heavy pot over high heat. Add the oil, and when it is hot, add the meat and any excess marinade. Stir-fry for about 5 minutes, until all sides of the meat have changed color. Add the onion and stir-fry another 2 to 3 minutes. Add the vinegar and the sake, vodka, or wine and bring to a boil. Stir-fry briefly, then cover and lower the heat to maintain a vigorous simmer. Cook for about 10 minutes, until the onion is very soft and the meat is tender.

Add the remaining ½ teaspoon salt and stir well, then taste and adjust if you wish. Serve hot.   SERVES 4

Serve with rice and a mild side dish, such as stir-fried greens or Aromatic Pumpkin and Coconut (page 160), or a sweet salad, such as Tomato, Red Onion, and Yellow Pepper Salad with Yogurt Dressing (page 71).

Women selling produce, including purple amaranth leaves, at a small market in Chowdy, in southern Goa

STREET FOODS,
SNACKS & DRINKS

IN THE SUBCONTINENT, LIFE ITSELF, IT SOMETIMES

seems, unfolds endlessly out on the street. In many areas of

larger towns and cities, people work on the sidewalks, they sleep

and cook on the sidewalks, they sell produce on the sidewalks.

For anyone who loves traveling in the Subcontinent, it's this life

of it. But street food here isn't the same as in neighboring Southeast Asia, where the street food vendors are legendary. In the Subcontinent, though restaurants often spill out onto the street, especially around bus stands and train stations, few exist entirely in the street. There are exceptions: A vendor may fry fresh hot pakoras (deep-fried vegetable fritters) on a Jaipur street corner, or roast *papads* (crispy crackers) over a small coal fire in Kathmandu, but generally between-meal eats and street food revolve more around chai shops, casual places where people drop in throughout the day for a snack and a cup of tea.

Chai shops are an institution in South Asia. They're everywhere, and they range in size and style from a few small stools with a vendor serving tea in tiny clay cups to a big, elaborate, brightly lit sweets store making special masala (spiced) tea served in stainless steel cups. Whatever the size and style of the shop, there will almost always be snacks, some fried, many of them

Tamarind-Mint Tea (page 313)

deep-fried, hot, and succulent. There are South Indian *vadas* (chickpea fritters), there are samosas and pakoras and much more.

When we get back home from a trip to the Subcontinent, we miss the quick eats and the liveliness of the chai shops. Though we're not the world's most frequent deep fryers, we make an exception for South Asian snacks, especially if we have friends over, for many of these snacks make wonderful appetizers. All it takes is a stable deep-frying arrangement (we use a large wok placed on a back burner) and several chutneys or salsas made ahead, and suddenly we are turning out treats quickly and deftly for a happy crowd.

The other half of the equation is drinks, drinks to go with all that flavor. They range here from two different versions of chai to lassi and dried apricot nectar to a world of inventive liquors and beers.

Tea picker at a plantation in the mountains of central Sri Lanka. She picks the leaves one by one, then puts them into the large basket that she carries with her.

SPICY CHICKPEA FRITTERS
. . . .

There are many different kinds of fritters, but our favorite is masala *vada*, sometimes called dal *vada*. It looks a bit like a small hamburger but is vegetarian. My number-one favorite meal in South India is a masala *dosa* (page 112) and a masala *vada*. Both come served with a *sambhar* (pages 186 or 187) and coconut chutney (page 39). The *dosa* (a crepelike bread, page 112) is the meal, while the *vada* is more like a snack to have along with the meal. There is something special about the two together, the *vada* dry and crunchy, the *dosa* (mixed with the soupy *sambhar*) all soft and squishy.

Vadas are also just a great snack on their own or with a cup of chai. When we make them at home, they fry up quickly in hot oil. Serve hot; or freeze them or some of them, and then reheat them in the microwave or oven.

2 cups chickpeas, soaked in cold water for at least 3 hours or overnight

About ³/₄ cup chopped onion

2 to 3 tablespoons minced green cayenne chiles

2 teaspoons minced ginger or ginger mashed to a paste

1¹/₂ teaspoons salt

1 cup loosely packed coriander leaves, roughly chopped

2 cups peanut oil for deep-frying

ACCOMPANIMENTS

Coconut Chutney (page 39), Tamarind Sauce (page 45), Tomato Chutney (page 44), Tart Mango Salsa (page 48), and/or another chutney or salsa

Drain the chickpeas and put them into a food processor with the onion, chiles, ginger, and salt (it will probably be easiest to do this in two batches). Process until the chickpeas are broken down but still coarse, not absolutely smooth. Add the coriander and process briefly to mix, then transfer to a bowl (if you worked in batches, mix them together).

Put the accompaniments you plan to serve in several condiment bowls and set aside.

Put out a slotted spoon and a platter lined with paper towels. Heat the oil in a stable wok or karhai (see Glossary) or a heavy pot over medium-high heat (325° to 350°F). Use a deep-frying thermometer to check the temperature, or stick a wooden chopstick or the handle of a wooden spoon into the oil: If bubbles rise around the wood, the oil is hot enough.

Wet your hands with water, scoop up about 2 tablespoons of the chickpea batter in one hand, and shape it in your palm into a golf ball–size round; the batter will be a little messy, but not unmanageable. Then, as if you were making a small hamburger patty, pat the ball into a flattened disk between your palms. Gently slide it into the hot oil and quickly shape two to four more (depending upon the size of your pan; you don't want them crowded). Fry until nicely browned, 3 to 4 minutes.

Lift the patties out of the oil with the slotted spoon and drain on the paper towel–lined platter. Continue until all the batter has been cooked, making sure that the oil is at 325° to 350°F before adding each new batch.

Serve hot or warm, with the accompaniments.

MAKES ABOUT 20 FRITTERS; SERVES 5 TO 6

Serve with one or more chutneys or salsas as a snack or appetizer, or as part of a meal.

SWEET SEV WITH RAISINS

. . . .

There's a huge category of savory snacks in India that goes by the name *chaat*. *Chaat* vendors sell small paper cones of crunchy snacks, assembled and flavored one by one.

A Muslim family in Udaipur taught us about this slightly crunchy blended snack, based on little dried noodles called *sev* that are made of deep-fried chickpea flour (*besan*). We make it a lot; it's been a hit in our house from the first, and it's very quick. Sometimes we have only one kind of raisin available, or we are out of pistachios; if you lack pistachios, increase the cashews to a generous ¼ cup. Keep the heat at medium or lower, so there's no risk of burning.

Sweet *sev* is often tinted yellow with a little food coloring. In a wealthy household, and probably in the Moghul court, where it apparently originated, the color would have come from saffron-tinted ghee, a sign of luxury that marked it as a special dish. We do use butter as the cooking medium, but we forego the coloring.

¼ cup golden raisins plus ¼ cup dark raisins, or ½ cup either one

¼ cup unblanched whole almonds

Scant ¼ cup pistachios (see headnote)

3 to 4 tablespoons ghee or butter

Scant ¼ cup cashews

½ cup fresh or frozen grated coconut or dried shredded coconut

2 cups dried chickpea flour noodles (see Glossary)

2 tablespoons sugar

ACCOMPANIMENT

About 10 *papads,* preferably black pepper–flavored, freshly toasted (page 289)

Wash the raisins in warm water. Cut the almonds lengthwise into halves or quarters, depending on their size. Cut the pistachios in half. Place all the ingredients near your stove top.

Heat a wok or karhai (see Glossary) or a large heavy skillet over medium heat. Add the ghee or butter and tilt the pan to swirl it and coat the pan as it melts. Add the raisins and all the nuts and cook gently for about a minute, stirring them to expose all sides to the hot pan. Add the coconut and stir to blend it in and break up lumps. After another minute or so, add the dried noodles and cook, stirring frequently to prevent burning, for about 5 minutes. (Lower the heat to medium-low if necessary to prevent the ingredients from crisping up or turning dark brown; they should stay pale. Resist the temptation to add water.) About a minute before you finish cooking, add the sugar and stir and toss gently to mix in.

Turn out onto a platter and mound in the center. Let cool to lukewarm or to room temperature before serving. (Prepare the *papads* while the mixture cools.)

Put out a small bowl or plate and a spoon for each guest (for those who don't want to eat with their hand), and a pair of serving spoons by the platter so guests can serve themselves. Stack the *papads* in a shallow bowl. Show your guests how to crumble a *papad* onto the *sev;* it gives a pleasing crispy crunch and a nice little jolt of black pepper heat.

SERVES 3 TO 4

Serve as a snack with tea, at any time of day.

CRISP-FRIED OKRA TIDBITS

· · · · · · · · · · · ·

We like okra whole and slightly slimy, we like it in stews, and we love it like this: crispy, melting, little bite-size slices. When fried rather than boiled or steamed, okra is both crisp and tender. These are great bar snacks, to accompany beer or cocktails, and they also make a delicious vegetable side.

¾ pound okra
2 green cayenne chiles (optional)
About ¼ cup peanut oil or raw sesame oil
About ½ teaspoon fine sea salt

Trim the ends from the okra and slice the okra into ¼-inch-thick slices (about 3 cups sliced). If using chiles, slit them lengthwise and scrape out the seeds. Slice crosswise into ¼-inch-thick slices. Line a plate with a paper towel.

Place a 10- to 11-inch cast-iron or other heavy skillet over medium-high heat and add the oil. When the oil is hot, add half the okra and spread it out over the hot surface of the pan. After 2 minutes, add half the chiles, if using. Continue to cook for about 5 minutes, or until the okra is browning on the first side, then use a spatula to flip the slices over. Fry on the other side until lightly browned, then use a slotted spoon to transfer to the paper towel–lined plate.

Use another paper towel to blot the okra and chiles well, then transfer to a clean plate or shallow bowl and sprinkle with about ¼ teaspoon salt, tossing to distribute the salt.

Repeat with the remaining okra (and chiles, if using). Add to the first batch of okra, sprinkle on another ¼ teaspoon salt, and toss. Taste for salt and add more, if you wish. Serve hot or at room temperature.

SERVES 6 TO 8

Serve as a snack with beer or a cold drink. Or serve as a vegetable side dish to accompany a meal of rice and a moist stew such as Cashew-Coconut Meatballs (page 262) or Zinet's Chicken with Tomato and Greens (page 244), or any of the dals on pages 178 to 198.

CAYENNE TIDBITS: If you don't have green chiles handy but want some chile heat, sprinkle on about ¼ teaspoon cayenne after you've seasoned the okra for the second time. You can also grind black pepper over, if you wish.

FRIED OKRA-YOGURT SALAD: These fried nuggets can become an ingredient to flavor a yogurt-based salad. Drain 2 cups plain (full- or low-fat) yogurt in a sieve for 20 minutes, then whisk in a little water (as described in the recipe for Cucumber Raita, page 67). Just before serving, stir in 1 cup or more fried okra, together with a little minced scallion, mint, or coriander, if you wish. Serve as a side salad with grilled meats.   YIELDS ABOUT 3 CUPS; SERVES 6 TO 8

FLAME-CRISPED PAPADS

. . . .

Papads—crisp, paper-thin flatbreads made from mung or urad dal—are sold in packages all over the Subcontinent. There was a time when each family would prepare its own dough at home, roll out the very thin rounds with a special grooved rolling pin, and dry them in the sun. Then the dried disks were gathered and stored, ready for use whenever needed. Many families still prepare homemade *papads* (sometimes called *pappadums*), but most people buy them already dried and packaged. Cottage industries now turn out good-quality inexpensive *papads* by the thousands.

If you've never bought a package of *papads* to cook at home, you have a wonderful surprise to look forward to. In an Indian grocery, you will generally find a wide variety for sale. Some will be flavored with cayenne pepper or black pepper, or garlic. Some will be brittle and so thin that they're almost translucent, while others will be relatively thick and made perhaps from a different kind of dal. We suggest buying a couple of different kinds, as they do differ quite a lot one from another. (And they are incredibly inexpensive, especially considering the amount of work that goes into producing them.) Package sizes vary, but *papads* usually come ten to twelve to a package and keep almost indefinitely, as long as they're sealed and kept in a cool, dry cupboard. They're an easy way to bring flavor and texture to a meal.

Padads need to be cooked before you can serve them. There are several different ways to bring them back to life. A common way is to deep-fry them, by sliding them one at a time into a karhai (see Glossary) or a skillet filled with a couple of inches of hot oil. They will instantly start to expand and change color. With a pair of tongs, try to hold each one under the surface of the oil until the whole disk has cooked, a process that should take no more than 10 seconds. Pull out the *papads* with the tongs, shake gently to remove excess oil, and stack them to cool and become crisp. Fried *papads* can be sprinkled with grated coconut, chopped coriander leaves, cayenne, or a spice powder, either garam masala (page 342 or store-bought) or Fragrant Sri Lankan Spice Powder (page 341).

Our favorite way of cooking them, though, is to hold them with tongs over a flame of a gas burner (or a grill), quickly exposing all sides and edges to the heat. They crinkle up into beautiful shapes almost at once, and as they cool, they become very crisp.

Serve hot or at room temperature, as a snack or before a meal with drinks, as they sometimes are offered in northern India. Or serve them to accompany a rice meal: Break off a piece and use it like a cracker to scoop up a little curry or rice, crumble them onto the rice for an added touch of texture, or serve with sweet sev (see page 287).

Packages of papads for sale at the weekly market in Karwa, a town in the state of Karnataka, on the west coast of India just south of Goa. OPPOSITE, CLOCKWISE FROM UPPER RIGHT: Goan Meat Tart (page 292), Fennel-Flecked Potato Samosas (page 296), and Tomato Chutney (page 44).

GOAN MEAT TARTS

· · · · · · · · · · · · ·

Goa, a small state on India's west coast, south of Mumbai, was colonized by the Portuguese. There are still, especially in the towns, clear signs of the Portuguese era: usually a Catholic church or two (some of them very grand), as well as colonial-style arcades, signs in Portuguese, and shop proprietors with surnames like Fernandes or da Silva.

Another remnant of the Portuguese era is the pastry shops, very good pastry shops. The meat pastries here were inspired by those we indulged in at a pastry shop near the central market in the town of Margao, in south Goa. They are delicious oven-baked little tarts filled with savory cooked meat, either beef or pork. The pastry is very short and a little sweet, the meat moist and lightly spiced. In Goa we often washed them down with a cool Limca (local lime-flavored soda), but at home we serve them with ice-cold beer or Tamarind-Mint Tea (page 313).

These freeze very well. Two make a filling snack. PHOTOGRAPH ON PAGE 291

PASTRY

2½ cups all-purpose flour or 3 cups pastry flour (see Note)

½ teaspoon salt

2 tablespoons sugar

¼ teaspoon baking powder

½ pound (1 cup) lard or 1 cup vegetable shortening

1 large egg

1 tablespoon rice vinegar

2 to 3 tablespoons cold water, if needed

1 egg, whisked with 1 tablespoon water, for a wash (optional)

FILLING

Double recipe Beef Filling or Pork Filling (page 293),

    or one recipe of each

Make the pastry at least an hour before you wish to start baking.

Combine all the dry ingredients in a bowl and stir to mix well. Cut in the lard or shortening until the mixture resembles coarse meal. Mix together the egg and vinegar and stir in. Try pulling the dough together. If it is still crumbly, add about 2 tablespoons cold water and mix. This should be enough to moisten the dough; if necessary, add a little more cold water. When the dough just comes together, pull it into a mass. Cut it into two pieces (each will weigh just over ½ pound). Place each piece in a heavy-duty plastic bag, flatten out to a disk, seal well, and refrigerate for at least 30 minutes. (The pastry keeps for 3 days in the refrigerator or for 1 month, well sealed in plastic, in the freezer. Defrost overnight in the refrigerator before using.)

Place a baking stone, if you have one, on a rack in the center of the oven. Preheat the oven to 375°F.

Lightly dust your work surface with flour. Turn out the pastry from one bag, keeping the other refrigerated. Roll out to a 17-by-nearly-7-inch rectangle. Use a 3¼-inch round cookie cutter or glass to cut out 10 rounds. Place them on a baking sheet. Reroll the scraps to make another 6 rounds. Place them on the sheet.

Lightly dust your work surface with flour again, and repeat with the other piece of pastry, but set the rounds aside on your work surface.

Spoon a scant 2 tablespoons filling in the center of one of the circles on the baking sheet. Brush the edges with cold water, then place one of the reserved rounds on top. Pinch the edges together all around or press down with a fork, to seal. Repeat with the remaining rounds. For a more golden crust, brush with a little egg wash. Cut two slits in the top of each pastry.

Bake for 20 minutes, or until very golden. Set the pastries on a rack to cool for several minutes before serving, or cool completely, seal in plastic bags, and freeze. Thaw overnight in the refrigerator, place on a baking sheet, and heat in the center of a 300°F oven for about 15 minutes.

MAKES 16 PASTRIES; SERVES 8

Serve as a snack, or as part of an easy lunch with a green salad or a tomato salad.

NOTE: *Maida,* the all-purpose white flour that is used to make these in India, is a little less strong than North American all-purpose flour. In fact, it's closer to pastry flour.

BEEF FILLING

4 dried red chiles, stemmed

$^1/_2$ teaspoon cumin seeds

2 cloves

$^1/_4$ teaspoon freshly grated nutmeg

$^1/_4$ teaspoon mace

1 tablespoon raw sesame, coconut, or peanut oil

$^1/_2$ cup minced shallots

1 tablespoon minced ginger or ginger mashed to a paste

$^1/_3$ pound fairly lean ground beef

$^1/_2$ teaspoon salt

$^1/_4$ teaspoon freshly ground black pepper

1 tablespoon rice vinegar

1 teaspoon sugar

Finely grind the dried chiles, cumin, and cloves in a spice/coffee grinder. Combine with the nutmeg and mace and set aside.

Heat the oil in a wok or karhai (see Glossary) or a wide heavy skillet over medium heat. Add the shallots, ginger, and spice mixture and cook for about 5 minutes, or until the shallots are softened. Add the meat and salt, stirring to break up any lumps in the meat. Add the pepper, vinegar, and sugar and cook over medium heat, partially covered, stirring occasionally, until the meat has changed color. You want a little moisture, so add a little water if necessary during cooking. Remove from the heat and set aside to cool. (Once cooled, the mixture can be frozen in a well-sealed container; thaw and bring to room temperature before using.)

MAKES 1 CUP FILLING, ENOUGH FOR 8 TARTS

PORK FILLING

1 tablespoon raw sesame, coconut, or peanut oil

$^1/_2$ cup minced onion

2 teaspoons minced garlic or garlic mashed to a paste

2 teaspoons minced ginger or ginger mashed to a paste

$^1/_4$ teaspoon ground cinnamon

2 pinches of ground cloves

$^1/_2$ teaspoon crushed cumin seeds or ground cumin

$^1/_4$ teaspoon freshly ground black pepper

2 tablespoons minced green cayenne chiles

$^1/_3$ pound ground pork or $^1/_3$ pound boneless pork butt or belly, finely chopped (see Note)

About $^1/_4$ cup water

1 tablespoon rice vinegar

1 tablespoon *feni* (Goan liquor, see page 310), or substitute sweet sake (rice wine)

In a wok or karhai (see Glossary) or wide heavy pot, heat the oil over medium-high heat. Add the onion and stir-fry until translucent, about 4 minutes. Add the garlic, ginger, cinnamon, cloves, cumin, and pepper and stir-fry for about 1 minute. Add the chiles, pork, and about 2 tablespoons water and stir-fry over medium heat, separating any clumps of meat, until the pork is almost cooked through, about 5 minutes. Add the vinegar, liquor, and another 2 tablespoons water, then simmer until just a little moisture remains, 3 to 5 minutes. Transfer to a bowl to cool to room temperature. (Once cooled, the mixture can be frozen in a well-sealed container; defrost and bring back to room temperature before using.)

MAKES A GENEROUS 1 CUP, ENOUGH FOR 8 TARTS

NOTE: If using pork butt or belly, we find it easiest to start with cold or half-frozen meat. Slice it into $^1/_4$-inch-thick slices. These can go into the processor to be coarsely ground or be chopped by hand into $^1/_4$-inch cubes.

Two morning views of the Taj Mahal, built by the Moghul emperor Shah Jahan as a mausoleum for his wife, Mumtaz Mahal, who died in 1631. The Taj is in the city of Agra, in the state of Uttar Pradesh, about three hours' drive from the Indian capital, New Delhi. It is probably the most famous monument in India. The Yamuna River flows below it, so there's often a mist in the early morning.

I'M NOT BIG ON BIG SITES and festivals. I think it's partly because over time I've been caught in frightening situations in the Subcontinent, where crowds were out of control. And I'm especially not big on the Taj Mahal, because my first time in Agra, where the Taj is located, I felt so overwhelmed by touts and hawkers and hasslers that I turned around and headed back to the station to catch the first train out of town.

But years later, traveling with my friend Lee, a photographer, whose only request was a visit to the Taj at sunrise, I had to give in. Lee agreed to be entirely in charge. He found us a good hotel nearby to sleep the night before, and we arose well before dawn and walked to the Taj. There was mist coming up from the river and there were, surprisingly, very few people. We walked peacefully by ourselves and photographed, and as the sun finally came up, the Taj was absolutely beautiful. I felt ashamed to have been such a curmudgeon.

To walk into the Taj, we had to check our shoes at the gate. In the chill of the dawn, the marble floors were cold and wet and wonderfully slippery. As morning came, the sun quickly heated things up, and then crowds gathered, and before long we were ready to leave, having had a very good time.

Back at the gate, however, among the hundreds and hundreds of pairs of shoes, mine were nowhere to be found.

It's not easy finding size elevens in Agra.

Taj Mahal

Man meditating in Pushkar, Rajasthan

FENNEL-FLECKED POTATO SAMOSAS

. . . .

Every morning in Udaipur at the chai stall by the temple, I'd watch Mohan and his cook make potato-filled samosas, pyramid-shape snacks wrapped in a thin dough and deep-fried. They made piles of them, several hundred each day, for they had a standing order from the primary school nearby that had to be filled by ten o'clock in the morning.

The wrappers here are made with all-purpose flour, flavored with salt and fennel seed, and softened with a little oil, just as Mohan made his wrappers. They're beautiful with the green seeds floating in the pale dough, and they're a wonderful complement to the spiced potato filling.

PHOTOGRAPH ON PAGE 291

DOUGH

1 cup all-purpose flour, plus extra for rolling

¹⁄₂ teaspoon salt

Scant 1 teaspoon fennel seeds

2 tablespoons vegetable oil or raw sesame oil

Scant ¹⁄₂ cup warm water

Spicy Potato Filling (page 131), at room temperature

Peanut oil for deep-frying

OPTIONAL ACCOMPANIMENT

Tamarind Sauce (page 45) or Fresh Coriander–Peanut Chutney (page 28)

Make the dough an hour before you wish to shape the samosas. Place the flour, salt, and fennel seeds in a large bowl or the bowl of a food processor.

To make by hand, add the oil and stir with a spoon or your hand to blend it into the dry ingredients. Add the warm water and stir to mix and moisten all the flour. Turn out onto a lightly floured surface and knead for about 5 minutes until very smooth. *To use a food processor,* with the machine running, pour the oil, then the water, through the feed tube. A ball of dough will form. Process for about 15 seconds, then turn out the dough onto a lightly floured surface and knead for about 1 minute until very smooth.

Cover the dough with plastic wrap and set aside to rest for at least 30 minutes, or as long as 3 hours.

When you are ready to proceed, cut the dough in half and set one half aside, covered. Cut the remaining dough in half. Roll each half under your palms into a rope about 10 inches long, and cut it in half. Flatten each piece on a lightly floured surface, then roll each one out to an oval about 10 inches long and 4 inches wide. The dough may resist rolling out; in that case, roll out one, then start rolling out another to give the first one time to relax before trying to roll it out further. Once you have the pieces rolled out, dust both sides lightly with flour and stack them. Repeat with the remaining half of the dough.

To shape the samosas, work with one piece of dough at a time. Place a small bowl of cold water, and a baking sheet or platter lightly dusted with flour, near your work surface. (The shaping explanation may look long, but just follow it to make your first samosa and then you'll understand how it works.) Use a knife or dough cutter to cut one piece of dough crosswise in half. Pick up one half and lay it on your palm, cut side near your fingertips. Wet half the length of the cut side with a little water, then fold the dough over and pinch the cut sides together to make a pocket. Turn the pocket on your palm so this new seam is facing up and the pocket looks V-shaped, with the point toward your fingertips. Fill the pocket with a generous tablespoon of potato filling. Fold the curved flap (the part of the dough nearest your wrist) over the filling and pinch it carefully all around onto the edge of the pocket to seal well. Lay the samosa on the prepared tray or sheet and repeat with the remaining dough.

By the time the sixteen samosas are shaped, you will have used almost 2 cups filling, having a generous ½ cup left over. You could eat the leftover filling as a little snack or use it to fill several Potato-Stuffed Parathas (page 130).

Let the samosas stand, uncovered, for about 30 minutes. This gives the wrappers time to firm and dry a little, which is better for deep-frying.

Place a slotted spoon near your stove top and set a wire rack over a baking sheet or large plate. Place a large stable wok or karhai (see Glossary) or a heavy pot on the stove and add peanut oil to come to a depth of 2 inches. Heat the oil to 325° to 350°F. Test the temperature with a deep-frying thermometer, or place a wooden chopstick or the handle of a wooden spoon vertically into the oil. If bubbles rise along the wood, the oil is at the right temperature.

Slide in one samosa and then a second one; if there's room, add another one or two, one at a time. (Each time you add a samosa, it lowers the oil temperature, so a little pause between additions keeps the temperature from dropping too far.) The oil will bubble around them as they sink to the bottom. After about 20 seconds, use the slotted spoon to turn them over. Continue to monitor them as they cook to ensure that all sides get touched with brown and firm up. The cooking time will depend on the size of your pan, oil temperature, and how many samosas you are cooking at a time. When they look well browned, lift each out with a slotted spoon, pausing at the edge of the pan to let oil drain off, then transfer it to the wire rack to drain. Repeat with the remaining samosas. Serve hot or warm with the sauce or chutney. (To reheat leftovers, drop the samosas again into very hot oil for about 30 seconds, or wrap them well in foil and reheat in a 300°F oven for 10 minutes.)

MAKES 16 SAMOSAS; SERVES 8

Serve as a snack or appetizer, or as part of a meal with Udaipur Urad Dal (page 189) or another dal and a green salad.

MUSHROOM PAKORAS
WITH FRESH HERB CHUTNEY
· · · · · · · · · · · ·

We first developed this recipe when we wrote an article on Asian street food for *Food & Wine* magazine, now almost fourteen years ago. To this day, the article is one of the most enjoyable articles we've ever worked on, because it was such a fun subject, and this recipe is one of our all-time favorites. Our first test of the recipe was at midnight one summer night, when Jeffrey was playing around in the kitchen. The pakoras went together quickly and easily. We made a fresh mint-coriander chutney to go along with them, then poured two glasses of cold beer—wow, what a late-night treat!

1¹/₂ cups (5 ounces) chickpea flour (*besan*)

1 teaspoon salt

1 teaspoon baking powder

¹/₂ teaspoon cayenne

1 cup warm water

3 cups peanut oil for deep-frying

1 pound medium white or portobello mushrooms, rinsed and dried

ACCOMPANIMENT

Mint-Coriander Chutney (recipe follows) or

   Fresh Coriander–Peanut Chutney (page 28)

In a small bowl, combine the chickpea flour, salt, baking powder, and cayenne. Make a well in the center and pour in the warm water. Stirring from the center, incorporate the dry ingredients to make a smooth, thick batter. If the mixture is lumpy, pass it through a coarse strainer.

In a stable wok or karhai (see Glossary) or a deep heavy pot, heat the oil over medium-high heat to 375°F. Use a deep-frying thermometer to check the temperature, or stick a wooden chopstick or the handle of a wooden spoon into the oil: If bubbles rise around the wood, the oil is hot enough. Line a plate with paper towels.

Drop 3 or 4 mushrooms into the batter and turn to coat well. Using chopsticks or tongs, lift them out and gently place them in the hot oil. Fry, turning occasionally, until golden brown all over, 2 to 3 minutes. Transfer to the paper towels to drain well. Repeat with the remaining mushrooms and batter.

Serve hot, with the chutney.　　　　　SERVES 6

Serve with drinks or as an appetizer.

MINT-CORIANDER CHUTNEY: The chutney has a little hit of chile heat. Feel free to cut back on the chiles, or to substitute a milder chile, say a jalapeño.

2 cups packed mint leaves

¹/₄ cup fresh lime juice

2 tablespoons coriander leaves

3 tablespoons sliced shallots

2 teaspoons minced green cayenne chile, or to taste

1 teaspoon sugar

¹/₂ teaspoon salt

Place all the ingredients in the food processor and process for about 15 seconds, until almost pureed. For the brightest flavor, serve immediately.　　　　　MAKES ABOUT ²/₃ CUP

Serve as a dip for the pakoras, or for Fennel-Flecked Potato Samosas (page 296). We also like this as a condiment for grills: Bangla-Flavored Fried Zucchini (page 144), Cumin-Coriander Beef Patties (page 268), or Grilled Fish Steaks with Black Pepper Rub (page 210).

Birthday in Jaisalmer

Monsoon scene in Bangladesh: A young man runs along a path near flooded rice fields.

WE HAVE MIDSUMMER BIRTHDAYS, July 9 and 15 to be exact. Summer birthdays are both good and bad. When we were kids, summer birthdays were a bit of a pain because school was out and that meant no birthday cupcakes to take to class, etc. But one upside of a summer birthday is that if you like to travel, then individual birthdays can be easier to remember later in life because they often take place away from home.

One birthday I remember was in the desert town of Jaisalmer, in western Rajasthan. July is the middle of the monsoon season, so Jaisalmer was wet, really wet, even though it's in the desert. Rain fell without stopping, morning and night. The lanes of the ancient town became rivers, several feet deep. But the lanes were narrow, and the buildings built up, so there were tiny "sidewalks," narrow ledges that ran alongside the lanes that had become rivers, and you could jump from one sidewalk to another and get around town like children on monkey bars. With all the rain, people were happy and laughing, despite the inconvenience.

I was the only foreigner in town, as far as I could tell, and I was staying put for a while, needing to recover from stomach troubles. So each day I'd leap around town, finding different tea shops to patronize, not eating much but happy to be where I was. On the afternoon of my birthday, the rain came down particularly heavily, and for several hours I was trapped in a corner tea shop, big leaps no longer possible, only swims. But it was hugely fun, the rivers whooshing by, and people almost giddy.

By evening the water went down, and I returned to my hotel. It was a good birthday.

The rain was there to greet me when I landed in the Bangladeshi capital, Dhaka. It poured down in buckets as I stood under the overhang in front of the airport, looking for the person from the guesthouse who was supposed to meet me. Handfuls of people were standing waiting, holding their saris and their trousers up out of the wet. A man made swooshing sounds with a large, coarse broom as he swept debris and swirls of water off to one side. The air was so thick with moisture that I felt I was breathing warm water.

Eventually I gave up waiting and found a taxi to take me into town. All was dull colored and muted in the downpour. The back wheels of the car *thrummed* whenever we drove through patches of deep water, and we left a wake behind us. The earth was red brown and the water, too, like mud pies, all messy and wet. Closer to town, suddenly there were splashes of bright color—rickshaws.

In the next few weeks, I saw a lot of rickshaws, not just in Dhaka, but in cities, towns, and villages everywhere. The cycle rickshaws of Bangladesh are like shiny painted baubles, gaudy and unlikely looking, a visual denial of the hard life of the men who pedal them. The rickshaw guys are tough, as rickshaw and cyclo drivers are everywhere. They're out in front pedaling, exposed to sun and rain. They wear a cotton cloth on their head to protect them from the sun. Their clothing just glues onto them in the rain. The passengers, one or two people usually, sit on a shallow padded seat, looking ahead past the back of the man whose work is to pedal them to where they want to go. The passengers can pull up the hood (like the hood on a baby stroller) to get shelter from the sun, and when it rains, the rickshaw man drapes them with a plastic sheet like a large bib that covers them up right to the chin.

The rickshaws move along smartly on the paved roads, anticipating and dodging in the complicated traffic of Dhaka. In traffic jams, they cram up tightly in a line, the front wheel of one bumping into the rear axle of the one in front, in turn being bumped from behind. In the heart of the city, there's no room for cars in the narrow streets, only rickshaws. They come into their own down there, and it's impossible to imagine how Dhaka could function without them. On one side street in the old town there's a row of rickshaw repair places, always busy. On the same stretch are several shops that sell rickshaw art, pictures of parrots, mosques, or rural scenes, painted on sheets of tin in brilliant acrylic colors, that rickshaw drivers attach to the back of their cab.

Wherever I am, I like to walk rather than being driven. I like the effort, and the chance I get to find life and to notice small details. But in Bangladesh, my being on foot was a problem. It didn't seem right to the rickshaw men who worked the area I was staying in. Why wouldn't I get a ride? Clearly, as a foreigner, I could afford it. So I learned to accommodate and take a rickshaw to the local market rather than walk. It was a matter of minutes, and pennies. The return trip was the same: As soon as I'd head off the main market street into the lanes of the neighborhood, a rickshaw guy would glide up and stop, available, needing the work. In I'd climb, with my camera bag and perhaps some shopping, and we'd travel slowly along the wet tree-lined streets.

RAIN & RICKSHAWS

At the Chai Shop

Cold drinks and fruit juices in a shop in Khajuraho, a small town that's famous for its temple carvings. It's located near the northern edge of the Indian state of Madhya Pradesh. PREVIOUS PAGE: *In central Dhaka, the Bangladeshi capital, the streets are narrow, making cycle rickshaws the most practical form of transport.*

IT'S GETTING LATE, close to nine in the evening. Many shopkeepers have closed for the night, but there's still lots of rickshaw traffic on the street and lots of people walking by. I'm sitting on a low stool, leaning against an alley wall, at a tea stall in Varanasi, the ancient holy city on the Ganges in northern India (see page 56). The tea stall is a restful and welcoming place in the dark night. There's a bare lightbulb hanging from a wire, and the blue flare of the gas flame that's bringing the large kettle of water to a boil and heating the brass pot of milk. Small clay cups shaped like little sake cups lie in nested lengths in a basket by the chai maker, a round man in his forties with a calm, good-natured face who never stops working. First he makes the tea, moistening the black loose leaves with hot water, stirring the tea, and bringing it back to a boil; once he has added the hot milk to it, and the sugar, he blends them together by pouring the mixture in a long swooping stream from kettle to pot, from pot to kettle. Then it's ready.

The chai man gracefully pours tea into fresh clay cups, one by one, passing them out to his waiting customers. We all sit, unhurried, holding our cups around the rim between curving thumb and forefinger, sipping occasionally, breathing in steam. Some people are chatting, others are lost in thought, several are reading newspapers by the light of the bare bulb. The tea man makes another batch of tea, the slight cardamom perfume of it wafting toward me as he starts pouring. He gives a questioning glance, an inquiring lift of the chin that asks each of us if we'd like another cupful. Some of us tender our cups to him, others give a shake of the head. Eventually, in ones and twos, each of us tosses his empty cup on the ground (where it will crumble back into the dust it was made from), pays the chai maker the two rupees (about four cents) owed for each cup of tea, and walks off into the warm night.

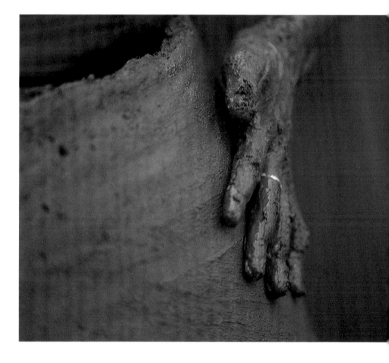

Two images from the kumahari *(potter caste) community in Udaipur, in southern Rajasthan: On the left, a man uses a wheel to shape a clay pot (in India we're always told that only men, not women, work with potter's wheels). On the right, a close-up of Sangana Bai's experienced hand (see "My First Tandoor," page 128).*

BENGALI PUFFED-RICE SNACK

· · · · · · · · · · · ·

It's found in Calcutta, in Dhaka, and in places in between, and it's called *murree* (or *muri*). It's eaten by the handful or, when you buy it from a street vendor, in tidy little mouthfuls, hot and sour and sweet, and oh so good.

You start with puffed rice (available in South Asian groceries), then flavor it. This Bangladeshi version is very like the *murree* I bought from a street vendor one afternoon in Mymensingh, in northeastern Bangladesh. Flavored with a tamarind-mustard sauce, minced onion, and chile, it came in a little paper cone. The vendor put the rice mixture into the cone, then drizzled the tamarind dressing over. The dressing moistened the rice, softening it with flavor.

This recipe produces a medium-hot mixture. You can reduce the heat by cutting back on the chiles.

Rice snack being wrapped by a street vendor in Dhaka

DRESSING

1 tablespoon tamarind pulp

¹/₄ cup hot water

3 tablespoons mustard oil or vegetable oil

¹/₂ teaspoon black mustard seeds

¹/₂ teaspoon cumin seeds or black cumin seeds

¹/₄ teaspoon nigella seeds

¹/₂ teaspoon salt, or to taste

2 cups puffed rice (see headnote)

3 to 4 tablespoons finely chopped shallots or red onion

2 green cayenne chiles, seeded and minced

Start preparing the dressing at least an hour before you wish to serve this. Chop the tamarind pulp and place it in a small bowl with the hot water. Let it stand for a few minutes to soak, then mash it with a fork or with your fingers. Pour it through a sieve into a bowl, pressing the pulp against the sieve to extract as much flavor as possible. Discard the pulp and set the tamarind liquid aside.

In a heavy skillet, heat the oil over medium-high heat. Add the mustard, cumin, and nigella seeds, stir briefly, then cover the pan until the mustard seeds have stopped popping. Add the tamarind liquid, lower the heat, and simmer for several minutes, until most of the water has boiled off. Stir in the salt, then pour the dressing into a small bowl and set aside to cool. (The dressing can be made a day ahead and stored in the refrigerator until needed.)

Place the puffed rice in a large bowl. Add the chopped shallots or onion and the minced chile and toss to mix well.

Just before serving, pour the tamarind-mustard dressing over the puffed rice, stirring and tossing to blend. Or put out the dressing separately, in one or more small condiment bowls with spoons. Pass the puffed rice mixture, then pass the dressing and invite guests to drizzle a little onto their puffed rice as they wish.   MAKES ABOUT 3 CUPS; SERVES 6

Serve as a snack or appetizer.

CARDAMOM CHAI

. . . .

This is our version of chai-shop chai (see "At the Chai Shop," page 302), flavored with a little cardamom and mellowed with hot milk and sugar.

About 6 cups water

¹/₂ cup whole or reduced-fat milk

Seeds from 1 green cardamom pod, ground

2 heaping tablespoons black tea leaves,
   preferably strong-tasting Assam tea

2 teaspoons sugar, or to taste

Heat the water to a boil. In a separate pan, heat the milk to a boil, stir in the cardamom, cover, and set aside.

Place the tea leaves in a heavy pot. Pour in a little of the hot water, then pour it off. Add the remaining hot water. Place over medium heat, bring to a boil, and boil for about 30 seconds, then pour the tea through a strainer into a pot.

Add the hot milk by pouring it through a cloth-lined strainer into the tea. Add the sugar and stir. If you wish to froth the tea (see "Throwing Tea," page 307), pour the mixture into another pot, then pour it back, continuing until it's frothy.

Place the pot back over the heat and bring the tea almost to the boil, then pour it into cups.   MAKES ABOUT 5 CUPS; SERVES 2 TO 4

SPICED CHAI FOR COLD MORNINGS

. . . .

One early December morning I headed out to explore the streets of Udaipur before sunrise. There was a chill in the air, and the sky was pale and clear, pearly and unwarmed. I went down a lane past the samosa stand I liked to stop at (see Fennel-Flecked Potato Samosas, page 296) and said a hello to Mohan as I walked by. "You look like you need warming up," he said. "Have a spiced tea."

It was a good offer. The tea was quickly made, and then I stood clasping the hot glass in my hands, breathing in the peppery, gingery steam and taking careful sips of the tea. It left a hot alive spot in my throat that lasted for several hours and kept any thought of chill or cold at bay.

1 heaping teaspoon tea leaves or 1 tea bag good black tea

About 1¹/₂ cups boiling water

¹/₄ teaspoon freshly ground black pepper

¹/₄ teaspoon powdered ginger or 1 teaspoon minced ginger

Sugar

Warm a small teapot by filling it with hot water, then emptying it. Place the tea in the pot, add the boiling water, and cover. Let it steep for several minutes, or until the tea has reached the strength you wish.

Place the pepper and ginger in the bottom of a large mug and pour in the tea. Stir thoroughly. Add sugar to taste and stir again. Drink hot, breathing in the aromatic steam.   MAKES A GENEROUS 1 CUP; SERVES 1

At a tea shop in Jaipur, in Rajasthan, a man "throws" hot milk from one pot into another.

Throwing Tea

"THROWING TEA" is a subcontinental tradition. A person making tea will often pour the milk and tea mixture from one container to another and then back again, over and over, in order to blend and froth the tea. You'll see people do this all over the Subcontinent, but nowhere as dramatically as in South India, where a tea maker will have an arc of milk tea that is three to four feet long flying through the air. An expert thrower never spills and can work with the smallest of containers, even while gazing in a completely different direction, making the performance even more impressive. The effect of all this is to froth the tea (and the same is often done with milk coffee) when it finally gets poured into individual cups, much like frothing milk for cappuccino. It tastes better.

After watching many tea throwers in the Subcontinent over the years, we finally decided to try it ourselves, and when we did we discovered that it isn't nearly as hard as it looks, at least when we work with smallish arcs. To learn to throw tea, try to find good-size containers that have strong handles and thin lips, and then practice outside, first with water. You'll soon find that the stream of water is landing just where it's supposed to land, and from there you can start to make your arc longer and longer. Before you know it, you'll be throwing hot milk tea for friends!

A farmer tosses water on a young rice crop in central Sri Lanka.

MANGO DRINK

. . . .

Our son Tashi is totally addicted to a mango drink in India called *Mazza*. It comes in small disposable cardboard containers and occasionally in recyclable bottles, stocked alongside the usual soft drink bottles of Limca and cola. The cardboard boxes are a familiar sight to anyone traveling by train, because they're commonly sold at railway station platforms and on the trains themselves.

Mazza is more or less straight mango and water, so one time after getting home from a trip, we promised Tashi that we would try to come up with our own version. We put fresh mango into a blender with water and a little sugar and we blended and, of course, we got pureed mango. And so we put in more water, and before long we got our mango drink: Mazza! As easy as that.

But then we felt that cook's impulse to make it somehow more complicated. We roasted cumin seeds, ground them, and added them. It was good. Then we added a pinch of salt, and it was interesting. But finally we looked at each other and agreed: The simplest version is the best: mango, water, and a little sugar.

2 large ripe mangoes

2 tablespoons sugar

2 cups water

Peel, pit, and slice the mangoes. Put into a blender or food processor with the sugar and water. Blend or process to a smooth liquid puree. Serve cold, with ice or not. MAKES ABOUT 4 CUPS; SERVES 3 TO 4

FROM LEFT TO RIGHT: *Sweet Lassi; juice made from Hunza Apricot Nectar (page 312); and Green Mango Cooler (page 313)*

SWEET LASSI

. . . .

Lassi is a very common drink made of yogurt whisked into water and enjoyed all across North India, but we're most familiar with this particular version, served in Kathmandu and made with a touch of rose water. One of the difficulties we've always had with drinking lassi is that it's generally made on the spot with local tap water, and while this is fine for everyone who's accustomed to the water, we usually try to drink only water that has been boiled or filtered.

Nowadays, bottled water is commonly available in many areas throughout the Subcontinent, which is wonderfully handy for travelers. But we don't like purchasing the blue plastic bottles of water, so we usually buy just two bottles to begin, then reuse them over and over again while we are traveling, using one as a bottle to filter into and one as a bottle to filter from. We use a Katadyne water filter, a Swiss-made filter that we have been taking with us on trips for almost twenty years. It looks like a small bicycle pump, and we pump to draw the water through a ceramic filter. It takes a little work each day if we're filtering for three or four people, but for only one person traveling, it's easy.

As far as this particular lassi goes, we first had it because the yogurt shopkeeper in Kathmandu not far from where we were staying used bottled water. Lassi is simple, easy, and great.

2 cups plain (full-or reduced-fat) yogurt

2 cups water

Pinch of salt

Sugar to taste

¹/₂ teaspoon rose water

Whisk the yogurt and water together in a deep bowl until frothy. Add the salt, sugar, and rose water and beat in. Serve cold over ice.

MAKES ABOUT 4 CUPS; SERVES 3 TO 4

BANANA LASSI: Add 1 or 2 coarsely chopped ripe bananas; omit the rose water. A blender whisks up the mixture in no time. SERVES 4

IN INDIA AND SRI LANKA, AS IN MOST PLACES AROUND THE WORLD, there's a history of production and consumption of alcoholic drinks, but for a traveler visiting the region it's oftentimes the absence of alcohol that is more conspicuous than a prevalence of drinking. Gujarat, for example, in northwest India, is a dry state, and if you're a tourist visiting, you must get a special permit stamped into your passport that allows you to buy beer, wine, or whiskey. My first six months' traveling in India, I don't remember having a single beer. I had no idea where to find one.

But things are changing. Liquor stores are now much more common than they were twenty years ago. We're told that it's the tax from liquor sales that's paying for the big new highways, and whether or not this is true, there are definitely a lot more beer and liquor stores around.

Of the many indigenous liquors in India and Sri Lanka, most have rural roots. A very common drink is something called *toddy,* which is the lightly fermented sap of the palmyra palm. The palm is tapped in a way similar to the tapping of a maple tree. The sap is drawn daily, then left to ferment briefly. Toddy is a natural addition to a cook's repertoire, used, for example, in Sri Lanka as an ingredient in making hoppers (see page 121). *Arrack,* the other major local liquor, is a distilled form of toddy. Arrack has an alcohol content less than that of foreign liquors but more than that of wine.

In Goa, famous throughout India for its liberal drinking laws, there's a local spirit distilled from cashew fruit called *feni* and that was supposedly first developed by Portuguese monks. Like any local liquor, it's a common ingredient in local lore—a maker of fortunes, a destroyer of families. It's also used in cooking (see Goan Pork Vindaloo, page 280). Where we stayed in Goa, one family had a still on the premises and made a good income from selling the *feni* to buyers from the neighboring state of Karnataka.

Khukri Rum, Raksi, Chang & Tungba

Harvested rice, still in the husk, needs to be dried in the sun (or by machinery) before it can be milled. Here in Bangladesh the traditional method is still in use: The rice is spread on a flat surface, and then the women walk through it to turn the grains and expose them to the heat of the sun.

WE HAVE ONLY A BASIC UNDERSTANDING of how these four alcoholic drinks are made, but when we're in Nepal, it doesn't stop us from enjoying them whenever we get the chance. *Khukri rum* is a commercially made rum available in the Kathmandu Valley and often also along trekking routes.

Raksi is sometimes commercially made and is easily found in any small shop in Kathmandu, but it is essentially a homemade liquor. It is made from millet, barley, or sometimes rice and tastes a little like whiskey. The grain is fermented and then distilled, but it's not overpoweringly strong. Because it's homemade hootch, *raksi* can taste quite different from region to region, even from household to household.

Chang is Tibetan in origin, and most often made from barley, less often from millet. Because it's fermented, not distilled, it resembles a beer. But it tastes nothing like beer; it has a more direct taste of grain.

Tungba is for us the most intriguing drink of the four, perhaps because we've had it the least, but also because it's served in a unique way. It is generally made from millet fermented in large wooden vats. When the large mass of millet is properly fermented, a portion is put into a large wooden (or perhaps bamboo) mug, and then boiling water is poured in. It's served with a wooden straw. You drink the hot, fermented, alcoholic *tungba* from the bottom up, using the straw. When you finish, more boiling water is poured over the millet, and you drink again. *Tungba* is not very alcoholic and it tastes great. We've had it in the Kathmandu Valley and also in the hills; to find it, you have to ask around.

We're sure there are many, many more ingenious types of liquor locally made in mountain valleys all across Nepal. But with just these four, we've enjoyed many a winter's night companionship, sitting with others around a fire in a hearth, or with a pot of hot coals at our feet.

HUNZA APRICOT NECTAR

· · · · · · · · · · · ·

We've been to the Hunza Valley only once, almost twenty years ago, but we'll never forget it. High up in the Karakoram Mountains in northern Pakistan, the valley is surrounded by rocky peaks, some of the highest mountain peaks in the world (see photograph, page 258), but the valley itself sits somewhat low and in June, when we were there, it's almost lush, albeit in a dry-air sort of way. Russian olive trees were in full blossom, filling every breeze with fragrance. And there were apricot trees, and fields of grain, and small fast streams with wildly fresh mountain water.

Hunzakots (see photograph, page 141) are said to live longer than anyone else on earth, but an anthropologist we met there said that that is an absolute myth. We believed him, but we had no difficulty understanding how such a myth could get started. Hunza, at least in June, is one of the most beautiful places on earth, a perfect place for myths and legends, a perfect place for fond memories!

The sweetness of this Hunza apricot nectar will vary depending on the apricots you start with. You may want to cut back the amount of sugar if your dried apricots are very sweet. The apricots are pureed with hot water, then cooked down with sugar to make a thick concentrate. The flavor is wonderfully intense. To serve, dilute it with three times the volume of water, hot or cold, or to taste. The nectar is also delicious as a topping for ice cream, or stirred into sweetened yogurt (see Sweet Yogurt Sundae with Saffron and Pistachios, page 323). PHOTOGRAPH ON PAGE 309

¾ pound (2 cups packed) best-quality dried apricots, preferably unsulfured, coarsely chopped
3 cups boiling water
2 cups water
About 1 cup sugar

Place the apricots in a bowl, pour the boiling water over, and let soak for 30 minutes to 1 hour.

Transfer the apricots and liquid to a processor or blender and process to a puree, as smooth as possible, 1 to 2 minutes. Pour into a heavy nonreactive pot, add the 2 cups water, and bring to a boil. Stir to blend together, then reduce the heat and simmer for 10 to 15 minutes. Add the sugar and stir to incorporate, then bring back to a simmer and cook for 20 minutes or so, until thickened, stirring occasionally to make sure it's not sticking.

Transfer to a heatproof glass jar and let cool, then store well sealed in the refrigerator for up to a week. Use as a concentrate to make juice: Place about ¼ cup of the syrup in a glass with about ¾ cup water, or to taste. MAKES 4 CUPS THICK CONCENTRATE, ENOUGH FOR 10 TO 12 GLASSES OF JUICE

TAMARIND-MINT TEA

. . . .

In Nepal, where this unusual drink comes from, tamarind-mint tea is made by steeping the ingredients in hot water and then straining the tea, a method that works well for us. But here at home, in the summer, we like to make it as sun tea, simply combining all the ingredients in a gallon jar and then putting the tea out in the sun for a few hours until it's ready.

After we strain the tea, we refrigerate it in the glass jar. With its unique balance of sour and sweet, combined with the fresh taste of the mint, it makes for a wonderful iced tea. PHOTOGRAPHS ON PAGES 17, 277, AND 284

2 cups loosely packed mint leaves

1/4 cup tamarind pulp, coarsely chopped

1/2 teaspoon ground cumin

1 tablespoon honey or sugar

1/2 teaspoon salt

8 cups boiling water

Wash out a 1-gallon glass jar with hot water to heat it, then place all the ingredients in the jar. Use a long spoon to break up the tamarind and help it blend with the water. Stir well and let it sit for at least 1 hour.

Mix the tea again well, then strain it through a sieve or strainer. Serve hot or cold, as you like.

This can also be made as sun tea, starting with cold water. Simply mix all the ingredients in the gallon glass jar and then put the jar out into the sun for a few hours to brew. Easy and fun. Serve over ice.

MAKES ABOUT 8 CUPS; SERVES 4 TO 8

GREEN MANGO COOLER

. . . .

Ayurveda, the Subcontinent's traditional approach to health, classifies foods into hot, cold, and neutral categories. Hot foods include meat, nuts, jaggery (crude or palm sugar), and ripe mango; cold foods include dairy products, green mango, sugarcane juice, cumin, and leafy green vegetables.

According to Ayurvedic thinking, in hot season it's important to eat cold and sweet foods and to stay cool and keep hydrated. That's when the green mango cooler comes into its own. People make it at home, and vendors do a brisk trade on the street. I saw vendors in Bhuj, in far western Gujarat, where the temperature was nearly one hundred degrees, and in Varanasi and Ahmadabad, pushing wheeled carts with cooked whole green mangoes hanging from a pole and a large earthenware container of cool spiced water underneath. The spiced water (an acquired taste of rock salt and cumin) quenches your thirst (and replenishes your electrolytes). Or you could add the green mango: The vendor peels the cooked green mangoes, mashes some of it, then whisks it into the spiced water, stirs in a little sugar, and serves it in a metal cup. The tartness and coolness are like a wake-up call to the system, galvanizing, refreshing in every way. PHOTOGRAPH ON PAGE 309

1 large green (unripe) mango (1 to 11/4 pounds)

1 teaspoon cumin seeds, toasted and ground

1/2 teaspoon salt (traditionally, sulfurous-tasting rock salt; we use sea salt)

2 tablespoons sugar, or to taste

About 4 cups cold water

Place the whole mango in a pot of cold water to cover and bring to a boil. Cook, covered, until the mango is softened and dull green, 10 to 15 minutes. Drain and let cool.

Peel the mango and cut the pulp into a blender or a food processor. Add the cumin, salt, and sugar and blend or process until smooth (you'll have about 1 cup). Add the water and process or blend to make drinks for all, or make individual servings, using about 1/4 cup of flavored pulp to 1 cup cold water. Serve plain or over ice cubes or chipped ice.

MAKES ABOUT 5 CUPS; SERVES 4 TO 5

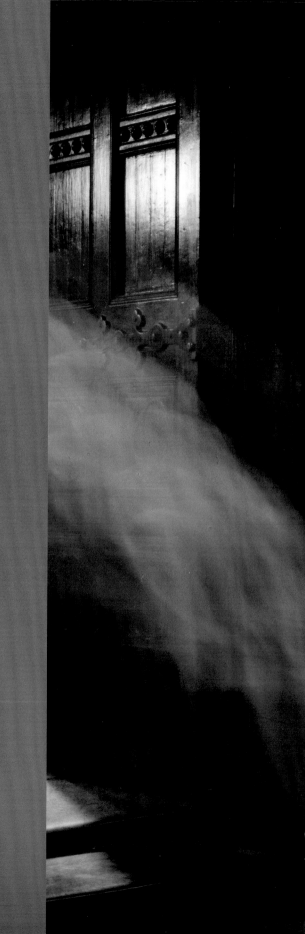

SWEETS

to my hotel after dark on a November evening in 1977. It was my
first time in India. I'd been there only ten days, but already I was
a cautious traveler. In Delhi, I'd been flimflammed out of $250
(enough for three and a half months' living!), and in Amritsar,
on the day I'd crossed into India from Pakistan, I'd found myself

year anniversary. I knew how a day could quickly spiral out of control, sometimes in a good way, sometimes in a bad way.

I wasn't happy to be walking after dark. It wasn't about being afraid; in the Subcontinent situations are seldom, in a personal-safety way, fear-making. But not entirely knowing my way home, and fresh from a bad experience, out alone after dark wasn't where I wanted to be. At one point, the road that I was walking on went under a big railway bridge, and so down I went, just as a train rumbled past overhead.

When I got to the other side, I was startled by an enormous bank of bright lights and something that looked like a carnival, or like an old Las Vegas casino sign, bright and colorful and complicated. There were rickshaws parked in scattered directions, and a few trucks and cars, and there was a crowd. As I got closer, the whole thing looked like nothing I had ever seen

Bhil woman. The Bhil are seminomadic people who live in the deserts of Rajasthan.

before. Display upon display, box upon box upon box, piles of bright colors and symmetrical shapes: I at last realized that I was looking at sweets! *Gulab jamun, rasgullah, sandesh, barfi, halwa* . . . Everyone was buying boxes of sweets, mixing and matching, like buying chocolates on Valentine's Day for someone you love, only more wonderfully chaotic, exuberant, festive.

One man came out of the crowd, walking in my direction, and caught sight of me. "Where are you from?" he asked.

"United States," I replied.

"Welcome," he said, smiling. He then opened the small cardboard box that he was carefully carrying and gently removed a syrup-coated golden brown ball. "*Gulab jamun*," he said as he handed me the sweet. "Happy Diwali!" (See the headnote, page 318.)

Small green mangoes

GULAB JAMUN

· · · · · · · · · · · ·

In the back streets of most old towns throughout the Subcontinent, there's almost always a small section of sweet makers, their shops containing large smoke- and spatter-blackened vats full of milk simmering down, milk that will then be fashioned into a range of brilliant sweets. Sweets are eaten as a snack rather than for dessert, and are given as gifts at Diwali, the lunar new year for Hindus (see Glossary).

Many of these sweets can be adapted to the home kitchen. One of the best is *gulab jamun*, milk blended with flour and shaped into round balls, slow fried, and then simmered in syrup. To double the recipe, double all the *jamun* ingredients; increase the syrup to 1½ cups each water and sugar, and use the same 2 teaspoons rose water.

JAMUN

½ cup buttermilk powder or regular milk powder

½ cup all-purpose flour

½ teaspoon baking soda

¼ cup milk

1 tablespoon ghee, plus more for deep-frying

SYRUP

1¼ cups sugar

1¼ cups water

2 teaspoons rose water

Mix the dry ingredients in a bowl. Add the milk and ghee and mix to a smooth dough. Let sit for a few minutes to firm up.

On a barely flour-dusted surface, roll out the dough to a cylinder about 8 inches long. Cut it into eight pieces with a sharp knife or dough scraper. Cup each piece under your palm and roll gently to shape it into a round ball.

In a wide (9-inch-diameter or more) saucepan, stir the sugar into the water. Bring to a boil and boil for a few minutes. Remove from the heat, stir in the rose water, and set aside.

Just before you start frying the first dough balls, place the syrup back over low heat.

Pour about 2 inches of ghee into a stable wok or deep heavy pot. Heat it to 325°F. Use a deep-frying thermometer to test the temperature, or stick a wooden chopstick or wooden spoon handle vertically into the pan; if bubbles start rising up the shaft, the ghee is at the right temperature. Carefully put in four dough balls; the balls should still have room to move around. Use a slotted spoon to stir the ghee and to keep the balls moving, though they should turn over by themselves, and fry until a deep golden brown, about 3 minutes.

Remove the pan of syrup from the heat. Use a slotted spoon to lift the *jamuns* out of the ghee, pausing for a moment to let it drain off them, and place them in the hot syrup, leaving space between them. Let stand for 30 minutes to an hour; as the balls soak up the syrup, they will expand to almost double their size.

Meanwhile, start frying a second batch. As long as there's room in the pan of syrup, you can add freshly fried *jamuns* to it; just make sure to soak them all for 30 minutes to an hour.

Lift the soaked *jamuns* carefully out of the syrup and set them on a plate. Serve warm or at room temperature, with a little syrup drizzled over them. **MAKES 8; SERVES 4**

Serve as a sweet snack to accompany tea or coffee, or for dessert.

HOME-STYLE JALEBIS

. . . .

Jalebis are casually coiled deep-fried sweets coated in syrup that are made and sold street side in many parts of India. The favorite *jalebi* maker in a market area has a steady line of customers outside his shop. I had never really understood why people had such a passion for *jalebis*, for I'd been too impatient to line up, so I'd only ever eaten cold (and tired) ones from places with no queuing public. Only when I finally tasted a *jalebi* fresh from the pan, in Ahmadabad, did I understand what all the fuss was about.

Good *jalebis* have a slightly crisp bite, an airy tender texture, and a sweetness that's not overpowering. Yogurt gives a touch of tartness that contrasts with the sugar syrup. Street-side *jalebis* are usually dyed orange-yellow. We don't color ours, but if you wish to, add a drop or two of food coloring to the batter when you stir in the water.

The cooked *jalebis* get dipped only briefly in syrup and don't need to soak, so once you start frying them, you'll have hot *jalebis* ready to eat in about five minutes. Mix the batter six hours (or as long as twenty-four hours ahead, if more convenient) before you wish to cook and serve them.

1 cup all-purpose flour

1 cup plain (full- or reduced-fat) yogurt

Up to ¼ cup water

2 tablespoons sugar

½ teaspoon salt

Ghee or vegetable oil for deep-frying

SYRUP

¾ cup sugar

¾ cup water

Place the flour in a bowl, add the yogurt, and blend together. Add a little water, a tablespoon at a time, just enough to make a thick, smooth, heavy batter; you don't want the batter runny, just smooth and very gloppy. Our yogurt is rather thick, so we need to add about 3 tablespoons water; you may need to add very little if your yogurt is more liquid. Set aside, covered, for 6 to 8 hours, or up to 24, if you wish.

When you are ready to proceed, make the syrup: Place the sugar in a wide heavy pot, add the water, and stir well with a wooden spoon. Place over medium heat and stir until the sugar has completely dissolved, then bring to a boil. Lower the heat slightly and let the syrup simmer for 5 to 10 minutes, then keep warm over very low heat.

Meanwhile, use scissors to cut a diagonal slice, smaller than a pencil in diameter, off one corner of a heavy plastic bag. Put out a slotted spoon, a wooden spatula, and a platter for the cooked *jalebis*.

Pour ghee or vegetable oil into a large stable wok or wide heavy pot to a depth of about 2 inches. Heat over medium-high heat to a temperature of about 325°F. Test the temperature with a deep-frying thermometer, or stick a wooden chopstick or wooden spoon handle vertically into the pan; if bubbles start rising up the shaft, the ghee or oil is the right temperature.

Stir in the sugar and salt into the batter. Transfer some or all of the batter to the plastic bag. First make only one *jalebi*, to get used to the technique. Once the ghee is hot, press the batter down to the cut corner of the bag and then, squeezing the bag firmly, pipe some batter into the ghee by moving the bag in a continuous circular motion above the hot ghee and piping out a twirly, irregular coiled shape 2 or 3 inches in diameter, making about three coils. (Leave gaps between the coils; the ghee can then bubble up in the gaps, cooking the *jalebi* more evenly.)

Let the *jalebi* bubble and cook until it is browning at the edges and puffed, about 1 minute. Use a slotted spoon to turn it over and let the other side cook until well browned. You may want to flip it back over to finish browning the first side. The *jalebi* should be a rich brown in color, and a little crispy. Use the slotted spoon to transfer the *jalebi* to the warm syrup. Immediately use the spatula to flip it over in the syrup and then to lift it out and onto the platter.

Repeat with the remaining batter and syrup. You may have room for up to four *jalebis* at a time in your pan without letting them touch. (You will have time to pipe in three or four before you need to start turning over the first one.)

Serve hot or warm, within half an hour of frying.

MAKES 15 TO 20 JALEBIS; SERVES 6 TO 10

Serve as a snack or for dessert.

MINI-CREPES IN SYRUP

· · · · · · · · · · · ·

Like *jalebis* (page 319), these small crepes, called *malpuas*, are made from a flour and yogurt batter. Let the batter sit for six to eight hours (or up to twenty-four hours, if you prefer) to ferment and get airy. After they are cooked in a skillet, the crepes, like *jalebis*, are bathed in a light sugar syrup. *Malpuas* are found in various versions across northern India, from Bengal to Gujarat. Unlike *jalebis*, they are flavored, usually with cardamom and perhaps a little fennel (as we do here); black pepper is another option. Two or three make an elegant and delicious dessert, accompanied by fresh heavy cream, or slices of fruit, or a scoop of sorbet or ice cream.

1 cup all-purpose flour

1 cup plain (full- or reduced-fat) yogurt

About ¼ cup water

2 teaspoons sugar

½ teaspoon ground fennel

Seeds from 2 green cardamom pods, ground (about ⅛ teaspoon)

⅛ teaspoon salt

3 to 4 tablespoons ghee, butter, or vegetable oil

SYRUP

1 cup sugar

1 cup water

OPTIONAL TOPPING

About ¼ cup toasted slivered almonds or chopped toasted pistachios

Mix together the flour and yogurt in a bowl. Add enough water to make a pourable loose batter, the texture of a crepe batter (the amount will depend on the thickness of your yogurt). Stir in the sugar, fennel, and cardamom. Set aside, covered, to ferment for 6 to 8 hours, or as long as 24 hours. (If you are leaving it for longer than 6 hours, refrigerate the batter, well covered, until an hour before you wish to use it.)

About an hour before you wish to serve the *malpuas*, make the syrup: Place the sugar in a wide pot, add the water, and bring to a boil, stirring to dissolve the sugar. Lower the heat and simmer for 5 minutes. Lower the heat to very low to keep the syrup warm.

Stir the salt into the batter and add a little more water if necessary to make the batter flow well. Put out two spatulas.

Place a wide heavy skillet over medium-high heat. (If you have two heavy pans, use both, to make the cooking go more quickly.) Add about 2 teaspoons ghee, butter, or oil to the pan and spread over the surface to grease it well. Stir the batter, then scoop up 1 tablespoon of it and pour it into the pan. Use the back of your spoon to lightly smooth it out to a round crepe 3 to 4 inches in diameter. If your pan is 12 inches in diameter, you will be able to fit at least one and probably two more crepes in the pan.

The crepes should first sizzle gently, as bubbles start to come up through them, and then in just over a minute the edges will start to brown and lift off the pan. As soon as they do, turn the crepes over and cook on the second side until nicely browned. One at a time, lift the crepes out and place in the pan of syrup. Use the second spatula to immediately turn each one over in the syrup and then transfer the crepe to a serving plate or platter. Repeat with the remaining batter, regreasing the pan(s) occasionally between batches.

Drizzle a little more syrup onto the crepes, then, if you wish, sprinkle on a scattering of nuts.

MAKES ABOUT 30 CREPES; SERVES 10 FOR DESSERT, 5 TO 6 FOR BREAKFAST

Serve for dessert with a little fresh cream or a tart sorbet. You can also serve these for breakfast or brunch, perhaps with fresh fruit on the side.

MINI-MALPUAS: We encountered a different version of *malpuas* in Bengal. The crepes were miniature, less than 2 inches across, and a little thicker. To make mini-*malpuas*, scoop up 2 teaspoons batter and drop it onto the hot pan; do not spread it out. The crepes will take a little longer to cook because they're thicker. Serve as easy finger food at a buffet or party.

Mini-Crepes in Syrup served with mango sorbet

SWEET YOGURT SUNDAE
WITH SAFFRON AND PISTACHIOS

· · · · · · · · · · · ·

Yogurt makes a simple and attractive sweet course or cooling snack-treat. This version of sweetened yogurt from Bengal is called *mishti doi*, *doi* being Bengali for "yogurt." The yogurt drains for an hour to lose its bitter whey and to thicken a little, then it is blended with jaggery (palm or crude sugar) and flavorings. Use good whole-milk yogurt, preferably organic. Serve in small bowls or tall sundae glasses and top with pistachios, or with pomegranate seeds or chopped toasted almonds.

1 quart plain full-fat yogurt

Generous ¼ teaspoon saffron strands (optional)

⅓ cup whole milk

¼ teaspoon ground cardamom or freshly grated nutmeg

⅓ cup finely chopped jaggery (palm or crude sugar), or more to taste, or substitute honey or brown sugar

About ¼ cup coarsely chopped pistachios, pomegranate seeds, or chopped toasted almonds

Line a large sieve or colander with cheesecloth or coarse cotton. Wet the cloth with water, then place the sieve or colander over a bowl. Place the yogurt in the sieve to drain for 1 hour in the refrigerator.

Turn the yogurt into a bowl and set aside. Use the whey for another purpose (it makes a refreshing drink and can also be used in place of lemon juice to curdle milk for making *chhana* and *paneer*; see page 344), or discard.

If using the saffron, lightly toast the strands in a small dry skillet over medium heat, until brittle. Add the milk and cardamom or nutmeg, or if not using saffron, heat the milk and cardamom in a small saucepan; bring to a simmer and simmer briefly, until the cardamom releases its scent (and the optional saffron gives off its color). Remove from the heat and stir in the sugar or honey until dissolved.

Whisk the mixture into the yogurt. Use a ladle to pour the yogurt into glasses or bowls. Top with a sprinkling of nuts or pomegranate seeds, and with a little more sugar if you wish. SERVES 8

Serve for dessert, perhaps with cookies or biscotti. This is also a good brunch option, served with Gita's Luchis (page 115) or other warm flatbreads.

GUJARATI YOGURT PUDDING: In Gujarat, there's a sweet called *shrikand* that, like *mishti doi*, is made of sweetened thickened yogurt. In fact, it's even thicker (the yogurt drains overnight) and sweeter. These desserts call out for individual adaptation, but here is a place to start with *shrikand*: Drain the yogurt overnight so it is very thick. Increase the sugar or honey to ½ cup and omit the saffron. Once you've whisked the milk mixture into the yogurt, stir in 1 cup chopped fruit, such as mangoes, or some berries. Chill before serving.

MANGO ICE CREAM WITH CARDAMOM

· · · · · · · · · · · ·

Indian ice cream, *kulfi*, is one of the world's great sweet inventions. It's so good and so simple to make. It may have been brought to India by the Moghuls, or perhaps they developed it once they reached India. *Kulfi* is traditionally made in small individual metal cones from a mixture of *khoa* (cooked-down milk) and flavorings.

Homemade *kulfi* is not tricky to make, needs no special equipment, and has a wonderful granular texture. This version is the simplest one we know. We learned it from our friend Sutapa, who starts with her mother's *kulfi* recipe, then simplifies it. (Her mother is from Bengal, and her recipe includes heavy cream, as well as the milks called for here.) We first tasted Sutapa's *kulfi* at a potluck birthday party. She'd made it in small old-style metal ice cube trays without the dividers in them, then cut it into squares to serve it, rather like a frozen version of fudge. Kids and adults all reached for it happily. The squares stayed cold and firm for a while, so they could easily be eaten by hand.

Use fresh ripe mangoes, peeled and chopped and pureed, or instead, canned mango puree (available from Asian groceries and well-stocked supermarkets) or frozen mango puree, now available in gourmet markets.

3 cups mango puree (see headnote)

1½ cups sweetened condensed milk

1⅓ cups evaporated milk

Scant ¼ teaspoon salt

Place all the ingredients in a blender or food processor and blend until smooth.

You can make trays of *kulfi*, or cubes, using molded plastic ice cube trays, or Popsicles, using a plastic Popsicle mold and wooden or plastic sticks. Pour the mixture into three ice cube trays or into Popsicle molds, filling them just three-quarters full, or else pour into small baking pans, again until just three-quarters full.

Place in the freezer. If using Popsicle molds, place a Popsicle stick in each mold once it's half-frozen, after about 45 minutes. Freeze until completely hardened. (The *kulfi* will take about 2 hours to harden if made in ice cube trays, and a little longer in larger shapes.) They can be frozen for as long as 1 month. **MAKES ABOUT 6 CUPS; 15 TO 18 POPSICLES**

MANGO-PISTACHIO ICE CREAM: Add ½ cup coarsely chopped pistachios to the ice cream mixture.

PEACH OR APRICOT ICE CREAM: Peaches or apricots, fresh and ripe or canned, are the temperate-climate fruits that most closely resemble mangoes. Not surprisingly, they make delicious *kulfi*. Follow the directions here, and if you wish, add a little pure vanilla extract to the mixture.

BANANA-PEPPER ROUNDS

· · · · · · · · · · · ·

These sweet treats couldn't be simpler. Slices of ripe banana are dipped in a smooth heavy batter made of egg and sugar whisked together, then dropped into hot oil and briefly fried. All you need is five minutes for whisking the batter and several minutes to get all the slices fried. They're served hot, topped with finely ground black pepper, a wonderful taste hit. Textures are both crisp (the caramelized fried batter) and melting (the hot banana within). Flavors are sweet and hot.

1 large egg

¼ cup sugar

½ to 1 cup coconut oil or peanut oil for frying

3 ripe bananas

Finely ground black pepper

Break the egg into a medium bowl, add the sugar, and whisk until thick, with small bubbles. This process always takes us a little longer than we want it to, about 5 minutes of whisking. The batter will be runny and thin for quite a while, then will start to get tiny bubbles in it and become thicker textured when dropped from the whisk. Set aside for the moment.

Place enough oil in a medium heavy skillet to come to a depth of just over ½ inch. Place over medium-high heat. Put a slotted spoon and two plates lined with paper towels near your stove top.

Peel the bananas and slice them crosswise into rounds; we usually make ours just under ½ inch thick. If the bananas are quite firm, you can slice them thinner.

Whisk the egg-sugar mixture briefly again, then set the whisk aside.

Pick up one banana round between your thumb and forefinger, drag it through the batter, and immediately drop it into the hot oil. Repeat with about ten more banana slices. The batter browns quickly: With your slotted spoon, start turning the slices over carefully, and then once you've done that, start lifting them out, pausing for a second as you do to allow extra oil to drain away. Place them on one of the paper towel–lined plates. Repeat, after whisking the batter briefly again, with the remaining banana slices and batter.

Transfer the rounds to a serving platter or plates and grind pepper on generously (we like a fine grind for this). Serve hot.   **SERVES 4 TO 6**

Serve as a sweet snack at any time of day, with tea or coffee, hot or iced. Or serve as a dessert, accompanied perhaps by a tart sorbet for a contrast in taste and temperature.

PAGE 327: *Near the end of the mango season in Rajshahi, in western Bangladesh, a young boy sells mangoes in the market on the main street.*

Hot season was over, and the rains had started in Bangladesh, so mango season was almost finished. I made a four-day trip to Rajshahi, a city on the Padma River (as the Ganges is called in Bangladesh) that is famous for its mangoes. I found large sweet ones there, called *posli,* and another variety called *nangra,* small ones, sweet and firm. But in fact the most memorable mango I had in Bangladesh was in Dhaka. I was having lunch with Hasna Begum and her daughter Lala (see "Remarkable Women," page 162), and at the end of the meal, Hasna Begum placed four mangoes on the table. "These are the last mangoes, you know. Nearly fifty years ago my parents planted mango trees by our house. After my parents died, the house was divided; my sister and I each had half the property. My sister plans to build a small building on her part of the land, so the mango trees will be cut down." The mangoes were green-skinned, some larger than others. She rinsed them in a basin of water, then sliced them into sections, leaving the peel on. The flesh was a beautiful golden orange-yellow, brilliant against the fine green peel, and, when I bit into it, oh-so-buttery, firm and smooth and lush, with no trace of fiber. The skin peeled off easily, too. It was one of the most delicious mango-eating experiences I've ever had.

Did the mangoes have an extra depth of flavor because it was their last year? Did Hasna Begum's affection for the trees, their shade, their bounty, their connection to her parents, deepen the taste of the fruit we ate that day?

IT WAS HOT SEASON IN PAKISTAN. We had flown from Islamabad to Karachi, where we had an overnight before our plane to Kathmandu the next day. We found beds at the travelers' dorm at the airport, a small separate building. At midnight, it was too hot to sleep, too hot to do anything but hang around, so we went looking for diversion. We found the small café that served airport workers, empty at that hour except for a man behind the counter. We asked if there was anything available to eat. "I'm sorry, we have only tea or coffee," said the man. "Oh, and we have mangoes. But I'm afraid they're cold," he said apologetically. "We keep them in the refrigerator. Do you mind?" We sat happily in the heavy night air, eating slices of cold mango and sipping hot tea.

IT WAS HOT SEASON IN NORTHERN INDIA. The first mangoes had arrived in Crawford Market in Mumbai. "Are they good?" I asked the vendor doubtfully. "Isn't it too early?" "They're *alfonsos* from Maharashtra," he said, "very good. Here, taste." I did, and then bought half a dozen medium-size yellow-orange-skinned mangoes with a little nub of a nose near one end. They were delicious, just like the sample he'd given me. Three weeks later I was in Varanasi and went looking for mangoes. There were none in the market. "Ah," said Todenji, who ran the guesthouse I stayed at. "No, mangoes won't be here for another three weeks or so. The *alfonsos* in Maharashtra come early. They're mostly exported, you know. Our mangoes are different." And then he described the mangoes that would be arriving in mid- to late April, after I was gone: the *langhra,* the *malda* ("sometimes as good as the *langhra,* sometimes better"), the *dusseri* from Lucknow, the big and rare *krishna blahg,* and the rarer and wonderful *mitua,* tiny and "sweet like honey" from neighboring Bihar. . . . Worth another trip.

MANGO TALES

SWEET AND CREAMY ROSE WATER DUMPLINGS TWO WAYS

· · · · · · · · · · · ·

Most milk-based sweets in the West are either ice cream in some form or milky puddings such as rice pudding. In the Subcontinent, there are two other categories. One is based on milk that is cooked down to a thick mass, rather like *dulce de leche*. The sweets in the other category, such as these, are made with *chhana*, a soft fresh cheese you can make at home from milk or buy in a South Asian grocery store.

In Bangladesh and Bengal, most people buy their sweets rather than making them. Sweet makers, called *moiras*, have beautifully arranged stalls and shops with stacks and rows of golden sweet round dumplings and disks, some topped with pistachio, most gleaming with sugar syrup and perfumed with cardamom or rose water. The displays are dizzying, so it's hard to choose which sweet to try. The other big fans of sweet shops, apart from children, and adults with a sweet tooth (who all give longing glances as they walk by), are wasps. Every sweet shop and stall has large wasps hovering. They don't seem to worry anyone. The shopkeepers just casually whisk them away from time to time.

These dumplings are round balls that are sweetened by a soaking in sugar syrup. They're not difficult to shape and cook once you have the fresh cheese on hand. Buy it or make it the day before, so it has time to drain well. We've found that when it's better drained and almost crumbly, the dumplings are more tender. Choose between plain or filled balls; both options are set out here. In addition, there are two basic styles of dumpling here. One is just simmered in aromatic sugar syrup, so it's creamy white, about an inch in diameter, and very tender. The other is golden and a little smaller, because the dumplings are briefly deep-fried before being soaked in the syrup.

We like the contrast of the golden and the pale, so we usually simmer eight and deep-fry the other eight, then serve them together on a plate. They go quickly!

2 cups chhana (page 344 or store-bought), drained overnight until crumbly
2 teaspoons all-purpose flour
Scant ¼ teaspoon salt
Peanut oil for deep-frying (optional)

OPTIONAL FILLING
1½ tablespoons ground pistachios or walnuts
2 teaspoons sugar
¼ teaspoon ground cardamom, nutmeg, or mace

SYRUP
4 cups water
4 cups sugar
2 tablespoons rose water

On a clean dry surface, knead the cheese until very smooth. The curds will break down and become one mass. Use a dough scraper to detach it from the counter if it sticks. Sprinkle on the flour and salt and knead well, another 2 minutes or so. Roll the dough under your flattened palms into a rope about 20 inches long. Cut it in half, then divide each half into eight pieces, to give you a total of sixteen pieces.

To shape plain balls, roll each piece into a ball between your palms. *To make filled balls,* mix all the filling ingredients together in a bowl. Flatten one piece of dough to a 2-inch round. Place a generous ¼ teaspoon filling on the center, then fold the edges up over the middle and roll lightly between your palms to make a ball.

Set the rolled balls aside, covered loosely to prevent drying out, while you prepare the syrup.

Place the water in a wide saucepan, stir in the sugar to dissolve it, and then bring to a rapid boil. Lower the heat to maintain a steady simmer. If making both simmered and fried balls, begin with the simmered ones.

To make simmered balls, add the balls to the syrup and simmer for 10 minutes. Be careful not to disturb them as they cook; they are fragile and can tear. The balls will expand to almost double and crowd one another; don't worry and don't flip them over. When they're done, turn off the heat and add the rose water. Let sit in the syrup for 2 hours. The balls will contract a little and become denser as they sit.

Serve at room temperature, in small bowls, with a little extra syrup drizzled over.

To make deep-fried balls (if you have not already made simmered balls), let the syrup simmer for 10 minutes. Remove from the heat, stir in the rose water, and set near your stove top.

Pour 3 inches of peanut oil into a stable wok or deep heavy pot. Heat to 325°F. To test the temperature, use a deep-frying thermometer, or stick a wooden chopstick or the handle of a wooden spoon into the oil vertically; if the oil bubbles up gently around it, it is the right temperature.

Gently slide the balls into the oil one by one; after 15 seconds, lower the heat slightly. Use a wooden spoon to keep the balls turning and moving around so they cook evenly. You want them to turn golden, but not dark brown, all over. Once they are golden, in 2 or 3 minutes, use a slotted spoon to lift them out of the oil and into the hot syrup. (If you already have some simmered balls soaking, just add the fried ones and let them soak together.) Soak for about 30 minutes.

Serve warm, at room temperature, or chilled, as above.

MAKES 16 DUMPLINGS; SERVES 5 TO 6

Serve for dessert. These are rich and melting, so either strong coffee or a dessert wine makes a welcome accompaniment.

In the enormous wholesale market in Chennai (Madras), there are deep-fried snacks to keep you going.

BANANA-JAGGERY FRITTERS

· · · · · · · · · · · ·

Another brilliantly simple dish that takes the sweetness and aroma of bananas a step beyond, these fritters from Assam make a great impromptu dessert. In Assam, they're called *koat pitha*. *Pitha* is the name given to a whole family of rice flour–based sweet fritters in Bengal, Orissa, and the northeast provinces, including Assam. These *pitha* are made of a blend of mashed ripe bananas, rice flour, and jaggery (palm or crude sugar). Each fritter is about two bites; allow four or more fritters per person.

Jaggery usually comes in hard blocks. Just use a cleaver to shave off thin slices of sugar, then chop them. It gives a slightly smoky flavor to the bananas. Demerara sugar, and brown sugar blended with maple sugar, are both good substitutes.

To make more fritters, proportionally increase all the ingredients.

PHOTOGRAPH ON PAGE 17

2 ripe bananas, peeled

⅓ cup chopped or grated jaggery (palm or crude sugar),
**   or substitute brown, maple, or demerara sugar**

Pinch of salt

⅓ cup rice flour (*not* sweet rice flour)

Coconut oil or peanut oil for deep-frying

Coarsely mash the bananas in a bowl. Add the sugar and salt and blend them in. Don't try to smooth out all the lumps of banana or sugar; you don't want a smooth puree. Sift the rice flour over the mixture, then use a wooden spoon to stir it in thoroughly.

Place a stable wok or a deep heavy pot on a burner and pour in 1 inch of oil. Heat over medium-high heat until hot (about 325°F). Test the oil by dropping a little batter into it: The batter should sink and then rise back up, and it should start to brown within about 20 seconds. If it turns very dark, lower the heat; if it doesn't rise back up, raise the heat a little or wait a little longer for the oil to heat up.

Put out two plates lined with paper towels, as well as a slotted spoon and two teaspoons. Use one teaspoon to scoop up a generous teaspoon of batter, then use the other teaspoon to scoop it off into the hot oil. Repeat with two to four more fritters, then start using the slotted spoon to turn each of them over. Within about 40 seconds they should be golden on one side; in another 30 seconds or so they will be cooked on both sides. As each gets cooked, lift it out with the slotted spoon, pausing to let the excess oil drain off, and place it on a paper towel–lined plate. Serve hot or warm. MAKES ABOUT 24 FRITTERS; SERVES 4 TO 6

Serve for dessert, perhaps with a tart sorbet on the side for a contrast of temperature and flavor. Or serve for brunch to accompany plain yogurt.

NOTE: In Kerala, we came across a morning chai snack made of white flour leavened with a little baking soda and yogurt and kneaded into a dough with ripe banana. The dough was shaped into ping-pong ball–size balls and deep-fried. Morning heaven, especially when dunked into hot chai.

SILKY GOAN PUDDING

· · · · · · · · · · · · ·

We shouldn't be surprised to find a brilliant custardlike pudding in the Goan repertoire: The Portuguese are famous for their custard tarts, and Goa was a Portuguese possession until 1975. This delectable Goan pudding is fusion food, a blend of local ingredients and Portuguese techniques. It's soft-textured, silky, and enticing, as you might expect from a custard made of coconut milk and eggs and scented with vanilla and cardamom.

NOTE: The pudding bakes in a bain-marie, or "water bath." You will need an 8-inch square or round cake pan or an ovenproof 8-inch bowl to hold the pudding, and a large pan (a roasting pan works well) that can hold it and some water, so the pudding can steam cook in the oven.

¾ pound (2 small to medium) baking potatoes

2 tablespoons rice flour (*not* sweet rice flour)

1¼ cups chopped or grated jaggery (palm or crude sugar),
   or substitute packed brown sugar

1½ cups canned or fresh coconut milk

3 large eggs

1 teaspoon pure vanilla extract

Seeds from 2 green cardamom pods, ground,
   or ⅛ teaspoon ground cardamom

¼ teaspoon salt

1 teaspoon butter or ghee for oiling the pan

Put a rack in the center of the oven and preheat the oven to 450°F. Bake the potatoes until cooked through and tender, about 1 hour. Set aside to cool. Reduce the oven temperature to 325°F.

Place the rice flour and sugar in a medium bowl and mix together. Add the coconut milk and whisk to mix well; use a fork if necessary to eliminate any lumps of sugar. The rice flour will soon be absorbed and all the lumps will disappear. Set aside.

Split the potatoes open and scoop the cooked potato into a bowl; discard the skins. Mash the potatoes until smooth, or pass them through a ricer into a bowl. Whisk the eggs into the potatoes until smooth. Add the coconut mixture and stir, then add the vanilla, cardamom, and salt and stir in.

Butter a round or square 8-inch cake pan or an ovenproof 8-inch bowl. Pour the batter into the pan or bowl. Pour 1 inch of hot water into a larger pan (see Note), then gently set the filled pan in the water.

Place in the center of the oven and bake for about 40 minutes, until there is no jiggle to the custard. It will brown slightly around the edges; be careful not to overbake it. The custard will be set on top but soft and silky underneath. Let cool before serving. The custard is too soft to unmold, but once cooled, it can be cut and served in slices or wedges.

SERVES 6 TO 8

Serve for dessert or as a sweet with tea or coffee, alone or with fresh fruit.

SILKY GOAN PUDDING WITH ROASTED NUTS: We like the smooth silkiness of the pudding on its own, but if you like a little texture, top it with ¼ cup or more chopped cashews, lightly toasted in a dry skillet until touched with brown. Sprinkle onto the pudding when it comes out of the oven, or onto each individual serving.

FOLLOWING PAGE: *Monkeys, cows, and pigeons share corn kernels that have been left as an offering at a shrine in Kathmandu's Durbar Square.*

THE MUNASINGHES

They were standing out on the front porch when I walked up. I recognized them immediately, and recognized the house, though I didn't think they recognized me. Twenty-six years is a long time.

"Hello, Mr. and Mrs. Munasinghe," I said. "Do you remember me? I lived with you for three months, twenty-six years ago. You let me have space in your kitchen to learn to cook, and I slept in the spare bedroom."

They looked uncomfortable for a moment, confused, but then Mr. Munasinghe suddenly shook his head, "Yes, Wyoming! Your parents live in Wyoming, in the United States." Mrs. Munasinghe still didn't recognize me, and she seemed frustrated, not recognizing. She is many years younger than Mr. Munasinghe (he is in his mid-eighties) and is not accustomed to her husband remembering something that she can't remember.

Standing there on the porch, watching the two of them, a giant wave of memories rushed through my head, intimate memories that are possible only when you have lived in very close quarters with other people. I remembered their anxieties, their love, their squabbles. I was twenty-three years old at the time, about ten years older than their two children. They'd rented out their bedroom to me to make extra money, while they slept together under a mosquito net in a little walled-off area of the dining room.

In the middle of the night, I would usually have to go to the toilet (having had a large ripe papaya or pineapple for dessert—not realizing at the time that they are diuretics), and so I'd walk through the dining room in the dark, and down the hallway to the back door, then open the door, hoping that it wouldn't squeak. The toilet was outside, and so, too,

were the ever-present monkeys that lived in the jungle that pressed up against the house.

"Do you still have monkeys?" I asked, standing there on the porch.

They both grimaced, and Mrs. Munasinghe suddenly relaxed. "We will always have monkeys, those terrible monkeys," Mrs. Munasinghe said laughingly. "I'm sure that we have even more than when you were here!"

Twenty-six years was a big part of their lifetime, too, and for nineteen of those years there has been a civil war in Sri Lanka. We went inside and had tea. The oldest son is again living at home, and there are grandchildren around. His wife is working in Saudi Arabia, and together they'd recently spent several years working in Laos. So we talked about food in Laos, and then we talked about Sri Lankan cooking. Mrs. Munasinghe started to remember, and she laughed, recalling my little table in the kitchen, my little kitchen within the kitchen that she had made for me. "Do you want to see?" she asked, and then we got up and walked into the kitchen.

"I don't think that it has changed," she said as we entered, her observations as precise as ever. And she was right. There were several large granite mortars and pestles, there was a stack of coconut husks used as fuel for the fire, and black-charred clay cooking pots, one for rice, and a *nambiliya*, a bowl with tiny grooves that's used to clean rice (as if panning for gold).

"What happened to the parrot?" I asked.

"Oh," said Mrs. Munasinghe, "the parrot died."

CREAMY PUDDING
WITH MACE AND CARDAMOM

· · · · · · · · · · · · ·

Known as *ravo* in the Parsi community, this lush dessert is smooth and creamy, subtly aromatic with rose water, cardamom, and mace and utterly delicious. It's one member of the family of subcontinental sweets that are made from cooked-down milk, as rice pudding is, except that here the thickener is not rice but a little semolina (coarsely ground, *not* semolina flour). You need to leave yourself an hour and a half for the cooking, but in fact it's best if you make the pudding ahead, when you're not rushed, perhaps when you have someone to chat with as you stir it, then refrigerate it and serve it chilled.

When warm or at room temperature, the pudding is thick and soft. When chilled, it's slightly denser in texture and feels even creamier in the mouth.

Perhaps because it's a distillation of good things, and a special treat, this pudding is often served topped with sultanas (golden raisins) and nuts. You may prefer yours plain. We don't like to add raisins, but we do enjoy the contrast of texture and flavor of lightly toasted almonds or pistachios on top.

About 3 tablespoons butter

3 tablespoons semolina (coarse, like Italian *semola*, *not* fine semolina flour)

1 cup water

¼ cup sugar

Pinch of salt

2½ cups whole milk

1 cup heavy cream

½ teaspoon rose water

¼ teaspoon coarsely chopped or ground mace

Seeds from 2 green cardamom pods, ground, or ⅛ teaspoon ground cardamom

OPTIONAL TOPPING

1 to 2 teaspoons butter

2 to 3 tablespoons slivered almonds or coarsely chopped pistachios

In a wide heavy pot, melt the butter over medium-high heat. Add the semolina and use a wooden spatula or a wooden spoon with a squared-off end to stir and blend the semolina with the butter. Cook the semolina-butter paste for 1 minute or so as it thickens, then add the water, sugar, and salt and stir to mix well. Continue stirring, taking care to scrape the end of the spatula across the bottom of the pot to prevent sticking and to reincorporate any semolina that is sticking. Once the mixture comes to a boil, lower the heat to maintain a simmer. Cook, stirring and scraping frequently; use a rubber scraper to clean off the sides of the pot and then blend the bits of semolina back into the liquid. The mixture will thicken after 10 to 15 minutes.

Add the milk and repeat: Bring to a simmer, stirring frequently, and continue to stir frequently as the liquid cooks down and thickens, about 20 minutes. You will need to lower the heat slightly as the mixture thickens; you want to maintain a very low simmer. The thicker the liquid, the thicker and larger the bubbles during simmering.

Once it thickens again, add the cream and repeat. When the pudding is thickened to the texture of a pourable pancake batter (it will have reduced to just over 2 cups in volume), another 20 minutes or so, remove from the heat. Stir in the rose water and spices. Keep stirring every once in a while, in order to prevent a skin or film from forming on top, until the mixture has cooled. Transfer to a ceramic or glass bowl.

Serve the pudding at room temperature or chilled. If you wish to serve it chilled, once the mixture has completely cooled, cover tightly with plastic wrap and refrigerate.

Just before serving, if topping the pudding with the nuts, melt the butter in a small heavy skillet over medium heat. Toss in the nuts and fry briefly, until just starting to be aromatic and to turn golden. Scatter the nuts on top of the pudding, and serve.   SERVES 6

Because the pudding is very rich, serving sizes are small. Serve for dessert in small bowls, perhaps with a wafer-thin cookie.

NOTE: The purpose of all the stirring and wiping down the sides of the pot is to prevent lumps from forming and to prevent the mixture from sticking or burning. If you end up with some lumps, pass the finished pudding through a fine sieve to break up any lumps, then return it to the pot for a minute or two, stirring constantly.

COCONUT CUSTARD

. . . .

This custard, made from coconut milk and jaggery (palm sugar or crude sugar), is Sri Lanka's most famous sweet, called *watalappan*. It's steam cooked on the stove top. *Watalappan* is rather like the *sankhaya* of Thailand, very easy to make and delicious. But then again, what combination of coconut milk and palm sugar isn't delicious?

1¼ cups chopped jaggery (8 ounces) (palm or crude sugar)
1½ cups canned or fresh coconut milk
4 large eggs, lightly beaten until foamy
¼ teaspoon ground cinnamon
¼ teaspoon nutmeg, preferably freshly grated
4 cloves, ground, or a pinch of ground cloves
Seeds from 2 green cardamom pods, ground,
   or ⅛ teaspoon ground cardamom

Set up a steaming arrangement: Place a 1-quart heatproof bowl in a wide pot with a tight-fitting lid. Add water to the pot to come partway up the sides of the bowl. Wrap the pot lid with a cotton cloth and check that it fits tightly, then set the pot of water and the lid aside, and place the bowl on the counter.

In a medium saucepan, melt the jaggery with 2 tablespoons of the coconut milk, stirring to blend. Remove from the heat, pour in the beaten eggs, and stir briefly. Add the remaining coconut milk and the spices and stir. Strain the liquid through a fine sieve into the bowl. Leave at least a 1-inch margin between the top of the liquid and the top of the bowl.

Place the bowl in the pot of water and bring the water to a boil. Cover the pot tightly with the cotton-lined lid, lower the heat to maintain a strong simmer, and cook for 40 minutes.

Remove from the heat. Protecting your hands and arms with oven mitts, lift off the lid, then lift the bowl out of the pot. Serve the pudding hot or at room temperature, in small individual bowls. If serving cooled, loosely cover with a cotton cloth until cooled.   SERVES 6

Serve for dessert after any type of meal.

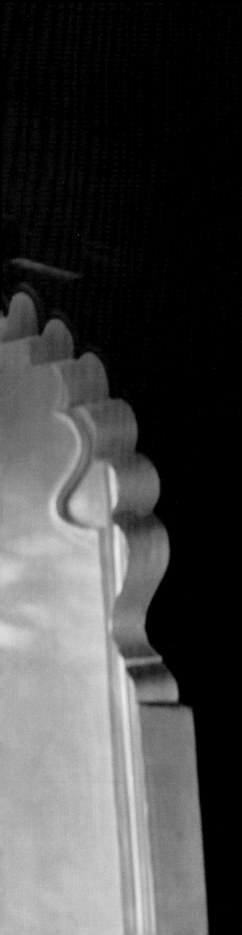

PANTRY

IN THE SUBCONTINENT, SPICES ARE TOSSED

into hot oil at the start of cooking, or added to a dish partway through cooking, or sprinkled on at the end. Like onions or garlic or fresh herbs, they're designed to heighten or deepen flavor, not to mask it. The whole and ground spices used early on (such as mustard seed or the Bengali Five-Spice Mixture) flavor the cooking oil and give the kitchen an appetizing aroma. Then they are joined in the oil by moist ingredients such as garlic, need to cook in the oil to release their flavors and aroma. Later, as the dish simmers, whole spices such as cinnamon sticks or bay leaves or dried red chiles may go in to flavor the broth.

The last spices to go in are often powdered. Masala powders, what the British in India came to call curry powders, are a blend made of whole spices that have been dry roasted or toasted and then ground to a powder. The best known in this category is garam masala. Others include rasam powder, Sri Lankan spice powder, and *sambhar* powder. Because they have already been cooked (during the dry roasting), the spices go into a dish near the end of cooking, a finishing of the seasoning process, rather like the last touch of salt or pepper in Western cookery.

These young women must be happy to be taking a break. They're part of a road crew working in rural Rajasthan, wielding heavy iron pick-axes in the heat of the day.

Spices keep their aroma and flavor best if they are stored whole, then ground just before being used. We use an electric coffee grinder to grind our spices or, if we just need them roughly crushed, a mortar and a pestle. We'll grind enough cumin or coriander seeds to use for a week, and we'll dry roast a small batch of blended whole spices for garam masala or *sambhar* masala, then grind them to have quickly at hand. If the blend gets to be more than a month old, we usually toss it and make a fresh batch.

We find glass jars, small jam jars, to be the most useful way to store our spices and spice blends. We can see what we have and reach for what we need quickly and without fuss.

Cayenne chiles, red and green

BENGALI FIVE-SPICE MIXTURE

. . . .

Called *panch phoron* (*panch* means "five" and *phoron* is "flavor" or "spice"), this mixture of whole untoasted spices gets tossed into hot oil before other ingredients are added. You can add a pinch of each spice every time the mixture is called for, but it's easy to assemble a batch of it, then keep it stored in a well-sealed jar.

There are several versions of *panch phoron*, because different people have different preferences. This is the easiest blend to remember, equal proportions of the five spices. We find it adds aroma and a subtle sweetness to the cooking oil, bringing forward the flavor of green vegetables or beef or whatever you are cooking. It's probably our most frequently used spice blend.

1 tablespoon nigella seeds
1 tablespoon cumin seeds
1 tablespoon black mustard seeds
1 tablespoon fenugreek seeds
1 tablespoon fennel seeds

Combine all the spices in a jar with a tight-fitting lid. Label and store away from heat and bright light.   MAKES JUST OVER ¼ CUP

OPTIONS: You can substitute anise seeds for the fennel seeds and you can, of course, alter the proportions.

CAYENNE

. . . .

We rely on store-bought cayenne, finely powdered dried red cayenne chiles, but sometimes we run out, and then we put dried red chiles in our coffee/spice grinder or food processor and grind them to a powder (the processor yields a slightly coarser texture). We tend to leave the seeds in, for extra heat, but you can sift them out. The powder tends to be slightly paler in color than the cayenne powder we buy, but it has a good chile heat and pleasant slightly sweet taste.

½ cup dried red chiles, stemmed

Place the chiles in a food processor or a spice/coffee grinder and grind to as fine a powder as possible. Be careful when you remove the lid: Try not to breathe in the chile dust (some people cover their mouths and noses with a cloth to protect themselves from the chile powder–laden air).

If you wish to sift out the seeds, use a fine sieve to do so. Transfer the powder to a wide-mouthed jar, cover tightly, label, and store in a cool, dark place.   MAKES ¼ CUP

FRAGRANT SRI LANKAN SPICE POWDER

· · · · · · · · · · · ·

There are in Sri Lanka, as in all parts of the Subcontinent, many types of dried spice blends to be used in different situations. This particular powder is used to bring forward flavors in a dish just as it has finished cooking. It is also sometimes sprinkled on simple salads and the like just for an extra little hit of flavor (try sprinkling it on lightly oiled or buttered hot corn on the cob). As in most Sri Lankan spice blends, the ingredients are roasted to a particularly dark color.

1 tablespoon raw white rice

One 2-inch piece cinnamon or cassia stick

3 to 4 cloves

2 tablespoons coriander seeds

2 sprigs fresh curry leaves (optional)

1 teaspoon black peppercorns

Seeds from 3 green cardamom pods

1 tablespoon cumin seeds

1 tablespoon fresh or frozen grated coconut

1 teaspoon black mustard seeds

Heat a medium or large cast-iron skillet over medium-high heat. Put in the rice and dry roast until just starting to brown. Add the cinnamon, cloves, coriander seeds, curry leaves, if using, black peppercorns, and cardamom and cumin seeds and roast, keeping an eye on the skillet to make sure the ingredients don't burn; shake the skillet every once in a while. Depending upon your skillet and the heat, the spices will need 5 to 6 minutes to get brown and smell great. Add the coconut and mustard seeds and continue to roast, shaking the skillet occasionally or stirring with a wooden spoon. The mustard seeds will pop and fly around, but not to worry. Roast until the spices are quite dark, but not burned. Turn out onto a plate and let cool a little.

Use a stone mortar for grinding, or use a spice/coffee grinder, and grind in batches until very fine. Place the powder in a sieve over a bowl and sift. Regrind again any spices not yet finely ground.

Store in a tightly sealed glass jar and remember to label the jar so that you know what it is! MAKES A SCANT ½ CUP

Use in specific recipes as directed and as a flavor powder to sprinkle on freshly cooked vegetables, grilled meats, or papads *(see page 289).*

GARAM MASALA

. . . .

Garam masala is a powdered spice blend that is added near the end of cooking to give a last-minute touch of flavor. A famous Indian cookbook from South Africa called *Indian Delights*, first published in 1961, calls it Pepping-Up Spice, and that's a good way to think of it.

Garam means "hot" or "heating," and *masala* means "spice blend." We think in this case the "hot" may refer to the fact that the spices are toasted, then ground, rather than to some hotness of flavor; this garam masala, like most, contains no chiles. On the other hand, it contains black pepper and cinnamon (or cassia), heating spices that are native to the Subcontinent, as well as cardamom, cloves, and coriander seed.

Different cooks have their favorite proportions. Here is one we like, which you can tweak as you please. The recipe yields about 1/3 cup, and it's best to make this smallish amount. Even if you use it regularly, most recipes call for only a little, a teaspoon or so. Keep it for no more than two months, for as it ages, the flavor balance changes (the cloves become more dominant, for example), so it's best to toss it out at that point and start again.

1 tablespoon black peppercorns

1/4 cup coriander seeds

1/2 teaspoon cloves

1 teaspoon seeds from green cardamom pods

One 1-inch piece cinnamon or cassia stick

Heat a medium cast-iron skillet over medium-high heat. Place the peppercorns in the skillet and dry roast, stirring frequently with a wooden spoon, until aromatic, 3 to 4 minutes. Turn out into a medium bowl. Repeat with the remaining ingredients, roasting them one ingredient at a time and stirring to prevent burning.

Grind the spices to a powder using a spice/coffee grinder (you will probably have to work in batches).

Let the powder cool completely in a bowl, then transfer to a jar, seal tightly, label, and date. Store in a cool, dark place for no more than 2 months. **MAKES ABOUT 1/3 CUP**

Use as directed in individual recipes; you can also sprinkle a little onto a hot papad (see page 289) or onto freshly boiled or grilled corn on the cob that has been brushed with butter or oil.

BROWNED ONIONS

. . . .

Onion slices fried in oil until browned are called *tarka* in Bangladesh and Pakistan and *birishta* in the Muslim community of Andhra Pradesh. Perhaps they traveled into the Subcontinent with other Central Asian Muslim dishes, such as *pulaos* and kebabs. Whatever the story, they make a wonderful extra layer of flavor for many dishes, especially rice dishes, slightly sweet. You can make a pile of it, then strew it on just before serving. The oil can be poured off, then used again for frying; the onions leave it richly flavored.

Use yellow onions (red onions are soft and floppy after frying, and white ones have less flavor). If you slice the onions ahead and place them on a baking sheet in the sun or in a 150°F oven to dry out a little, they'll have a little extra crispness after frying.

About 1 cup ghee or peanut oil

About 4 cups thinly sliced onions (see headnote)

Heat the ghee or oil in a large wok or karhai (see Glossary) or a wide heavy skillet over medium-high heat. Add the onions and fry, stirring frequently, until well touched with brown, 15 to 20 minutes. Lift out the onions, allow excess oil to run off, and drain on paper towels. Use the oil for any cooking or stir-frying.   MAKES ABOUT 1 CUP

Use as a topping for rice dishes such as Stir-fried Rice and Dal (page 96) or for unsauced simmered dishes such as Bangla Slow-Cooked Beef with Onion (page 273) or Slow-Cooked Wheat Berries and Lamb with Fresh Mint (page 266).

GHEE

. . . .

Ghee is a form of clarified butter used as a cooking oil and flavoring, as well as in Hindu religious rituals. It gives an enticing flavor to food when used for cooking or drizzled on at the last moment (see Chicken Biryani, Dum Style, page 102, for example).

When butter is clarified, it's heated until it melts, then it's heated over low temperature until the water it contains evaporates. The milk solids sink to the bottom of the pan and cook a little, giving the butter a lovely nutty taste; then the pure, clear butterfat is poured off. (The milk solids, which spoil quickly, are discarded.) The liquid butterfat solidifies as it cools and can be stored at room temperature without becoming rancid, an enormous advantage for people without refrigeration. (These days in the Subcontinent, the word *ghee* is used for any solid cooking fat, whether made from vegetable oil or from clarified butter.)

Ghee is sold in South Asian groceries, in well-stocked supermarkets, and in many health food stores. (Read the label carefully to see that you are getting butter ghee and not a vegetable oil–based product.) You can also make your own very easily. Start with good butter. Put out a large liquid measuring cup or other jug with a spout, and some cheesecloth for filtering the ghee, as well as a sterilized glass jar.

1 pound unsalted butter

Melt the butter in a heavy sauce pan over medium-low heat, then continue cooking, without letting it boil, for about half an hour. The moisture in the butter will evaporate and the milk solids will sink to the bottom of the pan. When the solids start to turn brown, pour off the clear clarified butter into a clean measuring cup or a jug.

Lay several layers of cheesecloth over the mouth of a sterilized glass jar and pour the butter through it. The cheesecloth will filter out any impurities, leaving the clear pale yellow liquid. When it cools, it will thicken into a soft yellow paste. It will keep for months in a well-sealed container. If you refrigerate it as we prefer to, it will harden, but, as butter does, it softens quickly at room temperature. MAKES ABOUT 1 1/2 CUPS

It may seem like a lot of work to make your own soft cheese, *chhana*, but it can all be done in less than half an hour, whenever you have a moment. (You can, of course, also buy *chhana* at South Asian groceries.) As with any cheese, the first time you make *chhana*, it will feel as if you're using a large quantity of milk to make what seems like a small amount of cheese.

8 cups whole or reduced-fat milk
3 to 4 tablespoons fresh lemon juice

Place the milk in a large pot and heat over medium heat, stirring occasionally to prevent sticking, until it's just below the boil. Take off the heat. Add the lemon juice, tablespoon by tablespoon, stirring with a clean wooden spoon after each addition. After the third or fourth tablespoon, you will see the curds separate out, looking like blobby bits floating on the surface. Keep on stirring the milk for several minutes, then set aside.

Moisten a piece of cheesecloth or loose-weave cotton cloth, place a sieve over a large bowl, and line it with the cloth (fold the cheesecloth so you have several layers to line the sieve). Pour in the milk mixture. Pour cold water over it to rinse off the taste of the souring agent, then let drain. The liquid will gradually drain through the curds into the bowl: Pull the cloth tightly around the curds to press out extra liquid, or tie the top of the cloth to make a bag and hang it on a hook over the bowl to drain. You will have soft moist cheese in about 30 minutes. If you want the cheese to make Sweet and Creamy Rose Water Dumplings (page 328), let the curds drain for 3 to 4 hours, or overnight, until quite crumbly.

Transfer to a small clean bowl and scrape any remaining curds off the cloth into the bowl (then rinse the cloth out thoroughly to use again).

Use immediately, or store, well covered, in the refrigerator for up to 3 days. **MAKES A GENEROUS 1/2 POUND, ABOUT 3/4 CUP**

Use as a version of cream cheese, spread on skillet breads such as Cumin-Flecked Skillet Breads (page 126) or on Chapatis (page 110), perhaps sprinkled with fresh herbs and sea salt.

In Assam, in the far northeast corner of India, there's a century-old national park called Kaziranga. It's one of the last preserves of the one-horned rhino; it also shelters tigers, wild water buffaloes, wild elephants, and other creatures. Visitors enter the park on elephants. The mahout (elephant keeper) and the elephant he cares for are a team for life; when her calf grows bigger, he'll have his own mahout. They're heading home for the evening after bathing in the river.

PANEER

· · · · · · · · · · · ·

Paneer is a pressed cheese with the texture of pressed tofu, firm and a little rubbery, and a very mild taste. You can find it (fresh or frozen) in South Asian groceries, but you can also make your own. It holds its shape rather than melting when heated, so it can be simmered in sauces.

Begin by making a double batch of *chhana* (page 344). Once it has drained, working with clean wet hands, shape the curds together into two small blocks about 4 inches square. Wrap each one tightly in cheesecloth or a clean cotton cloth and stack on a plate. Put a heavy weight on top (for example, a small cutting board weighed down by a large full jam jar); the weight will help press moisture out of the cheese. From time to time, pour off any liquid that has accumulated. After 4 hours or so, the cheese will be very firm and drier.

Rinse off and then store, well sealed, in the refrigerator for no more than 5 days. Slice to use.   **MAKES A SCANT 1 POUND**

Use to make Simmered Kashmiri Paneer (page 171), or brush slices with flavored oil (like that in Bangla-Flavored Grilled Zucchini, page 144) and grill until golden. You can also use paneer *in sandwiches, as you would another mild cheese.*

At a procession in Kochi (Cochin) in Kerala, the children riding on the elephants looked both pleased and very nervous.

ZINET'S YOUNG GINGER PICKLE

· · · · · · · · · · · ·

When fresh young ginger appears in the stores, take the opportunity to make these easy fresh pickles. (We also use regular ginger, if it's very fresh and nonfibrous.) We learned to make them from our neighbor Zinet (see Zinet's Chicken with Tomato and Greens, page 244). Buy plenty of ginger, for you'll lose some volume when you peel it and trim off any bumps or flaws.

4 cups thinly sliced peeled young ginger (about 1 pound)

2 teaspoons salt

2 teaspoons turmeric

½ cup fresh lemon juice

½ cup water

Place the sliced ginger in a wide bowl. Add the salt and turmeric and use a wooden spoon to toss and blend until the medallions are coated with salt and turmeric. Spread out on two baking sheets lined with wax paper or parchment paper and put in a warm, dry place to dry for 3 days, turning the slices once or twice. (You can also place them in a 150°F oven for 3 or 4 hours, then air dry them for another 2 days.) The drying will firm them up.

Mix together the lemon juice and water. Pack the ginger into two 1-cup jars and pour over the diluted lemon juice. Seal well and let stand for 1 week before using. Refrigerate once opened.   **MAKES 2 CUPS**

Serve as a pickle with any meal.

CHILE-GINGER PICKLE: Zinet, who eats a pickle every day as part of her evening meal, uses the same method with very fresh tender cauliflower florets; again, the liquid is not heated. Some people, she tells us, add dried red chiles to the pickling mixture, for more spice.

AFTER-DINNER FRESHENER

· · · · · · · · · · · ·

There are Ayurvedic explanations for the tradition, but really it comes down to pleasure, we think: After a meal comes the digestif. In France or Italy, the digestif is in liquid form: an after-dinner liqueur or perhaps a tisane; but in the Subcontinent, it's usually plain spices. Sometimes it's as simple as fennel seeds on a plate, green and inviting.

In Gujarat, the fennel seeds often come blended with coarse sugar or served alongside a bowl of coarse sugar so that diners can make a blend to their taste. The sugar is a wonderful sweetening balance for the intensity of the fennel. You pick up a pinch of seeds or seeds and sugar, put it in your mouth, and then bite down gently to release the flavors. Your mouth is left feeling freshened and invigorated; any stale remaining dinner flavors are chased away.

2 tablespoons fennel seeds

1 to 2 tablespoons coarse sugar, such as rock sugar (optional)

Place the fennel and sugar together in a small bowl, or separately in two small bowls, and put out on the table at the end of the meal so guests can help themselves. Allow about 1 teaspoon per person after a meal. Store in a sealed glass jar.   **MAKES 3 TO 4 TABLESPOONS**

OPPOSITE, LEFT: *In Madhya Pradesh, two sisters sit on steps in the village square, watching the commotion as we North Americans walk around their small village.* RIGHT: *A field of mustard in full bloom, in Uttar Pradesh. Mustard is eaten as a vegetable, its seeds are a valued spice, and its oil is widely used, especially in Nepal, Bengal, and Bangladesh.*

GLOSSARY

Ingredients, names, and unfamiliar terms

AJOWAN: *See* lovage.

AKOORI: A family of egg dishes from the Parsi community (see the recipes, pages 230 and 234).

AMARANTH: A plant (*Amaranthus hybridus*) native to South America that produces edible seeds and greens. In the Subcontinent, amaranth greens are widely used. Amaranth leaves may be green or partly purple; they are now widely available in well-stocked produce sections in North America.

AMCHOOR POWDER: A souring agent used in the northern part of the Subcontinent. It is processed from dried tart green mango and is sold in South Asian groceries.

ANARDANA: Dried sour pomegranate seeds, used in Pakistan and parts of northern India to give a tart flavoring. *Anardana* are sold in most South Asian grocery stores, usually in small plastic bags. Dark red to black, they must be ground to a powder or simmered in hot liquid to release their flavor.

ANDHRA PRADESH: An Indian state that lies south of the state of Orissa and north of Chennai (Madras), on the eastern coast. The principal city is Hyderabad, which is known for its Moghul-style cuisine adapted to tropical ingredients. Outside Hyderabad the state is primarily Hindu, with a cuisine that resembles that of Tamil Nadu, its neighbor to the south. It has its own versions of the crepelike breads called *dosas* (see Onion Skillet Breads, page 124) and of the dal called *sambhar* (page 187). See also page 14.

ANISE SEED: A spice (also called *aniseed*), the seed of the plant *Pimpinella anisum*, with a licoricelike flavor. In our experience, fennel is more common than anise in the Subcontinent; both are given the name *saunf* in Hindi. Anise has a dustier flavor than fennel has. The pale grayish thin long seeds are sold in well-stocked grocery stores; buy it whole rather than ground if possible, for fresher flavor.

ASAFOETIDA: A spice used in powdered form in savory dishes, especially in vegetarian Hindu cooking, often as a substitute for onions and garlic. Asafoetida is the resin collected from the root of a shrub (*Ferulla alliacea*) that grows in dry regions of India and in Iran and Afghanistan. Its Hindi name is *hing*. It has an unpleasant smell (the name means "stinky spice") when raw, but when added to hot oil at the early stages of cooking, it brings an aromatic oniony depth of flavor to the dish. It is usually sold as a pale yellow powder in small tins in South Asian groceries and some large supermarkets, but it may also come as a lump of hardened resin, which needs to be chopped into small pieces before it's used.

ATTA: Finely milled whole wheat flour from durum wheat, used in the making of chapatis (see page 110) and other flatbreads. Atta is pale yellow in color, with a high protein content. It is sold in large grocery stores and in South Asian groceries, sometimes labeled "durum flour for chapatis."

AYURVEDA: A system of traditional medicine that originated in India. In Ayurveda the balance in the body between opposites—hot and cold, acid and base—is maintained by eating appropriate foods and is considered the basis of good health. Ayurvedic ideas spread from India to become the basis of other traditional medicine systems, including the Tibetan and the Chinese.

BAGHAR: The Hindi term for the preliminary frying, in oil or ghee, of mustard seeds and/or other whole spices and onion and/or other aromatics, before adding the main ingredients; a common technique in many parts of the Subcontinent.

BAJRA: *See* millet flour.

BASH FUL: A parboiled rice from Bangladesh, with a mix of short and medium grains. See the recipe, page 87.

BASMATI: *See* rice.

BEAN SPROUTS: The tender new shoots of beans, most commonly mung beans or soybeans. The only bean sprouts called for in this book are mung bean sprouts. Barely sprouted legumes (soaked in warm water until just the tip of the sprout is showing) are used as an ingredient in the Subcontinent, but not in this book.

BELL PEPPERS: Bell peppers, often called *capsicums* in Britain and Australia, are a variety of sweet pepper, in the same family as chiles. They are eaten as a vegetable. *See also* chiles.

BENGAL: An Indian state, and also the name given to the whole region where the Bengali language is spoken, from the Indian state to the far border of Bangladesh. At times separated under the British into West and East Bengal, a division that approximates the present division between the Indian state of Bengal and the nation of Bangladesh, the region has a long history and a distinctive culinary and linguistic culture. The principal cities are Dhaka, the capital of Bangladesh, and Kolkata (formerly Calcutta), the capital of the Indian state of Bengal. Because it lies so far east, Bengal was conquered relatively late by the Moghuls, so its Muslim cooking is less marked by Moghul influence than that of other regions. Similarly, a strict version of Hinduism requiring vegetarianism was relatively late in arriving in Bengal (about two hundred years ago), so dals and legumes in general seem to play a lesser role in the cuisine than they do in other parts of India. Because the region is very fertile, a wide variety of fruits, vegetables, and fish is used in cooking. See the Index for recipes.

BENGALI FIVE-SPICE MIXTURE: See the recipe, page 340; *see also* panch phoron.

BESAN: *See* chickpea flour.

BETEL: A leaf bundle that is chewed as a kind of light stimulant and an aid to digestion in many parts of South Asia and Southeast Asia. The nut of the areca palm (*Areca catechu*) is cut into pieces and wrapped in a fresh leaf of a species of pepper vine (*Piper betle*), together with flavorings and some lime paste (an alkali) to release the alkaloids in the nut. The nut makes the chewer salivate and colors the saliva a deep red, staining the teeth. The wad may also include a little tobacco or spices in combination with the basic nut and lime. The whole combination is referred to as *paan* in Hindi and as *betel nut* in English, though *betel leaf* would be more accurate. *Paan* sellers set up in small markets all over the Subcontinent, with neat stacks of leaves and an array of ingredients ready to be assembled to order.

BIHAR: A conservative, predominantly Hindu state in northern India, located between the states of Uttar Pradesh and Bengal. Bihar has very fertile farmland and relatively dense population; its capital is Patna. Recently the southern, much more mountainous half of the state was separated off to create a new state called Jharkhand.

BILLING: Also called *belimbi* or *bilimbi*, the fruit of a tree (*Averrhoa bilimbi*) that is related to star fruit. It is used as a souring agent in Sri Lanka, as well as in Indonesia, Malaysia, and the Philippines.

BIRYANI: A rice and meat dish whose name comes from the Persian word for "rice," *birinj*. See the recipe, page 102; *see also* pulao.

BLACK CUMIN: *See* cumin.

BLACK MUSTARD SEED: *See* mustard.

BRAHMIN: The highest caste in Hinduism, often referred to as the priestly caste. Brahmins may be wealthy or poor, but because of their caste they have stricter requirements for purity and cleanliness in a Hindu sense; that is, a traditional Brahmin cannot eat food prepared by someone of a lower caste, or of no caste (such as a foreigner or a tribal person), nor can he or she share food or eat at the same table with such a person. Brahmin priests preside at Hindu rituals such as cremations, prayers for the dead, naming ceremonies, and weddings.

BROILING: The broiler element in modern ovens can be used as a substitute for grilling in many cases. The heat comes from above, and the meat or vegetables to be broiled are placed on a rack in the broiler about five inches below the heating element. When broiling, prop the oven door open a little to let the heat out or the food will roast in the oven's heat rather than being cooked from above by the direct heat of the broiler.

BROWN MUSTARD SEED: *See* mustard.

BUDDHISM: One of the major world religions, which began in India with the teachings of Gautama Buddha, who lived nearly 2,600 years ago, when the population of the Subcontinent was, obviously, much smaller and was either Hindu or animist. Buddhism spread across the northern part of the Subcontinent and northwest to Afghanistan and into China. It was also carried to Sri Lanka and Southeast Asia. Buddhism remains the dominant religion in Sri Lanka and in Bhutan, and an important religion in Nepal, as well as in Burma and Thailand. Although the number of Buddhists in India is now relatively small, India remains

an important pilgrimage place for Buddhists from all sects all over the world. Though the Buddha preached nonviolence, not all Buddhists are vegetarians.

BUTTER, CLARIFIED BUTTER: *See* ghee.

BUTTERMILK: Traditionally buttermilk is the liquid that remains when cream is cultured with the appropriate bacteria and churned into butter. Today, commercial buttermilk is made of cultured skim milk that is heat treated to stop fermentation. Buttermilk has a tart, refreshing taste, and traditional buttermilk is a common drink in the deserts of Pakistan, Rajasthan, and Gujarat. **Buttermilk powder** is sold in large grocery stores.

CARAMBOLA: *See* star fruit.

CARDAMOM: Cardamom is a bush that is native to South India and Sri Lanka. The seedpods are used as a spice. It is sold as whole pods or as a powder. Green cardamom is widely available; brown cardamom is available in South Asian groceries. **Green cardamom** (from the plant *Elettaria cardamomum*) has pale green pods that contain a number of small black seeds. Sometimes the pods have been bleached white; avoid these if possible. Most of the flavor is in the seeds. The pods may be used whole or crushed in simmered dishes, or the seeds may be ground to a powder and used when an intense flavor is desired—for example, in sweets such as Mango Ice Cream (page 324), or in the spice blend garam masala (see page 342). **Brown cardamom** has an earthier, more camphorous, and less intense flavor. Technically it is not true cardamom; it is from the *Ammomum aromaticum* plant. Its pods are a dull brown in color. Brown cardamom is grown in the Himalayan foothills and is used in *pulaos* and other savory dishes (see Pakistani Lamb Pulao, page 104). **Black cardamom** is an Ethiopian spice, again not a true cardamom; it is not used in the Subcontinent, as far as we know.

CASHEWS: Cashew trees (*Anacardium occidentale*) are native to Brazil and are now grown in subtropical parts of India and in Sri Lanka. Their fruit grows in a curious way: as a curved nut on the bottom of an edible fruit known as a *cashew apple*. In the Subcontinent, cashew nuts are used in savory dishes, to thicken sauces, or as a flavoring, as well as in sweet dishes as a garnish. Cashews are sold in well-stocked grocery stores and in South Asian groceries. (They are always sold shelled because the shells are toxic.) Because the nuts are rich in oils, they should be stored well sealed in plastic, in the refrigerator or freezer.

CASSIA, CINNAMON: These two spices, sold whole, as quills of bark, or in powdered form, are used in Moghul cooking and to flavor sweets. **Cassia** (*Cinnamomum cassia*) grows wild in northern India and is related to cinnamon, but it has a punchier, less delicate flavor. The Sanskrit name is *tvak*; in Bengal, we heard it called *taysbatta*. **Cassia leaves** are used in some parts of the Subcontinent as an aromatic; bay laurel leaves are a substitute. The **cinnamon tree** (*Cinnamomum zeylanicum*) grows wild in South India; the best-quality cinnamon is cultivated in Sri Lanka. Its Sanskrit name, *dar-chini*, means "Chinese bark." Much of the powdered cinnamon sold in North

America is in fact cassia. True cinnamon is tanner in color, whereas cassia is reddish brown. Though their flavors are not identical, you can substitute one for the other.

CASTE: A complicated belief system widespread in the Subcontinent, especially among Hindus, that individuals are born into a certain social class, a class that relates not to wealth but to the job or trade of the male members of the family. Strict observance of caste locks individuals and populations into the stratum of society they were born in, and successive governments, particularly in India, have attempted to loosen the rigidities that arise from caste. Outsiders, including tribal people and foreigners, have no caste. Many observant Hindus cannot share food or eat with, or have any kitchen utensil touched by, a low-caste or no-caste person. Elaborate rituals are required to purify or render clean any food or utensil that has been contaminated by contact with someone deemed unclean.

CATTLE: First domesticated in Baluchistan (western Pakistan) about seven thousand years ago, cattle in the Subcontinent are of several varieties, including the humped zebu cattle (*Bos indicus*), often used for farm work, and many newer crossbreeds bred for milk production. Water buffaloes (*Bubalus bubalis*) also produce milk, with a higher fat content than cow's milk. *See also* water buffalo.

CAYENNE POWDER: A powder made from dried red cayenne chiles. Cayenne is orange red to dark red, depending on whether the chiles it was made from were smoked or air dried. It adds heat to a dish and is sometimes referred to in the Subcontinent as *chile powder*. Cayenne is available in any grocery store. You can also make your own by grinding dried red chiles (see page 340). Store cayenne in a tightly sealed container in a cool, dark place and use sparingly until you know exactly how hot your particular batch is. *See also* chiles.

CHAI: The name for tea in most of the Subcontinent, very like the Chinese word *cha*, from which it is derived. It can mean tea of any kind, but in the West it has also come to mean specifically Indian-style tea, made with milk and sugar and perhaps scented with a little cardamom. See Spiced Chai for Cold Mornings, page 305, and Cardamom Chai, page 305; *see also* tea.

CHANA DAL: *See* dals.

CHAPATI: The Hindi name for an unleavened flatbread made of atta flour, rolled out to a thin round from four to eight inches across and cooked on a *tava*. In Urdu, the major language of Pakistan, and in some parts of India, the name is *roti*. See the recipes, pages 110 and 111.

CHHANA: A soft fresh cheese made in northern India and Pakistan from acidulated fresh cow's or water buffalo's milk (see page 344 for a recipe). *Chhana* is used in Bengal to make many sweet treats (see Sweet and Creamy Rose Water Dumplings Two Ways, page 328).

CHICKPEA FLOUR: A finely ground flour made from chickpeas (*chana* dal), widely used, especially in the northern half of the Subcontinent, to make both breads and batters for coating deep-fried vegetables and also to thicken sauces. (See the recipe for mushroom pakoras, page 298.) Chickpea flour is known in Hindi and Urdu as *besan*. It is available at any South Asian grocery. Store in a cool place, as you would whole wheat flour. *See also* chana dal *under* dals.

CHILES: **Chiles,** or **chile peppers,** grow on plants in the *Capsicum* genus. Most are annuals. They originated in Mexico and have become an important flavoring and ingredient of cuisines in many places, including most of the Subcontinent. Chiles may be used fresh or dried, left whole or slit, chopped, or minced. ("Slit" means a slash cut lengthwise from just below the stem end, without cutting the chile into pieces.) Dried chiles may be crumbled to a powder (*see* cayenne powder). The hotness of chiles is determined by the amount of capsaicin they contain. The seeds contain more capsaicin than the flesh, so some recipes call for stripping out the seeds and membrane to produce a milder dish. (Cooks who love chile heat tend to leave the seeds in.) *To strip chiles*, cut lengthwise, then use the tip of a small spoon to scrape out seeds and membranes. The capsaicin level depends not only on the variety of chile but also on the climate where it is grown: Hotter weather produces hotter chiles. Most chiles are green as they grow, turning to red as they ripen. The riper the chile, the hotter and sweeter it is. Chiles are rich in Vitamin C.

Banana: A sweet version of the Hungarian wax chile, the banana chile, or banana pepper, is pale yellow when ripe and has a mild flavor with only occasional hints of chile heat.

Bird chiles are used widely in Thai and Lao cooking, and are often called *Thai hot chiles* or, erroneously, *Tabasco chiles*. These small pointed chiles are very hot. They are sometimes sold dried, but are more and more available fresh, sold in small clear plastic packages. Unlike the other chiles listed here, these (and Tabasco peppers) are from a perennial species of chile plant called *Capsicum frutescens*.

Cayenne is very shiny-skinned, four to six inches long, and slender, tapering to a point, with marked heat. Cayenne is the most common chile in the Subcontinent, and the most commonly called for in this book. It is milder when green and immature, the form in which it is most often called for in these recipes; when ripe it is a strong red color (see photograph, page 339). In cookbooks from the Subcontinent, fresh green cayennes are commonly called *green chiles* and ripe ones are *red chiles*. Jalapeño chiles can be substituted: two jalapeños for each green cayenne chile, with a lessening of heat and a slightly different flavor. Serrano chiles can be substituted one for one when red cayenne chiles are called for in these recipes. *See also* cayenne powder.

Dried red chiles: Chiles dry well and can then be kept for a long time. In autumn, from Bhutan to China, Nepal, and northern India, chiles, most often red cayenne chiles, are laid out on the ground or on flat rooftops to dry. Dried red chiles are sold in South and Southeast Asian grocery stores and most large supermarkets. We use those from Thailand or India and store them in a glass jar. The heat of dried red chiles varies, so be cautious when you start using powder from a new batch.

Hungarian wax is a long, tapered chile that ripens from pale green to pale yellow, with some distinct heat, especially in the seeds.

Jalapeño: The snub-nosed, short, wide, deep green jalapeño, widely sold in North America, has a mild heat and a slightly sweet taste.

Pimentón: The dried powdered chile from Spain that is called *pimentón* has a smoky taste and a milder heat than cayenne; it is a good substitute for Kashmiri dried red chiles.

Serrano, a pointed red or green chile about two inches long, has a sharp heat, more than a red cayenne.

CILANTRO: *See* coriander.

CINNAMON: *See* cassia.

COCONUT: **Coconuts** grow on tall coconut palms (*Cocos nucifera*) in tropical and subtropical climates. Inside the hard exterior shell is a slightly sweet, watery liquid. The shell is lined with white oil-rich flesh that can be eaten raw, in chunks or grated. We substitute **frozen grated coconut** for fresh, because it is widely available in South and Southeast Asian groceries, as well as in some large supermarkets. Grated coconut can be used as an ingredient in cooked dishes, as is or dry roasted until golden, a process that brings out its flavor. When dry roasting grated coconut, if you start with the frozen version, it will give off liquid for a while before starting to get golden. **Dried** or **dessicated grated coconut** can be substituted; try to find the unsweetened version. **Coconut milk** is made by immersing grated coconut in warm water, then squeezing it; the warm water washes the oils out of the coconut, turning the water white and thickening it. The coconut meat is then squeezed dry and the milk poured off. This is the "first pressing," the richest milk. "Second pressing" is extracted by repeating the process. We usually substitute **canned (unsweetened) coconut milk**. Usually some of the thicker milk solidifies at the top of the can. Set this aside as the equivalent of first-pressing coconut milk. If your canned coconut milk is of even consistency, don't worry, and use it, as we do, as a substitute for either first or second pressing, whatever you need. Coconut milk will keep for only one to two days in the refrigerator. **Coconut oil** is the pure oil extracted from coconut flesh. It is loaded with flavor (and with saturated fats). It is widely used in the southern part of the Subcontinent for frying and gives incomparable taste. It is available in South Asian groceries. Store in the refrigerator once opened.

COFFEE: The coffee plant (*Coffea arabica* or *C. canephora*) is a perennial shrub. Its seeds, known as beans, turn bright red as they ripen. Coffee is grown in the mountainous areas of Sri Lanka and India, but it is not a major crop, nor is it nearly as widely consumed as tea in the Subcontinent.

CORIANDER: Coriander is an annual (*Coriandrum sativum*) that grows in temperate and subtropical climates. It provides to the cook both an herb, coriander leaves (known in Spanish and in parts of North America as *cilantro*), and a spice, coriander seed. Its root is also used in Thai-Lao cooking to flavor curry pastes and marinades.

For people who don't like **fresh coriander**, traveling in the Subcontinent can sometimes be a challenge, because it is so common. We love coriander, but we meet many people who feel just the opposite. When coriander appears outside its season, it can taste soapy, and we wonder whether people who don't like it first tasted it when it was out of season or less than very fresh. Mint leaves, although very different in taste, can often be substituted for coriander leaves when they are called for as a last-minute addition to a dish.

Coriander seeds are larger than peppercorns, round, and either light tan or grayish tan in color. Like other spices, coriander should be stored in a well-sealed container away from heat and light. We keep the whole seeds, then grind them when we need them. The seeds have a tough outer layer and can be difficult to grind fine, so we often keep a small supply of coriander powder, too. **Ground coriander** is used to flavor many savory dishes. It has a powerful warm, earthy taste. It's often used in combination with cumin seed, especially in dishes of Moghul origin. Coriander seed is rarely used whole, except to flavor pickles.

CORN, CORN FLOUR: Corn, often called *maize* in English in India, is native to the Americas but has become established as a grain in some parts of the Subcontinent. In the desert regions of Rajasthan and Gujarat, it is dried and ground to make corn flour, then used alone or in combination with wheat flour or ground dal to make skillet flatbreads and *dhokla* (see page 125). It is also used in the hills of Nepal and the Himalayan foothills area of West Bengal to make a polenta-type dish called *dero* (see Nepali Polenta with Himalayan Grilled Tomato Sauce, page 94).

CUMIN: Cumin, the seed of the plant *Cuminum cyminium*, is a spice that is called *jira* (sometimes written *jeera*) in Hindi and many other subcontinental languages. The most common variety has pale-tan long, narrow seeds and a flavor related to caraway, anise, and fennel. It is widely available. **Black cumin** has smaller, finer seeds and a more penetrating, more complex flavor. It is most often used in meat dishes, especially in Moghul-style cooking (see Pakistani Lamb Pulao, page 104). It is available in South Asian grocery stores, but regular cumin can be substituted. We keep whole cumin seeds on hand and grind them fresh when ground cumin is called for; they grind very easily in a mortar or a spice/coffee grinder.

CURRY: The widely used generic English name for wet, sauced, or spiced dishes from the Subcontinent. The origin of the word is in dispute: Some say it is a European adaptation of the Tamil word for pepper, *kari*, while others see it as deriving from *tarkari*, the Gujarati word for dishes that are served with rice or bread. Although it upsets purists, the term *curry* has become so widespread that we think it helps make cooked dishes from the Subcontinent feel more familiar to people getting acquainted with the cuisines of the region.

CURRY LEAVES: The leaves of a perennial bushy shrub, *Murraya koenigii*, native to southern India, these are an aromatic herb that is tossed into hot oil at the start of cooking, perfuming the air; the leaves may also be added later in the simmering process, just before the dish is served. They are widely used in the cuisines of southern India and Sri Lanka, as well as in some Gujarati dishes (see Eggs with Curry Leaves, page 234, and Potato White Curry, page 155). Curry leaves are sold fresh in large bundles in southern India and Sri Lanka; in North America, they can now be found fresh in many South Asian stores, especially Sri Lankan shops. Slightly shiny, deep green, tapered ovals that are smaller and less tough than bay leaves, the leaves grow in facing pairs along each stem. If you're not using them within two days, store them, well wrapped in plastic, in the freezer; use directly from the freezer as needed. Fresh-frozen curry leaves have much more life and flavor than dried curry leaves, which used to be the only version available in North America. The shrub can be grown successfully indoors in temperate climates. Place the plant in a partly sunny spot and water regularly.

CURRY POWDER: *See* garam masala *and* sambhar; see also Garam Masala (page 342) and Sambhar Powder (page 188).

DALS: *Dal* (sometimes transcribed *dhal*) is the term used in most of the northern parts of the Subcontinent for split legumes (often referred to as *pulses* by the British) such as **mung beans, chickpeas (garbanzo beans)**, and **lentils**. Whole unsplit dried legumes are sometimes referred to in English as *gram*; once split, they're called *dal*. Take dried mung beans, for example. When they're whole and dark green, they are referred to as *mung gram*. When they're split and skinned, they are a brilliant yellow color and are referred to as *mung dal*. Similarly, dried whole chickpeas, the small darker-skinned variety, as opposed to garbanzos, are called *Bengal gram*. What we in North America call *split peas*, yellow and hard, are generally known as *toovar* or *toor dal* in the Subcontinent. They're widely used in the southern regions for making *sambhar* (see pages 186 and 187) and also in Gujarat.

Dal is also the name given to the class of cooked legume dishes (for more detail, see Dals, page 175).

The world of dals is a huge one; in this book, we call for only a few different dried dals, all of which can be found in many health food stores, as well as in South Asian groceries. We buy in quantity and store our dried legumes in glass jars away from the light, where they keep well for six months, just drying out a little over time.

Chana dal: *Chana* comes in several types. The most common form of *chana* in the Subcontinent is smaller than a chickpea (garbanzo), darker skinned, and slightly wrinkled, the pea of the plant *Dolichos biflorus*. The type known as *Kabouli chana* is larger, paler, and smoother, and is like our chickpeas, the pea of the plant *Cicer arietinum*. Whole *chana* is also called *Bengal gram* in the Subcontinent. It is often sold split. Look for traditional *chana* in South Asian stores or substitute chickpeas available in grocery stores (cooking times will generally be longer). In the Subcontinent, especially in northern India, fresh *chana* is also eaten in season, like fresh soybeans. Larger than green peas, round and bright green, they need to be shucked. If you ever see them for sale in a South Asian grocery, do try them (you could substitute them for the soybeans in Simmered Spiced Soybeans, page 143).

Masur dal/masoor dal is a lentil-shape legume (*Lens culinaris* or *L. esculenta*) that is pale orange-red in color; it is sometimes called *red dal*. It cooks very quickly,

in about twenty minutes, so we think of it as the rushed cook's friend and as a necessary pantry staple. It is available in South Asian groceries and in well-stocked large groceries. See the Index for recipes.

Mung dal/moong dal comes from dried mung beans (the same beans that are sprouted to produce bean sprouts) from the plant *Phaseolus aureus*. Whole mung beans are small dull green peas that are known as *mung gram* or *green gram*; split mung beans are green on the outside and yellow on the inside. Most commonly, *mung dal* refers to hulled and split mung beans, which are bright golden yellow. In this book we call for only split hulled mung. When mung dal is cooked, it becomes thick and smooth, almost creamy in texture. It is supposedly the easiest of the dals to digest, and it is one the most commonly given to children. It is also the dal most often used to make *khichadi* (Stir-fried Rice and Dal, page 96).

Toovar dal, also called *toor* (sometimes written *tur*) or *archar*. Toovar dal is most widely used in southern India, especially for making *sambhars* (see pages 186 and 187) and Pepper-Tamarind Broth (page 198). It is split dried pigeon peas (from the plant *Cajanus cajan*) and a dark butterscotch in color; it looks like small golden chickpeas. Toovar dal is hard to find outside South Asian groceries. Like chickpeas, it takes a while to cook; allow two hours' boiling time to get it tender.

Urad dal, a small legume, is pale grayish white with a black skin. Whole *urad* is known as *black gram*, but it is usually sold split and skinned, looking like small pale gray to whitish pebbles. *Urad*, whose Sanskrit name is *masha*, is native to the Subcontinent and is related to mung beans. The plant's botanical name is *Phaseolus mungo*. Split *urad* is soaked, ground, and combined with rice to make the batter for *dosas* (see page 112) and *idlis* (see page 120), and it is also cooked as a dal (see Udaipur Urad Dal, page 189). Urad dal is widely available in South Asian stores.

DEEP-FRYING: Deep-frying requires oil that is stable at high temperatures (peanut oil is best, or use raw sesame oil), and a pot large enough to hold several inches or more of oil. The pot should be stable on the cooking surface so that it won't tip over. We often use a large wok for deep-frying, as is done in the Subcontinent (using a *karhai*; see page 355) and in China, but you can also use a deep fryer or a wide deep pot. You need a slotted or mesh spoon or spatula for lifting the food out of the hot oil. The oil needs to be deep enough to cover the food so it can cook evenly all over. After frying, the hot oil can be strained through a fine-mesh sieve to strain out impurities, then, once cooled, stored in a clean glass jar in the refrigerator. As long as the oil has not picked up any strong flavors from the food cooked in it, it can be used several times.

DHOTI: A length of cloth, traditionally made of homespun cotton, worn as a loincloth by men in earlier times. Gandhi repopularized the dhoti as a form of dress during the struggle for independence, to show respect for traditional values and skills.

DIWALI: A Hindu festival, a very joyous one, often called in English the "Festival of Light," that marks the lunar New Year. The dates vary, but it takes place in late

October or early November, at the new moon. At Diwali, people clean house and give gifts of sweets.

DOSA: *Dosas* are flatbreads made of a fermented batter cooked on a griddle; they look like large buckwheat crepes. Originally from southern India, *dosas* can now be found in many places in the Subcontinent, as street food or in restaurants. Most commonly the batter is made of soaked rice and urad dal. See the recipes, pages 112 and 114.

DRUMSTICK: A vegetable (*Moringa oleifera*) with long, slightly ridged slender pods, like elongated okra; it can be as long as two feet. Native to the Subcontinent, it is widely used, chopped into short lengths and simmered, especially in Bengal and in southern India, where it is often cooked in *sambhar* (see Sambhar with Drumsticks, page 186). The outer layer of the vegetable is rather tough, so the cooked pieces are eaten by being pulled between the front teeth to squeeze out the tender and delicious pulp, rather like eating artichoke leaves, and then the husks are discarded.

DUM: From the Persian *dumpukht*, meaning "air cooked" (the Anglo-Indians had *dumpoke*, a dish of boned stuffed duck). *Dum* refers to a method of steaming in a sealed closed pot so that textures become tender and aromas blended. See Chicken Biryani, Dum Style, page 102, and Cauliflower Dum, page 148.

FENNEL SEED: Fennel seeds are known as *saunf* in most of northern India and in Nepal (the same word, confusingly, is often used for anise seeds). They are long and rounded, pale green, and strongly aromatic, the seeds of sweet fennel (*Foeniculum vulgare*), which, like anise, is a member of the carrot family (Umbellifera). The anise/licorice taste is related to that of cumin, caraway, and anise but is more fresh and forward. Fennel is one of the spices in the Bengali five-spice mixture *panch phoron* (see page 358) and is also chewed as a digestive and breath freshener after a meal. Fennel seeds are widely available in grocery stores.

FENUGREEK: Fenugreek is an annual plant that is grown for both its leaves and its seeds. Its botanical name, *Trigonella foenum graecum*, means, literally, "triangular Greek hay," a reference to the shape of the seeds and an indication of how widespread the plant was in Greece at the time of the Romans. **Fenugreek leaves** are known as *methi* in Hindi and most of the languages of the northern part of the Subcontinent, where they are a fall and winter vegetable. In season, they are used as both a main ingredient and an herb or flavoring (see New Potatoes with Fresh Greens, page 154). **Fenugreek seeds** are actually a legume. Small, triangular, and golden tan in color, they are bitter tasting and aromatic, with a scent that reminds us of maple syrup. (In fact, fenugreek seed is used by the food processing industry to produce artificial maple flavor.) Fenugreek is most commonly used as a spice in the Subcontinent, either whole, when it is tossed into hot oil at the start of cooking (it is part of the Bengali Five-Spice Mixture, page 340), or ground. You will need a good spice grinder to grind the seeds, for they are very hard; or else keep a small supply of ground fenugreek. It is also used as a legume in *kirihodi*, Sri Lankan Fenugreek Dal (page 179).

FISH TAMARIND: This flavoring is not in fact related to tamarind—its English name refers to its culinary use as a souring agent in fish dishes, in Kerala. It is used as a souring agent in other dishes, as well, especially in Keralan and Gujarati cooking. Fish tamarind comes from a fruit (*Garcinia indica* or *G. cambogia*) that is cut into strips and then dried, so that it looks like blackened lumps of leather. Some pieces contain the edible sweet seeds of the fruit. Local recipes call for fish tamarind in terms of numbers of pieces, which are usually about an inch long and half an inch wide. They are added to simmering curries, especially fish curries, and, in Gujarat, are added to dals. Fish tamarind is known as *kokum* in Hindi; *pulam palli* in Malayalam, the language of Kerala; and *kachampuli* in Karnataka. The Sri Lankan souring agent called *goraka* (also known as *gambodge*) is either identical to or very closely related to fish tamarind, and it has a similar culinary function. Fish tamarind is not widely available in North America, but you may find it in most Sri Lankan and Indian grocery stores. True tamarind can be substituted for either fish tamarind or *goraka*, as we do in this book, using about 1 teaspoon tamarind pulp (dissolved in hot water and strained) for each piece of fish tamarind called for in the traditional recipe. *See also* tamarind.

FLATTENED RICE: Steamed or parboiled rice that is flattened into flakes and dried (see the photograph, page 90). Flattened rice keeps well in a sealed plastic bag in a cool, dark place and is a useful pantry item, for it cooks up very quickly (most commonly into *pulao*-like dishes) after a short soak in water. (See Mohan's Morning Rice, page 88, for example.) You can find it at South Asian groceries; ask for *poha* (the Hindi word), *aval* (the Tamil word), or *chira* (the Bengali word). See the Index for recipes.

GANGES: The holiest river for Hindus, and one of the major rivers of the Subcontinent. It rises in the Himalaya and flows east across the northern plains of India, past the cities of Lucknow, Varanasi, and Patna, and then into Bangladesh, where it is called the Padma River. It joins the Brahmaputra River in Bangladesh, just south of Dhaka, then flows south into the Bay of Bengal. Hindus believe that bathing in the Ganges confers blessings and that a person who has died will avoid the cycle of reincarnation if his ashes are scattered in the Ganges.

GARAM MASALA: Though most spices are heated and cooked in oil early in the cooking process to bring out their flavor and, in turn, flavor the oil, this powdered spice blend is generally added to a dish near the end of cooking. It is made of whole spices that are dry roasted, then ground to a powder (see page 342). Because the spices have already been heated, their essential oils and flavors have been released, so they can be added as a final flavoring. See also Sambhar Powder (page 188) and Fragrant Sri Lankan Spice Powder (page 341).

GARLIC: Garlic (*Allium sativum*) is widely used as a flavoring in the Subcontinent, most often in the form of garlic mashed to a paste, in a mortar. In a kitchen without a mortar, it's difficult to make a small quantity of **garlic paste** (though you can make a large quantity using a food processor or a mini-chopper). The best alternative to garlic paste is minced garlic or crushed garlic (crushed in a garlic press or with the flat side of a kitchen knife); in these recipes, we generally call for "minced garlic or garlic mashed to a paste."

GHEE: The word *ghee* is widely used in the Subcontinent for clarified butter and now, by extension, for any stable saturated cooking fat, whether vegetable or dairy based. The virtue of clarified butter is that it keeps well without refrigeration. It can be used for cooking and can also be drizzled or brushed on after cooking as a flavoring (for example, over freshly cooked rice or on flatbreads). In Hindu beliefs, ghee made with pure butter has cleansing and purifying qualities, and it is used in offerings and in the preparation of ritual foods. It was a major export from southern India to Rome in the first two centuries of the modern era, transported in leather bags. Ghee is widely available in health food stores and in South Asian groceries. See page 343 for a recipe.

GHUNDRUK: Fermented dried green leafy vegetables, a pantry staple in parts of Nepal and in the Himalayan foothills of west Bengal.

GINGER: Ginger is a rhizome, pale tan in color, that grows underground in temperate and tropical climates. The plant's Latin name is *Zingiber officinale*, and the Hindi word for ginger is *adhrak*. Select firm pieces of ginger, and store it in the refrigerator. **Young ginger** has thin pale skin; **mature ginger** has thicker tan skin and more fibrous flesh. To use, peel it, then thinly slice it, grate it, or crush it to a paste in a mortar, according to the recipes. Fresh (or "green") ginger has a warm intense flavor; dried ginger has an intense hot taste.

    Ginger paste is widely used in savory dishes in the Subcontinent. In Pakistan and the northern parts of India, it is most often added to hot oil, together with (or soon after) garlic paste, early in the cooking process. The easiest way to make ginger paste is with a mortar and a pestle; lacking one, mince the ginger. You can make up a large batch of ginger paste using a mini-chopper or processor and store well sealed in the refrigerator for up to several days, or freeze it in small amounts. **Powdered dried ginger** is a pungent and hot-tasting spice made from rhizomes that are dried, then ground to a powder and is used mainly in sweet baking. Kerala is a major producer, as is Jamaica.

GOA, GOAN: Goa is the smallest state in India, located on the west coast 150 miles south of Mumbai (Bombay), just north of Karnataka. It was colonized by the Portuguese. The local cuisine is fish-rich and often flavored with coconut, and uses vinegar as a souring agent. See the Index for recipes.

GORAKA: *See* fish tamarind.

GREEN MANGO: *See* mango.

GREEN PAPAYA: *See* papaya.

GRILLING: When grilling on a gas grill, remember not to be rushed, and when in doubt, opt for a lower temperature. If grilling over charcoal or hardwood, heat your grill well ahead and make sure you have plenty of coals and that they are not too hot—you don't want the outside of the meat or vegetable or bread scorching before the inside has had time to cook. Meat that is grilled on metal skewers cooks more quickly and evenly because the metal conducts heat into the center of the meat.

GRINDING: *See* mortar and pestle.

GUAVA: The fruit of the tree *Psidium guajava*, native to Central and South America. Guavas may be the size of large apples or as small as two inches in diameter. The peel is usually light yellow or green; the flesh is pink or pale green to white, with tiny seeds. The fruit is tart-sweet when ripe, with a pleasing penetrating aroma.

GUJARAT: The state of Gujarat lies north of Mumbai (Bombay) on India's west coast. Its desert area, called Katcch, borders Pakistan and has a long coastline. The major cities are Ahmadabad, the capital, and Surat, a busy commercial center. Gujarat is well known for its textile industry. Its cuisine is very distinctive, with an elaborate and inventive vegetarian repertoire, characterized by mild flavors and a hint of sweetness in many dishes. Perhaps because of Gujarat's location on the Arabian Sea, many Gujarati people have emigrated to other lands: Most of the South Asians who settled in eastern and southern Africa in the late nineteenth and early twentieth centuries were Gujarati, as Gandhi was, and their descendants now live all over the world. Consequently, Gujarati prepared foods and special ingredients are widely available in South Asian markets in North America and elsewhere.

HALAL: Muslims are required by the Koran to eat only meat that is *halal*, that is, permitted meat (not pork or certain seafood) from an animal that has been slaughtered by having its throat cut. Halal meat is similar to koshered meat, in that it has no blood in it. Most of the lamb and beef dishes in this book are traditionally made with halal meat. Most large cities in North America have at least one halal butcher.

HINDUISM: An ancient religion with many branches and sects, Hinduism is the major religion in India and Nepal. Over the centuries, rules and restrictions around the idea of cleanliness, expressed in the caste structure and in food proscriptions, came to play a defining role for Hindus. The rules of caste affect social relations and obligations: People of different castes generally don't eat together or intermarry and people of some lower castes are viewed by higher casts as unclean (*see also* caste). In modern times, the Indian government has tried to counteract the rigid and stratifying power of the caste system, in some places more successfully than in others. The food rules associated with Hinduism are complex and vary with the caste and beliefs of the family, but the most obvious one is that cattle are sacred and must not be killed, so beef is prohibited. Conversely, ghee (clarified butter) is viewed as cleansing and is a part of many ritual foods. The majority of Hindus are vegetarian, eating no meat or fish or eggs, but the restrictions vary among the different communities (Bengalis eat a lot of fish, for example, and the warrior Rajput caste in Rajasthan eats game and other meat). In traditional Hindu households, widows have a more restricted diet, being allowed no onions or garlic and very few legumes, nothing that might, in the traditional view, excite the passions. **Jains** are a special group of Hindus who follow a very strict vegetarianism and meticulous respect for life. There are Jain communities (and Jain temples) in many parts of India, especially in the western part of the country, most notably in Gujarat.

HOPPERS: Soft-textured leavened breads common in Sri Lanka and in Tamil Nadu and Kerala, made from rice batter cooked in a small circular pan like a small wok (see the recipe, page 121). The English name *hopper* is most likely an adaption of the Tamil word *appam*. Steamed nests of noodles made from a similar rice batter are called *string hoppers* in Sri Lanka and *idiappam* in southern India.

IDLIS: *Idlis* are flying saucer–shape steamed breads, white and a little absorbent; like *dosas*, *idlis* are from southern India, eaten as snack foods and for breakfast. They're made of a fermented rice and dal batter, which is cooked in an *idli steamer*, a stack of stainless steel pans, each with seven shallow indentations (like large egg poachers) and with perforations that allow steam to pass from one layer to the next. *Idli* steamers are sold in many South Asian groceries. *Idlis* are served with a *sambhar* (cooked soupy dal) and coconut chutney; see the recipe, page 120.

INDIAN MILLET FLOUR: *See* millet flour.

JACKFRUIT: A large subtropical fruit, jackfruit grows on tall trees (*Artocarpus heterophyllus*) from Bangladesh to Sri Lanka, as well as in Southeast Asia. The tree is thought to be native to India. The fruit can grow to a large long oval bigger than a large watermelon. It has a bumpy light brown, very hard outer skin, inside which are golden yellow segments. The taste is medium sweet and intensely aromatic, and the texture firm to soft but not very juicy; the seeds are flattened black rounds. Jackfruit flesh is not only eaten plain, as a fruit, but also used as an ingredient in savory dishes and as a flavoring for sweets. The seeds are used as a main ingredient in savory curries in Sri Lanka and southern India. The wood of the tree is an important building material, hard and fine grained and bright golden yellow in color.

JAGGERY: In many parts of the Subcontinent, palm sugar and crude (unrefined) cane sugar are both called *jaggery*. Both are medium to dark brown and sold in hard disks or blocks, or sometimes as a thick heavy paste. Jaggery is available in South Asian and Southeast Asian grocery stores. Its name in Hindi is *gur,* and in Tamil it's called *vellam*. Jaggery has a smoky taste, as traditionally made maple sugar does, from the cooking of the syrup (palm syrup or cane syrup) used to make it. Jaggery tastes less sweet per spoonful than brown or white sugar. You can substitute a blend of brown sugar and maple sugar, or just straight brown sugar, decreasing the quantity slightly.

JAIN: *See* Hinduism.

JOWAR: *See* sorghum.

KALIJIRA: *See* rice.

KALONJI: *See* nigella.

KARHAI: A *karhai* (sometimes transcribed *kadhai* or *karahi*; pronounced "ka-´rye") is a traditional woklike cooking pot with two handles; in Britain, it has recently come to be called a *Balti pan*. Anthropologists and archeologists say that it may be the precursor of the Chinese wok. It is used for stir-frying and simmering many dishes. A wok, heavy skillet, or wide heavy pot can be substituted.

KARNATAKA: The Indian state lying immediately south of Goa and north of Kerala on the west coast, with a narrow coastal plain and hilly interior. The main cities are Bangalore (now well known as an Indian Silicon Valley), Mangalore, and Mysore. The main language is Kannada. The population is primarily Hindu, and many of them are vegetarian. Rice is the staple food, but many wheat flour flatbreads, both plain and filled, also are eaten.

KASHMIR: A state in the far northwest of India, bordered on the west by Pakistan, on the north and east by (Chinese-controlled) Tibet, and on the south by the state of Punjab. Much of Kashmir is disputed territory: the border with Pakistan is a de facto line-of-control, not an agreed-upon border. Kashmir includes the mountainous region called Ladakh, once a Tibetan-ruled territory, through which the Indus River flows toward Pakistan; the fertile and temperate-climate Himalayan foothills, including the Srinagar Valley; and an area to the south in the plains where the Kashmiri winter capital, Jammu, is located. The majority of the population is Muslim, but at Partition and Independence in 1947, the ruler of Kashmir, who was Hindu, opted to have Kashmir become part of India rather than to join Pakistan.

Kashmiri food is famous in the Subcontinent for its delicacy and sophistication. It resembles Moghul cuisine, but with distinctive local characteristics. Rice is the staple food, served at meals in the form of *pulaos* as well as plain and drizzled with ghee. Flatbreads are inventive and are eaten as a snack or for breakfast. Tea is made in large samovars, as it is in Central Asia, a reminder that Kashmir is located on trade routes that caravans have followed for centuries to and from the heart of Asia. Both green tea and black tea are drunk, the black tea often scented with cardamom. Both Hindu Brahmins (Nehru, the first prime minister of India, was of this caste) and Muslims eat meat, especially lamb, and both communities cook with the mild bright red Kashmiri chile and with saffron, Kashmir's best-known crop. Muslims use onions and garlic to flavor dishes, whereas Hindus use ginger, fennel, fenugreek, and asafoetida.

KEBABS: *Kebab* is the word in the Turkic languages of Central Asia for meat cooked on a skewer, either in chunks or as a paste of ground meat with flavorings. Kebabs can be broiled or roasted in a tandoor oven, or grilled (our preference). See the Index for recipes.

KERALA: The Indian state that lies along the western coast in a long narrow strip ending at the country's tip and encompasses Malabar Coast. The capital of Kerala is Thiruvananthapuram (formerly Trivandrum); other notable cities and towns include Kochi (Cochin) and Calicut. Kerala has a tropical climate and is becoming a popular tourist destination for foreigners. It is known, among other things, for its very high literacy rate and population density, as well as for its production of black pepper and dried ginger. The spice trade between the Kerala coast and the Mediterranean goes back to Roman times. Perhaps as a consequence, Kerala is home to people of many different origins and religions, from Syrian Christians to Muslims, from Roman Catholics to Hindus.

KHICHADI: A class of mixed rice and dal dishes, known in Bengal as *kichuri* (see the recipe, page 96).

KINEMA: *See* soybeans.

LADAKH: *See* Kashmir.

LEGUMES: *See* dal.

LEMONGRASS: An aromatic grass, *Cymbopogon citratus,* that is sometimes called *citronella*. The lower stem is thick and woody and used as a spice in Southeast Asian cuisines and also in Sri Lanka. To use, trim off the tough root and then either slice very thinly or crush the bottom 2 to 3 inches of the stalk, where the flavor is. Citronella oil is used as a mosquito repellent.

LOVAGE: An herb with a strong celerylike taste, used in English and French cooking. The seeds of a related plant, *Carum copticum,* are often called *lovage seeds* and are known as *ajowan* in Hindi.

LUKEWARM: The temperature that the hand feels as just warm, meaning it is just at or above body temperature, around 100°F.

MACE: The lacy outer coating of nutmeg, which is removed and used as a separate spice. *See* nutmeg.

MAIDA: The common name in Hindi for all-purpose flour, as distinct from atta flour (*see* atta). Maida is made of a softer wheat than atta, so all-purpose, or all-purpose blended 2 to 1 with pastry flour, is a good substitute for it.

MALDIVE FISH: A widely used flavoring in Sri Lankan cooking, Maldive fish is small dried chunks of tuna that are crumbled or shredded and added to many dishes. It brings a smoky depth of flavor rather like that given by fish sauce or shrimp paste in Thai and other Southeast Asian cuisines. Maldive fish is sold in jars in Sri Lankan grocery stores. Bonito flakes (shaved dried tuna, used in Japanese cuisine) can be substituted, or the Maldive fish can be omitted altogether, with some loss of depth of flavor.

MANGO: Mangoes grow on tall shade-giving *Mangifera indica* trees in the tropics and subtropics, and they ripen in hot season, just before the rains. **Green mango,** small and firm-fleshed, is often called *raw mango* in English-language usage in the Subcontinent. In most cases, it is, in fact, unripe fruit, although there are also varieties of tart green mangoes that are hard to get in North America. Some green mangoes are very sour, some just tart and unripe tasting. Green mango has a crisper texture than ripe mango and is an ingredient in savory dishes, sometimes as a tart

flavoring (see Toovar Dal with Green Mango, page 197), sometimes as the main ingredient (see Gujarati Mango Chutney, page 40, and Tart Mango Salsa, page 48). Tart green mangoes are also dried and ground to a powder to make the souring agent called *amchur*. But to most people, the word *mango* conjures up ripe, juicy orange-yellow fruits, small or large. The best sweet mangoes have no fibers, just juicy sweet flesh, with a flat large oval pit. To eat a mango, you must cut the flesh from the pit. We usually peel first, then cut away the flesh; others peel after they've halved the mango. Suit yourself. *To cut the flesh off the pit,* set the fruit on one of its narrow sides and cut through it lengthwise just off the center line, running the knife edge down against the surface of the pit. Repeat on the other side, then trim off the edges. See "Mango Tales," page 326.

METHI: *See* fenugreek.

MILK: Milk has special status among Hindus and is treated with respect in most places in the Subcontinent, where it is an important food, especially in northern India, Pakistan, and Nepal. In Ayurveda it is viewed as cooling, sweet, and heavy; it should always be consumed warm. Milk products include yogurt, buttermilk, and the rich cream skimmed off milk that has been boiled and cooled. Because it doesn't keep well without refrigeration, many techniques have evolved to preserve milk or make it less likely to spoil. One is, of course, to make cheese with it (see *chhana* and *paneer,* pages 344 and 345), another to ferment it into yogurt (*see* yogurt). Ghee (*see* ghee), or clarified butter, is a way of preserving milk fats by eliminating the milk solids that can go rancid. If milk is cooked down, so that the milk sugars are very concentrated, it becomes thick with a concentrated sweetness that prevents spoilage (high concentrations of sugar discourage the growth of bacteria). Thick sweet milk products are used to make sweets of all kinds in the Subcontinent.

    Sweetened condensed milk, now sold in cans in grocery stores all over the world, can often be substituted for the Indian sweet cream called *khoa*. **Evaporated milk,** another product designed for long keeping, has been heat treated and is much less sweet and less thick than condensed milk. **Milk powder,** including **buttermilk powder,** which can be reconstituted by the addition of water, is usually low in fat.

MILLET FLOUR; INDIAN MILLET FLOUR: Several kinds of millet related to the grass *Panicum miliaceum* are grown in the Subcontinent and used for making flour for bread. Among them is the grain known in Hindi as *bajra,* which is used for making stove-top breads in the desert regions of northwest India (parts of Rajasthan and Gujarat) and in Pakistan. *Bajra* is sold in South Asian groceries. Store it in the refrigerator to keep it fresh; if it tastes bitter, it has fermented and should be discarded.

MINCE: To chop as fine as possible. In some recipes, we suggest mincing garlic and ginger as a substitute for crushing or grinding them to a paste with a mortar and a pestle.

MOGHUL: The Muslim rulers of Central and West Asia began invading the Subcontinent in about the tenth century. By the time the great Moroccan traveler

Ibn Battuta (see Bibliography) got to Delhi in 1338, most of northern India, from the Indus River to Lucknow, was controlled by a Muslim ruler based in Delhi. In the 1500s, the Moghuls, descendants of the Mongols, ruled Iran and parts of Afghanistan and took control of these northern kingdoms. Moghul culture, including its culinary traditions, was elaborate and refined, a blend of Central Asian and Persian cultural traditions. Moghul traditions were, of course, adapted and refined still further once they reached the Subcontinent, incorporating new ingredients. The cities of Delhi, Agra, Hyderabad, and Lucknow are particularly known for their Moghul-influenced cuisines. Because Moghul cuisine was the cuisine of the conquerors, it had, and still has, a special status in much of India and Pakistan—rather as French cuisine did, and still does, in much of Europe and North America. Dishes associated with Moghul tradition include biryani and *pulao*, and many sweets, from *jalebi* (see page 319) to *gulab jamun* (page 318) and *kulfi* (see Mango Ice Cream with Cardamom, page 324). Ingredients often include almonds, pistachios, or raisins, and spices such as cinnamon, cloves, and cardamom.

MORTAR AND PESTLE: Very useful tools in the traditional kitchens of the Subcontinent (and in many other places, from Mexico to Thailand), used to grind spices to a powder and fresh ingredients, such as ginger or garlic or herbs, to a paste. Though mortars are often bowl shape, for grinding, we find that the most effective mortar is a flat roughened stone tablet (known as a *shil* in Bengali), common in India and Bangladesh, with a heavy rough cylindrical stone pestle (*nora* in Bengali). The pestle can be used to crush a garlic clove or it can be rolled and rubbed against the surface of the mortar to grind either dry or moist ingredients. You can substitute a *spice/coffee grinder* for grinding dry spices. For grinding garlic or ginger to a paste, the best substitute is a *mini-chopper* or *small food mill*. *Food processors* work well only with larger quantities of garlic and ginger than are usually needed for one or two recipes; but you can process larger amounts of these, then store the extra in well-sealed containers in the refrigerator or freezer until needed. This is a practical solution if you cook subcontinental food regularly.

MUNG: *See* dals.

MUSLIM: The Muslim population of the Subcontinent is now more than 350 million. *Muslim* is the name given to followers of Islam. Islam began in the Arabian peninsula in 778 A.D. By the tenth century, there were Muslim populations in the Subcontinent who had arrived from the northwest as traders and as conquerors (*see also* Moghul). Both Pakistan and Bangladesh are Muslim countries (with less than 5 percent of their populations non-Muslim), as are the Maldives, the island nation off the coast of Sri Lanka. India has more Muslims than any other country in the Subcontinent, about 130 million, though they are a minority (about 12 percent of the total population). The Muslim population and culinary culture in India are particularly dominant in places that had Muslim rulers before Independence in 1947; these include Hyderabad, Lucknow, Delhi, and Agra. But, in fact, in most towns and all cities in India, and in Sri Lanka, there are sizable Muslim populations. There is a

long history of peaceful coexistence between different religious communities in India, but also examples, up to the present day, of violent confrontation between Hindus and Muslims, such as the killings in Gujarat in 2000 and the disputes and violence associated with the destruction of the mosque at Ayodhya in 1992.

MUSTARD: There are a number of varieties of mustard plants (*Brassica,* including *B. juncea*), most of them with intensely yellow flowers (see the photograph, page 347). They are eaten as greens; the seeds of some varieties are pressed for oil and also used as a spice. The name for **mustard greens** in much of the northern part of the Subcontinent is *sarson*. As in China, mustard greens are cooked and eaten like other leafy greens in the Subcontinent. They are sold in Asian grocery stores, specialty-produce and farmers' markets, and in some large supermarkets. **Mustard seeds** are small and round. Different varieties of mustard have seeds of different colors. In European cooking, yellow mustard seed is most common (and is the source of **yellow mustard powder**). In the Subcontinent, a purplish-brown seed from the plant *Brassica rapus*, most commonly referred to in English as **black mustard seed** but sometimes called **brown mustard seed,** is widely used as a spice. The seed is known as *rai* in the northern half of the Subcontinent. The seeds may be tossed into hot oil at the start of cooking, where they will pop (if you're using a shallow pan, it's a good idea to hold a lid over it so the spluttering seeds don't spread everywhere). They give a nutty toasted flavor. In Bengal, the seeds may also be ground as part of a curry paste. Black mustard seed is sold in South Asian shops and in well-stocked groceries. Mustard seeds harvested from several different kinds of mustard plant are pressed to produce **mustard oil**, the staple cooking oil in most of Nepal, Bengal, and Bangladesh. Mustard oil is sold in South Asian groceries, the bottles often marked "not for human consumption." We're told that this is a way of avoiding the labeling and testing that would be mandatory if it were imported as a food product (mustard oil can also be used as a liniment). We love the taste of the oil and the distinctive flavor it gives to dishes from Bengal and Nepal. Other oils can be substituted, but the dish will then lack the distinctive heat and aroma. You can also try using another oil together with 1 teaspoon mustard powder, to get some mustard heat and flavor. We were told that some people in Bengal who find the oil too rich are cutting it with canola or other vegetable oils, using them in a fifty-fifty blend.

MUTTON: The English word for meat from mature sheep; in the Subcontinent, *mutton* refers to meat from goats.

NAAN: Also transcribed *nan* or *non*, naan is the Central Asian word for "bread." In South Asia, it has come to mean the leavened tandoor-baked flatbreads that evolved from the breads brought to the Subcontinent by the Moghuls. See Home-Style Tandoor Naan, page 116.

NIGELLA: A small black teardrop-shaped spice with an oniony flavor—hence its other common name, *black onion seed*. In Hindi and related languages it is known as *kalonji* or as *kalajira*. It is not from the onion family, but instead is the seed of the *Nigella sativa* plant, which is related to Queen Anne's lace. Nigella is used sparingly on naan and to flavor hot oil at the start of cooking. One of the whole spices in the

Bengali five-spice mix *panch phoron* (see the recipe, page 340), it is available in South Asian groceries and some well-stocked groceries.

NUTMEG: One of the most highly prized spices in Europe in medieval times, nutmeg is the large, almost walnut-size nut of *Myristica fragrans*, a tree native to Indonesia. The nut is enclosed in a brittle lacy covering, called **mace,** that has a slightly different taste. Both nutmeg and mace are used to flavor sweets in the Subcontinent. For best flavor, buy whole nutmeg and grind it just before using. Ground nutmeg and mace are sold in grocery stores; whole nutmeg can be found in large grocery stores and in specialty shops.

OILS AND FATS: In the Subcontinent, oil is used alone or in combination with ghee (clarified butter) to fry flavorings at the start of cooking or to deep-fry. The oil used depends on the culture of the cook, as well as on her location and her economic circumstances. From our observation, the plant oils most widely used for cooking are **sesame oil** (raw, unroasted), **coconut oil,** and **mustard oil.** In addition, **cottonseed oil** and other inferior locally available oils may be used. When we call for vegetable oil, use any unflavored oil you wish, from **canola** to **safflower** to **corn oil.** When deep-frying, it's important to use an oil that is relatively stable at high temperatures; use **peanut oil,** or raw sesame or safflower oil. *See also under* coconut, mustard, *and* sesame.

To render fat, cut the fat into pieces and place it in a heavy skillet over medium heat. The fat will melt slowly, leaving delicious cracklings. Pour the melted fat off into a sterile container, and when completely cooled, store tightly covered in the refrigerator.

OKRA: Called *bindi* in Hindi and Urdu, *derosh* in Bengali, and *vendaikai* in Tamil, okra is commonly known as *ladies' fingers* in English in the Subcontinent. It is the pod of an annual plant, *Hibiscus esculentus,* and has light ridges down its length. Okra may be only an inch long, or as long as 5 or 6 inches; the pods taper to a point. Buy the smallest, most tender, and brightest green okra you can find. A staple of the African and southern American kitchen, where it often goes by the African name *gumbo,* okra is widely sold in North American groceries as well as in South Asian grocery stores. It can be cooked whole in salted water, rather like asparagus, then simply dressed with a vinaigrette, but in the Subcontinent it is simmered or fried in many inventive and delicious ways. It has a slightly mucilaginous texture when cooked that okra lovers find irresistible. See Spiced Tender Chopped Bindi, page 168, and Ladies' Fingers Curry, page 170.

ONION: Yellow cooking onions (*Allium cepa*) are commonly used in many parts of the Subcontinent in the early part of cooking, grated or chopped and cooked in hot oil until softened, or sometimes until lightly browned, before the main ingredient is added. They may also be used as a final flavoring or garnish, especially in Pakistani and Bangladeshi dishes (see Browned Onions, page 343). In some places milder onions are also used, for which we substitute shallots. Onions are believed by Buddhists and Hindus to be heating and to encourage base instincts; in Hinduism, they are forbidden to widows and to Brahmins, as is garlic. *See also* shallots.

ORISSA: A state on the coast of eastern India, bordered on the north by Bengal and on the south by Andhra Pradesh; the capital is Bubaneshwar. Orissa has a mountainous interior next to a narrow coastal plain. It has long been a producer and exporter of cotton textiles; it also has the largest concentration of ancient temples in the Subcontinent. Though the majority of the population is Hindu, there are important numbers of tribal people, mostly living in the thickly forested hills. See also "Orissa," page 274.

PAAN: *See* betel.

PALM SUGAR: *See* jaggery.

PANCH PHORON: A blend of five whole spices used in Bengali and Bangladeshi cooking. Traditionally they are nigella, fenugreek, fennel, cumin, and celery seed, for which we substitute the easier-to-find black mustard seed (see Bengali Five-Spice Mixture, page 340). The spices go into hot oil at the start of cooking.

PANEER: Fresh pressed cheese made from acidulated milk that has been drained and then pressed for several hours. See the recipe, page 344.

PAPAD, PAPPADUM: Crispy waferlike breads made from a paste of cooked dal, commonly urad dal, that is spread into thin disks and then dried. They are widely sold in South Asian groceries. They must be fried or toasted or grilled briefly before serving. See the recipe, page 289.

PAPAYA: In the Subcontinent, papayas are cheap and abundant. Versatile and very nutritious (they are extremely high in vitamin C and vitamin A), they're treated like vegetables when unripe, when they have a wet-crisp texture and slightly tart-acid flavor. (The closest substitute is Granny Smith apples.) Papayas grow on an unusual-looking tall skinny beanpole of a tree (*Carica papaya*), with a little umbrella of leaves at the top and a clump of oval-shape fruit growing and ripening just beneath the leaves. Unripe papayas are very firm to the touch, with green skin and pale green to pale yellow flesh. Ripe papayas are yellow- to orange-skinned, with orange to dark red flesh and jet-black seeds. To use, cut lengthwise in half and scrape out the seeds and pith. Green papaya flesh can be grated to make salads or chutney. Ripe papaya flesh is very sweet and is best balanced by a squeeze of lime juice.

PARBOILING: Generally, a process that refers to partially cooking foods, usually vegetables, in boiling water. In fact, though, parboiling has another meaning: Parboiling rice involves cooking it in the husk, then drying it. See page 86 for recipes; *see also* rice.

PARSI: A distinct community of people descended from refugees from Persia (Iran) who came to the Subcontinent about ten centuries ago. They settled in Gujarat and then in the Mumbai (Bombay) area. Their religion is Zoroastrianism. Their food is generally mild and subtle, with Persian and Gujarati elements. See page 230 for more information and the Index for recipes.

PATOL: *See* potol.

PEPPER: Pepper is a climbing vine (*Piper nigrum*) native to the Kerala region that thrives in tropical climates. **Black pepper** and **white pepper** are the dried unripe fruit (berries) of the pepper vine. For black pepper the berries are picked before they are ripe, then left out in the sun to ferment for several days, which turns them black. For white pepper, the berries are soaked after being picked ripe and then the whitish seed is removed and dried. White pepper has less aroma and flavor than black pepper. Kerala, in southern India, is a major grower and exporter of pepper. For centuries, black pepper was a very expensive spice in northern Europe; now we take it for granted as a flavoring and a way of adding heat to a dish.

PIMENTÓN: *See* chiles.

POMEGRANATE: The fruit of a small tree, *Punica granatum*. The fruit has long been a symbol of fertility, for inside its rather leathery skin are many seeds. Pomegranates may be sweet or tart. Sweet ones can be eaten out of hand, and have pink to red flesh and seed coatings; sour ones are used for making pomegranate molasses in the eastern Mediterranean, and their seeds are dried and used as a souring agent, called *anardana* in Pakistan and northern India.

POPPY SEEDS: The seeds of flowers of the *Papaver* genus. Known generally in the northern part of the Subcontinent as *khaskhas*, poppy seeds are sometimes, especially in Bangladesh and Bengal, ground to a paste to flavor a meat or vegetable dish (see Bangla Pea Shoots, page 165). (In Bengali, they are called *posto*, a pre-Sanskrit name, indicating that their use goes way back.) The seeds are white, unlike the black ones of European tradition.

POTATO: The potato (*Solanum tuberosum*) is native to the Americas but has become a staple crop in many parts of the world, including the Subcontinent. The starch content of all potatoes is high, but in some the texture is soft and crumbly when cooked (these are **floury potatoes**), while in others the cooked texture is smooth and firm (**waxy potatoes**). Floury potatoes are best for baking and for mashing; waxy potatoes are best for potato salad or curries, or wherever the potatoes need to hold their shape when chopped.

POTOL: "Pointed gourd"; a Bengali vegetable (see Bangla-Flavored Fried Zucchini, page 144). *Patol atol* is the Bengali name, *parwal* the Hindi word for this cucumberlike vegetable (*Trichosanthes dioica*). Like most members of the cucumber family, it is believed to have valuable cooling properties, so it is recommended as a food for the hot season.

PULAO: *Pulaos* (also called *pilaus* or *pilaffs*) are a category of flavored rice dishes that came to the Subcontinent with the Moghuls. They are related to the rice dishes of Iran and of Central Asia. Basmati or a similar rice is generally used. The rice is briefly boiled, drained, and then layered and steamed or simmered with meat or dal and seasoned oil or ghee. It absorbs flavors while cooking, much as paella or risotto rice absorbs flavors from the cooking broth. Biryani (see Chicken Biryani, Dum Style, page 102) is a kind of *pulao* that is cooked in the oven in a sealed pot. *See also* rice.

PULSES: *See* dals.

PUMPKIN: Pumpkin (*Cucurbita pepo*) is native to North America but is widely used as a vegetable in many parts of the world, including South Asia. The skin may be the familiar orange, or green or yellow-green, and the flesh may be orange, almost red, or a paler yellow-orange. Buy slices or wedges of pumpkin in Asian grocery stores or produce markets, or use small pie pumpkins or Japanese kabocha squash when pumpkin is called for. Deeper-colored flesh seems to have more flavor than pale flesh. Cut pumpkin will keep fairly well for up to a week, wrapped in plastic, in the refrigerator. Remove the seeds and pith and peel before using. See the Index for recipes.

PUNJAB: An area of the Subcontinent now divided between India and Pakistan, and the name of both the Indian state, whose capital is Chandigarh, and the Pakistani province, whose capital is Lahore. The name is derived from the Urdu word *panj*, meaning "five," and refers to the five large rivers that drain the region. Punjabi food, brought by immigrants, was the first subcontinental cuisine to become known to North Americans: a blend of Moghul-style dishes with tandoor-cooked breads and meats, and simple vegetable dishes such as *aloo ghobi* (cauliflower and potato) and *muttar paneer* (green peas with cheese).

PURI: A kind of unleavened flatbread found in the northern parts of the Subcontinent, made with atta flour and deep-fried. The breads emerge from the hot oil very puffed and tender and are usually served with chickpea stew or another dal. In Bengal, the local version of *puri* is made with all-purpose flour and is called *luchi*. See the recipe, page 115.

RAITA: The Hindi and Urdu name for a group of yogurt-based saucelike dishes traditional in the northern and northwestern regions of the Subcontinent, from Pakistan to Nepal and the Punjab. See Cucumber Raita, page 67.

RAJASTHAN: A traditional and rather conservative Indian state located to the west and north of Delhi and extending to the Pakistani border in the northwest and to Gujarat to the west; it is bordered by the state of Madhya Pradesh to the south and east. The capital and largest city is Jaipur; other notable cities are Jodhpur and Udaipur. Rajasthan is dry and desertlike, with some hilly ranges. In recent times, irrigation projects have made more of the land reliably cultivable, but the region still suffers from periodic droughts. Many people are nomadic or seminomadic. The majority of the population is Hindu, and there are important numbers of Muslims and Jains. The ruling class is Rajput, a warrior caste. Traditional dishes include game, grilled dishes, and many flatbreads, including breads made with sorghum or Indian millet or corn flour. There is also a very interesting unleavened bread called *batti* that is baked as a ball in the embers of the fire, then cracked open and eaten with ghee and sometimes a dal poured over it. Cooking traditions also include aromatic smoking, in which a dish of simmered meat or vegetables is finished off by being flavored with aromatic smoke: A piece of incense or burning juniper (we might use rosemary) is set in a holder in the pot, which is then covered tightly so the smoke can perfume the dish.

RASAM: A peppery tamarind and toovar dal–based liquid like a much thinner and more tart-tasting *sambhar* (*see* sambhar). A staple of Tamil cuisine, it is usually eaten early on in the meal, poured over rice. See the recipe, page 198.

RAW SESAME OIL: *See* sesame seed.

REMPEH: An aromatic long green leaf that is used in Sri Lankan cooking, called *pandanus* in Malaysia (where it is used primarily to perfume sweets); *pandan* is the name sometimes given to it in Sri Lanka. The plant is *Pandanus amaryllifolius, screw pine* in English. Rempeh can be found in Sri Lankan groceries. Omit it if it's not available; we know of no substitute.

RICE: There are many distinctive kinds of rice (the seeds of *Oryza sativa*) grown and sold in the Subcontinent: Botanists say there may be as many as twenty thousand different varieties, most of them grown and eaten locally. Rice is a staple in southern India and Sri Lanka, in Nepal, Bengal, and Bangladesh, and in parts of Pakistan and Bhutan. Plain rice is mostly cooked in plenty of boiling water, then drained, rather as pasta is cooked. Flavored rice dishes such as *pulao* and biryani are made by simmering the rice in flavored broth.

Very little **brown rice** is eaten in the Subcontinent. Instead, rice is normally milled (the bran is rubbed off), though in many places the milling is incomplete and some flecks of bran remain and color the rice. Some rice is parboiled before being milled; **parboiled rice** is referred to as *boiled rice* in English in the Subcontinent. The whole rice grains are soaked, then briefly boiled, then cooled and dried before milling. This drives nutrients from the bran into the rice, and also tints the white rice grains a little yellow. Parboiled rice is more nutritious than unboiled rice. It takes a little longer to cook because after they cool, the starches firm up to a hard glassy mass, and it has a firm separate texture once cooked. **Rice flakes**, also known as *flattened rice*, are made of parboiled rice that has been crushed flat. *See* flattened rice.

Parboiled rice is generally cooked plain, while flavored rice dishes are made with unboiled rice, which is better able to absorb liquid flavorings. Among all the rices of the Subcontinent, we give basic recipes for cooking six plain rices discussed below: basmati, kalijira, white and red samba, Bhutanese red, and rosematta. A number of them are also used in the flavored rice dishes here. (You can, of course, serve any plain rice you wish to accompany dishes from the Subcontinent.)

Basmati: The best known of the rices from the Subcontinent, basmati is used for *pulaos* and biryanis, for it absorbs flavors beautifully and yet keeps its shape during cooking. See the recipe, page 82. Patna rice (see below) may be substituted, or American-grown basmatilike rices such as Texmati.

Bhutanese red: A medium-grain rice that is only partly milled, leaving traces of its reddish bran, Bhutanese red is now available at specialty stores in North America. See the recipe, page 83.

Kalijira: A specialty rice from Bengal, *kalijira* is also known as *govindabog*. It's small and fine, like a smaller basmati. We've only seen it polished, as white rice. (In Bangladesh we were told that the rice's bran is black, not brown, hence its name:

kali, from the goddess with a blackened face; and *jira,* the word for "cumin seed.") See the recipe, page 83.

Kerala red: *See* rosematta.

Patna: Patna is the capital of Bihar State, located on the Ganges River downstream from Varanasi. It gives its name to a large category of long-grain rices. To some, basmati is a subcategory of Patna rice; to others, Patna is a less prized cousin of basmati. In any case, rice labeled "Patna" is a satisfactory substitute for basmati as a plain rice or in *pulaos* or biryanis. It is widely available in South Asian grocery stores.

Rosematta: A parboiled partially polished red rice from southern India; it may also be labeled "Kerala red rice." See the recipe, page 86.

Samba rice: A parboiled rice from Sri Lanka; both white and red (semimilled) are available in Sri Lankan shops. See page 87 for the basic recipe and more discussion.

SAFFRON: The dried stigma of the crocus flower, *Crocus sativus*, used as a spice and coloring agent. Saffron is called *kesar* in Hindi; the English name comes from the Persian and Arabic word *zaffran*. Food historians believe it originated in Greece, but it is now grown in Kashmir, where it was first grown fifteen hundred years ago, and in the past century has once again become an important crop. Saffron is expensive and prized by those who can afford it. It is sold in the form of threads, in very small quantities, in well-stocked supermarkets and in specialty stores. (Avoid powdered saffron.) To release its color and flavor, it should be very lightly dry roasted, then dissolved in a little milk or other liquid before being added to other ingredients, as directed in the recipes.

SAMBHAR: *Sambhar* is a soupy dish from southern India made of toovar dal and flavored with a distinctive dried spice blend known as *sambhar podi* (see Sambhar Powder, page 188). It often accompanies *dosas* or *idlis*. See the recipes, pages 112 and 120.

SAMBOL: The name of a category of Sri Lankan dishes that are like salsas. Sambols usually include onion and hot chiles, and are most often uncooked. They are served as condiments and as dips for hoppers or other breads. See the Index for recipes.

SAMOSA: A triangular deep-fried snack, made at home or as street food. Samosas consist of thin unleavened bread dough wrapped around a filling of vegetable or meat. They are related to the *somsa* of Central Asia and are associated with Moghul cuisine. In Bengal, they are known as *shingara* if they are vegetarian, *samosa* if the filling is meat. See Fennel-Flecked Potato Samosas, page 296.

SAWTOOTH HERB, SAW LEAF HERB: The long fresh green leaf of the *Eryngium foetidum* plant, with finely serrated edges (see photograph, page 52). Called *blandhania* in Hindi, it is widely used in Vietnamese cooking to flavor soups. It closely resembles the herb called *culantro* in Mexico and Puerto Rico and, like it, gives an aromatic and slightly tart edge of flavor. It can be chopped and stirred into hot dal about five minutes before serving, for an extra layer of flavor.

SEMOLINA: Widely called *rava*, the Hindi name, throughout the Subcontinent, semolina is coarsely ground hard wheat, the ingredient that the Italians call *semola* and that they use for making pasta. It is used in the Subcontinent to make the savory dish *uppuma* (see page 92), to thicken puddings, and to make sweets such as halvah.

SESAME SEED; SESAME OIL: Sesame is a bush (*Sesamum indicum*) that is native to the Subcontinent. Its seeds have long been an important food source; remnants of cooked sesame have been found in archaeological sites of the Harappan civilization (see page 8). The plant is prized for its seeds, which may be used as an ingredient in cooked dishes or as a topping for breads, or pressed for oil. The common name for **sesame seed** in Sanskrit-based languages such as Hindi is *til* or *tila*; in Tamil, it is known as *gingelly*. The sesame seeds used in the Subcontinent have a golden hull (black sesame is sometimes used in Japanese cooking). Hulled sesame seeds are pale, nearly white in color. Because of their high oil content, sesame seeds must be stored in the refrigerator or freezer. Always taste before using in cooking, to make sure they are fresh. If the seeds taste bitter, the oils have gone rancid and they should be discarded. **Sesame oil** is produced by grinding and pressing raw sesame seeds. The oil is widely used for cooking in the Subcontinent. It is clear and colorless, and it has a good nutritional profile. It keeps well and is stable at high temperatures, so it can be used for panfrying and deep-frying. The raw sesame oil used in the Subcontinent, and called for in recipes in this book, *is not to be confused with the roasted sesame oil,* pale brown in color and with a nutty toasted flavor, that is used in Japanese and Chinese dishes. Raw sesame oil is available in South Asian groceries; it is also used in French cooking, and sesame oil from France can often be found in grocery stores and health food stores.

SHALLOTS: Shallots are members of the onion (*allium*) family. **Asian shallots** have a purplish outer layer under their papery brown skin and a fairly pungent oniony flavor. **European shallots** are larger, the size of small onions, with a pale outer layer under their papery skin and a milder flavor. Both can be grown in many parts of North America. Shallots are peeled before using unless they are being grilled whole. Shallots may be sliced or minced; in Shallot Sambhar, page 187, they are simmered whole.

SHRIMP: Sometimes called *prawns*, shrimp are sold whole, with heads and shells on, or headless and peeled. **Tiger shrimp** have striped shells and tend to be larger than other kinds. There are about 35 medium shrimp to a pound and 50 small shrimp to a pound. In general, the larger the shrimp, the more expensive they are. In North America, most shrimp is flash-frozen immediately after being caught. Shrimp should smell sweet; if there is any fishy or off smell, avoid them. *To clean shrimp,* peel off the shell, pull off the head, and rinse well. When cooked, shrimp turn bright pink.

SIKHISM, SIKHS: A religion that was founded in the Punjab about five hundred years ago. The Sikh population is most dominant in the Punjab region, and its holy city is Amritsar, site of the Golden Temple. Sikhism espouses equality of all men and women, a reaction against and renunciation of the caste restrictions of Hinduism. Sikhs are permitted to eat meat of all kinds except beef. As a sign of their commitment to Sikhism, Sikh men keep their hair long and their beards unshaved, and coil their hair under a turban. There has been a Sikh independence movement in India, fighting for Kalistan (an independent Sikh nation), and some Hindu nationalist violence against Sikhs in Delhi and other places, but in general the Sikh population lives side by side with other communities.

SINHALESE/SINGHALESE: A people who form the majority population of Sri Lanka, and their language. The Sinhalese capital was at Kandy when the island of Sri Lanka (then known to Europeans as Ceylon) was conquered and colonized. Most Sinhalese are Buddhist; the Tamil population on the island is largely Hindu.

SORGHUM: Sorghum (*Sorghum bicolor*) is a grain related to millet. Some varieties are grown for their sugar content and used to produce sugar; others are milled into flour. In the United States, sorghum is grown in Mississippi, where it is also known as *milo*, and used primarily for animal feed. Known in Hindi as *jowar*, **sorghum flour** is used, alone or in combination with wheat flour, for making stove-top breads in the northwestern parts of the Subcontinent. It is sold in some South Asian grocery stores; it is also available from Bob's Red Mill, an American organic flour company, labeled both "sweet flour" and "sorghum flour." Sorghum flour contains no gluten.

SOYBEANS: We haven't encountered soybeans much in the Subcontinent except in Nepal and the mountainous area to the east of Nepal. There soybeans (the fruit of the plant *Glycine maximus*; also known as *edamame*) are used fresh and are also fermented, then stir-fried. Flash-frozen fresh soybeans are sold in many Japanese and other Asian stores, and now in gourmet stores/supermarkets, either in the pod or, more commonly, shelled and ready to be cooked and eaten. They're bright green ovals and cook quickly in boiling salted water or in a stir-fry. In Nepal and the surrounding area, soybeans are fermented to make *kinema*, a highly digestible, nutritionally valuable, and delicious pantry staple.

SPICES: Spices may be used whole or ground; they may be dry roasted, or toasted, in a skillet, then ground and added to a dish; in the Subcontinent, they are often tossed whole into hot oil at the start of cooking. Buy whole spices and store them in tightly sealed, labeled jars away from heat and light. Dry roast or grind them, if appropriate, just before using, to ensure freshness and intensity of flavor. We use a spice/coffee grinder or a mortar and a pestle to grind spices. *See also individual spices.*

STAR FRUIT: Known also as *carambola*, star fruit is a pale green to soft yellow oval fruit with well-incised ridges. The fruit of a small tree, *Averrhoa carambola*, that is native to southeast Asia, it is called star fruit because when it's sliced crosswise, the slices are an attractive star shape. The skin is edible (though sometimes the edges of the "wings," the tips of the stars, can be tough and need to be trimmed off). The flesh is firm and a little crisp, with a tart-sweet taste.

STIR-FRYING, FRYING: You can use a wok or the woklike pan from the Subcontinent called a *karhai* (*see* karhai) or a deep skillet for stir-frying. The process (familiar to many from Chinese cooking) involves heating a small amount of oil, adding flavorings, and then frying the main ingredients in the hot oil, keeping them moving around with a shovel-shaped metal spatula, pressing them against the hot surface of the pan to cook them, then lifting and moving them to prevent scorching (see Tamarind Potatoes, page 152, for example). In many cases in the Subcontinent the process takes place over less intense heat and is actually a cross between panfrying and stir-frying: The ingredients are moved around the pan, but with moderate heat, there's less risk of scorching. *See also* deep-frying.

SUMMER SQUASH: Thinner-skinned squashes such as zucchini, spaghetti squash, and delicata.

SWEETENED CONDENSED MILK: *See* milk.

SWORD BEAN: *Canavalia gladiata* has long flat pods that are eaten as green beans are, as a fresh-cooked vegetable. They can be sliced crosswise and used in place of green beans or long beans in dishes such as Hasna Begum's Mixed Vegetable Curry (page 164) or Shredded Green Bean Mallum (page 76). A similar New World bean is called *jack bean*. Sword beans are sold, when in season, at South Asian groceries (see photograph, page 140).

SYRIAN CHRISTIAN CHURCH: A form of Christianity that dates back to the early centuries of the modern era. A large number of people in Kerala are Syrian Christian, descendants of people who were converted to Christianity by St. Thomas, who came to Kerala in about A.D. 50. The scriptures were written in Syriac, hence the name given to the community. Syrian Christians, who eat meat of all kinds, have a culinary heritage distinct from that of the Hindus or Muslims of Kerala.

TADKA: *See* tempering.

TAMARIND: The name "tamarind" comes from the Arabic *tamar-ul-Hindi*, meaning "date or fruit from India." In Hindi it is called *imli*, in Tamil, *puli* (which also means "tart tasting"). The fruit of the tamarind tree (*Tamarindus indicus*) is used as a souring agent in many parts of the Subcontinent, especially in the south, as well as in Iranian and Georgian cooking and in Southeast Asia. The fruit grows as long pale brown pods with a dark brown sticky pulp inside. Tamarind pulp is now widely available in South Asian and Southeast Asian groceries, as well as in some large grocery stores. It is sold as small blocks wrapped in clear cellophane. It contains seeds and fibers, as well as the flavorful flesh, so it must be soaked and passed through a strainer before being used. The recipes give a brief set of instructions *for preparing tamarind*. Here is a more elaborate description of the process: Cut off a chunk of pulp (for most recipes you'll be using about a tablespoon) from the block of tamarind, then chop it into smaller pieces and place in a small bowl. Add a little hot water, about four times the volume of the pulp, and use a fork to help the tamarind pulp dissolve in the water. Let stand for 10 or 15 minutes, then place a

sieve over another small bowl and pour the tamarind mixture into the sieve. Press the tamarind through the sieve with a wooden spoon, and be sure to scrape off the tamarind liquid that clings to the underside of the sieve. Discard the pulp and seeds and use the liquid in recipes as directed (see, for example, Tamarind Potatoes, page 152, and Bangla Dal with a Hit of Lime, page 178).

TAMIL NADU, TAMIL: An Indian state lying on the east coast and extending from Chennai (Madras), the capital, to the southern tip of the country, Kanyakumari. Nadu is fertile and subtropical. In the Ghats, the steep hills that border Kerala to the west, the climate is more temperate, with cold nights. Tamil cooking is largely vegetarian, because the population is mainly Hindu, though fish is widely eaten. Tamil dishes such as *dosa, idli,* and hoppers (in Sri Lanka) have become popular all over the Subcontinent and in parts of England and North America. The Tamil population in Sri Lanka has its roots in two migrations from Tamil Nadu: one about 1,000 years ago, the source of the prosperous and highly educated Tamil community; the second in the nineteenth century under the British colonists who brought Tamil laborers to work on the tea plantations.

TANDOOR: A kind of oven that seems to have originated in Central Asia; the word is also sometimes written *tandur* or *tandir*. Tandoor ovens were introduced to the Subcontinent with the Moghul invasion and are associated with Moghul cuisine and traditions. They are commonly found in Pakistan and northern India, as well as in restaurants all over India that cater to tourists or truck drivers. The ovens are usually made of coarse clay that is sunbaked (see "My First Tandoor," page 128) and are barrel shaped, with an open top. A fire is built at the bottom of the oven (or the oven may be gas fired); when the walls are very hot, the fire is damped or lowered, and flattened pieces of bread dough, either leavened or unleavened, are slapped onto the inside oven walls, where they bake very quickly. Regular North American gas or electric ovens can be used for baking these breads, and we've given instructions in the recipes (see Home-Style Tandoor Naan, page 116, for example). Tandoors are also used for cooking meat, fish, and chicken; the meat is marinated or rubbed with flavorings, then threaded onto skewers and lowered into the oven.

TASTE: In Ayurveda, there are six tastes: sweet (*madhura* in Sanskrit), sour (*amla*), salty (*laana*), pungent (*katu*), bitter (*tikta*), and astringent (*kasaya*). Each is believed to consist of a combination of two of the five elements (earth, water, fire, air, and ether) and through them to act on the body in specific ways. Eating properly for health in the Ayurveda view involves balancing tastes, eating a slightly sweet dish to balance a sour or tart one, and so on.

TAVA: Sometimes transcribed *thava* or *thawa*, a *tava* is a round, slightly concave metal griddle that is placed over a fire or a stove-top flame and used for cooking chapatis and other flatbreads in the northern and central regions of the Subcontinent. It is eight to twelve inches across, with a handle on one side. Breads may be cooked without oil, or the surface may be greased with ghee or oil. *Tavas* are available from many South Asian groceries; a well-seasoned cast-iron skillet or griddle makes a good substitute.

TEA: Originally cultivated in China, tea (the bush *Camellia sinensis*) is now grown in many regions of the Subcontinent, notably Assam, west Bengal (around Darjeeling), and Sri Lanka. Tea bushes are kept trimmed to a low height so the leaves can be gathered by pickers standing on the ground (see photograph, page 285). The leaves are dried, or fermented and dried, then processed. Starting in the late 1800s, when the British ruled the Subcontinent, the merchants in Calcutta controlled the tea market in the Subcontinent, and they still do, we are told. Assam-style teas are stronger tasting than Bengal types and are generally preferred in the Subcontinent but less valued in other countries. Milder Darjeeling-style teas are largely grown for export. *See also* chai.

TEMPERING: The practice of adding a flavoring of spices and aromatics (such as onion) that have been separately cooked in oil to a cooked dish in order to heighten or round out flavors. The flavoring is known in Kerala as *kar'digarh*, meaning "mustard," because it usually contains whole or ground mustard seed; in the north, it's called a *tadka*. Many of the recipes in the dals chapter call for tempering. See also page 17.

THALI: The name of a metal tray on which a main meal is served throughout much of northern India; it is also the name of the meal, as in "*thali* meal." A *thali* meal is for one person and usually consists of a mound of rice, several flatbreads, small servings of one or two dals, several vegetables, and one or more chutneys. The side dishes are served in small bowls or in small piles on the tray beside the rice. Different regional cuisines have characteristic *thalis:* In Gujarat, for example, the rice is served at the end of the meal.

TURMERIC: A rhizome (*Cucurma longa*), related to ginger and native to the Subcontinent, that is widely used in its powdered dried form in many cuisines of the Subcontinent. Turmeric powder is a bright golden yellow in color and stains hands and clothing (it is a traditional dye as well as a culinary ingredient). It is believed to have antiflatulent properties, so it is an indispensable early addition in the cooking of dal or beans. In Ayurveda it is classed as warming. Sliced fresh turmeric is bright orange and is also used as an ingredient in some places: Rajasthan and Andhra Pradesh both have curried turmeric dishes. The Mundas, an aboriginal people of India, were known in the early Vedic literature as *nishada*, turmeric eaters. **Powdered turmeric,** made by boiling turmeric rhizomes, then drying them and grinding them to a powder, is widely available in grocery stores. **Fresh turmeric rhizomes,** the size of a small finger, pale brown outside and bright orange inside, are often available in Southeast Asian groceries.

VEDAS, VEDIC: The early writings in Sanskrit from the Subcontinent are known as *Vedas*. They deal with history, myth, food, and religion and date from a number of periods, starting in about 1700 B.C.E.

WATER BUFFALO: Large smooth-skinned black or gray, with curving horns, water buffalo (*Bubalus bubalis*) are native to the Subcontinent and have been domesticated for millennia. Wild herds still exist, especially in national parks in India, Nepal, and Sri Lanka. Water buffalo can tolerate hot temperatures but not extreme cold. They are used in the Subcontinent to pull plows or for other labor, as well as for their milk and their meat. Water buffalo's milk has a higher butterfat content than cow's milk and is pure white in color. The meat is comparable to beef.

WINTER MELON: A large cousin of the watermelon, eaten in savory dishes, as summer squash is. Winter melon is sold in large slices, wrapped in cellophane, in East Asian groceries. Look for melon with dark green peel and pale white-green interior, with tender flesh rather than hard. It is simmered in soups or used in quick stir-fries.

YARD-LONG BEANS: In the southern parts of the Subcontinent, as in Southeast Asia, yard-long beans are more common than regular green (or yellow) beans, which like a more temperate climate. Yard-longs are slender, dark green, and eighteen inches to two feet long (see photograph, page 229); they have a firmer texture than green beans. They are the pods of the cowpea (*Vigna unguiculata* ssp. *sesquipedelis*) and can be grown in North America in hot summer weather. They are now widely available in Asian groceries, sold in bundles. We like to cook them whole in boiling salted water, then slice them, if serving them as a simple dressed vegetable.

YOGURT: Known as *curd* in English in the Subcontinent and *dahi* in Hindi and many languages in the northern Subcontinent, yogurt, like all other dairy products, has an important place in Hindu cooking, and it is widely used in inventive ways, both savory and sweet, in almost all the cuisines of the Subcontinent. There yogurt is traditionally made from cow's or water buffalo's milk and is generally thicker and richer than all but the full-fat yogurts sold in North America. A yogurt culture (*Lactobacillus acidophilus*, usually in the form of some yogurt from the previous batch) is stirred into lukewarm milk and left to ferment in a slightly warm place. Yogurt can taste fairly tart, depending on the culture used, but the tartness can be relieved by draining off the whey. This is why many recipes call for draining yogurt briefly (fifteen minutes is enough) in a cloth-lined sieve or colander (see Cucumber Raita, page 67, for example). The remaining yogurt is thicker, richer, and milder tasting. You can use the thickened yogurt or, if you want the looser texture of the original, add water to get the consistency you wish. When used in cooked dishes, yogurt must be added late in the cooking and must not be boiled, or the sauce may separate (it will still taste good, but it will be less attractive).

Abdulla, Ummi. *Malabar Muslim Cookery*. Bombay: Orient Longman, 1993.

Achaya, K. T. *A Historical Dictionary of Indian Food*. New Delhi: Oxford University Press, 2002.

——. *Indian Food: A Historical Companion*. New Delhi: Oxford University Press, 1994.

Alford, Jeffrey, and Naomi Duguid. *Flatbreads and Flavors: A Baker's Atlas*. New York: William Morrow, 1995.

——. *HomeBaking: The Artful Mix of Flour and Tradition Around the World*. New York: Artisan, 2003.

——. *Seductions of Rice*. New York: Artisan, 1998.

Ammal, S. Meenakshi. *The Best of Samaithu Paar: The Classic Guide to Tamil Cuisine*. New Delhi: Penguin, 2001.

Anand, Gul. *The Three F's of Life: Films, Feasts and Fables*. Mumbai: PLA, 2000.

Arora, Neelaxi. *Assamese Cuisine*. New Delhi: Sterling, 1996.

Association of Nepalis in the Americas. *The Nepal Cookbook*. 1966. Reprint, New Delhi: New Age, 2003.

Babbar, Purobi. *Rotis and Naans of India*. Bombay: Vakils, Feffer and Simons, 1988.

Banerji, Chitrita. *Life and Food in Bengal.* India: Rupa, 1993.

Basham, A. L. *The Wonder That Was India*. Calcutta: Rupa, 1981.

Bender, Arnold E. *Dictionary of Nutrition and Food Technology*. New York: Academic Press, 1960.

Chapman, Pat. *Curry Club: Bangladeshi Restaurant Curries*. London: Piatkus, 1996.

Chowdary, Savitri. *Indian Cooking*. Bombay: Jaico, 1954.

Cooper, Arnie. "Biting the Hand That Feeds. How Globalization Cripples Small Farms: An Interview with Vandana Shiva." *The Sun* (Chapel Hill, NC), no. 338 (2004): pp. 4–12.

Dalal, Katy. *Jamva Chaloj— 2: More Parsi Delicacies to Tickle Your Palate*. Mumbai: Vakils, Feffer and Simons, 2003.

Dalal, Tarla. *Rajasthani Cookbook*. Mumbai: Sanjay and Company, 2003.

DasGupta, Minakshie. *Bangla Ranna: The Bengal Cookbook*. Rev. ed. New Delhi: UBS, 1998.

——, Bunny Gupta, and Jaya Chaliha. *The Calcutta Cookbook: A Treasury of Recipes from Pavement to Palace*. New Delhi: Penguin, 1995.

Davidson, Alan. *The Penguin Companion to Food*. London: Penguin, 2002.

Day, Harvey, with Sarojini Mudnani. *Curries of India*. Bombay: Jaico, 1991.

Deen, Hanifa. *Broken Bangles*. New Delhi: Penguin India, 1999.

Devi, Loke Rajye Laxmi. *Nepalese Kitchen*. New Delhi: Roli, 2000.

Devi, V. Niranjala. *Sumptuous 101 Veg. and Non Veg. Dishes*. Madras: Sura, n.d.

Dissanayake, Chandra. *Ceylon Cookery*. Colombo, Sri Lanka: n.p., 1976.

Farmer, B. H. *An Introduction to South Asia*, 2d ed. London: Routledge, 1993.

Fernandes, Jennifer. *100 Easy-to-Make Goan Dishes*. New Delhi: Vikas, 1992.

Foning, A. R. *Lepcha My Vanishing Tribe*. Kalimpong: n.p., 2003.

Fuchs, Stephen. *The Aboriginal Tribes of India*. London: Macmillan Press, 1977.

Gillow, John, and Nicholas Barnard. *Traditional Indian Textiles*. London: Thames & Hudson, 1995.

Gopalan, C., et al. *Nutritive Value of Indian Foods*. Hyderabad: National Institute of Nutrition, 2002.

Gupta, Niru. *Cooking the U.P. Way*. Hyderabad: Orient Longman, 2000.

Hegde, Saranya S. *Mangalorean Cuisine*. Bombay: IBH, 1988.

Hoffman, Dr. Jay M. *Hunza*. Valley Center, CA: Professional Press, 1985.

Inner Wheel Club of Darjeeling. *Himalayan Recipes*. Darjeeling: privately published, n.d.

Joseph, Rebecca. *Simplified Indian Cookery*. Bombay: Jaico, 1991.

Kabra, Kanchan G. *The Gujarat Cookbook: Authentic Vegetarian Cuisine*. New Delhi: UBS, 2000.

Kachru, Purnima. *Kashmiri Kitchen*. New Delhi: Roli, 2000.

Kalra, Jiggs, and Pushpesh Pant with Raminder Malhotra. *Classic Cooking of Punjab*. New Delhi: Allied Publishers, 2004.

Khokhar, Sabitha. *A Taste of Baltistan*. London: Merehurst, 1995.

Kornel, Das. *Tribal Cultural Heritage and Cult: The Gutob Gadaba Tribe of Orissa*. Bhubaneshwar: Modern Book Depot, 1999.

Kumar, Kamalini, and Sunanda Ray. *100 Traditional Recipes from Bengal*. New Delhi: Vikas, 1995.

Kuttaiah, Ranee Vijaya. *Cuisine from Coorg*. New Delhi: Sterling, 2000.

Lal, Premila. *Premila Lal's Indian Recipes*. New Delhi: Rupa, 1993.

——. *Vegetable Dishes*. Bombay: IBH, 1980.

Latif, Bilkees I. *The Essential Andhra Cookbook*. New Delhi: Penguin, 1999.

Majupuria, Indra. *Joys of Nepalese Cooking*. Lashkar (Gwalior): S. Devi, 1988.

Majupuria, Indra, and Diki Lobsang. *Tibetan Cooking*. Lashkar (Gwalior): S. Devi, 1994.

Manekshaw, Bhicoo J. *Parsi Food and Customs*. New Delhi: Penguin, 1996.

Mathew, Mrs. K. M. *Modern Kerala Dishes*. Kottayam: n.p., 1991.

Mayat, Zuleika, ed. *The Best of Indian Delights*. 1961. Reprint, Durban: Women's Cultural Group, 1989.

Mehta, Jeroo. *Enjoyable Parsi Cooking*. Bombay: Vakils, Feffer and Simons, 1992.

Mendonsa, Gilda. *The Best of Goan Cooking*. New Delhi: UBS, 1995.

Menezes, Maria Teresa. *The Essential Goa Cookbook*. New Delhi: Penguin, 2000.

Nadkarni, Shalini. *Saraswat Cookery*. Mumbai: Focus, 1997.

Nariman, Bapsi. *A Gourmet's Handbook of Parsi Cuisine*. New Delhi: Vikas, 1994.

Negi, B. S. *Regional Geography of India*. 3d ed. Meerut, India: Kedar Nath Ram Nath, 1990.

Norton, James K. *India and South Asia*. Guilford, CT: Dushkin, 1993.

Padmanabhan, Chandra. *Dakshin: Vegetarian Cuisine from South India*. San Francisco: Thorson's, 1994.

Patel, Ramesh. *Ayurvedic Cooking*. New Delhi: New Age, 2001.

Patil, Vimla. *A Cook's Tour of South India*. New Delhi: Sterling, 1991.

———. *Indian Cuisine: Dal Roti*. India: Rupa, 1997.

Patnaik, Nityananda. *Anthropological Studies on Indian Societies*. Bhubaneshwar: Modern Book Depot, 2001.

Peiris, Doreen. *A Ceylon Cookery Book*. 11th ed. Sri Lanka: n.p., 2003.

Pruthi, J. S. *Spices and Condiments*. Delhi: National Book Trust, 1976.

Radhakrishna, Sabita. *Aharam: Traditional Cuisine of Tamil Nadhu*. Mumbai: Zaika, 2000.

Rajalakshmi, U. B. *Udupi Cuisine*. Bangalore: Prism, 2000.

Rani. *Feast of India: A Legacy of Recipes and Fables*. New Delhi: Rupa, 1992.

Ratnatunga, Manel. *Sri Lankan Cookery*. New Delhi: Sterling, 2002.

Rawji, Tahera, and Hamida Suleman. *Simply India: Sweet and Spicy Recipes from India, Pakistan and East Africa*. Vancouver: Whitecap, 2003.

Reejhsinghani, Aroona. *Delights from Maharashtra*. Bombay: Jaico, 1987.

———. *Vegetarian Wonders from Gujarat*. Bombay: Jaico, 1975.

Santa Maria, Jack. *Indian Vegetarian Cookery*. New Delhi: BI, 1977.

Saussier, Gilles. *Living in the Fringe*. Netherlands: n.p., 1998.

Singh, Dharamjit. *Indian Cookery*. London: Penguin, 1970.

Singh, Pushpita. *Rajasthani Kitchen*. New Delhi: Roli, 2000.

Stackhouse, John. *Out of Poverty and Into Something More Comfortable*. Toronto: Random House Canada, 2000.

Subramanyam, Rajalakshmi. *101 Vegetarian Delicacies*. Madras: Sura, n.d.

Tannahill, Reay. *Food in History*. Rev .ed. New York: Crown, 1988.

Traditional Gourmet Delights. Montreal: Golden Agers of the Indian/Pakistani Community, n.d.

Varughese, Mrs. B. F. *Recipes for All Occasions*. Kottayam: privately printed, 1994.

Vaughan, J. G., and C. A. Geissler. *The New Oxford Book of Food Plants*. Oxford: Oxford University Press, 1997, 1999.

Vijay, G. Padma. *Indian & Mughlai Rice Treats*. New Delhi: Sterling, 1992.

von Furer-Haimendorf, Christoph. *Himalayan Traders: Life in Highland Nepal*. London: John Murray, 1975.

———. *Tribes of India: The Struggle for Survival*. Berkeley: University of California Press, 1982.

WEB SITES

http://www.ang.kfunigraz.ac.at/~katzer/engl/ : Gernot Katzer's spice pages.

http://www.seedman.com/ : A source for seeds, including for curry leaf plants.

READING LIST

A taste of the Subcontinent in fiction

Ali, Monica. *Brick Lane*. New York: Scribner's, 2003.

Anand, Mulk Raj. *Coolie*. Toronto: Bodley Head, 1972.

Desai, Anita. *Fasting Feasting*. London: Chatto & Windus, 1999.

——. *In Custody*. London: Vintage, 1999.

Gunesekera, Romesh. *Reef*. London: Granta, 1994.

Karmali, Sikeena. *A House by the Sea*. Toronto: Esplanade, 2003.

Markandaya, Kamala. *A Handful of Rice*. New York: John Day Co., 1966.

——. *Nectar in a Sieve*. New York: John Day Co., 1955.

Mistry, Rohinton. *Tales from Firozsha Baag*. Toronto: Penguin, 1987.

Narayan, R. K. *The Guide*. London: Penguin, 1980.

——. *The Vendor of Sweets*. London: Penguin, 1987.

Ondaatje, Michael. *Running in the Family*. Toronto: McClelland and Stewart, 1982.

Roy, Arundhati. *The God of Small Things*. Toronto: Random House, 1997.

Rushdie, Salman. *Midnight's Children*. Toronto: Knopf, 1980.

——. *The Moor's Last Sigh*. London: Cape, 1995.

——. *Shame*. London: Cape, 1983.

Selvadurai, Shyam, ed. *Story-wallah: A Celebration of South Asian Fiction*. Toronto: Thomas Allen, 2004.

Sidhwa, Bapsi. *Cracking India*. Milkweed Editions, 1991.

——. *The Crow Eaters*. Toronto: Cape, 1980.

Suleri, Sara. *Meatless Days*. Chicago: University of Chicago Press, 1989.

BIOREGIONALISM IN PUBLISHING

Years ago I went to a poetry reading by the poet Gary Snyder. After the reading, he gave a short talk about things that he was interested in at the time. One subject he talked about was "bioregionalism" as it applied to publishing. The notion was that we have natural "bioregions," regions within which we share common goals, common concerns, etc., and that publishing, like food distribution, would be better and more effective if it were more closely linked to these bioregions.

I was recently in Bhubaneshwar, the capital city of Orissa, scouring bookstores for information about the many tribal peoples who live in the state. I was having very little luck until I went into Modern Book Depot one afternoon and asked the man behind the desk if he could help me.

"Certainly," he replied, stepping out from behind the counter and going to the shelves. He proceeded to pull down almost a hundred books, stacking them on a nearby table where I could sit and look through them. I was in shock. As I started to look through the books, he suggested that when I had finished I might like to look in related topics such as agriculture that also have information about various peoples.

Many hours later I stumbled out of the bookstore in a daze. Not only was I carrying a large stack of books, but my head was spinning with all the titles I had looked through. Ninety-nine percent were books published in India, and probably three-quarters of those had been published locally, most of them by the very nice man behind the desk, Om Prakash.

Bioregionalism in publishing. Wonderful.

NOTES ON PHOTOGRAPHING IN THE SUBCONTINENT

We still work with 35 millimeter cameras and slide film. And these days we shoot only Fujichrome, primarily Provia 100, but also Velvia (which is very fine-grained 50 ASA film). We love transparencies; we love looking at them on the light table or even just in the archival plastic sheets we store them in. We love the way light travels through them, giving depth and radiance to shapes and colors.

Whether you shoot slide or print film or use a digital camera, you'll find the Subcontinent an exciting place to take photographs. As anywhere else, morning and evening light, with their warm tones and long slanting shadows, are most generous for photographs, especially of landscape. Because most of the Subcontinent has a hot season, many buildings and townscapes are constructed with shelter from the sun in mind. This means that there's lots of opportunity to shoot in shadow, using reflected indirect light, at times of the day when direct sunlight bleaches out the details. In rainy season, there's often bright overcast sky to work with, or radiant light spotlighting one point in the landscape dramatically, as the sun emerges from dark monsoon clouds. In the fall and early winter months (October to December–January), the light in the northern parts of the Subcontinent (Pakistan, Bangladesh, Nepal, the northern states of India including Gujarat, Bengal, Rajasthan, Kashmir) is generally crisp and clear, and very easy and generous for the photographer. In hot season there's a fair amount of dust, as well as penetrating heat, so film storage and keeping equipment clean require extra thought. Take plenty of camera cleaning tools and a number of heavy plastic bags, so you can store exposed film and raw film separately, preferably in a cool place (if your room isn't air-conditioned, remember that the floor is the coolest zone in the room).

In our experience, security people at airports in the Subcontinent are very accommodating and patient about hand-searching rolls of film rather than making us put them through the X-ray machine. We try to make their job easier by carrying the rolls of film in clear plastic bags so they can see easily and clearly what the film is.

THANKS

We have been making trips to the Subcontinent since the midseventies, but in the last few years we have traveled there especially for this book and have had help from some very generous people.

In Kochi, thanks to Asha Abraham of Lily Street. In Goa, thanks to Clem and Jai of the Rock-it in Palolem; to Jose; and to Faisal at the pepper farm. In Udaipur, many thanks to Indra, and also to his wife Pushpa, for market talk and roti lessons. Thanks for many discussions about village life in Rajasthan to Hansraj Pamar, Chatar Singh, Bhupendra Singh Chouhar, and Pushpendra Singh Bhati of Jagat Niwas. Thanks to Mohan. Warm thanks to Sangana Bai for lessons in tandoor making and patience, and to her daughters Jamna and Lalita for their generous lessons in "practicality" in the kitchen. Thanks too to her son Sanjay and his wife Monica, to her husband Lal Chand and younger son Bharat. Thanks to Laloo and his sister Mame Reshma Khan, and to their family.

In Ahmedabad, thanks to Shaola at the House of Mangaldas Girdhardas; to Shirag, Riku, and her parents for inviting us into their kitchen to learn and to their table to share a meal; and to Ragini. Thanks to the Kathiawari Ribari women for our encounter in the desert. Thanks to Sonabai and her daughter Likubai in Luria, north of Bhuj, for their hospitality; to Judy Frater, a scholar of Gujarati textiles and founder of Kala Raksha, a weaving center near Bhuj; and to Anand, for explanations. Thanks also to farmer Rajnikan Patel for sharing glimpses of his life and of the agricultural economy of northeastern Gujarat.

In Kalimpong, thanks to Sonam Gompu and his wife Donga Gompu for welcoming Naomi into their home and kitchen and for long discussions about food and culture. Thanks also to Anita Padan and Gita Das. In Darjeeling, thanks to Sonam Sherpa. In Varanasi, thanks to Tondenji and his wife Ratna Tonden, to flautist Hari Shankar and the other musicians, and to Jabbar the rickshaw driver.

In Orissa, many thanks to Gagan and Ranjan at Dove Tour.

In Sri Lanka, warm thanks again to the Munasinghes, who took good care of Jeffrey when he first lived in Kandy in the late seventies, and who welcomed him again when he returned twenty-six years later. Many thanks to Sam. Thanks also to Palitha Agalawatta and Shyamali Senanayake at the Winchester Café, and to Jayantha Kumara for inviting Jeffrey to the village and teaching him so much. Thanks also to the staff of the Queens Hotel.

In Bangladesh, thanks to Lala Rukh Selim and her mother Dr. Hasna Begum, for a delicious lunch and fascinating conversation. Thanks to Sylvia Islam for conversations about social change and rural development. Thank you to Kazi Siraz, and to Bulbul. And thanks to Tajul, Dulal, Alam, Baten, and Anwar at the Tropical Inn.

Sometimes we meet up with other foreigners in our travels, sometimes friends come and join us for part of the journey. We have enjoyed spending time with all of you. Especial thanks to Dom and Tashi, of course, and also to Ant, Sonia, Jahlia, and Taya; to Tashi's friend Jack; to Dawn Woodward; to Rajan Gill and Yasmine; and to Deb Olson. In Calcutta in 1999 we were generously welcomed and taken care of by our friends Oie and Supote Issarakura; thank you.

In the winter–spring of 2004 we spent time traveling and working in Sri Lanka and India with a film crew: Jacques Menard (director and coproducer), Louis Durocher (camera), Sanjay Mehta (sound), and Carol West (production assistant). They were filming for a one-hour documentary called *The Recipe Diaries*, about the creation of this cookbook. We tried to visualize ahead of time what it would be like to travel with a crew. The idea made us nervous, because we are used to traveling anonymously and improvising as we go. In fact it was a wonderful experience. We now cannot imagine more generous or fun traveling companions.

Back home from our travels we rely on the patience of friends, who contribute ideas, taste recipes we're working on, and give constructive feedback. Dawn Woodward was again a huge help in getting through the recipe work; Dina Fayerman's encouragement was, as always, an essential ingredient. Cassandra Kobayashi generously retested many recipes; her notes and suggestions, especially her ideas for substitutions, were invaluable. Thanks also to Philly Markowitz and Myke Dyer for retesting lamb recipes. Thanks to Zinet and Amin Dahrani for sharing thoughts on food and life, as well as some of their family recipes; and thanks to Sutapa Majumdar for her take on mango *kulfi*. Thanks to Alicia Peres for wide-ranging conversations about Subcontinental fiction and food, and for her reading list suggestions.

Our agent, Liv Blumer, while encouraging us all along the way (she has a real passion for the food of the Subcontinent), also ventured into a little recipe testing for the first time; thanks Liv, for everything.

We are very grateful for the encouragement given to us by friends at our Canadian publisher, Random House Canada, and especially Tanya Trafford, Anne Collins, and Sharon Klein.

Once we submit the manuscript, it gets turned into a book by a team of talented and very hardworking people. They include photographer Richard Jung, whose shots glow with life. This is the third book we have worked on together, and each time we are delighted. The food in the studio shots is styled by Susie Theodorou, assisted by Beth Pilar, with care and creativity; the prop stylist is Gabi Tubbs.

Copy editor Judith Sutton once again coped with our idiosyncrasies with diligence and good humor. Artisan executive editor Deborah Weiss Geline hand-held us through the tedious details of proofing and editing with her usual calm and grace.

Our last two books were designed by the gifted team at Level: Cliff Morgan and David Hughes. Cliff died suddenly in the spring of 2004, a terrible loss. We feel very fortunate that David, together with his wife Joleen, is continuing the Level tradition of creative design, and that he has given this book his usual meticulous and imaginative attention.

All of this creative work takes place under the caring eye of our wonderful editor and friend Ann Bramson, at Artisan, who cares so much about books. She begins by leaving us alone while we complete the manuscript, then edits it with a light and generous hand, making editing and organizational suggestions that always result in a stronger, clearer book. We are very grateful, and we feel so fortunate each time we get to work with her.

Thank you, all.

NOTE: The tsunami in late December 2004 hit the Subcontinent hard, especially Sri Lanka, the Maldives, and in India, the coastal areas of Tamil Nadu, Orissa, and southern Kerala, as well as the Andaman Islands. In the media coverage that followed, the world learned that in most of the region, unlike in Europe and North America, it is the poor who live on the shoreline, eking a living from the sea, while the wealthy live mostly on higher ground, at a safe distance from the ocean. Now, months later, the survivors are moving forward, creating life afresh, with resourcefulness and resilience.